NON SANZ DROICT.

William Shakespeare

The Tragedy of
TITUS ANDRONICUS

The Life of
TIMON OF ATHENS

With New Dramatic Criticism and
an Updated Bibliography

The Signet Classic Shakespeare
GENERAL EDITOR: SYLVAN BARNET

A SIGNET CLASSIC

SIGNET CLASSIC
Published by New American Library, a division of
Penguin Putnam Inc., 375 Hudson Street,
New York, New York 10014, U.S.A.
Penguin Books Ltd, 27 Wrights Lane,
London W8 5TZ, England
Penguin Books Australia Ltd, Ringwood,
Victoria, Australia
Penguin Books Canada Ltd, 10 Alcorn Avenue,
Toronto, Ontario, Canada M4V 3B2
Penguin Books (N.Z.) Ltd, 182–190 Wairau Road,
Auckland 10, New Zealand

Penguin Books Ltd, Registered Offices:
Harmondsworth, Middlesex, England

Published by Signet Classic, an imprint of New American Library,
a division of Penguin Putnam Inc.

First Signet Classic Printing, April 1989
11 10 9

 REGISTERED TRADEMARK—MARCA REGISTRADA

Library of Congress Catalog Card Number: 85-63519

Printed in the United States of America

BOOKS ARE AVAILABLE AT QUANTITY DISCOUNTS WHEN USED TO PROMOTE PRODUCTS OR SERVICES. FOR INFORMATION PLEASE WRITE TO PREMIUM MARKETING DIVISION, PENGUIN PUTNAM INC., 375 HUDSON STREET, NEW YORK, NEW YORK 10014.

Shakespeare: Prefatory Remarks

Between the record of his baptism in Stratford on 26 April 1564 and the record of his burial in Stratford on 25 April 1616, some forty documents name Shakespeare, and many others name his parents, his children, and his grandchildren. More facts are known about William Shakespeare than about any other playwright of the period except Ben Jonson. The facts should, however, be distinguished from the legends. The latter inevitably more engaging and better known, tell us that the Stratford boy killed a calf in high style, poached deer and rabbits, and was forced to flee to London, where he held horses outside a playhouse. These traditions are only traditions; they may be true, but no evidence supports them, and it is well to stick to the facts.

Mary Arden, the dramatist's mother, was the daughter of a substantial landowner; about 1557 she married John Shakespeare, who was a glove-maker and trader in various farm commodities. In 1557 John Shakespeare was a member of the Council (the governing body of Stratford), in 1558 a constable of the borough, in 1561 one of the two town chamberlains, in 1565 an alderman (entitling him to the appellation "Mr."), in 1568 high bailiff—the town's highest political office, equivalent to mayor. After 1577, for an unknown reason he drops out of local politics. The birthday of William Shakespeare, the eldest son of this locally prominent man, is unrecorded; but the Stratford parish register records that the infant was baptized on 26 April 1564. (It is quite possible that he was born on 23 April, but this date has probably been assigned by tradition because it is the date on which, fifty-two years later, he died.) The attendance records of the Stratford grammar school of the period are not extant, but it is reasonable to assume that the son of a local official attended the school and received substantial training in Latin. The masters of the school from Shakespeare's seventh to fifteenth years held Oxford degrees; the Elizabethan curriculum excluded mathematics and the natural sciences but taught a good deal of Latin rhetoric, logic, and literature. On 27 November 1582 a marriage license was issued to Shakespeare and Anne Hathaway, eight years his senior. The couple had a child in May, 1583. Perhaps the marriage was necessary, but perhaps the couple had earlier engaged in a formal "troth plight" which would render their children legitimate even if no further ceremony were performed. In 1585 Anne Hathaway bore Shakespeare twins.

That Shakespeare was born is excellent; that he married and had children is pleasant; but that we know nothing about his departure from Stratford to London, or about the beginning of his theatrical career, is lamentable and must be admitted. We would gladly sacrifice details about his children's baptism for details about his earliest days on the stage. Perhaps the poaching episode is true (but it is first reported almost a century after Shakespeare's death), or perhaps he first left Stratford to be a schoolteacher, as another tradition holds; perhaps he was moved by

> Such wind as scatters young men through the world,
> To seek their fortunes further than at home
> Where small experience grows.

In 1592, thanks to the cantankerousness of Robert Greene, a rival playwright and a pamphleteer, we have our first reference, a snarling one, to Shakespeare as an actor and playwright. Greene warns those of his own educated friends who wrote for the theater against an actor who has presumed to turn playwright:

> There is an upstart crow, beautified with our feathers, that with his *tiger's heart wrapped in a player's hide* supposes he is as well able to bombast out a blank verse as

the best of you, and being an absolute Johannes-factotum
is in his own conceit the only Shake-scene in a country.

The reference to the player, as well as the allusion to
Aesop's crow (who strutted in borrowed plumage, as an
actor struts in fine words not his own), makes it clear
that by this date Shakespeare had both acted and written.
That Shakespeare is meant is indicated not only by
"Shake-scene" but by the parody of a line from one of
Shakespeare's plays, *3 Henry VI:* "O, tiger's heart
wrapped in a woman's hide." If Shakespeare in 1592 was
prominent enough to be attacked by an envious dramatist, he probably had served an apprenticeship in the
theater for at least a few years.

In any case, by 1592 Shakespeare had acted and written, and there are a number of subsequent references to
him as an actor: documents indicate that in 1598 he
is a "principal comedian," in 1603 a "principal tragedian,"
in 1608 he is one of the "men players." The profession
of actor was not for a gentleman, and it occasionally drew
the scorn of university men who resented writing speeches
for persons less educated than themselves, but it was
respectable enough: players, if prosperous, were in effect
members of the bourgeoisie, and there is nothing to suggest that Stratford considered William Shakespeare less
than a solid citizen. When, in 1596, the Shakespeares
were granted a coat of arms, the grant was made to
Shakespeare's father, but probably William Shakespeare
(who the next year bought the second-largest house in
town) had arranged the matter on his own behalf. In subsequent transactions he is occasionally styled a gentleman.

Although in 1593 and 1594 Shakespeare published two
narrative poems dedicated to the Earl of Southampton,
Venus and Adonis and *The Rape of Lucrece*, and may
well have written most or all of his sonnets in the middle
nineties, Shakespeare's literary activity seems to have been
almost entirely devoted to the theater. (It may be significant that the two narrative poems were written in
years when the plague closed the theaters for several
months.) In 1594 he was a charter member of a the-

atrical company called the Chamberlain's Men (which in 1603 changed its name to the King's Men); until he retired to Stratford (about 1611, apparently), he was with this remarkably stable company. From 1599 the company acted primarily at the Globe Theatre, in which Shakespeare held a one-tenth interest. Other Elizabethan dramatists are known to have acted, but no other is known also to have been entitled to a share in the profits of the playhouse.

Shakespeare's first eight published plays did not have his name on them, but this is not remarkable; the most popular play of the sixteenth century, Thomas Kyd's *The Spanish Tragedy,* went through many editions without naming Kyd, and Kyd's authorship is known only because a book on the profession of acting happens to quote (and attribute to Kyd) some lines on the interest of Roman emperors in the drama. What is remarkable is that after 1598 Shakespeare's name commonly appears on printed plays—some of which are not his. Another indication of his popularity comes from Francis Meres, author of *Palladis Tamia: Wit's Treasury* (1598): in this anthology of snippets accompanied by an essay on literature, many playwrights are mentioned, but Shakespeare's name occurs more often than any other, and Shakespeare is the only playwright whose plays are listed.

From his acting, playwriting, and share in a theater, Shakespeare seems to have made considerable money. He put it to work, making substantial investments in Stratford real estate. When he made his will (less than a month before he died), he sought to leave his property intact to his descendants. Of small bequests to relatives and to friends (including three actors, Richard Burbage, John Heminges, and Henry Condell), that to his wife of the second-best bed has provoked the most comment; perhaps it was the bed the couple had slept in, the best being reserved for visitors. In any case, had Shakespeare not excepted it, the bed would have gone (with the rest of his household possessions) to his daughter and her husband. On 25 April 1616 he was buried within the chancel of the church at Stratford. An unattractive monument to his memory, placed on a wall near the grave, says he died on 23 April. Over the grave itself are the lines, perhaps by Shakespeare, that (more than his literary fame) have kept his bones undisturbed in the crowded burial ground where old bones were often dislodged to make way for new:

> Good friend, for Jesus' sake forbear
> To dig the dust enclosed here.
> Blessed be the man that spares these stones
> And cursed be he that moves my bones.

Thirty-seven plays, as well as some nondramatic poems, are held to constitute the Shakespeare canon. The dates of composition of most of the works are highly uncertain, but there is often evidence of a *terminus a quo* (starting point) and/or a *terminus ad quem* (terminal point) that provides a framework for intelligent guessing. For example, *Richard II* cannot be earlier than 1595, the publication date of some material to which it is indebted; *The Merchant of Venice* cannot be later than 1598, the year Francis Meres mentioned it. Sometimes arguments for a date hang on an alleged topical allusion, such as the lines about the unseasonable weather in *A Midsummer Night's Dream,* II.i.81–117, but such an allusion (if indeed it is an allusion) can be variously interpreted, and in any case there is always the possibility that a topical allusion was inserted during a revision, years after the composition of a play. Dates are often attributed on the basis of style, and although conjectures about style usually rest on other conjectures, sooner or later one must rely on one's literary sense. There is no real proof, for example, that *Othello* is not as early as *Romeo and Juliet,* but one feels *Othello* is later, and because the first record of its performance is 1604, one is glad enough to set its composition at that date and not push it back into Shakespeare's early years. The following chronology, then, is as much indebted to informed guesswork and sensitivity as it is to fact. The dates, necessarily imprecise, indicate something like a scholarly consensus.

PLAYS

1588–93	*The Comedy of Errors*
1588–94	*Love's Labor's Lost*
1590–91	*2 Henry VI*
1590–91	*3 Henry VI*
1591–92	*1 Henry VI*
1592–93	*Richard III*
1592–94	*Titus Andronicus*
1593–94	*The Taming of the Shrew*
1593–95	*The Two Gentlemen of Verona*
1594–96	*Romeo and Juliet*
1595	*Richard II*
1594–96	*A Midsummer Night's Dream*
1596–97	*King John*
1596–97	*The Merchant of Venice*
1597	*1 Henry IV*
1597–98	*2 Henry IV*
1598–1600	*Much Ado About Nothing*
1598–99	*Henry V*
1599	*Julius Caesar*
1599–1600	*As You Like It*
1599–1600	*Twelfth Night*
1600–01	*Hamlet*
1597–1601	*The Merry Wives of Windsor*
1601–02	*Troilus and Cressida*
1602–04	*All's Well That Ends Well*
1603–04	*Othello*
1604	*Measure for Measure*
1605–06	*King Lear*
1605–06	*Macbeth*
1606–07	*Antony and Cleopatra*
1605–08	*Timon of Athens*
1607–09	*Coriolanus*
1608–09	*Pericles*
1609–10	*Cymbeline*
1610–11	*The Winter's Tale*
1611	*The Tempest*
1612–13	*Henry VIII*

POEMS

1592	*Venus and Adonis*
1593–94	*The Rape of Lucrece*
1593–1600	*Sonnets*
1600–01	*The Phoenix and the Turtle*

Shakespeare's Theater

In Shakespeare's infancy, Elizabethan actors performed wherever they could—in great halls, at court, in the courtyards of inns. The innyards must have made rather unsatisfactory theaters: on some days they were unavailable because carters bringing goods to London used them as depots; when available, they had to be rented from the innkeeper; perhaps most important, London inns were subject to the Common Council of London, which was not well disposed toward theatricals. In 1574 the Common Council required that plays and playing places in London be licensed. It asserted that

> sundry great disorders and inconveniences have been found to ensue to this city by the inordinate haunting of great multitudes of people, specially youth, to plays, interludes, and shows, namely occasion of frays and quarrels, evil practices of incontinency in great inns having chambers and secret places adjoining to their open stages and galleries,

and ordered that innkeepers who wished licenses to hold performances put up a bond and make contributions to the poor.

The requirement that plays and innyard theaters be licensed, along with the other drawbacks of playing at inns, probably drove James Burbage (a carpenter-turned-actor) to rent in 1576 a plot of land northeast of the city walls and to build here—on property outside the jurisdiction of the city—England's first permanent construction designed for plays. He called it simply the Theatre. About all that is known of its construction is that it was wood. It soon had imitators, the most famous being the Globe (1599), built across the Thames (again outside the city's jurisdiction), out of timbers of the Theatre, which had been dismantled when Burbage's lease ran out.

There are three important sources of information about the structure of Elizabethan playhouses—drawings, a contract, and stage direction in plays. Of drawings, only the so-called De Witt drawing (c. 1596) of the Swan— really a friend's copy of De Witt's drawing—is of much significance. It shows a building of three tiers, with a stage jutting from a wall into the yard or center of the building. The tiers are roofed, and part of the stage is covered by a roof that projects from the rear and is supported at its front on two posts, but the groundlings, who paid a penny to stand in front of the stage, were exposed to the sky. (Performances in such a playhouse were held only in the daytime; artificial illumination was not used.) At the rear of the stage are two doors; above the stage is a gallery. The second major source of information, the contract for the Fortune, specifies that although the Globe is to be the model, the Fortune is to be square, eighty feet outside and fifty-five inside. The stage is to be forty-three feet broad, and is to extend into the middle of the yard (i.e., it is twenty-seven and a half feet deep). For patrons willing to pay more than the general admission charged of the groundlings, there were to be three galleries provided with seats. From the third chief source, stage directions, one learns that entrance to the stage was by doors, presumably spaced widely apart at the rear ("Enter one citizen at one door, and another at the other"), and that in addition to the platform stage there was occasionally some sort of curtained booth or alcove allowing for "discovery" scenes, and some sort of playing space "aloft" or "above" to represent (for example) the top of a city's walls or a room above the street. Doubtless each theater had its own peculiarities, but perhaps we can talk about a "typical" Elizabethan theater if we realize that no theater need exactly have fit the description, just as no father is the typical father with 3.7 children. This hypothetical theater is wooden, round or polygonal (in *Henry V* Shakespeare calls it a "wooden *O*"), capable of holding some eight hundred spectators standing in the yard around the projecting elevated stage and some fifteen hundred additional spectators seated in the three roofed galleries. The stage, protected by a "shadow" or "heavens" or roof, is entered by two doors; behind the doors is the "tiring house" (attiring house, i.e., dressing room), and above the doors is some sort of gallery that may sometimes hold spectators but that can be used (for example) as the bedroom from which Romeo—according to a stage direction in one text—"goeth down." Some evidence suggests that a throne can be lowered onto the platform stage, perhaps from the "shadow"; certainly characters can descend from the stage through a trap or traps into the cellar or "hell." Sometimes this space beneath the platform accommodates a sound-effects man or musician (in *Antony and Cleopatra* "music of the hautboys is under the stage") or an actor (in *Hamlet* the "Ghost cries under the stage") Most characters simply walk on and off, but because there is no curtain in front of the platform, corpses will have to be carried off (Hamlet must lug Polonius' guts into the neighbor room), or will have to fall at the rear, where the curtain on the alcove or booth can be drawn to conceal them.

Such may have been the so-called "public theater." Another kind of theater, called the "private theater" because its much greater admission charge limited its audience to the wealthy or the prodigal, must be briefly mentioned. The private theater was basically a large room, entirely roofed and therefore artificially illuminated, with a stage at one end. In 1576 one such theater was established in Blackfriars, a Dominican priory in London that had been suppressed in 1538 and confiscated by the Crown and thus was not under the city's jurisdiction. All the actors in the Blackfriars theater were boys about eight to thirteen years old (in the public theaters similar boys played female parts; a boy Lady Macbeth played to a man Macbeth). This private theater had a precarious existence, and ceased operations in 1584. In 1596 James

Burbage, who had already made theatrical history by building the Theatre, began to construct a second Blackfriars theater. He died in 1597, and for several years this second Blackfriars theater was used by a troupe of boys, but in 1608 two of Burbage's sons and five other actors (including Shakespeare) became joint operators of the theater, using it in the winter when the open-air Globe was unsuitable. Perhaps such a smaller theater, roofed, artificially illuminated, and with a tradition of a courtly audience, exerted an influence on Shakespeare's late plays.

Performances in the private theaters may well have had intermissions during which music was played, but in the public theaters the action was probably uninterrupted, flowing from scene to scene almost without a break. Actors would enter, speak, exit, and others would immediately enter and establish (if necessary) the new locale by a few properties and by words and gestures. Here are some samples of Shakespeare's scene painting:

> This is Illyria, lady.

> Well, this is the Forest of Arden.

> This castle hath a pleasant seat; the air
> Nimbly and sweetly recommends itself
> Unto our gentle senses.

On the other hand, it is a mistake to conceive of the Elizabethan stage as bare. Although Shakespeare's Chorus in *Henry V* calls the stage an "unworthy scaffold" and urges the spectators to eke out our performance with your mind," there was considerable spectacle. The last act of *Macbeth,* for example, has five stage directions calling for "drum and colors," and another sort of appeal to the eye is indicated by the stage direction "Enter Macduff, with Macbeth's head." Some scenery and properties may have been substantial; doubtless a throne was used, and in one play of the period we encounter this direction: "Hector takes up a great piece of rock and casts at Ajax, who tears up a young tree by the roots and assails

Hector." The matter is of some importance, and will be glanced at again in the next section.

The Texts of Shakespeare

Though eighteen of his plays were published during his lifetime, Shakespeare seems never to have supervised their publication. There is nothing unusual here; when a playwright sold a play to a theatrical company he surrendered his ownership of it. Normally a company would not publish the play, because to publish it meant to allow competitors to acquire the piece. Some plays, however, did get published: apparently, treacherous actors sometimes pieced together a play for a publisher, sometimes a company in need of money sold a play, and sometimes a company allowed a play to be published that no longer drew audiences. That Shakespeare did not concern himself with publication, then, is scarcely remarkable; of his contemporaries only Ben Jonson carefully supervised the publication of his own plays. In 1623, seven years after Shakespeare's death, John Heminges and Henry Condell (two senior members of Shakespeare's company, who had performed with him for about twenty years) collected his plays—published and unpublished—into a large volume, commonly called the First Folio. (A folio is a volume consisting of sheets that have been folded once, each sheet thus making two leaves, or four pages. The eighteen plays published during Shakespeare's lifetime had been issued one play per volume in small books called quartos. Each sheet in a quarto had been folded twice, making four leaves, or eight pages.) The First Folio contains thirty-six plays; a thirty-seventh, *Pericles,* though not in the Folio is regarded as canonical. Heminges and Condell suggest in an address "To the great variety of readers" that the republished plays are presented in better form than in the quartos: "Before you were abused with diverse stolen and surreptitious copies, maimed and deformed by the frauds and stealths of injurious impostors that exposed them; even those, are now offered to your view cured and perfect of their limbs, and all the rest absolute in their numbers, as he [i.e., Shakespeare] conceived them."

Whoever was assigned to prepare the texts for publication in the First Folio seems to have taken his job seriously and yet not to have performed it with uniform care. The sources of the texts seem to have been, in general, good unpublished copies or the best published copies. The first play in the collection, *The Tempest,* is divided into acts and scenes, has usually full stage directions and descriptions of spectacle, and concludes with a list of the characters, but the editor was not able (or willing) to present all of the succeeding texts so fully dressed. Later texts occasionally show signs of carelessness: in one scene of *Much Ado About Nothing* the names of actors, instead of characters, appear as speech prefixes, as they had in the quarto, which the Folio reprints; proofreading throughout the Folio is spotty and apparently was done without reference to the printer's copy; the pagination of *Hamlet* jumps from 156 to 257.

A modern editor of Shakespeare must first select his copy; no problem if the play exists only in the Folio, but a considerable problem if the relationship between a quarto and the Folio—or an early quarto and a later one—is unclear. When an editor has chosen what seems to him to be the most authoritative text or texts for his copy, he has not done with making decisions. First of all, he must reckon with Elizabethan spelling. If he is not producing a facsimile, he probably modernizes it, but ought he to preserve the old form of words that apparently were pronounced quite unlike their modern forms—"lanthorn," "alablaster"? If he preserves these forms, is he really preserving Shakespeare's forms or perhaps those of a compositor in the printing house? What is one to do when one finds "lanthorn" and "lantern" in adjacent lines? (The editors of this series in general, but not invariably, assume that words should be spelled in their modern form.) Elizabethan punctuation, too, presents problems. For example in the First Folio, the only text for the play, Macbeth rejects his wife's idea that he can wash the blood from his hand:

> no: this my Hand will rather
> The multitudinous Seas incarnardine,
> Making the Greene one, Red.

Obviously an editor will remove the superfluous capitals, and he will probably alter the spelling to "incarnadine," but will he leave the comma before "red," letting Macbeth speak of the sea as "the green one," or will he (like most modern editors) remove the comma and thus have Macbeth say that his hand will make the ocean *uniformly* red?

An editor will sometimes have to change more than spelling or punctuation. Macbeth says to his wife:

> I dare do all that may become a man,
> Who dares no more, is none.

For two centuries editors have agreed that the second line is unsatisfactory, and have emended "no" to "do": "Who dares do more is none." But when in the same play Ross says that fearful persons

> floate vpon a wilde and violent Sea
> Each way, and moue,

need "move" be emended to "none," as it often is, on the hunch that the compositor misread the manuscript? The editors of the Signet Classic Shakespeare have restrained themselves from making abundant emendations. In their minds they hear Dr. Johnson on the dangers of emending: "I have adopted the Roman sentiment, that it is more honorable to save a citizen than to kill an enemy." Some departures (in addition to spelling, punctuation, and lineation) from the copy text have of course been made, but the original readings are listed in a note following the play, so that the reader can evaluate them for himself.

The editors of the Signet Classic Shakespeare, following tradition, have added line numbers and in many cases act and scene divisions as well as indications of locale at the beginning of scenes. The Folio divided most of the plays into acts and some into scenes. Early eighteenth-century editors increased the divisions. These divisions, which provide a convenient way of referring to passages in the plays, have been retained, but when not in the text chosen as the basis for the Signet Classic text they are enclosed in square brackets [ ] to indicate that they are editorial editions. Similarly, although no play of Shakespeare's published during his lifetime was equipped with indications of locale at the heads of scene divisions, locales have here been added in square brackets for the convenience of the reader, who lacks the information afforded to spectators by costumes, properties, and gestures. The spectator can tell at a glance he is in the throne room, but without an editorial indication the reader may be puzzled for a while. It should be mentioned, incidentally, that there are a few authentic stage directions—perhaps Shakespeare's, perhaps a prompter's—that suggest locales: for example, "Enter Brutus in his orchard," and "They go up into the Senate house." It is hoped that the bracketed additions provide the reader with the sort of help provided in these two authentic directions, but it is equally hoped that the reader will remember that the stage was not loaded with scenery.

No editor during the course of his work can fail to recollect some words Heminges and Condell prefixed to the Folio:

> It had been a thing, we confess, worthy to have been wished, that the author himself had lived to have set forth and overseen his own writings. But since it hath been ordained otherwise, and he by death departed from that right, we pray you do not envy his friends the office of their care and pain to have collected and published them.

Nor can an editor, after he has done his best, forget Heminges and Condell's final words: "And so we leave you to other of his friends, whom if you need can be your guides. If you need them not, you can lead yourselves, and others. And such readers we wish him."

SYLVAN BARNET
Tufts University

William Shakespeare

The Tragedy of
TITUS ANDRONICUS

Edited by Sylvan Barnet

Contents

Introduction

Titus Andronicus has had few admirers and numerous detractors. T. S. Eliot states the detractors' case as directly as any: *Titus* is "one of the stupidest and most uninspired plays ever written, a play in which it is incredible that Shakespeare had any hand at all, a play in which the best passages would be too highly honored by the signature of Peele." Unlike Eliot's notably original view that *Hamlet* "so far from being Shakespeare's masterpiece . . . is most certainly an artistic failure," his remark on *Titus* is a commonplace: Dr. Johnson, Hazlitt, Coleridge, and the editor of the Yale edition denied Shakespeare's authorship of most of the play; the editor of the New Cambridge edition gives much of it to Peele and saves some of the Shakespearean passages only by the desperate expedient of claiming that they are not really bad but are a clever burlesque of bad writing.

The idea that *Titus* may not be entirely Shakespeare's is at least as old as 1687, when Thomas Ravenscroft, who had recently given the stage his adaptation of the play, recorded that he had been told that Shakespeare "only gave some master-touches to one or two of the principal parts or characters." But the evidence that Shakespeare wrote *Titus* is weighty. In 1598 Francis Meres listed it as one of Shakespeare's plays, and in 1623 Heminges and Condell, who had acted with Shakespeare for some twenty years, included *Titus* in the Folio collection of his plays. However displeased we may be by part or all of *Titus*, there is no evidence that it is not his.

There are, of course, some inconsistencies that have been offered as proof that Shakespeare was revising an older play. We are told in II.iii.86 that Tamora's infidelity to the Emperor has "made him noted [i.e., notorious] long," although Tamora and the Emperor have been married only one night. But such an inconsistency proves no more about dual authorship than the similar treatment of time in *Othello,* or the apparently contradictory remarks about Macbeth's children. More serious is the shift of the villain's role from Tamora to Aaron, but again it does not prove that Shakespeare is revising an earlier play; probably he found the Moor Aaron coming to life as he worked on him, and Tamora simply fell into the background until the last act, when her part is stronger.

There is no sense trying to dissociate Shakespeare from *Titus;* all the available evidence insists that it is canonical. But neither is there any sense in emphasizing, as has recently been done, its connection with Shakespeare's early historical plays or with his later Roman tragedies. A good deal has been written about the Elizabethan history play as a dramatized sermon on the wounds of civil war, a sermon of special interest to Englishmen whose monarch was an aging and heirless queen. The later Roman plays, too, are seen to have political subjects. It is true, of course, that *Julius Caesar, Antony and Cleopatra,* and *Coriolanus* are all concerned in part with civil war, but it is hard to believe that while witnessing a performance of, say, *Antony and Cleopatra,* Shakespeare's audience fretted about the possibility that England would find itself the battlefield of triumvirs; rather it must have been watching with interest a story in which political themes are subordinated to the doings of a "lass unparalleled" and a general who becomes "the noble ruin of her magic." *Titus* does indeed concern itself, in part of the first scene, with establishing the succession in Rome; Titus is asked (I.i.186) to "help to set a head on headless Rome." But thereafter the motif fades from view until the fifth act, when Lucius, one of Titus' sons, leads an army against the vicious emperor whom Titus in the first scene

helped to establish. In V.iii.67 ff. there is a speech stress-
ing the horror of civil war, but it can scarcely be said to
be closely related to what has preceded it, and its ascrip-
tion to a nameless "Roman Lord" suggests that it may
well have been an afterthought. There is, furthermore,
a curious bit of evidence that Shakespeare regarded the
play as less political than did the earliest recorded inter-
preter, the printer or editor of the second quarto (1600).
The first quarto (1594) concludes—as presumably Shakespeare concluded—with some lines about the deceased
wicked queen:

> As for that ravenous tiger, Tamora,
> No funeral rite, nor man in mourning weed,
> No mournful bell shall ring her burial;
> But throw her forth to beasts and birds to prey.
> Her life was beastly and devoid of pity,
> And being dead, let birds on her take pity.

When a second edition was called for, it was apparently
set up from a copy that had suffered some damage to the
foot of the last leaf of text; the person overseeing the
publication seems to have mistakenly thought that some
lines had been lost at the foot, though in fact nothing was
lost but "Finis the Tragedy of Titus Andronicus." He
added four lines:

> See justice done on Aaron, that damned Moor,
> By whom our heavy haps had their beginning;
> Then afterwards to order well the state,
> That like events may ne'er it ruinate.

The last two lines, though bad, are appropriate enough
and have their parallels in later plays when rather colorless characters assure their fellows that some sort of order
is returning to the state, but certainly neither these lines
nor the first scene should turn our minds from characters
and passions to politics. Shakespeare himself ended the
play by calling attention not to political concerns but to

the pitiless queen whose body will be left for scavenging birds.

To say that Shakespeare ended his play with a comment on the Queen and not on the state is not to deny that there are substantial passages devoted to the state. But the final lines emphasize the central concern of the play—the passions and deeds that are the stuff of tragedy. Critics tend to suggest that we go to a tragedy so that we may draw political and ethical conclusions, but the tragic dramatists tend to emphasize deeds of horror and passionate responses to these deeds. Even at the end of a play, the emphasis is not on drawing conclusions, but on experiencing emotions. Nobody who witnesses *Hamlet* can feel that the entrance of Fortinbras shifts attention from tragic experiences to ethics and politics; attention is kept on the catastrophic happenings in Denmark.

Ambassador.   The sight is dismal;
  And our affairs from England come too late.
  The ears are senseless that should give us hearing. . . .

Horatio. But since, so jump upon this bloody question,
  You from the Polack wars, and you from England,
  Are here arrived, give order that these bodies
  High on a stage be placèd to the view,
  And let me speak to th' yet unknowing world
  How these things came about. So shall you hear
  Of carnal, bloody, and unnatural acts,
  Of accidental judgments, casual slaughters,
  Of deaths put on by cunning and forced cause,
  And, in this upshot, purposes mistook
  Fall'n on th' inventors' heads.

                (*Hamlet* V.ii. 368–86)

The violence of *Titus* has often aroused condemnation, as though tragedy did not customarily dramatize violence. It is true that *Titus* has more than its share, but if, for example, we find especially abhorrent the introduction of the severed heads of two of Titus' sons, it is perhaps because we have forgotten (since directors customarily omit the business) a stage direction in the last act of

Macbeth, "Enter Macduff, with Macbeth's head." Repulsive happenings are not something Shakespeare dramatized in his youth and then outgrew; *Hamlet* concludes with four corpses (there would be a fifth if Horatio had his way), to say nothing of the earlier deaths or the skulls the gravediggers unearth; *King Lear* calls for Gloucester to be blinded before the audience, and it concludes with the (to modern taste) gratuitous introduction of the corpses of Goneril and Regan, who have had the grace to die offstage. The dozen or so deaths in *Titus* are about double the number in *Lear*, and the rape and cannibalism in Titus are unparalleled elsewhere in Shakespeare, but they are not incompatible with the idea of tragedy. Nor are they mere Elizabethan sensationalism. If we recall Clytemnestra exulting over her slaughtered husband, or the incestuous Oedipus entering on the stage with bloody eyeless sockets, or the lecherous Pentheus, whose mother will in a frenzy exult over his severed head, we remember that none of the world's four great tragic dramatists shrinks from dramatizing the demonic and the horrible. We tend, especially if we are readers rather than spectators, to emphasize the wisdom and patience that are allegedly achieved through heroic suffering, but surely we ought to recall, for example, that Hamlet in the last act forces poison down Claudius' throat. Again, we can talk of purgation and reconciliation in *King Lear*, but we must recall that the cries and horrors do not disappear toward the end of the play; it is only seventy-five lines before the end that Lear enters with the dead Cordelia in his arms ("Howl, howl, howl, howl"), and the play closes with a dead march.

Of Shakespeare's early tragedies—*Richard III, Titus, Richard II*, and *Romeo and Juliet*—*Titus* is certainly the poorest, but it alone has a protagonist who is both noble and flawed, and thus it looks forward to *Julius Caesar* and to the greater tragedies. *Romeo and Juliet*, perhaps the best of Shakespeare's early tragedies, is an incomparably finer piece of work than *Titus*, but its vision of star-crossed lovers is quite different from the tragic vision of *Hamlet, Othello, Lear, Macbeth, Antony and Cleopatra*, and

Coriolanus, whose protagonists in a significant way resemble Titus. In *Romeo and Juliet* the lack of any vigorous presentation of evil (in most of the greater tragedies Shakespeare did not hesitate to draw potent villains), the decisive role played by chance, the youth and innocence of the lovers, and the emphasis on reconciliation at the end, all work together to produce a tragedy that strikes us as substantially different from the later tragedies. Of course one can say that the lovers are in some measure responsible for their fates—if they had not loved they might have outlived their parents—but the overall impression is one of innocence destroyed by destiny and released from this transitory world to a timeless realm. *Titus* is something else; in it, as in the great tragedies, deeds recoil on the head of the doers and even well-intentioned deeds may have their painful consequences. Titus offers up Alarbus as a sacrifice to the souls of the dead, and he thereby incurs the hatred of Tamora. Declining to accept the title of emperor, Titus helps to establish Saturninus, who quickly proves to be his foe. Titus nominates Saturninus apparently because he is the elder son—a reasonable basis—but the first two speeches of the play suggest to the hearer that Bassianus rather than Saturninus is the fitter. What Shakespeare is doing, of course, is dramatizing what seems to be an essential tragic fact—a man doing something according to his best lights and according to an impressive but, as it proves, mistaken code. In his dealings with his sons, as well as with Tamora and Saturninus, Titus prefigures the great tragic heroes: Titus' inflexible conception of honor alienates him even from those he loves. He moves, a Titan, in a world of his own, at times heroically silent when lesser men would weep, at times loudly lamenting to the stones, when lesser men would be silent. At the start it is said of him,

> A nobler man, a braver warrior,
> Lives not this day within the city walls.

(I.i.25–26)

His nobility, his bravery, sets him off from others, even from his own sons, and (like Othello's high vision of Desdemona that leads him to kill her when he thinks her unchaste) Titus' virtues themselves become oppressive. His code of honor sets him apart from other men; he becomes increasingly aware of a painful isolation, and he speaks of it grandly, as a tragic hero should. Juliet comes to realize that her "dismal scene [she] needs must act alone"; Macbeth, plotting Banquo's death, keeps even his wife "innocent of the knowledge"; Hamlet speaks "wild and whirling words" and is markedly detached from Horatio, as well as from Claudius, Gertrude, and Ophelia; Lear will "abjure all roofs"; Coriolanus, told that he is banished from Rome, will reply "I banish you." Titus, the earliest of these protagonists, says of himself:

> For now I stand as one upon a rock,
> Environed with a wilderness of sea,
> Who marks the waxing tide grow wave by wave,
> Expecting ever when some envious surge
> Will in his brinish bowels swallow him.
> This way to death my wretched sons are gone,
> Here stands my other son, a banished man,
> And here my brother weeping at my woes:
> But that which gives my soul the greatest spurn
> Is dear Lavinia, dearer than my soul.
>
> (III.i.93–102)

Like Shakespeare's other tragic figures, he wears the shirt of Nessus and gives vent to his feelings. The speech is a little too self-conscious, the assonance, alliteration, and other repetitions are a little too insistent (*waxing, wave by wave; expecting, ever, envious; brinish bowels; stands, son; weeping, woes; soul, spurn, dear, dearer, soul*), but one would be hard pressed to point to a better passage in the work of any of Shakespeare's early contemporaries other than Marlowe.

Shakespeare must have felt that his chief problem was one of style, not of plot: What sort of rhetoric could effectively present the bloody and unnatural horrors that

were the substance of Elizabethan tragedy and of classical
tragedy as he knew it? There was, of course, no question
of presenting tragic happenings "realistically"; tragedy was
concerned with unusual people in unusual situations; its
medium was verse, not prose. *Titus* contains a few brief
exchanges in prose, and indeed the Clown's prose is notable ("God forbid I should be so bold to press to heaven
in my young days"), but when he wrote *Titus*, Shakespeare must have been unable to conceive of the significant role that prose might play in his tragedies. Even
half a century or so after Shakespeare's great achievements in tragic prose, England's best dramatic critic of
the time believed that because tragedy shows us "nature
wrought up to a higher pitch" it ought to be in verse.
(Dryden advocated heroic couplets, however, not blank
verse.) The verse drama of Shakespeare's infancy and
much of that of his youth was rhymed, heavily allitera-
tive, and rich in laments built on apostrophes, rhetorical
questions, and exclamations. To us it seems stiff and foolish, even in the hands of, say, George Gascoigne, who
was educated at Cambridge, and who wrote some lyric
and satiric verse of considerable merit. Here is a passage
from Gascoigne's tragedy *Jocasta,* produced at Gray's
Inn in 1566:

Antigone. O doleful day, wherein my sorry sire
　　Was born, and yet O more unhappy hour
　　When he was crownèd king of stately Thebes.
　　The Hymenei, in unhappy bed
　　And wicked wedlock, wittingly did join
　　The guiltless mother with her guilty son,
　　Out of which root we be the branches born
　　To bear the scourge of their so foul offense.

If a passage with less narrative content is wanted, the
following will do to show the tragic lament full-blown:

Antigone. O weary life, why bid'st thou in my breast
　　And I contented be that these mine eyes
　　Should see her die that gave to me this life,

And I not 'venge her death by loss of life?
Who can me give a fountain made of moan,
That I may weep as much as is my will,
To souse this sorrow up in swelling tears?

Finally:

Oedipus. O wife, O mother, O both woeful names,
  O woeful mother, and O woeful wife,
  O would to God, alas, O would to God
  Thou ne'er had been my mother, nor my wife.

That Gascoigne is translating does not obscure the kind
or the quality of his verse. Shakespeare must have been
very familiar with this sort of writing; in *A Midsummer
Night's Dream* he neatly parodies (through Bottom's
speech) the lament of the previous generation:

        But stay, O spite!
        But mark, poor knight,
   What dreadful dole is here!
        Eyes, do you see?
        How can it be?
  O dainty duck! O dear!
        Thy mantle good,
        What, stained with blood!
  Approach, ye Furies fell!
        O Fates, come, come,
        Cut thread and thrum;
  Quail, crush, conclude, and quell!

                  (V.i.268–79)

More subtle, Hotspur's dying words in *1 Henry IV*
have a touch of the same absurd apostrophe and alliteration that marked the older drama and that are appropriate to this anachronistic young knight:

O Harry, thou hast robbed me of my youth!
I better brook the loss of brittle life
Than those proud titles thou hast won of me.

They wound my thoughts worse than thy sword my flesh.
But thoughts, the slaves of life, and life, Time's fool. . . .
(V.iv.80–84)

In *Titus* there is a good deal of alliteration, balance,
and parallelism, especially in the first two acts:

Patient yourself, madam, and pardon me

(I.i.121)

Rome's readiest champions, repose you here in rest

(I.i.151)

Clear up, fair Queen, that cloudy countenance.
Though chance of war hath wrought this change of cheer
(I.i.263–64)

And curtained with a counsel-keeping cave

(II.iii.24)

On the whole the impression is not that of naïveté; or if
there is a suggestion of naïveté, it is that of a highly tal-
ented writer infatuated with his medium and occasionally
forgetful of the dramatic ends that every speech ought
to serve. Despite the abundant (almost comically frequent) horrors, the atmosphere is more that of the hot-
house than the slaughterhouse; the horrors exist in ele-
gant luxuriance, and though the groundlings probably
were delighted, the author must have felt he was creating
a drama that would appeal also to the cultivated, who
knew Seneca and Ovid.

The Latin quotations that dot the play are the most
apparent sign of the lamp, but the fifty-odd mythological
allusions are scarcely less apparent. Despite the classical
setting, Shakespeare did not have to strew his play with
references to Pyramus, Vulcan, Cerberus, Prometheus,
Hecuba, the Styx, Dido and Aeneas, Priam, Virginius,
and a host of others. *Julius Caesar* has only a tenth as
many mythological allusions, but when he wrote *Titus,*
Shakespeare evidently was aiming at something quite different from the spare style he was to use in *Julius Caesar*.

In *Titus* he seeks to capture grandeur by abundance. Here
is a sample:

> Now climbeth Tamora Olympus' top,
> Safe out of fortune's shot, and sits aloft,
> Secure of thunder's crack or lightning flash,
> Advanced above pale envy's threat'ning reach.
> As when the golden sun salutes the morn,
> And having gilt the ocean with his beams,
> Gallops the zodiac in his glistering coach,
> And overlooks the highest-peering hills;
> So Tamora:
> Upon her wit doth earthly honor wait,
> And virtue stoops and trembles at her frown.
>
> (II.i.1–11)

The simile beginning in line 5 is markedly introduced by
the prominent position that "As" occupies in the line,
and it is markedly concluded by the similarly prominent
"So" in line 9; the explicit allusion to Olympus and the
only barely less explicit allusion to Phoebus suggest that
Shakespeare is attempting to climb, in Sidney's phrase, to
"the height of Seneca his style." (Before the speech is
over there will be a reference to Prometheus, and another
to Semiramis.) Sidney was speaking, about 1585, of
Gorboduc (1562), but his words apply to the infinitely
superior *Titus:* "it is full of stately speeches and well-
sounding phrases."

This heightened style, as well as the conception of a
tragic hero pushed beyond the limits of endurance, surely
owes something to Seneca, but Ovid, too, helped shape
Titus. The grisly business of cooking Chiron and Demetrius and serving them as a meat pie to a parent is Ovidian
as well as Senecan; Seneca's *Thyestes* includes such a
feast, but so too does Ovid's tale of Procne in *Metamorphoses*. In a sense, the stories are inseparable; in *Thyestes*,
Atreus himself compares the feast to that in the legend
of Procne, and the basic idea of a parent dining on the
flesh of his offspring (a vestige of rituals in which the
father killed his son as his son became a competitor?)

exists in various myths. In *Titus,* Shakespeare quotes—
rather misquotes—bits of Seneca, but he alludes directly
not only to the legend of Procne but to its rendition in
the *Metamorphoses*. The strong Ovidian influence on
Shakespeare's early writing, especially on the narrative
poems, is beyond all doubt; Francis Meres said in 1598
what must have seemed commonplace: "The sweet witty
soul of Ovid lives in mellifluous and honey-tongued Shakespeare; witness his *Venus and Adonis,* his *Lucrece,* his
sugared sonnets." In *Love's Labor's Lost* a pedant, Holofernes, speaks of Ovid, and though Holofernes can
scarcely be regarded as a reliable mouthpiece, here he
seems to be voicing Shakespeare's opinion, though perhaps a little bumptiously: "For the elegancy, facility, and
golden cadence of poesy, . . . Ovidius Naso was the man"
(IV.ii.127).

Ovid's elegancy, facility, and golden cadence had been
famous even in antiquity (Quintilian said Ovid was unable
to curb his luxuriance—even as Ben Jonson was later to
say that Shakespeare "flowed with that facility that sometime it was necessary he should be stopped"), and to
English playwrights in the latter part of the sixteenth
century Ovid must have seemed with Seneca to be the
man to add dignity to the blatant huffings of earlier
English tragedy. The earlier tragedies with their abundant
"O's" were notably direct; Ovid is often equally direct,
but he is also rich in comparisons. Philomela's severed
tongue "writhed convulsively," a recent translation says,
"like a snake's tail when it has been newly cut off and,
dying, tried to reach its mistress' feet." In Arthur Golding's version of Ovid, which Shakespeare surely knew,
the passage runs thus:

> And with a pair of pinsons fast did catch her by the
>   tongue,
> And with his sword did cut it off. The stump whereon
>   it hung
> Did patter still. The tip fell down, and quivering on the
>   ground
> As though that it had murmured it made a certain sound,

And as an adder's tail cut off doth skip a while, even so
The tip of Philomela's tongue did wriggle to and fro,
And nearer to her mistressward in dying still did go.

Here is Ovid's description (in Golding's words) of
Pyramus' wound: Pyramus drew

His sword, the which among his guts he thrust, and by
    and by
Did draw it from the bleeding wound beginning for to
    die,
And cast himself upon his back. The blood did spin
    on high
As when a conduit pipe is cracked, the water bursting
    out
Doth shoot itself a great way off and pierce the air about.

Probably Shakespeare felt that his description of the
mutilated Lavinia was in the best Ovidian manner:

> Why dost not speak to me?
> Alas, a crimson river of warm blood,
> Like to a bubbling fountain stirred with wind,
> Doth rise and fall between thy rosèd lips,
> Coming and going with thy honey breath.
>   (II.iv.21–25)

In *Lucrece*, probably written in 1593, within three or four
years of *Titus* and possibly within the same year, Shakespeare wrote:

> And from the purple fountain Brutus drew
>   The murd'rous knife, and, as it left the place,
>   Her blood, in poor revenge, held it in chase.
>   (1734–36)

To defend *Lucrece* would be even more difficult than to
defend *Titus*, but it ought to be evident that Shakespeare
is attempting to make art out of violence. For naked violence we must turn, say, to *Lear*, where a woman plucks

an old man's beard, urges her husband to gouge out the old man's eyes, and stabs a servant in the back. In *Titus* the horror is for the most part elevated, or at least veiled by ingenuity.

This is not to say that Shakespeare's treatment of horror is successful in *Titus:* the testimony of generations of readers (few playgoers have had the chance to see *Titus*) strongly suggests that it is unsuccessful. The elaborate treatment occasionally disgusts us, though perhaps it was meant to distance the horror and thereby make it acceptable. But in its day, and for a couple of decades after, the play was popular; as late as 1614 Ben Jonson grumbled that *Titus* still had its admirers. It is a remarkable achievement, superior in character, in plot, and in language to *The Spanish Tragedy,* and it rivals Marlowe, whose plays are the only other major plays of the period. Its exuberance, though in places distressing, is a sign of imaginative fertility that was later to be splendidly husbanded. It is, of course, a play that is of its age, but if we strongly have this impression, is it not partly because Shakespeare went on to write plays that are not of an age but for all time?

SYLVAN BARNET

The Most Lamentable Roman Tragedy
of
Titus Andronicus

[*Dramatis Personae*

Saturninus, son to the late Emperor of Rome,
    afterward Emperor
Bassianus, brother to Saturninus
Titus Andronicus, a noble Roman
Marcus Andronicus, Tribune, and brother to Titus
Lucius }
Quintus }
Martius } sons to Titus Andronicus
Mutius }
Young Lucius, a boy, son to Lucius
Publius, son to Marcus Andronicus
Sempronius }
Caius } kinsmen to Titus Andronicus
Valentine }
Aemilius, a noble Roman
Alarbus }
Demetrius } sons to Tamora
Chiron }
Aaron, a Moor, beloved by Tamora
A Captain
A Messenger
A Clown
Tamora, Queen of the Goths
Lavinia, daughter to Titus Andronicus
Nurse, and a blackamoor Infant
Romans, Goths, Senators, Tribunes, Officers,
    Soldiers, and Attendants

Scene: Rome, and the countryside near it]

The Most Lamentable Roman Tragedy of Titus Andronicus

[ACT I

Scene I. *Rome. Before the Capitol.*]

[Flourish.°1] Enter the Tribunes and Senators aloft; and then enter Saturninus and his followers at one door, and Bassianus and his followers [at the other,] with drums and trumpets.

Saturninus. Noble patricians, patrons of my right,
　Defend the justice of my cause with arms;
　And, countrymen, my loving followers,
　Plead my successive title° with your swords.
　I am his first-born son that was the last　　　　　　　*5*
　That ware the imperial diadem of Rome;
　Then let my father's honors live in me,
　Nor wrong mine age° with this indignity.

Bassianus. Romans, friends, followers, favorers of my right,
　If ever Bassianus, Caesar's son,　　　　　　　　　　　*10*

Were gracious° in the eyes of royal Rome,
Keep° then this passage to the Capitol,
And suffer not dishonor to approach
The imperial seat, to virtue consecrate,
15   To justice, continence,° and nobility;
But let desert in pure election shine,
And, Romans, fight for freedom in your choice.

Marcus. (*With the crown*) Princes, that strive by fac-
       tions and by friends
Ambitiously for rule and empery,°
20   Know that the people of Rome, for whom we stand
A special party, have by common voice,
In election for the Roman empery,
Chosen Andronicus, surnamèd Pius
For many good and great deserts to Rome.
25   A nobler man, a braver warrior,
Lives not this day within the city walls.
He by the senate is accited° home
From weary wars against the barbarous Goths;
That with his sons, a terror to our foes,
30   Hath yoked° a nation strong, trained up in arms.
Ten years are spent since first he undertook
This cause of Rome, and chastisèd with arms
Our enemies' pride: five times he hath returned
Bleeding to Rome, bearing his valiant sons
35   In coffins from the field.°
And now at last, laden with honor's spoils,
Returns the good Andronicus to Rome,
Renownèd Titus, flourishing in arms.
Let us entreat, by honor of his name,
40   Whom worthily you would have now succeed,

11 *gracious* acceptable   12 *Keep* guard   15 *continence* restraint
19 *empery* dominion (but in line 22 *empery* = emperor)   27 *accited*
summoned   30 *yoked* subjugated   35 *field* (this word is followed
by: "and at this day/To the monument of that Andronici/Done
sacrifice of expiation,/And slain the noblest prisoner of the Goths."
These lines, omitted from the second and third quartos and from
the Folio, are inconsistent with the ensuing action, in which Alarbus
is sacrificed. Perhaps Shakespeare neglected to cancel them in the
manuscript after deciding to make Alarbus' execution part of the
action)

And in the Capitol and Senate's right,°
Whom you pretend° to honor and adore,
That you withdraw you and abate your strength,
Dismiss your followers, and, as suitors should,
Plead your deserts in peace and humbleness.   45

Saturninus. How fair° the tribune speaks to calm my
        thoughts!

Bassianus. Marcus Andronicus, so I do affy°
In thy uprightness and integrity,
And so I love and honor thee and thine,
Thy noble brother Titus and his sons,   50
And her to whom my thoughts are humbled all,
Gracious Lavinia, Rome's rich ornament,
That I will here dismiss my loving friends;
And to my fortunes and the people's favor
Commit my cause in balance to be weighed.   55
                        Exit [his] soldiers.

Saturninus. Friends, that have been thus forward in
        my right,
I thank you all, and here dismiss you all,
And to the love and favor of my country
Commit myself, my person, and the cause.°
                        [*Exeunt his followers.*]
Rome, be as just and gracious unto me   60
As I am confident and kind° to thee.
Open the gates and let me in.

Bassianus. Tribunes, and me, a poor competitor.°
        [*Flourish.*] *They go up into the Senate house.*

                Enter a Captain.

Captain. Romans, make way! The good Andronicus,
Patron° of virtue, Rome's best champion,   65
Successful in the battles that he fights,
With honor and with fortune is returned
From where he circumscribèd with his sword

41 *the Capitol and Senate's right* the right of the Capitol and the
Senate   42 *pretend* claim   46 *fair* courteously   47 *affy* trust   59
cause affair   61 *confident and kind* trusting and natural(ly devoted)
63 *competitor* candidate   65 *Patron* representative

And brought to yoke the enemies of Rome.

Sound drums and trumpets, and then enter two of Titus' sons, and then two men bearing a coffin covered with black, then two other sons, then Titus Andronicus, and then Tamora, the Queen of Goths, and her three sons, [Alarbus,] Chiron, and Demetrius, with Aaron the Moor, and others as many as can be; then set down the coffin, and Titus speaks.

70   *Titus.* Hail, Rome, victorious in thy mourning weeds!°
Lo, as the bark that hath discharged his fraught°
Returns with precious lading to the bay
From whence at first she weighed her anchorage,°
Cometh Andronicus, bound with laurel boughs,
75   To re-salute his country with his tears,
Tears of true joy for his return to Rome.
Thou° great defender of this Capitol,
Stand gracious to the rites that we intend!
Romans, of five and twenty valiant sons,
80   Half of the number that King Priam had,
Behold the poor remains, alive and dead!
These that survive let Rome reward with love;
These that I bring unto their latest° home,
With burial amongst their ancestors.
85   Here Goths have given me leave to sheathe my
      sword.
Titus, unkind° and careless of thine own,
Why suffer'st thou thy sons, unburied yet,
To hover on the dreadful shore of Styx?°
Make way to lay them by their brethren.°
                          They open the tomb.
90   There greet in silence, as the dead are wont,
And sleep in peace, slain in your country's wars!
O sacred receptacle of my joys,
Sweet cell of virtue and nobility,

---

70 *weeds* apparel   71 *his fraught* its freight   73 *anchorage* anchors
77 *Thou* i.e., Jupiter   83 *latest* last   86 *unkind* unnatural   88 *Styx*
river surrounding Hades   89 *brethren* (trisyllabic here and occasionally elsewhere: "breth-e-rin")

How many sons hast thou of mine in store,
That thou wilt never render to me more!　　　95

Lucius. Give us the proudest prisoner of the Goths,
That we may hew his limbs, and on a pile
Ad manes fratrum° sacrifice his flesh,
Before this earthy prison of their bones,
That so the shadows be not unappeased,　　　100
Nor we disturbed with prodigies° on earth.

Titus. I give him you, the noblest that survives,
The eldest son of this distressèd queen.

Tamora. Stay, Roman brethren! Gracious conqueror,　105
Victorious Titus, rue the tears I shed,
A mother's tears in passion° for her son:
And if thy sons were ever dear to thee,
O, think my son to be as dear to me!
Sufficeth not that we are brought to Rome,
To beautify thy triumphs° and return,　　　110
Captive to thee and to thy Roman yoke,
But must my sons be slaughtered in the streets,
For valiant doings in their country's cause?
O, if to fight for king and commonweal
Were piety in thine, it is in these.　　　115
Andronicus, stain not thy tomb with blood.
Wilt thou draw near the nature of the gods?
Draw near them then in being merciful;
Sweet mercy is nobility's true badge.
Thrice-noble Titus, spare my first-born son.　　120

Titus. Patient° yourself, madam, and pardon me.
These are their brethren, whom your Goths beheld
Alive and dead, and for their brethren slain
Religiously they ask a sacrifice.
To this your son is marked, and die he must,　125
T' appease their groaning shadows that are gone.

Lucius. Away with him! And make a fire straight,

---

98 *Ad manes fratrum* to the ghosts of our brothers (Latin)
101 *prodigies* ominous disturbances　106 *passion* violent emotion
110 *triumphs* triumphal processions　121 *Patient* calm

And with our swords, upon a pile of wood,
Let's hew his limbs till they be clean consumed.
                    Exit Titus' sons with Alarbus.

130   *Tamora.* O cruel, irreligious piety!

Chiron. Was never Scythia° half so barbarous.

Demetrius. Oppose° not Scythia to ambitious Rome.
      Alarbus goes to rest, and we survive
      To tremble under Titus' threat'ning look.
135   Then, madam, stand resolved, but hope withal°
      The selfsame gods that armed the Queen of Troy°
      With opportunity of sharp revenge
      Upon the Thracian tyrant in his tent
      May favor Tamora, the Queen of Goths,
140   (When Goths were Goths and Tamora was queen)
      To quit° the bloody wrongs upon her foes.

                Enter the sons of Andronicus again.

Lucius. See, lord and father, how we have performed
      Our Roman rites! Alarbus' limbs are lopped,
      And entrails feed the sacrificing fire,
145   Whose smoke like incense doth perfume the sky.
      Remaineth naught but to inter our brethren,
      And with loud 'larums° welcome them to Rome.

Titus. Let it be so, and let Andronicus
      Make this his latest farewell to their souls.
                    *Sound trumpets, and lay the coffin
                              in the tomb.*
150   In peace and honor rest you here, my sons,
      Rome's readiest champions, repose you here in rest,
      Secure from worldly chances and mishaps!
      Here lurks no treason, here no envy° swells,
      Here grow no damnèd drugs,° here are no storms,

---

131 *Scythia* a region in southern Russia noted for its savage inhabitants   132 *Oppose* compare   135 *withal* with this   136 *Queen of Troy* Hecuba (who murdered the sons of Polymnestor—*the Thracian tyrant* of line 138—in revenge for his murder of her son)   141 *quit* requite, repay   147 *'larums* alarums, calls to arms   153 *envy* malice   154 *drugs* poisonous plants

No noise, but silence and eternal sleep: *155*
In peace and honor rest you here, my sons!

Enter Lavinia.

Lavinia. In peace and honor live Lord Titus long,
My noble lord and father, live in fame!
Lo, at this tomb my tributary° tears
I render for my brethren's obsequies,   *160*
And at thy feet I kneel, with tears of joy
Shed on this earth for thy return to Rome.
O, bless me here with thy victorious hand,
Whose fortunes Rome's best citizens applaud.

Titus. Kind Rome, that hast thus lovingly reserved   *165*
The cordial° of mine age to glad my heart!
Lavinia, live, outlive thy father's days
And fame's eternal date,° for virtue's praise!

[*Enter above Marcus Andronicus, Saturninus,
Bassianus, and others.*]

Marcus. Long live Lord Titus, my belovèd brother,
Gracious triumpher in the eyes of Rome!   *170*

Titus. Thanks, gentle tribune, noble brother Marcus.

Marcus. And welcome, nephews, from successful wars,
You that survive, and you that sleep in fame!
Fair lords, your fortunes are alike in all,
That in your country's service drew your swords,   *175*
But safer triumph is this funeral pomp,
That hath aspired° to Solon's happiness°
And triumphs over chance in honor's bed.
Titus Andronicus, the people of Rome,
Whose friend in justice thou hast ever been,   *180*
Send thee by me, their tribune and their trust,
This palliament° of white and spotless hue,
And name thee in election for the empire
With these our late-deceasèd emperor's sons:

159 *tributary* given as tribute   166 *cordial* comfort (literally: stimulant to the heart)   168 *date* duration   177 *aspired* risen   177 *Solon's happiness* (Solon said: "Call no man happy until he is dead")   182 *palliament* robe

185 Be *candidatus*° then, and put it on,
And help to set a head on headless Rome.

Titus. A better head her glorious body fits
Than his that shakes for age and feebleness:
What° should I don this robe and trouble you?
190 Be chosen with proclamations today,
Tomorrow yield up rule, resign my life,
And set abroad new business for you all?
Rome, I have been thy soldier forty years,
And led my country's strength successfully,
195 And buried one and twenty valiant sons,
Knighted in field, slain manfully in arms,
In right and service of their noble country:
Give me a staff of honor for mine age,
But not a scepter to control the world.
200 Upright he held it, lords, that held it last.

Marcus. Titus, thou shalt obtain and ask° the empery.

Saturninus. Proud and ambitious tribune, canst thou
tell?

Titus. Patience, Prince Saturninus.

Saturninus.   Romans, do me right.
Patricians, draw your swords and sheathe them not
205 Till Saturninus be Rome's emperor.
Andronicus, would thou were shipped to hell
Rather than rob me of the people's hearts.

Lucius. Proud Saturnine, interrupter of the good
That noble-minded Titus means to thee!

210 *Titus.* Content thee, Prince, I will restore to thee
The people's hearts, and wean them from themselves.

Bassianus. Andronicus, I do not flatter thee,
But honor thee, and will do till I die.
My faction if thou strengthen with thy friends,

185 *candidatus* candidate (Latin; literally: clad in white)   189
What why   201 *obtain and ask* i.e., obtain if you ask for

I will most thankful be, and thanks to men   215
Of noble minds is honorable meed.°

Titus. People of Rome, and people's tribunes here,
I ask your voices and your suffrages:
Will ye bestow them friendly on Andronicus?

Tribunes. To gratify the good Andronicus,   220
And gratulate° his safe return to Rome,
The people will accept whom he admits.°

Titus. Tribunes, I thank you, and this suit I make,
That you create our emperor's eldest son,
Lord Saturnine; whose virtues will, I hope,   225
Reflect on Rome as Titan's° rays on earth,
And ripen justice in this commonweal:
Then, if you will elect by my advice,
Crown him and say, "Long live our emperor!"

Marcus. With voices and applause of every sort,   230
Patricians and plebeians, we create
Lord Saturninus Rome's great emperor,
And say "Long live our Emperor Saturnine!"
                    [*A long flourish till they come down.*]

Saturninus. Titus Andronicus, for thy favors done
To us in our election° this day,   235
I give thee thanks in° part of thy deserts,
And will with deeds requite thy gentleness:°
And for an onset,° Titus, to advance
Thy name and honorable family,
Lavinia will I make my empress,°   240
Rome's royal mistress, mistress of my heart,
And in the sacred Pantheon° her espouse.
Tell me, Andronicus, doth this motion° please thee?

Titus. It doth, my worthy lord, and in this match

216 *meed* reward   221 *gratulate* rejoice at   222 *admits* approves
226 *Titan's* the sun god's   235 *election* (here, as often in Shakespeare, *-ion* is disyllabic)   236 *in* as   237 *gentleness* nobility
238 *onset* beginning   240 *empress* (here, and often elsewhere in
Titus, trisyllabic: "em-per-es")   242 *Pantheon* temple dedicated to
all the gods   243 *motion* proposal

245 I hold me highly honored of your grace,
And here in sight of Rome to Saturnine,
King and commander of our commonweal,
The wide world's emperor, do I consecrate
My sword, my chariot, and my prisoners,
250 Presents well worthy Rome's imperious° lord.
Receive them then, the tribute that I owe,
Mine honor's ensigns° humbled at thy feet.

Saturninus. Thanks, noble Titus, father of my life!
How proud I am of thee and of thy gifts
255 Rome shall record, and when I do forget
The least of these unspeakable deserts,
Romans, forget your fealty° to me.

Titus. [*To Tamora*] Now, madam, are you prisoner to
an emperor,
To him that, for your honor and your state,
260 Will use you nobly and your followers.

Saturninus. [*Aside*] A goodly lady, trust me, of the
hue
That I would choose, were I to choose anew.
[*Aloud*] Clear up, fair Queen, that cloudy coun-
tenance.
Though chance of war hath wrought this change
of cheer,°
265 Thou com'st not to be made a scorn in Rome.
Princely shall be thy usage every way.
Rest on my word, and let not discontent
Daunt all your hopes. Madam, he° comforts you
Can make you greater than the Queen of Goths.
270 Lavinia, you are not displeased with this?

Lavinia. Not I, my lord, sith° true nobility
Warrants° these words in princely courtesy.

Saturninus. Thanks, sweet Lavinia. Romans, let us go.

---

250 *imperious* imperial 252 *ensigns* tokens 257 *fealty* loyalty
264 *cheer* countenance 268 *he* he who 271 *sith* since 272 *Warrants* justifies

Ransomless here we set our prisoners free.
Proclaim our honors, lords, with trump and drum.   275

Bassianus. Lord Titus, by your leave, this maid is
  mine.

Titus. How, sir! Are you in earnest then, my lord?

Bassianus. Ay, noble Titus, and resolved withal
  To do myself this reason and this right.

Marcus. Suum cuique° is our Roman justice.   280
  This prince in justice seizeth but his own.

Lucius. And that he will, and shall, if Lucius live.

Titus. Traitors, avaunt!° Where is the Emperor's
  guard?
  Treason, my lord! Lavinia is surprised!°

Saturninus. Surprised! By whom?

Bassianus.   By him that justly may   285
  Bear his betrothed from all the world away.
      [*Exeunt Marcus and Bassianus, with Lavinia.*]

Mutius. Brothers, help to convey her hence away,
  And with my sword I'll keep this door° safe.
      [*Exeunt Lucius, Quintus, and Martius.*]

Titus. Follow, my lord, and I'll soon bring her back.
      [*During the fray, exeunt Saturninus, Tamora,
          Demetrius, Chiron, and Aaron.*]

Mutius. My lord, you pass not here.   290

Titus. What, villain boy! Barr'st me my way in Rome?
      [*He stabs Mutius.*]

Mutius. [*Dying*] Help, Lucius, help!

          [*Enter Lucius.*]

Lucius. My lord, you are unjust; and more than so,

280 *Suum cuique* to each his own (Latin)   283 *avaunt* be gone
284 *surprised* suddenly taken   288 *door* (disyllabic)

In wrongful quarrel you have slain your son.

295 *Titus.* Nor thou, nor he, are any sons of mine:
My sons would never so dishonor me.
Traitor, restore Lavinia to the Emperor.

Lucius. Dead if you will, but not to be his wife
That is another's lawful promised love.   [*Exit.*]

*Enter aloft the Emperor with Tamora and her
two sons and Aaron the Moor.*

300 *Saturninus.* No, Titus, no; the Emperor needs her not,
Nor her, nor thee, nor any of thy stock:
I'll trust by leisure° him that mocks me once;
Thee never, nor thy traitorous haughty sons,
Confederates all thus to dishonor me.
305 Was none in Rome to make a stale°
But Saturnine? Full well, Andronicus,
Agree these deeds with that proud brag of thine,
That saidst I begged the empire at thy hands.

Titus. O monstrous! What reproachful words are
these?

Saturninus. But go thy ways, go, give that changing
310 piece°
To him that flourished for her with his sword:
A valiant son-in-law thou shalt enjoy,
One fit to bandy° with thy lawless sons,
To ruffle° in the commonwealth of Rome.

315 *Titus.* These words are razors to my wounded heart.

Saturninus. And therefore, lovely Tamora, Queen of
Goths,
That like the stately Phoebe° 'mongst her nymphs
Dost overshine the gallant'st dames of Rome,
If thou be pleased with this my sudden choice,
320 Behold, I choose thee, Tamora, for my bride,

302 *by leisure* slowly   305 *stale* laughingstock   310 *changing piece*
fickle wench   313 *bandy* contend, bicker   314 *ruffle* brawl   317
Phoebe Diana, goddess of the moon

And will create thee Empress of Rome.
Speak, Queen of Goths, dost thou applaud my
    choice?
And here I swear by all the Roman gods,
Sith priest and holy water are so near,
And tapers burn so bright, and everything   325
In readiness for Hymenaeus° stand,
I will not re-salute the streets of Rome,
Or climb my palace, till from forth this place
I lead espoused my bride along with me.

Tamora. And here in sight of heaven to Rome I
    swear,   330
If Saturnine advance the Queen of Goths,
She will a handmaid be to his desires,
A loving nurse, a mother to his youth.

Saturninus. Ascend, fair Queen, Pantheon. Lords, ac-
    company
Your noble emperor and his lovely bride,   335
Sent by the heavens for Prince Saturnine,
Whose wisdom hath her fortune conquerèd.
There shall we consummate our spousal rites.
                          Exeunt omnes° [*except Titus*].

Titus. I am not bid° to wait upon this bride.
Titus, when wert thou wont to walk alone,   340
Dishonored thus and challengèd° of wrongs?

        *Enter Marcus and Titus' sons [Lucius,
             Quintus, and Martius].*

Marcus. O Titus, see, O, see, what thou hast done!
In a bad quarrel slain a virtuous son.

Titus. No, foolish tribune, no; no son of mine,
Nor thou, nor these, confederates in the deed   345
That hath dishonored all our family,
Unworthy brother, and unworthy sons!

326 *Hymenaeus* god of marriage 338 s.d. *omnes* all (Latin) 339
bid asked 341 *challengèd* accused

Lucius. But let us give him burial as becomes;°
Give Mutius burial with our brethren.

350 *Titus.* Traitors, away! He rests not in this tomb:
This monument five hundred years hath stood,
Which I have sumptuously re-edified:°
Here none but soldiers and Rome's servitors
Repose in fame; none basely slain in brawls.
355 Bury him where you can, he comes not here.

Marcus. My lord, this is impiety in you.
My nephew Mutius' deeds do plead for him;
He must be buried with his brethren.

Titus' two sons speak:

[*Quintus, Martius.*] And shall, or him we will accom-
pany.

360 *Titus.* And shall? What villain was it spake that word?

Titus' son speaks.

[*Quintus.*] He that would vouch it in any place but
here.

Titus. What, would you bury him in my despite?°

Marcus. No, noble Titus, but entreat of thee
To pardon Mutius and to bury him.

365 *Titus.* Marcus, even thou hast stroke upon my crest,
And with these boys mine honor thou hast wounded.
My foes I do repute° you every one,
So trouble me no more, but get you gone.

Martius. He is not with himself; let us withdraw.

370 *Quintus.* Not I, till Mutius' bones be buried.
                    The brother and the sons kneel.

Marcus. Brother, for in that name doth nature plead—

Quintus. Father, and in that name doth nature speak—

348 *becomes* is fitting   352 *re-edified* rebuilt   362 *in my despite* in
spite of me   367 *repute* consider

Titus. Speak thou no more, if all the rest will speed.°

Marcus. Renownèd Titus, more than half my soul—

Lucius. Dear father, soul and substance of us all—   373

Marcus. Suffer° thy brother Marcus to inter
His noble nephew here in virtue's nest,
That died in honor and Lavinia's cause.
Thou art a Roman, be not barbarous:
The Greeks upon advice° did bury Ajax°   380
That slew himself; and wise Laertes' son°
Did graciously plead for his funerals:
Let not young Mutius then, that was thy joy,
Be barred his entrance here.

Titus.   Rise, Marcus, rise.
The dismal'st day is this that e'er I saw,   385
To be dishonored by my sons in Rome!
Well, bury him, and bury me the next.
                    They put him in the tomb.

Lucius. There lie thy bones, sweet Mutius, with thy
    friends,
Till we with trophies do adorn thy tomb.

                They all kneel and say:

[*All.*] No man shed tears for noble Mutius,   390
He lives in fame that died in virtue's cause.

Marcus. My lord, to step out of these dreary dumps,°
How comes it that the subtle Queen of Goths
Is of a sudden thus advanced in Rome?

Titus. I know not, Marcus, but I know it is;   395
(Whether° by device° or no, the heavens can tell.)
Is she not then beholding° to the man
That brought her for this high good turn so far?
Yes, and will nobly him remunerate.

373 *if all the rest will speed* if the rest is to go well (?) if the rest of
you wish to live (?)   376 *Suffer* allow   380 *advice* deliberation
380 *Ajax* (when Achilles' arms were given to Odysseus, Ajax in a
fury stabbed himself)   381 *Laertes' son* Odysseus   392 *dumps* blues,
melancholy state   396 *Whether* (probably pronounced "where")
396 *device* plot   397 *beholding* beholden, indebted

*Enter the Emperor, Tamora and her two sons, with
the Moor at one door. Enter at the other door
Bassianus and Lavinia, with others.*

400 *Saturninus.* So Bassianus, you have played your prize:°
    God give you joy, sir, of your gallant bride!

Bassianus. And you of yours, my lord! I say no more,
    Nor wish no less, and so I take my leave.

Saturninus. Traitor, if Rome have law, or we have
    power,
405   Thou and thy faction shall repent this rape.

Bassianus. Rape, call you it, my lord, to seize my own,
    My true-betrothèd love, and now my wife?
    But let the laws of Rome determine all;
    Meanwhile am I possessed of that is mine.

410 *Saturninus.* 'Tis good, sir; you are very short with us,
    But if we live we'll be as sharp with you.

Bassianus. My lord, what I have done, as best I may
    Answer I must, and shall do with my life.
    Only thus much I give your grace to know—
415   By all the duties that I owe to Rome,
    This noble gentleman, Lord Titus here,
    Is in opinion° and in honor wronged,
    That, in the rescue of Lavinia,
    With his own hand did slay his youngest son,
420   In zeal to you, and highly moved to wrath
    To be controlled° in that he frankly° gave.
    Receive him then to favor, Saturnine,
    That hath expressed himself in all his deeds
    A father and a friend to thee and Rome.

425 *Titus.* Prince Bassianus, leave to plead° my deeds;
    'Tis thou and those that have dishonored me.
    Rome and the righteous heavens be my judge,
    How I have loved and honored Saturnine!

---

400 *played your prize* won your contest   417 *opinion* reputation
421 *controlled* opposed   421 *frankly* generously   425 *leave to
plead* cease pleading

Tamora. My worthy lord, if ever Tamora
    Were gracious in those princely eyes of thine,   *430*
    Then hear me speak indifferently° for all;
    And at my suit, sweet, pardon what is past.

Saturninus. What, madam! Be dishonored openly,
    And basely put it up° without revenge?

Tamora. Not so, my lord, the gods of Rome forfend°   *435*
    I should be author° to dishonor you!
    But on mine honor dare I undertake°
    For good Lord Titus' innocence in all,
    Whose fury not dissembled speaks his griefs:
    Then at my suit look graciously on him;   *440*
    Lose not so noble a friend on vain suppose,°
    Nor with sour looks afflict his gentle heart.
    [*Aside*] My lord, be ruled by me, be won at last,
    Dissemble all your griefs and discontents—
    You are but newly planted in your throne—   *445*
    Lest then the people, and patricians too,
    Upon a just survey, take Titus' part,
    And so supplant you for ingratitude,
    Which Rome reputes to be a heinous sin.
    Yield at entreats:° and then let me alone.°   *450*
    I'll find a day to massacre them all,
    And race° their faction and their family,
    The cruel father and his traitorous sons,
    To whom I suèd for my dear son's life;
    And make them know what 'tis to let a queen   *455*
    Kneel in the streets and beg for grace in vain.
    [*Aloud*] Come, come, sweet Emperor—come, Andronicus—
    Take up this good old man, and cheer the heart
    That dies in tempest of thy angry frown.

Saturninus. Rise, Titus, rise, my empress hath prevailed.   *460*

431 *indifferently* impartially   434 *put it up* (the figure is of putting
up, or sheathing, a sword)   435 *forfend* forbid   436 *author* agent
437 *undertake* assert   441 *vain suppose* empty supposition   450 *at
entreats* to entreaties   450 *let me alone* i.e., leave it to me   452 *race*
root out

Titus. I thank your Majesty, and her, my lord.
These words, these looks, infuse new life in me.

Tamora. Titus, I am incorporate in Rome,
A Roman now adopted happily,
465 And must advise the Emperor for his good.
This day all quarrels die, Andronicus.
And let it be mine honor, good my lord,
That I have reconciled your friends and you.
For you, Prince Bassianus, I have passed
470 My word and promise to the Emperor
That you will be more mild and tractable.
And fear not, lords, and you, Lavinia;
By my advice, all humbled on your knees,
You shall ask pardon of his Majesty.

[*Lucius.*] We do, and vow to heaven, and to his high-
475 ness,
That what we did was mildly as we might,°
Tend'ring° our sister's honor and our own.

Marcus. That on mine honor here do I protest.

Saturninus. Away, and talk not, trouble us no more.

Tamora. Nay, nay, sweet Emperor, we must all be
480 friends.
The tribune and his nephews kneel for grace.
I will not be denied. Sweet heart, look back.

Saturninus. Marcus, for thy sake, and thy brother's
here,
And at my lovely Tamora's entreats,
485 I do remit these young men's heinous faults.
Stand up.
Lavinia, though you left me like a churl,
I found a friend, and sure as death I swore
I would not part° a bachelor from the priest.
490 Come, if the Emperor's court can feast two brides,
You are my guest, Lavinia, and your friends.

476 *mildly as we might* as mild as we might do   477 *Tend'ring*
having regard for   489 *part* depart

This day shall be a love-day,° Tamora.

Titus. Tomorrow, and° it please your Majesty
To hunt the panther and the hart with me,
With horn and hound we'll give your Grace bon-
jour.°   *495*

Saturninus. Be it so, Titus, and gramercy° too.

                                        Exeunt.

Sound trumpets. Manet° [Aaron the] Moor.

---

492 *love-day* day appointed to settle disputes (with a pun on day
for love)   493 *and* if   495 *bonjour* good morning (French)   496
gramercy thanks   496 s.d. *Manet* remains (Latin. Clearly this and
the next scene are continuous; the Folio's incorrect division into
acts is retained merely to facilitate reference)

[ACT II

Scene I. *Rome. Before the palace.*
Aaron alone.]

Aaron. Now climbeth Tamora Olympus'° top,
    Safe out of fortune's shot, and sits aloft,
    Secure of° thunder's crack or lightning flash,
    Advanced above pale envy's° threat'ning reach.
5   As when the golden sun salutes the morn,
    And having gilt the ocean with his beams,
    Gallops° the zodiac in his glistering coach,
    And overlooks° the highest-peering hills;
    So Tamora:
10   Upon her wit doth earthly honor wait,
    And virtue stoops and trembles at her frown.
    Then, Aaron, arm thy heart, and fit thy thoughts
    To mount aloft with thy imperial mistress,
    And mount her pitch,° whom thou in triumph long
15   Hast prisoner held, fettered in amorous chains,
    And faster bound to Aaron's charming° eyes
    Than is Prometheus° tied to Caucasus.
    Away with slavish weeds° and servile thoughts!
    I will be bright and shine in pearl and gold
20   To wait upon this new-made empress.
    To wait, said I? To wanton with this queen,

II.i.1 *Olympus* Mount Olympus (reputed home of the gods)   3 *of*
from 4 *envy's* hate's 7 *Gallops* gallops through 8 *overlooks*
looks down upon 14 *mount her pitch* rise to the highest point of
her flight (a term from falconry) 16 *charming* spellbinding 17
Prometheus a Titan fettered to a rock in the Caucasus because he
stole fire from heaven 18 *weeds* apparel

This goddess, this Semiramis,° this nymph,
This siren, that will charm Rome's Saturnine
And see his shipwrack and his commonweal's.
Hollo! What storm is this?　　　　　　　　　25

Enter Chiron and Demetrius, braving.°

Demetrius. Chiron, thy years wants° wit, thy wits
　　wants edge,
And manners, to intrude where I am graced,°
And may for aught thou knowest affected° be.

Chiron. Demetrius, thou dost overween° in all,
And so in this, to bear me down with braves.°　　30
'Tis not the difference of a year or two
Makes me less gracious,° or thee more fortunate;
I am as able and as fit as thou
To serve, and to deserve my mistress' grace;
And that my sword upon thee shall approve,°　　35
And plead my passions for Lavinia's love.

Aaron. Clubs, clubs!° These lovers will not keep the
　　peace.

Demetrius. Why, boy, although our mother, unad-
　　vised,°
Gave you a dancing-rapier° by your side,
Are you so desperate grown, to threat your friends?　40
Go to; have your lath° glued within your sheath,
Till you know better how to handle it.

Chiron. Meanwhile, sir, with the little skill I have,
Full well shalt thou perceive how much I dare.
　　　　　　　　　　　　　　　They draw.

Demetrius. Ay, boy, grow ye so brave?

Aaron.　　　　　　　　　Why, how now, lords!　45

22 *Semiramis* legendary Assyrian queen, noted for her lust and
beauty　25 s.d. *braving* challenging　26 *wants* (the ending -*s* is
frequently found with a plural subject)　27 *graced* favored　28
affected loved　29 *overween* arrogantly presume　30 *braves* threats
32 *gracious* acceptable　35 *approve* prove　37 *Clubs, clubs* (the
cry raised to call the watch to separate brawlers in London)
38 *unadvised* unwisely　39 *dancing-rapier* ornamental light sword
41 *lath* wooden (stage) sword

So near the Emperor's palace dare ye draw,
And maintain such a quarrel openly?
Full well I wot° the ground of all this grudge.
I would not for a million of gold
50 The cause were known to them it most concerns,
Nor would your noble mother for much more
Be so dishonored in the court of Rome.
For shame, put up.°

Demetrius.   Not I, till I have sheathed
My rapier in his bosom, and withal
55 Thrust those reproachful speeches down his throat,
That he hath breathed in my dishonor here.

Chiron. For that I am prepared and full resolved,
Foul-spoken coward, that thund'rest with thy tongue
And with thy weapon nothing dar'st perform.

60 *Aaron.* Away, I say!
Now, by the gods that warlike Goths adore,
This petty brabble° will undo us all.
Why, lords, and think you not how dangerous
It is to jet° upon a prince's right?
65 What, is Lavinia then become so loose,
Or Bassianus so degenerate,
That for her love such quarrels may be broached
Without controlment, justice, or revenge?
Young lords, beware! And should the Empress
know
70 This discord's ground,° the music would not please.

Chiron. I care not, I, knew she and all the world:
I love Lavinia more than all the world.

Demetrius. Youngling, learn thou to make some
meaner° choice.
Lavinia is thine elder brother's hope.

75 *Aaron.* Why, are ye mad? Or know ye not, in Rome
How furious and impatient they be,

---

48 *wot* know   **53** *put up* sheathe your weapons   **62** *brabble* brawl
64 *jet* encroach   **70** *ground* reason (with a pun on the musical
meaning: bass to a descant)   **73** *meaner* lower

And cannot brook competitors in love?
I tell you, lords, you do but plot your deaths
By this device.

Chiron.　　　　　Aaron, a thousand deaths
Would I propose° to achieve her whom I love.　　　*80*

Aaron. To achieve her how?

Demetrius.　　　　Why makes thou it so strange?°
She is a woman, therefore may be wooed;
She is a woman, therefore may be won;
She is Lavinia, therefore must be loved.
What, man! More water glideth by the mill　　　*85*
Than wots the miller of, and easy it is
Of a cut loaf to steal a shive,° we know:
Though Bassianus be the Emperor's brother,
Better than he have worn Vulcan's badge.°

Aaron. [*Aside*] Ay, and as good as Saturninus may.　　*90*

Demetrius. Then why should he despair that knows
　　to court it
With words, fair looks, and liberality?
What, hast not thou full often stroke a doe,
And borne her cleanly by the keeper's nose?

Aaron. Why then, it seems, some certain snatch° or so　*95*
Would serve your turns.

Chiron.　　　　　Ay, so the turn were served.

Demetrius. Aaron, thou hast hit it.

Aaron.　　　　　　Would you had hit it too,
Then should not we be tired with this ado.
Why, hark ye, hark ye! And are you such fools
To square° for this? Would it offend you then　　*100*
That both should speed?°

80 *propose* be willing to meet　81 *Why makes thou it so strange*
why do you seem surprised　87 *shive* slice　89 *Vulcan's badge* i.e.,
the horns of cuckoldry (Vulcan's wife, Venus, deceived him with
Mars)　95 *snatch* catch (the likelihood that there is also a sexual
meaning here is increased by *turns* in the next line, a word often
denoting sexual acts)　100 *square* quarrel　101 *speed* prosper

Chiron.   Faith, not me.

Demetrius. Nor me, so I were one.

Aaron. For shame, be friends, and join for that you
    jar.°

'Tis policy° and stratagem must do
105   That you affect,° and so must you resolve,
That what you cannot as you would achieve,
You must perforce° accomplish as you may.
Take this of me, Lucrece° was not more chaste
Than this Lavinia, Bassianus' love.
110   A speedier course than ling'ring languishment
Must we pursue, and I have found the path.
My lords, a solemn° hunting is in hand.
There will the lovely Roman ladies troop:
The forest walks are wide and spacious,
115   And many unfrequented plots° there are
Fitted by kind° for rape and villainy.
Single° you thither then this dainty doe,
And strike her home by force, if not by words:
This way, or not at all, stand you in hope.
120   Come, come, our empress, with her sacred wit
To villainy and vengeance consecrate,
Will we acquaint withal what we intend,
And she shall file our engines° with advice,
That will not suffer you to square yourselves,
125   But to your wishes' height advance you both.
The Emperor's court is like the House of Fame,°
The palace full of tongues, of eyes, and ears:
The woods are ruthless,° dreadful, deaf, and dull;
There speak, and strike, brave boys, and take your
    turns,
130   There serve your lust shadowed from heaven's eye,
And revel in Lavinia's treasury.

103 *for that you jar* to get what you quarrel over   104 *policy* cunning   105 *affect* desire   107 *perforce* necessarily   108 *Lucrece*
Roman lady noted for her chastity; she killed herself when Sextus
Tarquinius raped her   112 *solemn* ceremonious   115 *unfrequented
plots* unvisited areas   116 *kind* nature   117 *Single* single out (a
hunting term)   123 *file our engines* sharpen our minds   126 *House
of Fame* (Ovid and Chaucer have notable poems on it; Fame =
Rumor, and the House of Fame is full of gossip)   128 *ruthless*
pitiless

Chiron. Thy counsel, lad, smells of no cow

Demetrius. Sit *fas aut nefas,*° till I find the strea
  To cool this heat, a charm to calm these fits,
  Per Stygia, per manes vehor.°   *Exeunt.* *133*

[Scene II. *A forest near Rome.*]

*Enter Titus Andronicus and his three sons [and
Marcus], making a noise with hounds and horns.*

Titus. The hunt is up, the morn is bright and gray,°
  The fields are fragrant, and the woods are green:
  Uncouple° here, and let us make a bay,°
  And wake the Emperor and his lovely bride,
  And rouse the Prince, and ring a hunter's peal,   *5*
  That all the court may echo with the noise.
  Sons, let it be your charge, as it is ours,
  To attend the Emperor's person carefully:
  I have been troubled in my sleep this night,
  But dawning day new comfort hath inspired.   *10*

Here a cry° *of hounds, and wind horns in a peal: then
enter Saturninus, Tamora, Bassianus, Lavinia,
Chiron, Demetrius, and their attendants.*

Many good morrows to your Majesty!
Madam, to you as many and as good!
I promisèd your Grace a hunter's peal.

Saturninus. And you have rung it lustily, my lords,
  Somewhat too early for new-married ladies.   *15*

Bassianus. Lavinia, how say you?

133 *Sit fas aut nefas* be it right or wrong (Latin) 135 *Per Stygia,
per manes vehor* I am carried through Stygian (infernal) regions,
through ghosts (Latin, derived from Seneca's *Hippolytus,* line 1177)
II.ii.1 *gray* sky blue (?)   3 *Uncouple* unleash the hounds   3 *make a
bay* keep up the cry of the hounds   10 s.d. *cry* deep barking

Lavinia.   I say, no;
   I have been broad awake two hours and more.

Saturninus. Come on then, horse and chariots let us
      have,
   And to our sport. [*To Tamora*] Madam, now shall
      ye see
   Our Roman hunting.

20 *Marcus.*   I have dogs, my lord,
   Will rouse the proudest panther in the chase,
   And climb the highest promontory top.

Titus. And I have horse will follow where the game
   Makes way and runs like swallows o'er the plain.

Demetrius. Chiron, we hunt not, we, with horse nor
25   hound,
   But hope to pluck a dainty doe to ground.   *Exeunt.*

[Scene III. *The forest.*]

Enter Aaron alone, [*with a bag of gold*].

Aaron. He that had wit would think that I had none,
   To bury so much gold under a tree
   And never after to inherit° it.
   Let him that thinks of me so abjectly°
5 Know that this gold must coin a stratagem,
   Which, cunningly effected, will beget
   A very excellent piece of villainy.
   And so repose, sweet gold, for their unrest,
   That have their alms out of the Empress' chest.
                                    [*Hides the gold.*]

Enter Tamora alone to the Moor.

10 *Tamora.* My lovely Aaron, wherefore look'st thou sad

II.iii.3 *inherit* possess   4 *abjectly* contemptuously

When every thing doth make a gleeful boast,
The birds chaunt melody on every bush,
The snakes lies rollèd in the cheerful sun,
The green leaves quiver with the cooling wind,
And make a checkered shadow on the ground: 15
Under their sweet shade, Aaron, let us sit,
And whilst the babbling echo mocks the hounds,
Replying shrilly to the well-tuned horns
As if a double hunt were heard at once,
Let us sit down and mark their yellowing° noise: 20
And after conflict such as was supposed
The wandering prince and Dido° once enjoyed,
When with a happy storm they were surprised
And curtained with a counsel-keeping cave,
We may, each wreathèd in the other's arms,   25
(Our pastimes done) possess a golden slumber,
Whiles hounds and horns and sweet melodious birds
Be unto us as is a nurse's song
Of lullaby to bring her babe asleep.

Aaron. Madam, though Venus govern your desires,   30
Saturn is dominator° over mine:
What signifies my deadly-standing° eye,
My silence and my cloudy melancholy,
My fleece of woolly hair that now uncurls
Even as an adder when she doth unroll   35
To do some fatal execution?
No, madam, these are no venereal° signs:
Vengeance is in my heart, death in my hand,
Blood and revenge are hammering in my head.
Hark, Tamora, the empress of my soul,   40
Which never hopes more heaven than rests in thee,
This is the day of doom for Bassianus:
His Philomel° must lose her tongue today,

11 *boast* display   20 *yellowing* loudly calling   22 *The wandering
prince and Dido* Aeneas and the Queen of Carthage (see Virgil's
Aeneid IV)   31 *Saturn is dominator* the planet Saturn (whose influence allegedly caused sluggishness) dominates   32 *deadly-stand-
ing* fixed in a deathlike stare (?)   37 *venereal* erotic   43 *Philomel*
(Philomela was ravished by Tereus, who then cut out her tongue;
later she communicated her plight by weaving the story into a
tapestry. See II.iv.26-27, 38-39; IV.i.47-48; V.ii.200)

Thy sons make pillage of her chastity,
45 And wash their hands in Bassianus' blood.
Seest thou this letter? Take it up, I pray thee,
And give the King this fatal-plotted scroll.
Now question me no more; we are espied.
Here comes a parcel of our hopeful booty,°
50 Which dreads not yet their lives' destruction.

Enter Bassianus and Lavinia.

Tamora. Ah, my sweet Moor, sweeter to me than life!

Aaron. No more, great Empress, Bassianus comes.
Be cross with him, and I'll go fetch thy sons
To back thy quarrels whatsoe'er they be.   [*Exit.*]

55 *Bassianus.* Who have we here? Rome's royal Empress,
Unfurnished of° her well-beseeming troop?
Or is it Dian, habited° like her,
Who hath abandonèd her holy groves
To see the general hunting in this forest?

60 *Tamora.* Saucy controller° of my private steps!
Had I the power that some say Dian had,
Thy temples should be planted presently°
With horns, as was Actaeon's,° and the hounds
Should drive upon thy new-transformèd limbs,
65 Unmannerly intruder as thou art!

Lavinia. Under your patience, gentle Empress,
'Tis thought you have a goodly gift in horning,°
And to be doubted° that your Moor and you
Are singled forth to try experiments:
70 Jove shield your husband from his hounds today!
'Tis pity they should take him for a stag.

Bassianus. Believe me, Queen, your swart Cimmerian°

49 *parcel of our hopeful booty* part of the victims we hope for
56 *Unfurnished of* unaccompanied by   57 *habited* dressed   60 *controller* critic   62 *presently* immediately   63 *Actaeon* legendary hunter who spied on Diana bathing; she transformed him into a stag and his own hounds killed him   67 *horning* (an unfaithful wife was said to give her husband horns)   68 *doubted* suspected
72 *Cimmerian* dweller in darkness

    Doth make your honor of his body's hue,
    Spotted,° detested, and abominable.
    Why are you sequest'rèd from all your train,   75
    Dismounted from your snow-white goodly steed,
    And wand'red hither to an obscure plot,
    Accompanied but with a barbarous Moor,
    If foul desire had not conducted you?

Lavinia. And, being intercepted in your sport,   80
    Great reason that my noble lord be rated°
    For sauciness. I pray you, let us hence,
    And let her joy° her raven-colored love;
    This valley fits the purpose passing well.

Bassianus. The King my brother shall have notice° of
    this.   85

Lavinia. Ay, for these slips have made him noted°
    long.
    Good king, to be so mightily abused!

Tamora. Why, I have patience to endure all this.

        Enter Chiron and Demetrius.

Demetrius. How now, dear sovereign, and our gra-
    cious mother,
    Why doth your Highness look so pale and wan?   90

Tamora. Have I not reason, think you, to look pale?
    These two have ticed° me hither to this place,
    A barren detested vale, you see it is;
    The trees, though summer, yet forlorn and lean,
    Overcome with moss and baleful mistletoe: 95
    Here never shines the sun; here nothing breeds,
    Unless the nightly owl or fatal raven:
    And when they showed me this abhorrèd pit,
    They told me, here, at dead time of the night
    A thousand fiends, a thousand hissing snakes,   100
    Ten thousand swelling toads, as many urchins,°
    Would make such fearful and confusèd cries,

74 *Spotted* infected 81 *rated* berated, rebuked 83 *joy* enjoy 85
notice (monosyllabic, pronounced "notes") 86 *noted* notorious
92 *ticed* enticed 101 *urchins* hedgehogs

As any mortal body hearing it
Should straight fall mad, or else die suddenly.
105 No sooner had they told this hellish tale,
But straight they told me they would bind me here
Unto the body of a dismal yew,
And leave me to this miserable death.
And then they called me foul adulteress,
110 Lascivious Goth,° and all the bitterest terms
That ever ear did hear to such effect.
And, had you not by wondrous fortune come,
This vengeance on me had they executed:
Revenge it, as you love your mother's life,
115 Or be ye not henceforth called my children.

Demetrius. This is a witness that I am thy son.
                                    Stab[s] him.

Chiron. And this for me, struck home to show my
        strength.   [*Stabs Bassianus.*]

Lavinia. Ay come, Semiramis, nay, barbarous
        Tamora!
For no name fits thy nature but thy own!

Tamora. Give me the poniard! You shall know, my
120   boys,
Your mother's hand shall right your mother's
        wrong.

Demetrius. Stay, madam; here is more belongs to her.
First thrash the corn, then after burn the straw.
This minion stood upon° her chastity,
125 Upon her nuptial vow, her loyalty,
And with that painted° hope braves your mighti-
        ness:
And shall she carry this unto her grave?

Chiron. And if she do, I would I were an eunuch.
Drag hence her husband to some secret hole,

110 *Goth* (possibly a pun on "goat," an animal believed to be
lascivious)   124 *minion stood upon* hussy made a fuss about   126
painted specious, unreal

And make his dead trunk pillow to our lust.   *130*

Tamora. But when ye have the honey we desire,
Let not this wasp outlive us both to sting.

Chiron. I warrant you, madam, we will make that
sure.
Come, mistress, now perforce we will enjoy
That nice-preservèd honesty° of yours.   *135*

Lavinia. O Tamora! Thou bearest a woman's face—

Tamora. I will not hear her speak; away with her.

Lavinia. Sweet lords, entreat her hear me but a word.

Demetrius. Listen, fair madam, let it be your glory
To see her tears, but be your heart to them   *140*
As unrelenting flint to drops of rain.

Lavinia. When did the tiger's young ones teach the
dam?°
O, do not learn° her wrath; she taught it thee.
The milk thou suck'st from her did turn to marble;
Even at thy teat thou hadst thy tyranny.   *145*
Yet every mother breeds not sons alike,
[*To Chiron*] Do thou entreat her show a woman's
pity.

Chiron. What! Wouldst thou have me prove myself
a bastard?

Lavinia. 'Tis true; the raven doth not hatch a lark:
Yet have I heard—O could I find it now!—   *150*
The lion, moved with pity, did endure
To have his princely paws pared all away.
Some say that ravens foster forlorn children,
The whilst their own birds famish in their nests:
O, be to me, though thy hard heart say no,   *155*
Nothing so kind but something pitiful!°

135 *nice-preserved honesty* fastidiously guarded chastity   142 *dam*
mother   143 *learn* teach   156 *Nothing so kind but something pitiful* i.e., not so kind as the raven, but somewhat pitying

Tamora. I know not what it means; away with her!

Lavinia. O, let me teach thee for my father's sake,
 That gave thee life when well he might have slain
  thee.
160 Be not obdurate, open thy deaf ears.

Tamora. Hadst thou in person ne'er offended me,
 Even for his sake am I pitiless.
 Remember, boys, I poured forth tears in vain
 To save your brother from the sacrifice,
165 But fierce Andronicus would not relent.
 Therefore away with her, and use her as you will;
 The worse to her, the better loved of me.

Lavinia. O Tamora, be called a gentle queen,
 And with thine own hands kill me in this place!
170 For 'tis not life that I have begged so long;
 Poor I was slain when Bassianus died.

Tamora. What begg'st thou then? Fond° woman, let
 me go.

Lavinia. 'Tis present death I beg, and one thing more
 That womanhood denies° my tongue to tell.
175 O, keep me from their worse than killing lust,
 And tumble me into some loathsome pit,
 Where never man's eye may behold my body.
 Do this, and be a charitable murderer.

Tamora. So should I rob my sweet sons of their fee.
180 No, let them satisfice their lust on thee.

Demetrius. Away! For thou hast stayed us here too
 long.

Lavinia. No grace? No womanhood? Ah beastly crea-
 ture!
 The blot and enemy to our general name!°
 Confusion° fall—

Chiron. Nay, then I'll stop your mouth. Bring thou
185 her husband.

172 *Fond* foolish 174 *denies* forbids 183 *our general name* i.e.,
womankind 184 *Confusion* destruction

This is the hole where Aaron bid us hide him.
[*Demetrius throws the corpse into a pit and then
covers it with branches. Exeunt Demetrius and
Chiron, dragging Lavinia.*]

Tamora. Farewell, my sons, see that you make her
    sure.
  Ne'er let my heart know merry cheer indeed
  Till all the Andronici be made away.°
  Now will I hence to seek my lovely Moor,   190
  And let my spleenful° sons this trull° deflower.
                          [*Exit.*]

*Enter Aaron with two of Titus' sons [Quintus and
Martius].*

[*Aaron.*] Come on, my lords, the better foot before!
  Straight will I bring you to the loathesome pit
  Where I espied the panther fast asleep.

Quintus. My sight is very dull, whate'er it bodes.   195

Martius. And mine, I promise you. Were it not for
    shame,
  Well could I leave our sport to sleep awhile.
                [*He falls into the pit.*]

Quintus. What, art thou fallen? What subtle hole is
    this,
  Whose mouth is covered with rude-growing briers,
  Upon whose leaves are drops of new-shed blood   200
  As fresh as morning dew distilled on flowers?
  A very fatal place it seems to me.
  Speak, brother, hast thou hurt thee with the fall?

Martius. O, brother, with the dismal'st object hurt
  That ever eye with sight made heart lament.   205

Aaron. [*Aside*] Now will I fetch the King to find them
    here,
  That he thereby may have a likely guess
  How these were they that made away his brother.
                     Exit.

189 *made away* killed   191 *spleenful* lustful   191 *trull* strumpet

Martius. Why dost not comfort me and help me out
210   From this unhallowed and bloodstainèd hole?

Quintus. I am surprisèd° with an uncouth° fear,
        A chilling sweat o'erruns my trembling joints;
        My heart suspects more than mine eye can see.

Martius. To prove thou hast a true-divining heart,
215   Aaron and thou look down into this den
        And see a fearful sight of blood and death.

Quintus. Aaron is gone, and my compassionate heart
        Will not permit mine eyes once to behold
        The thing whereat it trembles by surmise.
220   O, tell me who it is, for ne'er till now
        Was I a child to fear I know not what.

Martius. Lord Bassianus lies berayed° in blood,
        All on a heap, like to a slaughtered lamb,
        In this detested, dark, blood-drinking pit.

225 *Quintus.* If it be dark, how dost thou know 'tis he?

Martius. Upon his bloody finger he doth wear
        A precious ring that lightens all this hole,
        Which, like a taper in some monument,
        Doth shine upon the dead man's earthy cheeks,
230   And shows the ragged entrails° of this pit:
        So pale did shine the moon on Pyramus,
        When he by night lay bathed in maiden blood.
        O brother, help me with thy fainting hand—
        If fear hath made thee faint, as me it hath—
235   Out of this fell° devouring receptacle,
        As hateful as Cocytus'° misty mouth.

Quintus. Reach me thy hand, that I may help thee out;
        Or, wanting° strength to do thee so much good,
        I may be plucked into the swallowing womb
240   Of this deep pit, poor Bassianus' grave.
        I have no strength to pluck thee to the brink.

---

211 *surprisèd* dumfounded   211 *uncouth* strange   222 *berayed* defiled   230 *ragged entrails* rugged interior   235 *fell* savage   236
Cocytus river in Hades   238 *wanting* lacking

Martius. Nor I no strength to climb without thy help.

Quintus. Thy hand once more; I will not loose again
　　Till thou art here aloft or I below:
　　Thou canst not come to me; I come to thee.   245
　　　　　　　　　　　　　　　　[*Falls in.*]

　　Enter the Emperor and Aaron the Moor.

Saturninus. Along with me! I'll see what hole is here,
　　And what he is that now is leaped into it.
　　Say, who art thou, that lately didst descend
　　Into this gaping hollow of the earth?

Martius. The unhappy sons of old Andronicus,   250
　　Brought hither in a most unlucky hour,
　　To find thy brother Bassianus dead.

Saturninus. My brother dead! I know thou dost but
　　jest:
　　He and his lady both are at the lodge,
　　Upon the north side of this pleasant chase;   255
　　'Tis not an hour since I left them there.

Martius. We know not where you left them all alive,
　　But, out alas! Here have we found him dead.

　　Enter Tamora, Andronicus, and Lucius.

Tamora. Where is my lord the King?

Saturninus. Here, Tamora, though grieved with killing
　　grief.   260

Tamora. Where is thy brother, Bassianus?

Saturninus. Now to the bottom dost thou search° my
　　wound;
　　Poor Bassianus here lies murderèd.

Tamora. Then all too late I bring this fatal writ,
　　The complot° of this timeless° tragedy;   265
　　And wonder greatly that man's face can fold°

262 *search* probe　265 *complot* plot　265 *timeless* untimely　266
fold hide (in the creases of a hypocritical smile)

In pleasing smiles such murderous tyranny.
                    She giveth Saturnine a letter.

Saturninus. (*Reads the letter.*) "And if° we miss to
        meet him handsomely°—
        Sweet huntsman, Bassianus 'tis we mean—
270   Do thou so much as dig the grave for him.
        Thou know'st our meaning. Look for thy reward
        Among the nettles at the elder tree
        Which overshades the mouth of that same pit
        Where we decreed to bury Bassianus.
275   Do this and purchase us thy lasting friends."
        O, Tamora! Was ever heard the like?
        This is the pit, and this the elder tree.
        Look, sirs, if you can find the huntsman out
        That should° have murdered Bassianus here.

280 *Aaron.* My gracious lord, here is the bag of gold.

Saturninus. [*To Titus*] Two of thy whelps, fell° curs
        of bloody kind,°
        Have here bereft my brother of his life.
        Sirs, drag them from the pit unto the prison,
        There let them bide until we have devised
285   Some never-heard-of torturing pain for them.

Tamora. What, are they in this pit? O wondrous thing!
        How easily murder is discoverèd!

Titus. High Emperor, upon my feeble knee
        I beg this boon, with tears not lightly shed,
290   That this fell fault of my accursèd sons,
        Accursèd, if the faults be proved in them—

Saturninus. If it be proved! You see, it is apparent.°
        Who found this letter? Tamora, was it you?

Tamora. Andronicus himself did take it up.

295 *Titus.* I did, my lord, yet let me be their bail,
        For by my father's reverend tomb I vow
        They shall be ready at your Highness' will

268 *And if* if   268 *handsomely* handily   279 *should* was to   281
fell savage   281 *kind* nature   292 *apparent* obvious

To answer their suspicion° with their lives.

Saturninus. Thou shalt not bail them; see thou follow
    me.
Some bring the murdered body, some the murderers.   300
Let them not speak a word; the guilt is plain,
For by my soul were there worse end than death,
That end upon them should be executed.

Tamora. Andronicus, I will entreat the King.
Fear not° thy sons; they shall do well enough.   305

Titus. Come, Lucius, come, stay not to talk with them.
                                        [*Exeunt.*]

[Scene IV. *The forest.*]

*Enter the Empress' sons with Lavinia, her hands cut
off, and her tongue cut out, and ravished.*

Demetrius. So, now go tell, and if° thy tongue can
    speak,
Who 'twas that cut thy tongue and ravished thee.

Chiron. Write down thy mind, bewray° thy meaning
    so,
And if thy stumps will let thee play the scribe.

Demetrius. See how with signs and tokens she can
    scrowl.°   5

Chiron. Go home, call for sweet° water, wash thy
    hands.

Demetrius. She hath no tongue to call nor hands to
    wash,
And so let's leave her to her silent walks.

298 *their suspicion* i.e., the suspicion they are under   305 *Fear not*
do not fear for   II.iv.1 *and if* if (as in line 4)   3 *bewray* reveal   5
scrowl scrawl (with a pun on "scroll"?)   6 *sweet* perfumed

Chiron. And 'twere my cause,° I should go hang
    myself.

Demetrius. If thou hadst hands to help thee knit the
10   cord.   *Exeunt [Chiron and Demetrius].*

        Enter Marcus from hunting.

Marcus. Who is this? My niece, that flies away so fast!
    Cousin,° a word, where is your husband?
    If I do dream, would all my wealth would wake me!
    If I do wake, some planet strike me down,
15   That I may slumber an eternal sleep!
    Speak, gentle niece, what stern ungentle hands
    Hath lopped and hewed and made thy body bare
    Of her two branches, those sweet ornaments,
    Whose circling shadows kings have sought to sleep
      in,
20   And might not gain so great a happiness
    As half thy love? Why dost not speak to me?
    Alas, a crimson river of warm blood,
    Like to a bubbling fountain stirred with wind,
    Doth rise and fall between thy rosèd lips,
25   Coming and going with thy honey breath.
    But, sure, some Tereus° hath deflowered thee,
    And, lest thou shouldst detect° him, cut thy tongue.
    Ah, now thou turn'st away thy face for shame!
    And, notwithstanding all this loss of blood,
30   As from a conduit with three issuing spouts,
    Yet do thy cheeks look red as Titan's° face
    Blushing to be encount'red with a cloud.
    Shall I speak for thee? Shall I say 'tis so?
    O, that I knew thy heart, and knew the beast,
35   That I might rail at him to ease my mind!
    Sorrow concealèd, like an oven stopped,
    Doth burn the heart to cinders where it is.
    Fair Philomela, why she but lost her tongue,

---

9 *cause* case   12 *Cousin* (commonly used of any near relative other
than a parent, child, or sibling)   26 *Tereus* ravisher of Philomela
(see note to II.iii.43)   27 *detect* expose   31 *Titan's* the sun god's

And in a tedious sampler° sewed her mind:
But lovely niece, that mean is cut from thee;   40
A craftier Tereus, cousin, hast thou met,
And he hath cut those pretty fingers off,
That could have better sewed than Philomel.
O, had the monster seen those lily hands
Tremble like aspen leaves upon a lute,   45
And make the silken strings delight to kiss them,
He would not then have touched them for his life!
Or, had he heard the heavenly harmony
Which that sweet tongue hath made,
He would have dropped his knife, and fell asleep   50
As Cerberus° at the Thracian poet's feet.
Come, let us go and make thy father blind,
For such a sight will blind a father's eye.
One hour's storm will drown the fragrant meads;
What will whole months of tears thy father's eyes?   55
Do not draw back, for we will mourn with thee:
O, could our mourning ease thy misery!   *Exeunt.*

39 *tedious sampler* laboriously executed tapestry   51 *Cerberus*
three-headed dog who guarded the entrance to Hades; he was lulled
by Orpheus, *the Thracian poet*

[ACT III

Scene I. *Rome. A street.*]

*Enter the Judges and Senators with Titus' two
sons bound, passing on the stage to the place of
execution, and Titus going before, pleading.*

Titus. Hear me, grave fathers! Noble tribunes, stay!
  For pity of mine age, whose youth was spent
  In dangerous wars, whilst you securely slept;
  For all my blood in Rome's great quarrel shed,
5 For all the frosty nights that I have watched,
  And for these bitter tears, which now you see
  Filling the agèd wrinkles in my cheeks,
  Be pitiful to my condemnèd sons,
  Whose souls is not corrupted as 'tis thought.
10 For two and twenty sons I never wept,
  Because they died in honor's lofty bed;

Andronicus lieth down° and the Judges pass by him.

  For these, tribunes, in the dust I write
  My heart's deep languor° and my soul's sad tears:
  Let my tears staunch° the earth's dry appetite;
15 My sons' sweet blood will make it shame and blush.
  O earth, I will befriend thee more with rain,
  That shall distill from these two ancient ruins,
  Than youthful April shall with all his show'rs:
  In summer's drought I'll drop upon thee still,°

III.i.11 s.d. *lieth down* i.e., prostrates himself   13 *languor* grief
14 *staunch* satisfy, satiate   19 *still* continuously

In winter with warm tears I'll melt the snow,　　20
And keep eternal springtime on thy face,
So° thou refuse to drink my dear sons' blood.

Enter Lucius, with his weapon drawn.

O reverend tribunes! O gentle agèd men!
Unbind my sons, reverse the doom° of death,
And let me say, that never wept before,　　25
My tears are now prevailing orators.

Lucius. O noble father, you lament in vain,
The tribunes hear you not, no man is by,
And you recount your sorrows to a stone.

Titus. Ah, Lucius, for thy brothers let me plead.　　30
Grave tribunes, once more I entreat of you.

Lucius. My gracious lord, no tribune hears you speak.

Titus. Why, 'tis no matter, man, if they did hear
They would not mark me, if they did mark
They would not pity me, yet plead I must,　　35
And bootless° unto them.
Therefore I tell my sorrows to the stones,
Who though they cannot answer my distress,
Yet in some sort they are better than the tribunes,
For that they will not intercept° my tale:　　40
When I do weep they humbly at my feet
Receive my tears and seem to weep with me;
And were they but attirèd in grave weeds,°
Rome could afford no tribunes like to these.
A stone is soft as wax, tribunes more hard than
　stones:　　45
A stone is silent and offendeth not,
And tribunes with their tongues doom men to death.
But wherefore stand'st thou with thy weapon
　drawn?

Lucius. To rescue my two brothers from their death,
For which attempt the judges have pronounced　　50

22 *So* provided that　24 *doom* judgment　36 *bootless* in vain　40
intercept interrupt　43 *grave weeds* solemn apparel

My everlasting doom of banishment.

Titus. O happy man! They have befriended thee.
Why, foolish Lucius, dost thou not perceive
That Rome is but a wilderness of tigers?
55   Tigers must prey, and Rome affords no prey
But me and mine. How happy art thou then,
From these devourers to be banishèd!
But who comes with our brother Marcus here?

Enter Marcus with Lavinia.

Marcus. Titus, prepare thy agèd eyes to weep,
60   Or if not so, thy noble heart to break.
I bring consuming sorrow to thine age.

Titus. Will it consume me? Let me see it then.

Marcus. This was thy daughter.

Titus.   Why, Marcus, so she is.

Lucius. Ay me! This object° kills me!

65 *Titus.* Faint-hearted boy, arise, and look upon her.
Speak, Lavinia, what accursèd hand
Hath made thee handless in thy father's sight?
What fool hath added water to the sea,
Or brought a faggot to bright-burning Troy?
70   My grief was at the height before thou cam'st,
And now like Nilus° it disdaineth bounds.
Give me a sword, I'll chop off my hands too,
For they have fought for Rome, and all in vain;
And they have nursed this woe, in feeding life;
75   In bootless prayer have they been held up,
And they have served me to effectless use.
Now all the service I require of them
Is that the one will help to cut the other.
'Tis well, Lavinia, that thou hast no hands,
80   For hands to do Rome service is but vain.

Lucius. Speak, gentle sister, who hath mart'red° thee?

Marcus. O, that delightful engine° of her thoughts,

64 *object* sight   71 *Nilus* the Nile   81 *mart'red* mutilated   82 *engine* instrument

That blabbed° them with such pleasing eloquence,
Is torn from forth that pretty hollow cage,
Where like a sweet melodious bird it sung   85
Sweet varied notes, enchanting every ear!

Lucius. O, say thou for her, who hath done this deed?

Marcus. O, thus I found her, straying in the park,
Seeking to hide herself, as doth the deer
That hath received some unrecuring° wound.   90

Titus. It was my dear, and he that wounded her
Hath hurt me more than had he killed me dead:
For now I stand as one upon a rock,
Environed with a wilderness of sea,
Who marks the waxing tide grow wave by wave,   95
Expecting ever when some envious° surge
Will in his brinish bowels swallow him.
This way to death my wretched sons are gone,
Here stands my other son, a banished man,
And here my brother weeping at my woes: 100
But that which gives my soul the greatest spurn°
Is dear Lavinia, dearer than my soul.
Had I but seen thy picture in this plight,
It would have madded me: what shall I do
Now I behold thy lively° body so?   105
Thou hast no hands to wipe away thy tears,
Nor tongue to tell me who hath mart'red thee.
Thy husband he is dead, and for his death
Thy brothers are condemned, and dead by this.°
Look, Marcus! Ah, son Lucius, look on her!   110
When I did name her brothers, then fresh tears
Stood on her cheeks, as doth the honey-dew
Upon a gath'red lily almost withered.

Marcus. Perchance she weeps because they killed her
    husband,
Perchance because she knows them innocent.   115

---

83 *blabbed* freely spoke   90 *unrecuring* incurable   96 *envious* malicious   101 *spurn* thrust   105 *lively* living   109 *by this* by this time

Titus. If they did kill thy husband, then be joyful,
 Because the law hath ta'en revenge on them.
 No, no, they would not do so foul a deed;
 Witness the sorrow that their sister makes.
120 Gentle Lavinia, let me kiss thy lips,
 Or make some sign how I may do thee ease.°
 Shall thy good uncle, and thy brother Lucius,
 And thou, and I, sit round about some fountain,
 Looking all downwards, to behold our cheeks
125 How they are stained, like meadows yet not dry
 With miry slime left on them by a flood?
 And in the fountain shall we gaze so long
 Till the fresh taste be taken from that clearness,°
 And made a brine-pit with our bitter tears?
130 Or shall we cut away our hands, like thine?
 Or shall we bite our tongues, and in dumb shows°
 Pass the remainder of our hateful days?
 What shall we do? Let us, that have our tongues,
 Plot some device of further misery,
135 To make us wondered at in time to come.

Lucius. Sweet father, cease your tears, for at your grief
 See how my wretched sister sobs and weeps.

Marcus. Patience, dear niece. Good Titus, dry thine eyes.

Titus. Ah, Marcus, Marcus! Brother, well I wot
140 Thy napkin° cannot drink a tear of mine,
 For thou, poor man, hast drowned it with thine own.

Lucius. Ah, my Lavinia, I will wipe thy cheeks.

Titus. Mark, Marcus, mark! I understand her signs:
 Had she a tongue to speak, now would she say
145 That to her brother which I said to thee:
 His napkin, with his true tears all bewet,
 Can do no service on her sorrowful cheeks.
 O, what a sympathy° of woe is this!

121 *do thee ease* bring you relief 128 *clearness* i.e., clear pool 131 *dumb shows* silent signs 140 *napkin* handkerchief 148 *sympathy* agreement

As far from help as Limbo is from bliss!

Enter Aaron the Moor alone.

Aaron. Titus Andronicus, my lord the Emperor   150
　Sends thee this word, that, if thou love thy sons,
　Let Marcus, Lucius, or thyself, old Titus,
　Or any one of you, chop off your hand
　And send it to the King: he for the same
　Will send thee hither both thy sons alive,   155
　And that shall be the ransom for their fault.

Titus. O, gracious Emperor! O, gentle Aaron!
　Did ever raven sing so like a lark,
　That gives sweet tidings of the sun's uprise?
　With all my heart, I'll send the Emperor my hand.   160
　Good Aaron, wilt thou help to chop it off?

Lucius. Stay, father! For that noble hand of thine
　That hath thrown down so many enemies
　Shall not be sent; my hand will serve the turn.
　My youth can better spare my blood than you,   165
　And therefore mine shall save my brothers' lives.

Marcus. Which of your hands hath not defended Rome
　And reared aloft the bloody battle-ax,
　Writing destruction on the enemy's castle?
　O, none of both but are of high desert: 170
　My hand hath been but idle; let it serve
　To ransom my two nephews from their death,
　Then have I kept it to a worthy end.

Aaron. Nay, come, agree whose hand shall go along,
　For fear they die before their pardon come.   175

Marcus. My hand shall go.

Lucius. 　　　　　　By heaven, it shall not go.

Titus. Sirs, strive no more; such with'red herbs as these
　Are meet° for plucking up, and therefore mine.

Lucius. Sweet father, if I shall be thought thy son,
　Let me redeem my brothers both from death.   180

178 *meet* fit

Marcus. And, for our father's sake and mother's care,
　Now let me show a brother's love to thee.

Titus. Agree between you; I will spare my hand.

Lucius. Then I'll go fetch an ax.

185　*Marcus.* But I will use the ax.
　　　　　　　　　　Exeunt [*Lucius and Marcus*].

Titus. Come hither, Aaron. I'll deceive them both;
　Lend me thy hand, and I will give thee mine.

Aaron. [*Aside*] If that be called deceit, I will be honest,
　And never whilst I live deceive men so:
190　But I'll deceive you in another sort,
　And that you'll say, ere half an hour pass.
　　　　　　　　　　He cuts off Titus' hand.

Enter Lucius and Marcus again.

Titus. Now stay your strife, what shall be is dis-
　　patched.
　Good Aaron, give his Majesty my hand;
　Tell him it was a hand that warded° him
195　From thousand dangers; bid him bury it;
　More hath it merited, that let it have.
　As for my sons, say I account of them
　As jewels purchased at an easy price,
　And yet dear too because I bought mine own.

200　*Aaron.* I go, Andronicus, and for thy hand
　Look by and by to have thy sons with thee.
　[*Aside*] Their heads, I mean. O, how this villainy
　Doth fat° me with the very thoughts of it!
　Let fools do good, and fair men call for grace,
205　Aaron will have his soul black like his face.　*Exit.*

Titus. O, here I lift this one hand up to heaven,
　And bow this feeble ruin to the earth.
　If any power pities wretched tears,
　To that I call! [*To Lavinia*] What, wouldst thou
　　kneel with me?

194 *warded* guarded　203 *fat* delight (literally: "nourish")

Do then, dear heart, for heaven shall hear our
   prayers,   210
Or with our sighs we'll breathe the welkin dim,°
And stain the sun with fog, as sometime clouds
When they do hug him in their melting bosoms.

Marcus. O brother, speak with possibility,
   And do not break into these deep extremes.   215

Titus. Is not my sorrow deep, having no bottom?
   Then be my passions° bottomless with them.

Marcus. But yet let reason govern thy lament.

Titus. If there were reason for these miseries,
   Then into limits could I bind my woes: 220
When heaven doth weep, doth not the earth
   o'erflow?
If the winds rage, doth not the sea wax mad,
Threat'ning the welkin with his big-swoll'n face?
And wilt thou have a reason for this coil?°
I am the sea; hark, how her sighs doth flow!   225
She is the weeping welkin, I the earth:
Then must my sea be movèd with her sighs,
Then must my earth with her continual tears
Become a deluge, overflowed and drowned,
For why° my bowels° cannot hide her woes,   230
But like a drunkard must I vomit them.
Then give me leave, for losers will have leave
To ease their stomachs° with their bitter tongues.

Enter a Messenger, with two heads and a hand.

Messenger. Worthy Andronicus, ill art thou repaid
   For that good hand thou sent'st the Emperor.   235
Here are the heads of thy two noble sons,
And here's thy hand in scorn to thee sent back;
Thy grief their sports, thy resolution mocked:

211 *breathe the welkin dim* becloud the heavens with our breath
217 *passions* outbursts   224 *coil* fuss   230 *For why* because   230
bowels (thought to be the seat of compassion; akin to the modern
use of "heart")   233 *stomachs* feeling

That° woe is me to think upon thy woes,
240 More than remembrance of my father's death.

[Exit.]

Marcus. Now let hot Etna cool in Sicily,
And be my heart an ever-burning hell!
These miseries are more than may be borne!
To weep with them that weep doth ease some deal,°
245 But sorrow flouted at is double death.

Lucius. Ah, that this sight should make so deep a
wound,
And yet detested life not shrink° thereat!
That ever death should let life bear his name,°
Where life hath no more interest but to breathe!

[Lavinia kisses Titus.]

250 *Marcus.* Alas, poor heart, that kiss is comfortless
As frozen water to a starvèd° snake.

Titus. When will this fearful slumber° have an end?

Marcus. Now, farewell, flatt'ry, die Andronicus,
Thou dost not slumber: see thy two sons' heads,
255 Thy warlike hand, thy mangled daughter here,
Thy other banished son with this dear° sight
Struck pale and bloodless, and thy brother, I,
Even like a stony image cold and numb.
Ah! Now no more will I control thy griefs:
260 Rend off thy silver hair, thy other hand
Gnawing with thy teeth, and be this dismal sight
The closing up of our most wretched eyes:
Now is a time to storm; why art thou still?

Titus. Ha, ha, ha!

Marcus. Why dost thou laugh? It fits not with this
265 hour.

Titus. Why, I have not another tear to shed.
Besides, this sorrow is an enemy,

239 *That* so that   244 *some deal* somewhat   247 *shrink* slip away
248 *bear his name* i.e., be called "life"   251 *starvèd* numbed
252 *fearful slumber* i.e., nightmare existence   256 *dear* heartfelt

And would usurp upon my wat'ry eyes
And make them blind with tributary° tears;
Then which way shall I find Revenge's Cave?   270
For these two heads do seem to speak to me,
And threat me I shall never come to bliss
Till all these mischiefs be returned again,
Even in their throats that hath committed them.
Come, let me see what task I have to do.   275
You heavy° people, circle me about,
That I may turn me to each one of you,
And swear unto my soul to right your wrongs.
The vow is made. Come, brother, take a head;
And in this hand the other will I bear.   280
And Lavinia, thou shalt be employed in these arms,
Bear thou my hand, sweet wench, between thy
    teeth:°
As for thee, boy, go, get thee from my sight.
Thou art an exile, and thou must not stay.
Hie to the Goths, and raise an army there,   285
And, if ye love me, as I think you do,
Let's kiss and part, for we have much to do.
                          Exeunt [all but Lucius].

Lucius. Farewell, Andronicus, my noble father,
    The woefull'st man that ever lived in Rome!
    Farewell, proud Rome, till Lucius come again;   290
    He loves his pledges dearer than his life.
    Farewell, Lavinia, my noble sister;
    O, would thou wert as thou tofore° hast been!
    But now nor Lucius nor° Lavinia lives
    But in oblivion and hateful griefs.   295
    If Lucius live, he will requite your wrongs,
    And make proud Saturnine and his empress
    Beg at the gates, like Tarquin° and his queen.

269 *tributary* paid as tribute   276 *heavy* sad   282 *teeth* (possibly
Shakespeare intended to delete "teeth" from the manuscript, and
substituted the less grotesque "arms" above it; if so, the compositor
mistakenly took "arms" to be part of the previous line, and to make
sense of it he perhaps altered something like "employed in this" to
"employed in these arms")   293 *tofore* formerly   294 *nor . . . nor*
neither . . . nor   298 *Tarquin* Roman king whose rule was overthrown when his son (of the same name) raped Lucrece

Now will I to the Goths and raise a pow'r,
300   To be revenged on Rome and Saturnine.

Exit Lucius.

[Scene II. *Rome. Within Titus' house.*]

*A banket.° Enter Andronicus, Marcus, Lavinia,
and the boy [Lucius].*

Titus. So, so, now sit, and look you eat no more
    Than will preserve just so much strength in us
    As will revenge these bitter woes of ours.
    Marcus, unknit that sorrow-wreathen knot:°
5   Thy niece and I, poor creatures, want our hands,
    And cannot passionate° our tenfold grief
    With folded arms. This poor right hand of mine
    Is left to tyrannize upon my breast;
    Who, when my heart all mad with misery
10   Beats in this hollow prison of my flesh,
    Then thus I thump it down.
    [*To Lavinia*] Thou map° of woe, that thus dost talk
       in signs,
    When thy poor heart beats with outrageous beating,
    Thou canst not strike it thus to make it still.
15   Wound it with sighing,° girl, kill it with groans;
    Or get some little knife between thy teeth,
    And just against thy heart make thou a hole,
    That all the tears that thy poor eyes let fall
    May run into that sink,° and soaking in
20   Drown the lamenting fool° in sea-salt tears.

Marcus. Fie, brother, fie! Teach her not thus to lay
    Such violent hands upon her tender life.

III.ii.s.d. *banket* light meal   4 *knot* i.e., Marcus' folded arms, a sign
of heavy thoughts   6 *passionate* passionately express   12 *map* picture   15 *wound it with sighing* (sighing was believed to shorten life)
19 *sink* sewer   20 *fool* (here, as often, implying affection and pity)

Titus. How now! Has sorrow made thee dote already?
Why, Marcus, no man should be mad but I.
What violent hands can she lay on her life!   25
Ah, wherefore dost thou urge the name of hands,
To bid Aeneas° tell the tale twice o'er,
How Troy was burnt and he made miserable?
O, handle not the theme, to talk of hands,
Lest we remember still that we have none.   30
Fie, fie, how franticly I square° my talk,
As if we should forget we had no hands,
If Marcus did not name the word of hands!
Come, let's fall to; and, gentle girl, eat this.
Here is no drink? Hark, Marcus, what she says—   35
I can interpret all her martyred signs—
She says she drinks no other drink but tears,
Brewed with her sorrow, meshed° upon her cheeks.
Speechless complainer, I will learn thy thought;
In thy dumb action will I be as perfect°   40
As begging hermits in their holy prayers:
Thou shalt not sigh, nor hold thy stumps to heaven,
Nor wink,° nor nod, nor kneel, nor make a sign,
But I of these will wrest an alphabet,
And by still° practice learn to know thy meaning.   45

Boy. Good grandsire, leave these bitter deep laments.
Make my aunt merry with some pleasing tale.

Marcus. Alas, the tender boy, in passion moved,
Doth weep to see his grandsire's heaviness.

Titus. Peace, tender sapling, thou art made of tears,   50
And tears will quickly melt thy life away.
          Marcus strikes the dish with a knife.
What dost thou strike at, Marcus, with thy knife?

Marcus. At that that I have killed, my lord—a fly.

Titus. Out on thee, murderer! Thou kill'st my heart;
Mine eyes are cloyed with view of tyranny: 55
A deed of death done on the innocent

27 *Aeneas* (see Virgil's *Aeneid* II.2)   31 *square* shape   38 *meshed*
mashed, brewed   40 *perfect* fully knowing   43 *wink* shut the eyes
45 *still* constant

Becomes not Titus' brother. Get thee gone;
I see thou art not for my company.

Marcus. Alas, my lord, I have but killed a fly.

60 *Titus.* "But!" How, if that fly had a father and mother?
How would he hang his slender gilded wings,
And buzz lamenting doings in the air!
Poor harmless fly,
That, with his pretty buzzing melody,
65 Came here to make us merry! And thou hast killed
him.

Marcus. Pardon me, sir; it was a black ill-favored°
fly,
Like to the Empress' Moor. Therefore I killed him.

Titus. O, O, O,
Then pardon me for reprehending thee,
70 For thou hast done a charitable deed.
Give me thy knife, I will insult on° him,
Flattering myself, as if it were the Moor,
Come hither purposely to poison me.
                    [*He strikes at it.*]
There's for thyself, and that's for Tamora.
75 Ah, sirrah!°
Yet I think we are not brought so low
But that between us we can kill a fly
That comes in likeness of a coal-black Moor.

Marcus. Alas, poor man! Grief has so wrought on
him,
80 He takes false shadows for true substances.

Titus. Come, take away.° Lavinia, go with me:
I'll to thy closet,° and go read with thee
Sad stories chancèd° in the times of old.
Come, boy, and go with me; thy sight is young,
85 And thou shalt read when mine begin to dazzle.
                    Exeunt.

66 *ill-favored* ugly   71 *insult on* exult over   75 *sirrah* (common
term of address to an inferior)   81 *take away* clear the table   82
closet private room   83 *chancèd* that happened

[ACT IV

Scene I. *Rome. Before Titus' house.*]

*Enter Lucius' son and Lavinia running after him;
and the boy flies from her with his books under
his arm. Enter Titus and Marcus.*

Boy. Help, grandsire, help! My aunt Lavinia
   Follows me everywhere, I know not why.
   Good uncle Marcus, see how swift she comes.
   Alas, sweet aunt, I know not what you mean.

Marcus. Stand by me, Lucius, do not fear thine aunt.   *5*

Titus. She loves thee, boy, too well to do thee harm.

Boy. Ay, when my father was in Rome she did.

Marcus. What means my niece Lavinia by these signs?

Titus. Fear her not, Lucius. Somewhat doth she mean.
   See, Lucius, see, how much she makes of thee: *10*
   Somewhither would she have thee go with her.
   Ah, boy, Cornelia° never with more care
   Read to her sons than she hath read to thee
   Sweet poetry and Tully's *Orator*.°
   Canst thou not guess wherefore she plies thee thus?   *15*

Boy. My lord, I know not, I, nor can I guess,
   Unless some fit or frenzy do possess her:
   For I have heard my grandsire say full oft,

IV.i.12 *Cornelia* mother of the Gracchi, two famous tribunes 14
Tully's Orator Cicero's *De oratore* (or his *Orator ad M. Brutum*)

Extremity of griefs would make men mad;
20 And I have read that Hecuba of Troy
Ran mad for sorrow. That made me to fear,
Although, my lord, I know my noble aunt
Loves me as dear as e'er my mother did,
And would not, but in fury,° fright my youth,
25 Which made me down to throw my books and fly,
Causeless perhaps. But pardon me, sweet aunt:
And, madam, if my uncle Marcus go,
I will most willingly attend° your ladyship.

Marcus. Lucius, I will.

30 *Titus.* How now, Lavinia? Marcus, what means this?
Some book there is that she desires to see.
Which is it, girl, of these? Open them, boy.
But thou art deeper read, and better skilled.
Come, and take choice of all my library,
35 And so beguile thy sorrow, till the heavens
Reveal the damned contriver of this deed.
Why lifts she up her arms in sequence thus?

Marcus. I think she means that there were more than
one
Confederate in the fact.° Ay, more there was,
40 Or else to heaven she heaves them for revenge.

Titus. Lucius, what book is that she tosseth° so?

Boy. Grandsire, 'tis Ovid's *Metamorphosis;*°
My mother gave it me.

Marcus.   For love of her that's gone,
Perhaps she culled it from among the rest.

45 *Titus.* Soft! So busily she turns the leaves!
Help her! What would she find? Lavinia, shall I
read?
This is the tragic tale of Philomel,
And treats of Tereus' treason and his rape;

24 *but in fury* except in madness   28 *attend* wait on   39 *fact* crime
41 *tosseth* turns the pages of   42 *Metamorphosis* (so spelled in the
title of an Elizabethan translation by Golding, with which Shakespeare was familiar; properly *Metamorphoses*)

And rape, I fear, was root of thy annoy.

Marcus. See, brother, see, note how she quotes° the
    leaves.   50

Titus. Lavinia, wert thou thus surprised, sweet girl,
    Ravished and wronged, as Philomela was,
    Forced in the ruthless, vast,° and gloomy woods?
    See, see!
    Ay, such a place there is, where we did hunt—   55
    O, had we never, never hunted there—
    Patterned by° that the poet here describes,
    By nature made for murders and for rapes.

Marcus. O, why should nature build so foul a den,
    Unless the gods delight in tragedies?   60

Titus. Give signs, sweet girl, for here are none but
    friends,
    What Roman lord it was durst do the deed:
    Or slunk not Saturnine, as Tarquin erst,°
    That left the camp to sin in Lucrece' bed?

Marcus. Sit down, sweet niece: brother, sit down by
    me.   65
    Apollo, Pallas, Jove, or Mercury,
    Inspire me, that I may this treason find!
    My lord, look here: look here, Lavinia.
                He writes his name with his staff,
                 and guides it with feet and mouth.
    This sandy plot is plain;° guide if thou canst,
    This after me.° I have writ my name   70
    Without the help of any hand at all.
    Cursed be that heart that forced us to this shift!°
    Write thou, good niece, and here display at last
    What God will have discovered° for revenge.
    Heaven guide thy pen to print thy sorrows plain,   75
    That we may know the traitors and the truth!
                She takes the staff in her mouth and guides
                  it with her stumps and writes.

---

50 *quotes* examines 53 *vast* desolate 57 *Patterned by* after the
pattern 63 *erst* once 69 *plain* flat 70 *after me* as I do 72 *shift*
device 74 *discovered* revealed

O, do ye read, my lord, what she hath writ?

[*Titus.*] "*Stuprum.*° Chiron. Demetrius."

Marcus. What, what! The lustful sons of Tamora
80 Performers of this heinous, bloody deed?

Titus. Magni Dominator poli,
     Tam lentus audis scelera? tam lentus vides?°

Marcus. O, calm thee, gentle lord! Although I know
     There is enough written upon this earth
85 To stir a mutiny in the mildest thoughts,
     And arm the minds of infants to exclaims.°
     My lord, kneel down with me; Lavinia, kneel;
     And kneel, sweet boy, the Roman Hector's° hope;
     And swear with me, as, with the woeful fere°
90 And father of that chaste dishonored dame,
     Lord Junius Brutus° sware for Lucrece' rape,
     That we will prosecute by good advice°
     Mortal revenge upon these traitorous Goths,
     And see their blood, or die with this reproach.

95 *Titus.* 'Tis sure enough, and you knew how,
     But if you hunt these bear-whelps, then beware:
     The dam will wake; and if she wind ye° once,
     She's with the lion deeply still in league,
     And lulls him whilst she playeth on her back,
100 And when he sleeps will she do what she list.°
     You are a young huntsman, Marcus, let alone;
     And, come, I will go get a leaf of brass,
     And with a gad° of steel will write these words,
     And lay it by. The angry northern wind
105 Will blow these sands like Sibyl's leaves° abroad,
     And where's our lesson then? Boy, what say you?

Boy. I say, my lord, that if I were a man,

78 *Stuprum* rape (Latin)   81–82 *Magni Dominator . . . lentus
vides?* ruler of the great heavens, are you so slow to hear and to see
crimes? (Latin; derived from Seneca's *Hippolytus*, lines 668–69)
86 *exclaims* exclamations   88 *the Roman Hector's* i.e., Andronicus
(Titus is compared to Hector, Troy's champion)   89 *fere* spouse
91 *Junius Brutus* chief of those who drove the Tarquins from Rome
92 *by good advice* after careful deliberation   97 *and if she wind ye*
if she get wind of (smell) you   100 *list* please   103 *gad* spike,
stylus   105 *Sibyl's leaves* leaves on which the Sibyl wrote prophecies

Their mother's bedchamber should not be safe
For these base bondmen to the yoke of Rome.

Marcus. Ay, that's my boy! Thy father hath full oft   110
For his ungrateful country done the like.

Boy. And, uncle, so will I, and if I live.

Titus. Come, go with me into mine armory:
Lucius, I'll fit thee, and withal my boy
Shall carry from me to the Empress' sons   115
Presents that I intend to send them both.
Come, come; thou'lt do my message, wilt thou not?

Boy. Ay, with my dagger in their bosoms, grandsire.

Titus. No, boy, not so; I'll teach thee another course.
Lavinia, come. Marcus, look to my house.   120
Lucius and I'll go brave it° at the court;
Ay, marry,° will we, sir; and we'll be waited on.°
                                        Exeunt.

Marcus. O heavens, can you hear a good man groan,
And not relent, or not compassion him?
Marcus, attend him in his ecstasy,°   125
That hath more scars of sorrow in his heart
Than foemen's marks upon his batt'red shield,
But yet so just that he will not revenge.
Revenge the heavens° for old Andronicus!   *Exit.*

121 *brave it* behave defiantly   122 *marry* (an interjection, from "By
the Virgin Mary")   122 *be waited on* i.e., not be ignored   125
ecstasy fit of madness   129 *Revenge the heavens* may the heavens
take revenge

[Scene II. *Rome. Within the palace.*]

Enter Aaron, Chiron, and Demetrius, at one door, and at the other door young Lucius and another, with a bundle of weapons and verses writ upon them.

Chiron. Demetrius, here's the son of Lucius,
He hath some message to deliver us.

Aaron. Ay, some mad message from his mad grandfather.

Boy. My lords, with all the humbleness I may,
5   I greet your honors from Andronicus.
[*Aside*] And pray the Roman gods confound° you
both.

Demetrius. Gramercy,° lovely Lucius, what's the
news?

Boy. [*Aside*] That you are both deciphered, that's the
news,
For villains marked with rape. [*Aloud*] May it
please you,
10   My grandsire, well-advised,° hath sent by me
The goodliest weapons of his armory
To gratify your honorable youth,
The hope of Rome; for so he bid me say;
And so I do, and with his gifts present
15   Your lordships; whenever you have need,
You may be armèd and appointed° well.
And so I leave you both, [*aside*] like bloody villains.
Exit.

Demetrius. What's here? A scroll, and written round
about?

IV.ii.6 *confound* destroy   7 *Gramercy* thanks   10 *well-advised* in
sound mind   16 *appointed* equipped

Let's see:

    Integer vitae, scelerisque purus,   20
    Non eget Mauri jaculis, nec arcu.°

Chiron. O, 'tis a verse in Horace; I know it well:
I read it in the grammar long ago.

Aaron. Ay, just; a verse in Horace; right, you have it.
[*Aside*] Now, what a thing it is to be an ass!   25
Here's no sound jest! The old man hath found their
    guilt,
And sends them weapons wrapped about with lines
That wound, beyond their feeling, to the quick.
But were our witty° empress well afoot,
She would applaud Andronicus' conceit.°   30
But let her rest in her unrest awhile.
[*Aloud*] And now, young lords, was't not a happy
    star
Led us to Rome, strangers, and more than so,
Captives, to be advancèd to this height?
It did me good, before the palace gate   35
To brave the tribune in his brother's hearing.

Demetrius. But me more good, to see so great a lord
Basely insinuate° and send us gifts.

Aaron. Had he not reason, Lord Demetrius?
Did you not use his daughter very friendly?   40

Demetrius. I would we had a thousand Roman dames
At such a bay,° by turn to serve our lust.

Chiron. A charitable wish and full of love.

Aaron. Here lacks but your mother for to say amen.

Chiron. And that would she for twenty thousand
more.   45

Demetrius. Come, let us go, and pray to all the gods
For our belovèd mother in her pains.

20–21 *Integer vitae . . . nec arcu* the man of upright life and free
from crime has no need of a Moor's javelins or bow (Latin; from
Horace, *Odes,* I.xxii.1–2) 29 *witty* wise 30 *conceit* idea, design
38 *insinuate* curry favor 42 *At such a bay* thus cornered

Aaron. [*Aside*] Pray to the devils, the gods have given
   us over.

                          Trumpets sound.

Demetrius. Why do the Emperor's trumpets flourish
   thus?

50   *Chiron.* Belike,° for joy the Emperor hath a son.

Demetrius. Soft! Who comes here?

         Enter Nurse with a blackamoor child.

Nurse.   God morrow, lords.
   O, tell me, did you see Aaron the Moor?

Aaron. Well, more or less, or ne'er a whit at all,
   Here Aaron is; and what with Aaron now?

55   *Nurse.* O gentle Aaron, we are all undone!
   Now help, or woe betide thee evermore!

Aaron. Why, what a caterwauling dost thou keep!
   What dost thou wrap and fumble° in thy arms?

Nurse. O, that which I would hide from heaven's eye,
60   Our empress' shame and stately Rome's disgrace!
   She is delivered, lords, she is delivered.

Aaron. To whom?

Nurse.   I mean, she is brought abed.

Aaron. Well, God give her good rest! What hath he
   sent her?

Nurse. A devil.

Aaron.   Why, then she is the devil's dam;°
65   A joyful issue.

Nurse. A joyless, dismal, black, and sorrowful issue!
   Here is the babe, as loathsome as a toad
   Amongst the fair-faced breeders of our clime.
   The Empress sends it thee, thy stamp, thy seal,

---

50 *Belike* probably   58 *fumble* clumsily bundle up   64 *dam* mother

And bids thee christen it with thy dagger's point. *70*

Aaron. Zounds,° ye whore! Is black so base a hue?
Sweet blowse,° you are a beauteous blossom, sure.

Demetrius. Villain, what hast thou done?

Aaron. That which thou canst not undo.

Chiron. Thou hast undone our mother. *75*

Aaron. Villain, I have done° thy mother.

Demetrius. And therein, hellish dog, thou hast undone
    her.
Woe to her chance,° and damned her loathèd
    choice!
Accursed the offspring of so foul a fiend!

Chiron. It shall not live. *80*

Aaron. It shall not die.

Nurse. Aaron, it must; the mother wills it so.

Aaron. What, must it, nurse? Then let no man but I
Do execution on my flesh and blood.

Demetrius. I'll broach° the tadpole on my rapier's
    point. *85*
Nurse, give it me; my sword shall soon dispatch it.

Aaron. Sooner this sword shall plow thy bowels up.
Stay, murderous villains! Will you kill your brother?
Now, by the burning tapers of the sky,
That shone so brightly when this boy was got,° *90*
He dies upon my scimitar's sharp point
That touches this my first-born son and heir!
I tell you, younglings, not Enceladus,°
With all his threat'ning band of Typhon's brood,
Nor great Alcides,° nor the god of war, *95*
Shall seize this prey out of his father's hands.

71 *Zounds* (an interjection, from "By God's wounds") 72 *blowse*
ruddy wench (here, ironic) 76 *done* had sexual intercourse with
78 *chance* luck 85 *broach* impale 90 *got* begat 93 *Enceladus*
one of the Titans (sons of Typhon) who fought the Olympians 95
Alcides Hercules

What, what, ye sanguine,° shallow-hearted boys!
Ye white-limed walls!° Ye alehouse painted signs!
Coal-black is better than another hue,
100 In that it scorns to bear another hue;
For all the water in the ocean
Can never turn the swan's black legs to white,
Although she lave° them hourly in the flood.
Tell the Empress from me, I am of age
105 To keep mine own, excuse it how she can.

Demetrius. Wilt thou betray thy noble mistress thus?

Aaron. My mistress is my mistress, this my self,
The vigor and the picture of my youth:
This before all the world do I prefer;
110 This mauger° all the world will I keep safe,
Or some of you shall smoke° for it in Rome.

Demetrius. By this our mother is forever shamed.

Chiron. Rome will despise her for this foul escape.°

Nurse. The Emperor in his rage will doom her death.

115 *Chiron.* I blush to think upon this ignomy.°

Aaron. Why, there's the privilege your beauty bears:
Fie, treacherous hue, that will betray with blushing
The close enacts° and counsels of thy heart!
Here's a young lad framed of another leer:°
120 Look, how the black slave smiles upon the father,
As who should say, "Old lad, I am thine own."
He is your brother, lords, sensibly fed
Of that self blood° that first gave life to you,
And from your womb where you imprisoned were
125 He is enfranchisèd and come to light:
Nay, he is your brother by the surer side,°
Although my seal be stampèd in his face.

97 *sanguine* pink-cheeked 98 *white-limed walls* (perhaps a reference to the "whited sepulchers" of Matthew 23:27) 103 *lave* wash 110 *mauger* in spite of 111 *smoke* suffer 113 *escape* escapade 115 *ignomy* ignominy 118 *close enacts* secret resolutions 119 *leer* complexion 122–23 *sensibly fed/Of that self blood* i.e., his body draws on the same blood 126 *the surer side* i.e., the mother's side

Nurse. Aaron, what shall I say unto the Empress?

Demetrius. Advise thee, Aaron, what is to be done,
And we will all subscribe° to thy advice: *130*
Save thou the child, so° we may all be safe.

Aaron. Then sit we down and let us all consult.
My son and I will have the wind of you:°
Keep there; now talk at pleasure of your safety.

Demetrius. How many women saw this child of his? *135*

Aaron. Why, so, brave lords! When we join in league,
I am a lamb: but if you brave the Moor,
The chafèd° boar, the mountain lioness,
The ocean swells not so as Aaron storms.
But say again, how many saw the child?   *140*

Nurse. Cornelia the midwife, and myself,
And no one else but the delivered Empress.

Aaron. The Empress, the midwife, and yourself:
Two may keep counsel when the third's away.
Go to the Empress, tell her this I said.   *145*
                            He kills her.
Wheak, wheak!
So cries a pig preparèd to the spit.

Demetrius. What mean'st thou, Aaron? Wherefore
    didst thou this?

Aaron. O, lord, sir, 'tis a deed of policy!°
Shall she live to betray this guilt of ours?   *150*
A long-tongued babbling gossip? No, lords, no.
And now be it known to you my full intent.
Not far one Muliteus my countryman
His° wife but yesternight was brought to bed;
His child is like to her, fair as you are.   *155*
Go pack° with him, and give the mother gold,
And tell them both the circumstance of all,°

130 *subscribe* agree   131 *so* provided that   133 *have the wind of
you* i.e., keep you safely in our view (as game is watched, down
wind)   138 *chafèd* enraged   149 *policy* cunning   153–54 *country-
man/His* countryman's   156 *pack* conspire   157 *circumstance of
all* all the details

And how by this their child shall be advanced,
And be receivèd for the Emperor's heir,
160 And substituted in the place of mine,
To calm this tempest whirling in the court;
And let the Emperor dandle him for his own.
Hark ye, lords; you see I have given her physic,°
And you must needs bestow her funeral;
165 The fields are near, and you are gallant grooms.
This done, see that you take no longer days,°
But send the midwife presently to me.
The midwife and the nurse well made away,
Then let the ladies tattle what they please.

170 *Chiron.* Aaron, I see, thou wilt not trust the air
With secrets.

Demetrius.   For this care of Tamora,
Herself and hers are highly bound to thee. *Exeunt.*

Aaron. Now to the Goths, as swift as swallow flies,
There to dispose this treasure in mine arms,
175 And secretly to greet the Empress' friends.
Come on, you thick-lipped slave, I'll bear you
hence;
For it is you that puts us to our shifts.°
I'll make you feed on berries and on roots,
And feed on curds and whey, and suck the goat,
180 And cabin° in a cave, and bring you up
To be a warrior and command a camp.   *Exit.*

---

163 *physic* medicine   166 *days* time   177 *puts us to our shifts* causes us to use stratagems   180 *cabin* dwell

[Scene III. *Rome. A street.*]

*Enter Titus, old Marcus, [his son Publius,] young
Lucius, and other gentlemen, with bows; and
Titus bears the arrows with letters on the ends
of them.*

Titus. Come, Marcus, come; kinsmen, this is the way.
　Sir boy, let me see your archery;
　Look ye draw home° enough, and 'tis there straight.
　Terras Astraea reliquit.°
　Be you rememb'red,° Marcus: she's gone, she's
　　fled.　　　　　　　　　　　　　　　　　　　　　*3*
　Sirs, take you to your tools. You, cousins, shall
　Go sound the ocean, and cast your nets;
　Happily° you may catch her in the sea;
　Yet there's as little justice as at land:
　No, Publius and Sempronius, you must do it;　　*10*
　'Tis you must dig with mattock and with spade,
　And pierce the inmost center of the earth:
　Then, when you come to Pluto's region,°
　I pray you deliver him this petition:　　　　　*15*
　Tell him, it is for justice and for aid,
　And that it comes from old Andronicus,
　Shaken with sorrows in ungrateful Rome.
　Ah, Rome! Well, well; I made thee miserable
　What time° I threw the people's suffrages
　On him that thus doth tyrannize o'er me.　　　*20*
　Go, get you gone, and pray be careful all,
　And leave you not a man of war unsearched:
　This wicked emperor may have shipped her hence,
　And, kinsmen, then we may go pipe for° justice.

Marcus. O, Publius, is not this a heavy case,　　*25*

IV.iii.3 *home* fully　4 *Terras Astraea reliquit* Astraea (goddess of
justice) has left the earth (Latin; from Ovid, *Metamorphoses,* I.150)
5 *Be you rememb'red* remember　8 *Happily* perhaps　13 *Pluto's
region* Hades　19 *What time* when　24 *pipe for* i.e., whistle vainly
for

    To see thy noble uncle thus distract?

Publius. Therefore, my lords, it highly us concerns
    By day and night t' attend him carefully,
    And feed his humor° kindly as we may,
30   Till time beget some careful remedy.

Marcus. Kinsmen, his sorrows are past remedy.
    But° . . .
    Join with the Goths, and with revengeful war
    Take wreak° on Rome for this ingratitude,
35   And vengeance on the traitor Saturnine.

Titus. Publius, how now! How now, my masters!
    What, have you met with her?

Publius. No, my good lord, but Pluto sends you word,
    If you will have revenge from hell, you shall:
40   Marry, for Justice, she is so employed,
    He thinks, with Jove in heaven, or somewhere else,
    So that perforce you must needs stay a time.

Titus. He doth me wrong to feed me with delays.
    I'll dive into the burning lake below,
45   And pull her out of Acheron° by the heels.
    Marcus, we are but shrubs, no cedars we,
    No big-boned men framed of the Cyclops'° size;
    But metal, Marcus, steel to the very back,
    Yet wrung with wrongs more than our backs can
        bear:
50   And sith° there's no justice in earth nor hell,
    We will solicit heaven, and move the gods
    To send down Justice for to wreak° our wrongs.
    Come, to this gear.° You are a good archer, Marcus.
                     He gives them the arrows.
    Ad Jovem, that's for you: here, *Ad Apollinem:*
55   *Ad Martem,*° that's for myself:

29 *humor* mood, caprice   32 *But* (a catchword indicates that the
line begins "But," though the line itself was omitted)   34 *wreak*
vengeance   45 *Acheron* river in Hades   47 *Cyclops* giants (in
Homer's *Odyssey*)   50 *sith* since   52 *wreak* avenge   53 *gear* affair
54–55 *Ad Jovem . . . Ad Apollinem:/Ad Martem* to Jove . . . to
Apollo; to Mars (Latin)

Here, boy, to Pallas: here, to Mercury:
To Saturn, Caius, not to Saturnine;
You were as good to shoot° against the wind.
To it, boy! Marcus, loose when I bid.
Of my word, I have written to effect;   *60*
There's not a god left unsolicited.

Marcus. Kinsmen, shoot all your shafts into the court:
We will afflict the Emperor in his pride.

Titus. Now, masters, draw. O, well said, Lucius!
Good boy, in Virgo's° lap; give it Pallas.   *65*

Marcus. My lord, I aim a mile beyond the moon;
Your letter is with Jupiter by this.

Titus. Ha, ha!
Publius, Publius, what hast thou done!
See, see, thou hast shot off one of Taurus' horns.   *70*

Marcus. This was the sport, my lord: when Publius
shot,
The bull being galled, gave Aries such a knock
That down fell both the Ram's horns in the court,
And who should find them but the Empress' villain?
She laughed, and told the Moor he should not
choose   *75*
But give them to his master for a present.

Titus. Why, there it goes! God give his lordship joy!

Enter the Clown,° with a basket and two pigeons in it.

News, news from heaven! Marcus, the post is come.
Sirrah, what tidings? Have you any letters?
Shall I have justice? What says Jupiter?   *80*

Clown. Ho, the gibbet maker!° He says that he hath

---

58 *You were as good to shoot* you would do as much good by shooting   65 *Virgo's* the Virgin's (sign of the zodiac, as are *Taurus*—the
bull—in line 70, and *Aries*—the ram—in line 72)   77 s.d. *Clown*
rustic fellow   81 *gibbet maker* (apparently "Jupiter"—which in the
original text is spelled "Jubiter"—was pronounced rather like "gib-
beter," i.e., gibbet maker)

taken them down again, for the man must not be
hanged till the next week.

Titus. But what says Jupiter, I ask thee?

85 *Clown.* Alas, sir, I know not Jubiter; I never drank
with him in all my life.

Titus. Why, villain, art not thou the carrier?

Clown. Ay, of my pigeons, sir, nothing else.

Titus. Why, didst thou not come from heaven?

90 *Clown.* From heaven? Alas, sir, I never came there!
God forbid, I should be so bold to press to heaven
in my young days. Why, I am going with my
pigeons to the tribunal plebs,° to take up a matter
of brawl betwixt my uncle and one of the Emperal's
95 men.

Marcus. Why, sir, that is as fit as can be to serve for
your oration; and let him deliver the pigeons to the
Emperor from you.

Titus. Tell me, can you deliver an oration to the
100 Emperor with a grace?

Clown. Nay, truly, sir, I could never say grace in all
my life.

Titus. Sirrah, come hither: make no more ado,
But give your pigeons to the Emperor:
105 By me thou shalt have justice at his hands.
Hold, hold, meanwhile, here's money for thy
charges.°
Give me pen and ink. Sirrah, can you with a grace
deliver up a supplication?

Clown. Ay, sir.

110 *Titus.* Then here is a supplication for you. And when
you come to him, at the first approach you must

93 *tribunal plebs* (malaprop for *tribunus plebis*, "Tribune of the
plebs"; *Emperal*, later in the sentence, is another malaprop) 106
charges i.e., pigeons

kneel, then kiss his foot, then deliver up your
pigeons, and then look for your reward. I'll be at
hand, sir! See you do it bravely.°

Clown. I warrant you, sir, let me alone.　　　　　　115

Titus. Sirrah, hast thou a knife? Come, let me see it.
Here, Marcus, fold it in the oration,
For thou hast made it like an humble suppliant.
And when thou hast given it to the Emperor,
Knock at my door, and tell me what he says.　　　120

Clown. God be with you, sir; I will.　　　　　　*Exit.*

Titus. Come, Marcus, let us go. Publius, follow me.
　　　　　　　　　　　　　　　　　　Exeunt.

[Scene IV. *Rome. Before the palace.*]

*Enter Emperor and Empress and her two sons.
The Emperor brings the arrows in his hand that
　　　　　Titus shot at him.*

Saturninus. Why, lords, what wrongs are these! Was
　　　ever seen
An emperor in Rome thus overborne,
Troubled, confronted thus, and for the extent°
Of egal° justice used in such contempt?
My lords, you know, as know the mightful gods,　　5
However these disturbers of our peace
Buzz in the people's ears, there naught hath passed
But even° with law against the willful sons
Of old Andronicus. And what and if
His sorrows have so overwhelmed his wits,　　　10
Shall we be thus afflicted in his wreaks,°
His fits, his frenzy, and his bitterness?

114 *bravely* well　IV.iv.3 *extent* exercise　4 *egal* equal　8 *even*
agreeing　11 *wreaks* vengeful acts

And now he writes to heaven for his redress!
See, here's to Jove, and this to Mercury,
15   This to Apollo, this to the god of war.
Sweet scrolls to fly about the streets of Rome!
What's this but libeling against the Senate,
And blazoning° our unjustice everywhere?
A goodly humor, is it not, my lords?
20   As who would say, in Rome no justice were.
But if I live, his feignèd ecstasies°
Shall be no shelter to these outrages,
But he and his shall know that justice lives
In Saturninus' health; whom, if he sleep,
25   He'll so awake, as he in fury shall
Cut off the proud'st conspirator that lives.

Tamora. My gracious lord, my lovely Saturnine,
Lord of my life, commander of my thoughts,
Calm thee, and bear the faults of Titus' age,
30   Th' effects of sorrow for his valiant sons,
Whose loss hath pierced him deep and scarred his heart,
And rather comfort his distressèd plight
Than prosecute the meanest or the best
For these contempts. [*Aside*] Why, thus it shall become
35   High-witted Tamora to gloze° with all.
But, Titus, I have touched thee to the quick,
Thy lifeblood out:° if Aaron now be wise,
Then is all safe, the anchor in the port.

Enter Clown.

How now, good fellow? Wouldst thou speak with us?

40   *Clown.* Yea, forsooth, and your mistress-ship be emperial.

Tamora. Empress I am, but yonder sits the Emperor.

Clown. 'Tis he. God and Saint Stephen give you

18 *blazoning* proclaiming   21 *ecstasies* fits of madness   35 *gloze* use specious words   37 *Thy lifeblood out* when your blood is out

godden.° I have brought you a letter and a couple
of pigeons here.   45

> *He [i.e., Saturninus] reads the letter.*

Saturninus. Go, take him away, and hang him presently.

Clown. How much money must I have?

Tamora. Come, sirrah, you must be hanged.

Clown. Hanged! By lady,° then I have brought up a
neck° to a fair end.   *Exit [with guards].*   50

Saturninus. Despiteful and intolerable wrongs!
Shall I endure this monstrous villainy?
I know from whence this same device proceeds.
May this be borne as if his traitorous sons,
That died by law for murder of our brother,   55
Have by my means been butchered wrongfully.
Go, drag the villain hither by the hair,
Nor age nor honor shall shape privilege:°
For this proud mock I'll be thy slaughter-man—
Sly frantic wretch, that holp'st to make me great,   60
In hope thyself should govern Rome and me.

> *Enter nuntius,° Aemilius.*

What news with thee, Aemilius?

Aemilius. Arm, my lords. Rome never had more
cause.
The Goths have gathered head,° and with a power°
Of high-resolvèd men, bent to the spoil,   65
They hither march amain, under conduct°
Of Lucius, son to old Andronicus;
Who threats, in course of this revenge, to do
As much as ever Coriolanus° did.

---

44 *godden* good evening   49 *By lady* (an interjection, from "By
Our Lady")   50 *neck* (possibly with a pun on "knack," which means
"deceitful trick")   58 *shape privilege* provide immunity   61 s.d.
nuntius messenger (Latin)   64 *gathered head* raised an army   64
power army   66 *conduct* leadership   69 *Coriolanus* (this Roman
hero who became Rome's enemy is the protagonist in Shakespeare's
last tragedy)

70 *Saturninus.* Is warlike Lucius general of the Goths?
       These tidings nip me, and I hang the head
       As flowers with frost or grass beat down with
             storms.
       Ay, now begins our sorrows to approach:
       'Tis he the common people love so much;
75   Myself hath often heard them say,
       When I have walkèd like a private man,
       That Lucius' banishment was wrongfully,
       And they have wished that Lucius were their
             emperor.

   Tamora. Why should you fear? Is not your city
       strong?

80 *Saturninus.* Ay, but the citizens favor Lucius,
       And will revolt from me to succor him.

   Tamora. King, be thy thoughts imperious, like thy
       name.
       Is the sun dimmed, that gnats do fly in it?
       The eagle suffers little birds to sing
85   And is not careful° what they mean thereby,
       Knowing that with the shadow of his wings
       He can at pleasure stint° their melody:
       Even so mayst thou the giddy men of Rome.
       Then cheer thy spirit: for know, thou Emperor,
90   I will enchant the old Andronicus
       With words more sweet, and yet more dangerous,
       Than baits to fish, or honey-stalks° to sheep;
       Whenas the one is wounded with the bait,
       The other rotted with delicious feed.

95 *Saturninus.* But he will not entreat his son for us.

   Tamora. If Tamora entreat him, then he will:
       For I can smooth, and fill his agèd ears
       With golden promises, that, were his heart
       Almost impregnable, his old ears deaf,
100   Yet should both ear and heart obey my tongue.

85 *careful* worried   87 *stint* stop   92 *honey-stalks* clover

[*To Aemilius*] Go thou before to be our ambassa-
   dor:
Say that the Emperor requests a parley
Of warlike Lucius, and appoint the meeting
Even at his father's house, the old Andronicus.

Saturninus. Aemilius, do this message honorably,   105
   And if he stand in° hostage for his safety,
   Bid him demand what pledge will please him best.

Aemilius. Your bidding shall I do effectually.   *Exit.*

Tamora. Now will I to that old Andronicus,
   And temper° him with all the art I have,   110
   To pluck proud Lucius from the warlike Goths.
   And now, sweet Emperor, be blithe again,
   And bury all thy fear in my devices.

Saturninus. Then go successantly,° and plead to him.
                               Exeunt.

---

106 *stand in* insist upon   110 *temper* work upon   114 *successantly*
one after the other(?)

[ACT V

Scene I. *A plain near Rome.*]

*Enter Lucius, with an army of Goths, with drums
and soldiers.*

Lucius. Approvèd° warriors, and my faithful friends,
I have receivèd letters from great Rome,
Which signifies what hate they bear their emperor,
And how desirous of our sight they are.
5 Therefore, great lords, be, as your titles witness,
Imperious, and impatient of your wrongs;
And wherein Rome hath done you any scath,°
Let him make treble satisfaction.

Goth. Brave slip,° sprung from the great Andronicus,
10 Whose name was once our terror, now our comfort,
Whose high exploits and honorable deeds
Ingrateful Rome requites with foul contempt,
Be bold° in us: we'll follow where thou lead'st,
Like stinging bees in hottest summer's day,
15 Led by their master to the flow'rèd fields,
And be advengèd on cursèd Tamora.

[*Other Goths.*] And as he saith, so say we all with him.

Lucius. I humbly thank him, and I thank you all.
But who comes here, led by a lusty Goth?

V.i.1 *Approvèd* tested   7 *scath* harm   9 *slip* offshoot   13 *bold* confident

*Enter a Goth, leading of Aaron with his child
in his arms.*

Goth. Renownèd Lucius, from our troops I strayed   20
    To gaze upon a ruinous monastery,
    And, as I earnestly did fix mine eye
    Upon the wasted° building, suddenly
    I heard a child cry underneath a wall.
    I made unto the noise, when soon I heard   25
    The crying babe controlled with this discourse:
    "Peace, tawny° slave, half me and half thy dame.°
    Did not thy hue bewray° whose brat° thou art,
    Had nature lent thee but thy mother's look,
    Villain, thou mightst have been an emperor: 30
    But where the bull and cow are both milk-white,
    They never do beget a coal-black calf.
    Peace, villain, peace!" Even thus he rates° the
      babe,
    "For I must bear thee to a trusty Goth,
    Who, when he knows thou art the Empress' babe,   35
    Will hold thee dearly for thy mother's sake."
    With this, my weapon drawn, I rushed upon him,
    Surprised him suddenly, and brought him hither,
    To use as you think needful of the man.

Lucius. O worthy Goth, this is the incarnate devil   40
    That robbed Andronicus of his good hand.
    This is the pearl that pleased your empress' eye,
    And here's the base fruit of her burning lust.
    Say, wall-eyed° slave, whither wouldst thou convey
    This growing image of thy fiendlike face?   45
    Why dost not speak? What, deaf? Not a word?
    A halter, soldiers! Hang him on this tree,
    And by his side his fruit of bastardy.

Aaron. Touch not the boy; he is of royal blood.

Lucius. Too like the sire for ever being good.   50
    First hang the child, that he may see it sprawl—

23 *wasted* ruined   27 *tawny* black   27 *dame* mother   28 *bewray*
reveal   28 *brat* young offspring   33 *rates* berates   44 *wall-eyed*
glaring (literally: having a whitish iris)

A sight to vex the father's soul withal.

Aaron. Get me a ladder.° Lucius, save the child,
And bear it from me to the Empress.
55 If thou do this, I'll show thee wondrous things
That highly may advantage thee to hear.
If thou wilt not, befall what may befall,
I'll speak no more but "Vengeance rot you all!"

Lucius. Say on, and if it please me which thou
  speak'st,
60 Thy child shall live, and I will see it nourished.

Aaron. And if it please thee! Why, assure thee,
  Lucius,
'Twill vex thy soul to hear what I shall speak;
For I must talk of murders, rapes, and massacres,
Acts of black night, abominable deeds,
65 Complots of mischief, treason, villainies
Ruthful° to hear, yet piteously performed:°
And this shall all be buried in my death,
Unless thou swear to me my child shall live.

Lucius. Tell on thy mind, I say thy child shall live.

70 *Aaron.* Swear that he shall, and then I will begin.

Lucius. Who should I swear by? Thou believest no
  god:
That granted, how canst thou believe an oath?

Aaron. What if I do not? As indeed I do not;
Yet, for I know thou art religious,
75 And hast a thing within thee callèd conscience,
With twenty popish tricks and ceremonies,
Which I have seen thee careful to observe,
Therefore I urge thy oath; for that I know
An idiot holds his bauble° for a god,
80 And keeps the oath which by that god he swears,
To that I'll urge him: therefore thou shalt vow
By that same god, what god soe'er it be,

---

53 *Get me a ladder* i.e., hang me rather than the child   66 *Ruthful*
pitiful   66 *piteously performed* i.e., performed, which excites pity
79 *bauble* carved head at the end of a court fool's stick

That thou adorest and hast in reverence,
To save my boy, to nourish and bring him up;
Or else I will discover naught to thee.   85

Lucius. Even by my god I swear to thee I will.

Aaron. First know thou, I begot him on the Empress.

Lucius. O most insatiate and luxurious° woman!

Aaron. Tut, Lucius, this was but a deed of charity
To° that which thou shalt hear of me anon.   90
'Twas her two sons that murdered Bassianus;
They cut thy sister's tongue and ravished her,
And cut her hands, and trimmed her as thou sawest.

Lucius. O detestable villain! Call'st thou that trim-
     ming?

Aaron. Why, she was washed, and cut, and trimmed,
     and 'twas   95
Trim sport for them which had the doing of it.

Lucius. O barbarous, beastly villains, like thyself!

Aaron. Indeed, I was their tutor to instruct them.
That codding° spirit had they from their mother,
As sure a card as ever won the set.°
That bloody mind, I think, they learned of me,   100
As true a dog as ever fought at head.°
Well, let my deeds be witness of my worth.
I trained° thy brethren to that guileful hole,
Where the dead corpse of Bassianus lay;   105
I wrote the letter that thy father found,
And hid the gold within that letter mentioned,
Confederate with the Queen and her two sons;
And what not done, that thou hast cause to rue,
Wherein I had no stroke of mischief in it?   110
I played the cheater° for thy father's hand,
And when I had it drew myself apart,

---

88 *luxurious* lustful   90   *To* in comparison with   99 *codding* lustful   100 *set* game   102 *at head* (a courageous bulldog went for
the bull's nose)   104 *trained* lured   111 *cheater* officer appointed
to look after escheats or property forfeited to the Crown

And almost broke my heart with extreme laughter.
I pried me through the crevice of a wall,
115 When for his hand he had his two sons' heads;
Beheld his tears and laughed so heartily
That both mine eyes were rainy like to his:
And when I told the Empress of this sport,
She sounded° almost at my pleasing tale,
120 And for my tidings gave me twenty kisses.

Goth. What, canst thou say all this and never blush?

Aaron. Ay, like a black dog, as the saying is.

Lucius. Art thou not sorry for these heinous deeds?

Aaron. Ay, that I had not done a thousand more.
125 Even now I curse the day—and yet, I think,
Few come within the compass of my curse—
Wherein I did not some notorious ill:
As kill a man or else devise his death,
Ravish a maid or plot the way to do it,
130 Accuse some innocent and forswear° myself,
Set deadly enmity between two friends,
Make poor men's cattle break their necks,
Set fire on barns and haystalks in the night,
And bid the owners quench them with their tears.
135 Oft have I digged up dead men from their graves
And set them upright at their dear friends' door,
Even when their sorrows almost was forgot,
And on their skins, as on the bark of trees,
Have with my knife carvèd in Roman letters,
140 "Let not your sorrow die, though I am dead."
But, I have done a thousand dreadful things
As willingly as one would kill a fly,
And nothing grieves me heartily indeed,
But that I cannot do ten thousand more.

145 *Lucius.* Bring down the devil, for he must not die
So sweet a death as hanging presently.

Aaron. If there be devils, would I were a devil,
To live and burn in everlasting fire,

119 *sounded* swooned   130 *forswear* perjure

So I might have your company in hell,
But to torment you with my bitter tongue!   *150*

Lucius. Sirs, stop his mouth, and let him speak no
   more.
                Enter Aemilius.

Goth. My lord, there is a messenger from Rome   *155*
   Desires to be admitted to your presence.

Lucius. Let him come near.
   Welcome, Aemilius, what's the news from Rome?

Aemilius. Lord Lucius, and you princes of the Goths,
   The Roman Emperor greets you all by me;
   And, for he understands you are in arms,
   He craves a parley at your father's house,
   Willing you to demand your hostages,   *160*
   And they shall be immediately delivered.

Goth. What says our general?

Lucius. Aemilius, let the Emperor give his pledges
   Unto my father and my uncle Marcus,
   And we will come. March away.   [*Exeunt.*] *165*

[Scene II. *Rome. Before Titus' house.*]

*Enter Tamora and her two sons, disguised [as
   Revenge attended by Rape and Murder].*

Tamora. Thus, in this strange and sad habiliment,°
   I will encounter with Andronicus,
   And say I am Revenge, sent from below
   To join with him and right his heinous wrongs.
   Knock at his study, where, they say, he keeps°   *5*
   To ruminate strange plots of dire revenge;
   Tell him Revenge is come to join with him,
   And work confusion° on his enemies.

V.ii.1 *sad habiliment* dismal apparel 5 *keeps* dwells 8 *confusion*
destruction

They knock, and Titus [above] opens his study door.

Titus. Who doth molest my contemplation?
10   Is it your trick to make me ope the door,
That so my sad decrees may fly away,
And all my study be to no effect?
You are deceived: for what I mean to do
See here in bloody lines I have set down.
15   And what is written shall be executed.

Tamora. Titus, I am come to talk with thee.

Titus. No, not a word. How can I grace my talk,
Wanting a hand to give that accord?°
Thou hast the odds of° me, therefore no more.

Tamora. If thou didst know me, thou wouldst talk
20   with me.

Titus. I am not mad, I know thee well enough.
Witness this wretched stump, witness these crimson
    lines,
Witness these trenches made by grief and care,
Witness the tiring day and heavy night,
25   Witness all sorrow, that I know thee well
For our proud empress, mighty Tamora:
Is not thy coming for my other hand?

Tamora. Know thou, sad man, I am not Tamora;
She is thy enemy, and I thy friend.
30   I am Revenge, sent from th' infernal kingdom
To ease the gnawing vulture of thy mind,
By working wreakful° vengeance on thy foes.
Come down and welcome me to this world's light;
Confer with me of murder and of death:
35   There's not a hollow cave or lurking place,
No vast obscurity or misty vale,
Where bloody murder or detested rape
Can couch° for fear, but I will find them out,

---

18 *give that accord* i.e., provide appropriate gestures   19 *odds of*
advantage over   32 *wreakful* avenging   38 *couch* lie hidden

And in their ears tell them my dreadful name,
Revenge, which makes the foul offender quake.   **40**

Titus. Art thou Revenge? And art thou sent to me,
To be a torment to mine enemies?

Tamora. I am, therefore come down and welcome me.

Titus. Do me some service ere I come to thee.
Lo, by thy side where Rape and Murder stands;   **45**
Now give some surance° that thou art Revenge;
Stab them, or tear them on thy chariot wheels;
And then I'll come and be thy wagoner,
And whirl along with thee about the globes.
Provide thee two proper palfreys,° black as jet,   **50**
To hale thy vengeful wagon swift away,
And find out murder in their guilty caves:
And when thy car° is loaden with their heads,
I will dismount, and by thy wagon wheel
Trot like a servile footman all day long,   **55**
Even from Hyperion's° rising in the east,
Until his very downfall in the sea.
And day by day I'll do this heavy task,
So° thou destroy Rapine° and Murder there.

Tamora. These are my ministers and come with me.   **60**

Titus. Are them thy ministers? What are they called?

Tamora. Rape and Murder; therefore callèd so,
'Cause they take vengeance of such kind of men.

Titus. Good Lord, how like the Empress' sons they are!
And you the Empress! But we worldly° men   **65**
Have miserable, mad, mistaking eyes.
O sweet Revenge, now do I come to thee:
And, if one arm's embracement will content thee,
I will embrace thee in it by and by. [*Exit above.*]

Tamora. This closing° with him fits his lunacy.   **70**

46 *surance* assurance   50 *proper palfreys* excellent horses   53 *car* chariot   56 *Hyperion's* the sun god's   59 *So* provided that   59 *Rapine* rape   65 *worldly* mortal, of this world   70 *closing* agreement

Whate'er I forge° to feed his brainsick humors,
Do you uphold and maintain in your speeches,
For now he firmly takes me for Revenge,
And, being credulous in this mad thought,
75 I'll make him send for Lucius his son;
And, whilst I at a banket hold him sure,
I'll find some cunning practice° out of hand,°
To scatter and disperse the giddy Goths,
Or at the least make them his enemies.
80 See, here he comes, and I must ply my theme.

[*Enter Titus.*]

Titus. Long have I been forlorn, and all for thee.
Welcome, dread Fury, to my woeful house:
Rapine and Murder, you are welcome too:
How like the Empress and her sons you are!
85 Well are you fitted, had you but a Moor:
Could not all hell afford you such a devil?
For well I wot the Empress never wags°
But in her company there is a Moor;
And, would you represent our queen aright,
90 It were convenient° you had such a devil:
But welcome, as you are. What shall we do?

Tamora. What wouldst thou have us do, Andronicus?

Demetrius. Show me a murderer, I'll deal with him.

Chiron. Show me a villain that hath done a rape,
95 And I am sent to be revenged on him.

Tamora. Show me a thousand that hath done thee
wrong,
And I will be revengèd on them all.

Titus. Look round about the wicked streets of Rome,
And when thou find'st a man that's like thyself,
100 Good Murder, stab him; he's a murderer.
Go thou with him, and when it is thy hap°
To find another that is like to thee,

71 *forge* invent 77 *practice* scheme 77 *out of hand* on the spur
of the moment 87 *wags* moves 90 *convenient* fitting 101 *hap*
chance

Good Rapine, stab him; he is a ravisher.
Go thou with them, and in the Emperor's court
There is a queen attended by a Moor;   105
Well shalt thou know her by thine own proportion,
For up and down she doth resemble thee;
I pray thee, do on them some violent death;
They have been violent to me and mine.

Tamora. Well hast thou lessoned us; this shall we do. 110
But would it please thee, good Andronicus,
To send for Lucius, thy thrice valiant son,
Who leads towards Rome a band of warlike Goths,
And bid him come and banquet at thy house:
When he is here, even at thy solemn° feast,   113
I will bring in the Empress and her sons,
The Emperor himself, and all thy foes,
And at thy mercy shall they stoop and kneel,
And on them shalt thou ease thy angry heart.
What says Andronicus to this device?   120

Titus. Marcus, my brother! 'Tis sad Titus calls.

Enter Marcus.

Go, gentle Marcus, to thy nephew Lucius;
Thou shalt inquire him out among the Goths.
Bid him repair° to me and bring with him
Some of the chiefest princes of the Goths: 125
Bid him encamp his soldiers where they are;
Tell him the Emperor and the Empress too
Feast at my house, and he shall feast with them.
This do thou for my love, and so let him,
As he regards his agèd father's life.   130

Marcus. This will I do, and soon return again. [*Exit.*]

Tamora. Now will I hence about thy business,
And take my ministers along with me.

Titus. Nay, nay, let Rape and Murder stay with me,
Or else I'll call my brother back again,   135
And cleave to no revenge but Lucius.

115 *solemn* ceremonious   124 *repair* come

Tamora. [*Aside to her sons*] What say you, boys? Will
    you abide with him,
    Whiles I go tell my lord the Emperor
    How I have governed our determined jest?°
140   Yield to his humor, smooth and speak him fair,°
    And tarry with him till I turn again.

Titus. [*Aside*] I knew them all, though they supposed
    me mad;
    And will o'erreach them in their own devices,
    A pair of cursèd hellhounds and their dame.

145 *Demetrius.* Madam, depart at pleasure, leave us here.

Tamora. Farewell, Andronicus: Revenge now goes
    To lay a complot° to betray thy foes.

Titus. I know thou dost; and, sweet Revenge, farewell.
                    [*Exit Tamora.*]

Chiron. Tell us, old man, how shall we be employed?

150 *Titus.* Tut, I have work enough for you to do.
    Publius, come hither, Caius, and Valentine!

        [*Enter Publius and others.*]

Publius. What is your will?

Titus. Know you these two?

Publius. The Empress' sons, I take them: Chiron,
155   Demetrius.

Titus. Fie, Publius, fie! Thou art too much deceived;
    The one is Murder, and Rape is the other's name:
    And therefore bind them, gentle Publius:
    Caius and Valentine, lay hands on them:
160   Oft have you heard me wish for such an hour,
    And now I find it: therefore bind them sure;
    And stop their mouths if they begin to cry. [*Exit.*]

---

139 *governed our determined jest* managed the jest we agreed ("determined") upon   140 *smooth and speak him fair* flatter and speak
courteously to him   147 *complot* plot

Chiron. Villains, forbear! We are the Empress' sons.

Publius. And therefore do we what we are commanded.
   Stop close their mouths, let them not speak a word: 165
   Is he sure bound? Look that you bind them fast.

*Enter Titus Andronicus with a knife, and Lavinia with
a basin.*

Titus. Come, come, Lavinia; look, thy foes are bound.
   Sirs, stop their mouths, let them not speak to me,
   But let them hear what fearful words I utter.
   O villains, Chiron and Demetrius!   170
   Here stands the spring whom you have stained with
      mud,
   This goodly summer with your winter mixed.
   You killed her husband, and, for that vile fault
   Two of her brothers were condemned to death,
   My hand cut off and made a merry jest: 175
   Both her sweet hands, her tongue, and that more dear
   Than hands or tongue, her spotless chastity,
   Inhuman traitors, you constrained and forced.
   What would you say if I should let you speak?
   Villains, for shame you could not beg for grace.   180
   Hark, wretches, how I mean to martyr you.
   This one hand yet is left to cut your throats,
   Whiles that Lavinia 'tween her stumps doth hold
   The basin that receives your guilty blood.
   You know your mother means to feast with me,   185
   And calls herself Revenge, and thinks me mad:
   Hark, villains, I will grind your bones to dust,
   And with your blood and it I'll make a paste,
   And of the paste a coffin° I will rear,
   And make two pasties of your shameful heads,   190
   And bid that strumpet, your unhallowed dam,
   Like to the earth, swallow her own increase.°
   This is the feast that I have bid her to,
   And this the banket she shall surfeit on;
   For worse than Philomel you used my daughter,   195

189 *coffin* pie crust   192 *increase* offspring

    And worse than Progne° I will be revenged.
    And now prepare your throats. Lavinia, come,
    Receive the blood; and when that they are dead,
    Let me go grind their bones to powder small,
200   And with this hateful liquor temper° it,
    And in that paste let their vile heads be baked.
    Come, come, be every one officious°
    To make this banket, which I wish may prove
    More stern and bloody than the Centaurs' feast.°
                  He cuts their throats.
205   So, now bring them in, for I'll play the cook,
    And see them ready against° their mother comes.
                          Exeunt.

[Scene III. *Rome. Within Titus' house.*]

Enter Lucius, Marcus, and the Goths [*with Aaron a prisoner, and an Attendant bearing Aaron's child*].

Lucius. Uncle Marcus, since 'tis my father's mind
    That I repair° to Rome, I am content.

Goth. And ours with thine, befall what fortune will.

Lucius. Good uncle, take you in this barbarous Moor,
5   This ravenous tiger, this accursèd devil;
    Let him receive no sust'nance, fetter him,
    Till he be brought unto the Empress' face
    For testimony of her foul proceedings:
    And see the ambush of our friends be strong;
10   I fear the Emperor means no good to us.

---

196 *Progne* wife of Tereus (Tereus raped and mutilated Progne's sister, Philomela, and in revenge Progne slaughtered Tereus' and her own—son and served him to Tereus) 200 *temper* mix 202 *officious* busy 204 *Centaurs' feast* (a battle followed the marriage feast to which the Lapiths invited the Centaurs) 206 *against* in preparation for the time when V.iii.2 *repair* return

Aaron. Some devil whisper curses in my ear,
    And prompt me, that my tongue may utter forth
    The venomous malice of my swelling heart!

Lucius. Away, inhuman dog! Unhallowed slave!
    Sirs, help our uncle to convey him in.   15
            [*Goths lead Aaron in. Trumpets sound.*]
    The trumpets show the Emperor is at hand.

*Sound trumpets. Enter Emperor and Empress, with
        Tribunes and others.*

Saturninus. What, hath the firmament mo° suns than
    one?

Lucius. What boots° it thee to call thyself a sun?

Marcus. Rome's Emperor, and nephew, break the
    parle;°
    These quarrels must be quietly debated.   20
    The feast is ready, which the careful° Titus
    Hath ordained to an honorable end,
    For peace, for love, for league, and good to Rome.
    Please you, therefore, draw nigh, and take your
    places.

Saturninus. Marcus, we will.   25

*Trumpets sounding, enter Titus, like a cook,
    placing the dishes, and Lavinia with a veil over
    her face, [young Lucius, and others].*

Titus. Welcome, my lord; welcome, dread Queen;
    Welcome, ye warlike Goths; welcome, Lucius;
    And welcome, all: although the cheer° be poor,
    'Twill fill your stomachs; please you eat of it.

Saturninus. Why art thou thus attired, Andronicus?   30

Titus. Because I would be sure to have all well,
    To entertain your Highness and your empress.

Tamora. We are beholding to you, good Andronicus.

17 *mo* more   18 *boots* avails   19 *break the parle* interrupt the talk
(i.e., cease quarreling)   21 *careful* full of sorrow   28 *cheer* hospitality

Titus. And if your Highness knew my heart, you were.
35   My lord the Emperor, resolve° me this:
   Was it well done of rash Virginius
   To slay his daughter with his own right hand,
   Because she was enforced,° stained, and deflow'r'd?

Saturninus. It was, Andronicus.

40 *Titus.* Your reason, mighty lord!

Saturninus. Because the girl should not survive her
   shame,
   And by her presence still renew his sorrows.

Titus. A reason mighty, strong, and effectual,
   A pattern, precedent, and lively warrant,
45   For me, most wretched, to perform the like.
   Die, die, Lavinia, and thy shame with thee,
   And with thy shame thy father's sorrow die!
                         [*He kills her.*]

Saturninus. What hast thou done, unnatural and unkind?°

Titus. Killed her for whom my tears have made me
   blind.
50   I am as woeful as Virginius was,
   And have a thousand times more cause than he
   To do this outrage, and it now is done.

Saturninus. What, was she ravished? Tell who did the
   deed.

Titus. Will't please you eat? Will't please your Highness
   feed?

55 *Tamora.* Why hast thou slain thine only daughter thus?

Titus. Not I; 'twas Chiron and Demetrius:
   They ravished her and cut away her tongue;
   And they, 'twas they, that did her all this wrong.

Saturninus. Go, fetch them hither to us presently.

---

35 *resolve* answer   38 *enforced* forced, raped   48 *unkind* (1) unnatural (2) cruel

Titus. Why, there they are, both bakèd in this pie,   60
    Whereof their mother daintily hath fed,
    Eating the flesh that she herself hath bred.
    'Tis true, 'tis true; witness my knife's sharp point.
                  He stabs the Empress.

Saturninus. Die, frantic wretch, for this accursèd deed.
                        [Kills Titus.]

Lucius. Can the son's eye behold his father bleed?   65
    There's meed for meed,° death for a deadly deed.
                    [Kills Saturninus.]

Marcus. You sad-faced men, people and sons of Rome,
    By uproars severed, as a flight of fowl
    Scattered by winds and high tempestuous gusts,
    O, let me teach you how to knit again   70
    This scattered corn into one mutual sheaf,
    These broken limbs again into one body.

Roman Lord. Let Rome herself be bane° unto herself,
    And she whom mighty kingdoms curtsy to,
    Like a forlorn and desperate castaway,   75
    Do shameful execution on herself,
    But if° my frosty signs and chaps of age,°
    Grave witnesses of true experience,
    Cannot induce you to attend my words.
    [To Lucius] Speak, Rome's dear friend, as erst°
       our ancestor,°   80
    When with his solemn tongue he did discourse
    To lovesick Dido's sad attending° ear
    The story of that baleful° burning night,
    When subtle Greeks surprised King Priam's Troy;
    Tell us what Sinon° hath bewitched our ears,   85
    Or who hath brought the fatal engine in
    That gives our Troy, our Rome, the civil wound.
    My heart is not compact° of flint nor steel;

---

66 *meed for meed* measure for measure   73 *bane* destruction   77 *But if* unless   77 *frosty signs and chaps of age* i.e., white hair and cracked (wrinkled) skin   80 *erst* formerly   80 *our ancestor* i.e., Aeneas   82 *sad attending* seriously listening   83 *baleful* injurious 85 *Sinon* Greek who persuaded the Trojans to admit the wooden horse   88 *compact* composed

Nor can I utter all our bitter grief,
90 But floods of tears will drown my oratory
And break my utt'rance, even in the time
When it should move ye to attend me most,
And force you to commiseration.
Here's Rome's young captain, let him tell the tale,
95 While I stand by and weep to hear him speak.

Lucius. Then, gracious auditory, be it known to you
That Chiron and the damned Demetrius
Were they that murd'red our emperor's brother;
And they it were that ravishèd our sister.
100 For their fell° faults our brothers were beheaded,
Our father's tears despised, and basely cozened°
Of that true hand that fought Rome's quarrel out
And sent her enemies unto the grave.
Lastly, myself unkindly banishèd,
105 The gates shut on me, and turned weeping out,
To beg relief among Rome's enemies,
Who drowned their enmity in my true tears
And oped their arms to embrace me as a friend:
I am the turned-forth, be it known to you,
110 That have preserved her welfare in my blood,
And from her bosom took the enemy's point,
Sheathing the steel in my advent'rous body.
Alas, you know I am no vaunter,° I;
My scars can witness, dumb although they are,
115 That my report is just and full of truth.
But, soft!° Methinks, I do digress too much,
Citing my worthless praise. O, pardon me,
For when no friends are by, men praise themselves.

Marcus. Now is my turn to speak. Behold the child:
120 Of this was Tamora deliverèd,
The issue of an irreligious Moor,
Chief architect and plotter of these woes:
The villain is alive in Titus' house,
And as he is to witness, this is true.
125 Now judge what cause had Titus to revenge

100 *fell* savage   101 *cozened* cheated   113 *vaunter* braggart   116 *soft* hold (a common interjection)

These wrongs, unspeakable, past patience,
Or more than any living man could bear.
Now have you heard the truth. What say you,
    Romans?
Have we done aught amiss, show us wherein,
And, from the place where you behold us pleading,   130
The poor remainder of Andronici
Will, hand in hand, all headlong hurl ourselves
And on the ragged° stones beat forth our souls,
And make a mutual closure° of our house.
Speak, Romans, speak, and if you say we shall,   135
Lo, hand in hand, Lucius and I will fall.

Aemilius. Come, come, thou reverend man of Rome,
And bring our emperor gently in thy hand,
Lucius our emperor; for well I know
The common voice do cry it shall be so.   140

Marcus. Lucius, all hail, Rome's royal Emperor!
    [*To soldiers*] Go, go into old Titus' sorrowful
        house,
And hither hale that misbelieving Moor,
To be adjudged some direful slaught'ring death,
As punishment for his most wicked life.   145
                    [*Exeunt Attendants.*]
Lucius, all hail, Rome's gracious governor!
                    [*Cries of approval.*]

Lucius. Thanks, gentle Romans: may I govern so,
To heal Rome's harms and wipe away her woe!
But, gentle people, give me aim° awhile,
For nature puts me to a heavy task.   150
Stand all aloof; but, uncle, draw you near
To shed obsequious° tears upon this trunk.
O, take this warm kiss on thy pale cold lips,
These sorrowful drops upon thy bloodstained face,
The last true duties of thy noble son!   155

Marcus. Tear for tear and loving kiss for kiss
Thy brother Marcus tenders on thy lips:

133 *ragged* rugged   134 *mutual closure* common end   149 *give me
aim* assist me   152 *obsequious* mourning

O, were the sum of these that I should pay
Countless and infinite, yet would I pay them!

160 *Lucius.* Come hither, boy; come, come, and learn of us
To melt in showers. Thy grandsire loved thee well;
Many a time he danced thee on his knee,
Sung thee asleep, his loving breast thy pillow;
Many a story hath he told to thee,
165 And bid thee bear his pretty tales in mind,
And talk of them when he was dead and gone.

Marcus. How many thousand times hath these poor
lips,
When they were living, warmed themselves on thine!
O, now, sweet boy, give them their latest° kiss.
170 Bid him farewell; commit him to the grave;
Do them° that kindness, and take leave of them.

Boy. O, grandsire, grandsire! Ev'n with all my heart
Would I were dead, so you did live again!
O Lord, I cannot speak to him for weeping;
175 My tears will choke me if I ope my mouth.

[*Enter Attendants with Aaron.*]

Roman. You sad Andronici, have done with woes;
Give sentence on this execrable wretch
That hath been breeder of these dire events.

Lucius. Set him breast-deep in earth and famish him;
180 There let him stand and rave and cry for food:
If anyone relieves or pities him,
For the offense he dies. This is our doom.°
Some stay, to see him fast'ned in the earth.

Aaron. Ah, why should wrath be mute, and fury dumb?
185 I am no baby, I, that with base prayers
I should repent the evils I have done:
Ten thousand worse than ever yet I did
Would I perform, if I might have my will:
If one good deed in all my life I did,

169 *latest* last   171 *them* i.e., "these poor lips" of line 167   182
doom sentence

I do repent it from my very soul.   190

Lucius. Some loving friends convey the Emperor hence,
　　And give him burial in his father's grave:
　　My father and Lavinia shall forthwith
　　Be closèd in our household's monument.
　　As for that ravenous tiger, Tamora,   195
　　No funeral rite, nor man in mourning weed,
　　No mournful bell shall ring her burial;
　　But throw her forth to beasts and birds to prey.
　　Her life was beastly and devoid of pity,
　　And being dead, let birds on her take pity.   *Exeunt.*   200

Finis the Tragedy of Titus Andronicus.

Textual Note

There is an allusion to a Roman hero named Titus in *A Knack to Know a Knave,* acted in June 1592. Though the allusion may, of course, be to an earlier play on the subject rather than to Shakespeare's play, there is no need to multiply entities; Shakespeare's *Titus Andronicus* may have been on the stage before 1592. The next bit of evidence is a reference of 23 January 1594 in Henslowe's *Diary* to the effect that Sussex's men acted a new piece, "titus & ondronicus." If the allusion in *A Knave* is not to Shakespeare's play, quite possibly *Titus Andronicus* was indeed new in 1594, but it is equally possible that it was "new" only to Sussex's company, or that it had been newly revised. On 6 February 1594 the Stationers' Register entered "a book intituled a Noble Roman Historye of Titus Andronicus." Perhaps this entry alludes to the play, which indeed was published in 1594, though possibly the entry is to some other piece on the same subject. In 1614 Ben Jonson, in the Induction to *Bartholomew Fair,* mentions that Andronicus was seen on the stage as long ago as "fiue and twentie or thirtie yeeres"; strictly, Jonson's reference would date the play 1584–89, though probably he is speaking loosely and his evidence surely does not prohibit a date in the early nineties. The date widely favored is 1592–94, but there is no compelling reason to believe that *Titus* could not have been written in the late eighties.

Only one copy of the first quarto (1594) is known to be extant. Apparently Q1 (i.e., the first quarto) was printed from Shakespeare's manuscript or from a copy of it; a number of stage directions—such as "Enter . . . as many as can be"—suggest an author's hand. In 1600 a second quarto (Q2) was issued. It omits a few lines, adds some, and alters a good deal of punctuation. There is no reason to believe that the alterations represent Shakespeare's revisions; probably all the revisions are a compositor's tamperings. Q3, issued in 1611, was set up from Q2 and therefore has no authority. The version in the First Folio (F) is based on Q3 but makes numerous small alterations (especially in stage directions) and adds the entire scene (III.ii). The new scene is of sufficient excellence to be Shakespeare's, and though the other changes in F do not suggest that great effort was made to give the play in a version much different from that of Q3, the new scene shows that the editors had access to some unpublished material. The present edition is based on Q1, except for III.ii, which is, of course, based on F. It regularizes speech prefixes (for example, Q1's "Saturnine," "Saturninus," "King," "Satur," are all given here as "Saturninus"); it slightly alters the position of a few stage directions, and it modernizes spelling and punctuation. The act divisions were first established by F; the scene divisions are the work of later editors and though of no authenticity they provide a convenient device for reference. Departures from Q1, other than those mentioned above and corrections of obvious typographical errors, are listed below, the adopted reading first, in *italic* type, followed by the original reading in roman. If the adopted reading is from Q2, Q3, or F, that fact is indicated in a bracket following the reading. If there is no such indication, the adopted reading is an editor's conjecture.

I.i.35 [for the three and a half lines that follow these words in Q1 see footnote to the line] 69 s.d. *her three sons* her two sonnes 98 *manes* manus 226 *Titan's* [Q2] Tytus 242 *Pantheon* Pathan 264 *chance* [Q2] change 280 *cuique* cuiqum 317 *Phoebe* Thebe 358 s.d. *speak* speakes 369 *Martius* 3. Sonne 370 *Quintus* 2. Sonne 372 *Quintus* 2. sonne 391 [Q1 follows with s.d.:

"Exit all but Marcus and Titus," and the other early texts also indicate an exit]   399 *Yes ... remunerate* [F; omitted in the quartos]

II.i.110 *than* this

II.ii.1 *morn* [F] Moone

II.iii.69 *try* [Q2] trie thy   72 *swart* swartie   160 *ears* [Q3] yeares
210 *unhallowed* [F] vnhollow   222 *berayed* bereaud   231 *Pyramus*
[Q2] Priamus   236 *Cocytus* Ocitus

II.iv.27 *him* them   30 *three* their

III.i.146 *his true* her true

III.ii [this scene is found only in F]   39 *complainer* complayne
52 *thy knife* knife   53 *fly* Flys   55 *are cloyed* cloi'd   72 *myself*
my selfes

IV.i.50 *quotes* [Q2] coats   88 *hope* [Q2] hop [or "I op"]

IV.ii.95 *Alcides* [Q2] Alciades

IV.iii.57 *Saturn* Saturnine   78 *News* [Q2] Clowne. Newes

IV.iv.5 *know, as know* know   49 *By* be   99 *ears* [F] yeares

V.ii.52 *caves* cares   56 *Hyperion's* Epeons   65 *worldly* [Q2]
wordlie

V.iii. 125 *cause* course   144 *adjudged* [F] adiudge   154 *bloodstained* blood slaine   163 *Sung* [Q2] Song

A Note on the Source of
Titus Andronicus

Those Shakespeareans who are embarrassed by *Titus*
(but who cannot overlook the strong evidence that he
wrote it) sometimes assume that it represents his rework-
ing of an older, and presumably worse, play. No such play
has come to light, and though it is possible that Shakespeare's source was a play now extant only in Shakespeare's revision, it is more than possible—even likely—
that his source was a prose tale regarded as history. The
Folger Shakespeare Library has a unique copy of a mid-
eighteenth-century booklet entitled *The History of Titus
Andronicus,* which contains a prose narrative (reprinted
below) and a ballad. The ballad, of no interest to us, is
an abbreviated metrical version of the prose narrative,
but this latter seems to be a reprint of a much older
piece—quite possibly of a late-sixteenth-century version
that may have been Shakespeare's source. Certainly the
prose narrative is not indebted to the play: it makes no
reference to Shakespeare—as it surely would if it had
been written in the eighteenth century—and it includes a
good deal of alleged history that Shakespeare does not.
Furthermore, some of its characters are unnamed; if the
narrative were based on the play, Aaron, for example,

would doubtless be mentioned by name, but he is merely called "the wicked Moor."

Put it this way: the extant *History of Titus Andronicus* is almost surely a reprint of a much older piece, quite possibly a reprint of the tale that Shakespeare dramatized. There is no opposing evidence. The *History* is reprinted below, from the only known copy, and for the first time since its publication in the middle of the eighteenth century. Spelling and punctuation have been modernized, and manifest typographical errors have been corrected.

The

History

OF

Titus Andronicus,

The Renowned Roman General

who, after he had saved Rome by his valor from being destroyed by the barbarous Goths and lost two and twenty of his valiant sons in ten years' war, was, upon the Emperor's marrying the Queen of the Goths, put to disgrace and banished; but being recalled, the Emperor's son by a first wife was murdered by the Empress' sons and a bloody Moor, and how charging it upon Andronicus' sons, though he cut off his hand to redeem their lives, they were murdered in prison; how his fair daughter Lavinia, being ravished by the Empress' sons, they cut out her tongue, and hands off, etc.; how Andronicus slew them, made pies of their flesh, and presented them to the Emperor and Empress; and then slew them also; with the miserable death he put the wicked Moor to; then at her request slew his daughter and himself to avoid torment.

Reprinted by permission of The Folger Shakespeare Library.

The
Tragical History
of
Titus Andronicus, etc.

Chapter 1

How Rome being besieged by the barbarous Goths and being at the point to yield through famine, it was unexpectedly rescued by Andronicus, with the utter defeat of the enemy, for which he was received in triumph.

When the Roman Empire was grown to its height and the greatest part of the world was subjected to its imperial throne, in the time of Theodosius, a barbarous northern people out of Swedeland, Denmark, and Gothland came into Italy in such numbers, under the leading of Tottilius, their king, that they overrun it with fire and sword, plundering churches, ripping up women with child, and deflowering virgins in so horrid and barbarous a manner that the people fled before them like flocks of sheep.

To oppose this destroying torrent of the Goths, a barbarous people, strangers to Christianity, the Emperor raised a mighty army in Greece, Italy, France, Spain, Germany, and England, and gave battle under the passage of the Alpine mountains, but was overthrown, with the loss of threescore thousand of his men, and flying to Rome, was besieged in it by a numerous host of these barbarians, who pressed so hard to beat down the walls and enter with a miserable slaughter of the citizens that such as could get over the River Tiber fled in a fearful manner to a distant country. The siege lasting ten months, such a famine arose that no unclean thing was left uneaten; dogs, cats, horses, rats and mice were curious dainties; thousands died in the streets of hunger, and most of those that were alive looked more like glass than living creatures; so that being brought to the last extremity, the vulgar sort came about the Emperor's palace and with piteous cries implored him either to find some means to get them food, to stay their fleeting lives, or make the best terms he could and open the gates to the enemy.

This greatly perplexed him; the former he could not do, and the latter he knew would not only uncrown him, if he escaped with his life, but be the ruin of the Roman Empire; yet in the greatest of this extremity he unexpectedly found relief.

Titus Andronicus, a Roman senator and a true lover of his country, hearing in Graecia, where he was governor of the province of Achaia, what straits Rome and his sovereign were brought into by the barbarous nations, got together friends and sold whatever he had of value to hire soldiers; so that with his small army he secretly marched away, and falling upon the mighty army of the enemy (when they were drowned as it were in security, wine, and sleep, resolved to make a general storm the next day, in which they had undoubtedly carried the city), he and his sons, entering their camp, and followed by the rest, made such a slaughter that the cry and confusion were exceeding great; some changed sleep into death, others vomited wine and blood mixed together, through the wounds they received; some lost heads at once, others arms: Tottilius, in this confusion being awakened, had his first care to convey away his queen and two sons, who were newly come to the camp, and then labored to rally his flying men; but being desperately charged by Andronicus, he was thrown from his horse and much wounded, many lives being lost in remounting him; whereupon seeing the slaughter so great by the pale beams of the moon, and not knowing the number of his adversaries, having caused the retreat to be sounded, he fled in great confusion and left the rich spoils of his camp, the wealth of many plundered nations, to Andronicus and his soldiers; who being expert in war, would not meddle with them that night, but stood to their arms till the morning.

Chapter II

How in ten years' war, with the loss of two and twenty of his valiant sons, he won many famous battles, slew Tottilius, King of the Goths, and did many other brave exploits, etc.

The watch upon the walls of Rome, having heard a confused cry and the clashing of arms, were greatly astonished, but could not think what it should mean; for the camps of the barbarous Goths extended in a large circuit about the famous city; however, the captains of the guards advertised the Emperor of it, who sent out scouts, but they, fearful of approaching too near the enemy in the night, could get certain intelligence only that they heard the groans and cries, as they thought, of dying men. However, the shades of night being dispelled, and the glorious sun raising [?] forth a cheerful light, the porters of the gate espying three men coming towards it, and soon after being come up, knocked with great earnestness, they took the courage to demand what they were and what they required.

"I am," said one of them, "Andronicus, your friend, and desire admittance to speak with the Emperor, since the news I bring will no doubt be pleasing to him."

Upon this, lifting up his helmet, they knew him with joy, knowing him to be a very worthy patriot, thinking he came to do them good, as he had often done in their great distress when the Huns and Vandals invaded the empire some years before and were beaten out by him.

The Emperor no sooner heard he was come, but he ran from his palace to meet him and would not suffer him to kneel, but embraced him tenderly as a brother, saying, "Welcome, Andronicus, in this the time of our greatest misery; it was thy counsel I wanted, to know how to free us from this barbarous enemy, against whose force the city cannot long hold out."

"May it please your Majesty," replied Andronicus, "let

those fears be banished, the work is done to you unknown; I and my twenty-five sons, and what friends and
soldiers I could get, have this night fallen into their quar-
ters, cut off fifty thousand of them, and their scattered
remains with their king are fled."

At this the Emperor was astonished and scarce could
believe it, though he very well knew the integrity of Andronicus, till his own captains came and told him the
siege was raised with a miserable slaughter, but by whom
they knew not, unless the enemy had fallen out among
themselves, and the troops they could yet see in view
were but inconsiderable. Now these were those that be-
longed to Andronicus, who as soon as it was day were in
pursuit of the enemy under the command of his five-and-
twenty sons.

This surprising news was no sooner spread in the city
but the joy of the people was exceeding great; and when
they knew who was their deliverer, they went in proces-
sion and sung his praises. After that he rode in a triumphant chariot through the city, crowned with an oaken
garland, the people shouting, trumpets sounding, and all
other expressions and demonstrations of joy that a grateful people could afford their deliverer, in which he behaved himself so humble that he gained the love of all.

This was no sooner over, but he desired the Emperor
to join what forces he could with those that he had
brought and speedily pursue the enemy before he could
gather new strength, that he might beat him out of Italy
and his other countries where he yet held strong garrisons.
This was embraced as good counsel, and the senators, by
the Emperor's mandate, assembled with joy, who chose
with one consent Andronicus their general. He was not
slow in mustering his forces, nor in the speedy pursuit; he
found they had passed the Alps and that their army was
increased by new supplies, yet he gave them battle, and
charging through the thickest of their squadrons hand to
hand, slew Tottilius and beat down his standard. Whereupon the Goths fled, and the slaughter continued for many
miles, covering all the lanes and roads with the bodies of
the dead; and in the pursuit he took the Queen of the

Goths captive and brought her to Rome, for which signal
victory he had a second triumph and was styled the deliverer of his country. But his joy was a little eclipsed by
the loss of five of his sons, who died courageously fighting
in battle.

Chapter III

*How the Emperor, weary of so tedious a war, contrary
to the mind and persuasions of Andronicus, married the
Queen of the Goths and concluded a peace; how she
tyrannized and her sons slew the Prince that was betrothed to Andronicus' daughter and hid him in the forest.*

The Goths, having found the pleasantness of these fruitful countries, resolved not so to give them over, but, en-
couraged by Tottilius' two sons, Alaricus and Abonus,
sent for fresh forces and made a desolation in the Roman
provinces, continuing a ten years' war, wherein the valiant
Andronicus, Captain-General of the Empire, gained many
victories over them, with great effusion of blood on either
side; but those barbarous people still increasing in their
numbers, the Emperor, desiring peace, it was agreed to,
in consideration he should marry Attava, Queen of the
Goths, and in case he should die without issue, her sons
might succeed in the Empire. Andronicus opposed this
very much, as did many other, knowing, through the
Emperor's weakness, that she, being an imperious woman
and of a haughty spirit, would govern him as she pleased
and enslave the noble Empire to strangers. However, it
was carried on with a high hand, and great preparations
were made for the royal nuptials, though with very little
rejoicing among the people, for what they expected soon
followed.

The Queen of the Goths being made Empress, soon began to show her disposition, according to the cruelty of
her nation and temper, persuading the easy Emperor to
place the Goths in the places of his most trusty friends;

and having above all vowed revenge on Andronicus, who most opposed her proceedings, she procured him to be banished; but the people, whose deliverer he had been in their greatest extremity, calling to mind that and his many other good services, rose unanimously in arms and went clamoring to the palace, threatening to fire it and revenge so base an indignity on the Queen, if the decree which had been passed against all reason was not speedily revoked. This put her and the Emperor into such a fears [sic] that their request was granted; and now she plotted by more private ways to bring the effects of revenge and implacable hatred about more secretly.

She had a Moor as revengeful as herself, whom she trusted in many great affairs and was usually privy to her secrets, so far that from private dalliances she grew pregnant and brought forth a blackamoor child. This grieved the Emperor extremely, but she allayed his anger by telling him it was conceived by the force of imagination, and brought many suborned women and physicians to testify the like had often happened. This made the Emperor send the Moor into banishment, upon pain of death never to return to Rome. But her lust and the confidence she had put in him as the main engine to bring about her devilish designs made her plot to have that decree revoked; when having got the Emperor into a pleasant humor, she feigned herself sick, telling him withal she had seen a vision which commanded her to call back the innocent Moor from banishment or she should never recover of that sickness. The kind, good-natured Emperor, who could not resist her tears and entreaties, with some difficulty consented to it, provided he should be commanded to keep always out of her sight, lest the like mischance might happen as had been before. This she seemingly consented to, and he was immediately sent for, and the former familiarities continued between them, though more privately.

Andronicus, besides his sons, had a very fair and beautiful daughter, named Lavinia, brought up in all singular virtues, humble, courteous, and modest, insomuch that the Emperor's only son, by a former wife, fell extremely in love with her, seeking her favor by all virtuous and honorable ways, insomuch that after a long courtship, with her father and the Emperor's consent she was betrothed to him.

The Queen of the Goths, hearing this, was much enraged, because from such a marriage might spring princes that might frustrate her ambitious designs, which was to make her sons emperors jointly. Wherefore she labored all she could to frustrate it, by declaring what a disgrace it would be to the Emperor to marry his son to the daughter of a subject, who might have a queen with a kingdom to her dowry. But finding the Prince constant, she resolved to take him out of the way; so it was plotted between her, the Moor, and her two sons that they should invite him to hunt in the great forest on the banks of the River Tiber, and there murder him. This was effected, by shooting him through the back with a poisoned arrow, which came out at his breast, of which wound he fell from his horse and immediately died. Then they digged a very deep pit in a pathway and threw him in, covering it lightly with boughs and sprinkling earth on it; and so returning reported they had lost the Prince in the forest, and though they had sought and called everywhere, they could not find him.

Chapter IV

How the wicked Moor, who had laid with the Empress and got into her favor above all others, betrayed Andronicus' three sons and charged the Prince's murder on them, for which they were cast into a dungeon, and after their father had cut off his hand to save them were beheaded.

The fair Lavinia no sooner heard the Prince was missing but she fell into great sorrow and lamentation, her heart misgiving her of some treachery, and thereupon she entreated her brothers to go in search of him, which they did with all speed. But being dogged by the Moor and the Queen of Goths's two sons, they unluckily coming in the way where the pit was digged, they fell both in upon the dead body and could not by reason of the great depth get out. Their cruel enemies no sooner saw this, but they hasted to the court and sent the guards in search of the murdered Prince, who found Andronicus' two sons with the dead body, which they drew up and carried prisoners to the court, where the Moor and the other two falsely swore against them that they had often heard them threaten revenge on the Prince, because he had put them to the foil, in a tournament at jousting. This, and the circumstances of their being found, with the vehement aggravation, was a sufficient ground to the Emperor to believe, who loved his son entirely and was much grieved for his death, and though they denied it with all the protestations imaginable, and pleaded their innocence, demanded the combat against their accusers, which by the law of arms they ought to have been allowed, they were immediately loaden with irons and cast into a deep dungeon among noisome creatures, as frogs, toads, serpents, and the like, where notwithstanding all the intercessions that were made they continued eating the filth that they found in that place.

At last the Queen, designing to work her revenge on Andronicus, sent the Moor in the Emperor's name, to tell him, if he designed to save his sons from the misery and death that would ensue, he should cut off his right hand and send it to court. This the good-natured father scrupled not to do, no, nor had it been his life to ransom them, he would have freely parted with it; whereupon laying his hand on a block, he gave the wicked Moor his sword, who immediately struck it off and inwardly laughed at the villainy. Then departing with it, he told him his sons should be sent to him in a few hours. But whilst he was rejoicing with the hopes of their delivery, a hearse came to his door with guards, which made his aged heart to tremble. The first thing they presented him was his hand, which they said would not be accepted; and the next was his three sons beheaded. At this woeful sight, overcome with grief, he fainted away on the dead bodies; and when he recovered again, he tore his hoary hair, which age and his lying in winter camps for the defense of his country had made as white as snow, pouring out floods of tears; but found no pity from the hardened villains, who left him with scoffs in the midst of his woeful lamentations with his sorrowful daughter. Yet this was not all, for soon after another to be deplored affliction followed, as shall in the next chapter be shown.

Chapter V

How the two lustful sons of the Empress, with the assistance of the Moor, in a barbarous manner ravished Lavinia, Andronicus' beautiful daughter, and cut out her tongue and cut off her hands, to prevent discovery; yet she did it by writing in the dust with a wand, etc.

The fair and beautiful Lavinia, for the loss of her lovers [sic] and brothers, so basely murdered by treachery, tore her golden hair, shed floods of tears, and with her nails offered violence to that lovely face kings had adored and beheld with admiration. She shunned all company, retiring to woods and groves, to utter her piteous complaints and cries to the senseless trees, when one day, being watched thither by the Moor, he gave notice of it to the Queen's two sons, who, like the wicked Elders and chaste Susanna, had a long time burned in lust yet knew her virtues were proof against all temptations, and therefore it could not be obtained but by violence. So thinking this an opportunity to serve their turns, immediately repaired to the grove and setting the Moor to watch on the outborders, soon found her pensive and sorrowful, yet comely and beautiful in tears, when unawares, before she saw them, like two ravenous tigers, they seized the trembling lady, who struggled all she could and cried out piteously for help; and seeing what their wicked intentions bent at, she offered them her throat, desiring they would bereave her of her life, but not of her honor. However, in a villainous manner, staking her down by the hair of her

head and binding her hands behind her, they turned up
her nakedness and forced their way into her closet of
chastity, taking it by turns, the elder beginning first and
the younger seconding him as they had before agreed
on; and having tired themselves in satiating their beastly
appetites, they began to consider how they should come
off when such a villainy was discovered. Whereupon, calling the Moor to them, they asked his advice, who wickedly
counseled them to make all sure, seeing they had gone
thus far, by cutting out her tongue to hinder her telling
tales and her hands off to prevent her writing a discovery.
This the cruel wretches did, whilst she in vain entreated
them to take away her life, since they had bereaved her
of her honor, which was dearer to her. And in this woeful
condition they left the lady, who had expired for the loss
of blood had not her uncle Marcus happened accidentally,
soon after, to come in search of her, who at the woeful
sight, overcome with sorrow, could hardly keep life in
himself; yet recovering his spirits, he bound up her
wounds and conveyed her home.

Poor Andronicus' grief for this sad disaster was so
great that no pen can write or words express; much ado
they had to restrain him from doing violence upon himself; he cursed the day he was born to see such miseries
fall on himself and family, entreating her to tell him, if
she could any ways do it by signs, who had so villainously
abused her. At last the poor lady, with a flood of tears
gushing from her eyes, taking a wand between her stumps,
wrote these lines:

> The lustful sons of the proud Empress
> Are doers of this hateful wickedness.

Hereupon he vowed revenge, at the hazard of his own
and all their lives, comforting his daughter with this when
nothing else would do.

Chapter VI

How Andronicus, feigning himself mad, found means to entrap the Empress' two sons in a forest, where, binding them to a tree, he cut their throats, made pies of their flesh, and served them up to the Emperor and Empress, then slew them, set the Moor quick in the ground, and then killed his daughter and himself.

Andronicus, upon these calamities, feigned himself distracted and went raving about the city, shooting his arrows towards heaven, as in defiance, calling to hell for vengeance, which mainly pleased the Empress and her sons, who thought themselves now secure; and though his friends required justice of the Emperor against the ravishers, yet they could have no redress, he rather threatening them, if they insisted on it; so that finding they were in a bad case and that in all probability their lives would be the next, they conspired together to prevent that mischief and revenge themselves; lying in ambush in the forest when the two sons went a-hunting, they surprised them, and binding them to a tree pitifully crying out for mercy, though they would give none to others, Andronicus cut their throats whilst Lavinia, by his command, held a bowl between her stumps to receive the blood; then conveying the bodies home to his own house privately, he cut the flesh into fit pieces and ground the bones to powder and made of them two mighty pasties, and invited the Emperor and Empress to dinner, who, thinking to make sport with his frantic humor, came; but when they had eat of the pasties, he told them what it was; and thereupon giving the watchword to his friends, they immediately issued out, slew the Emperor's guards, and, lastly, the Emperor and his cruel wife, after they had sufficiently upbraided them with the wicked deeds they had done. Then seizing on the wicked Moor, the fearful villain fell on his knees, promising to discover all. But when he had told how he had killed the Prince, betrayed the three sons of Andronicus by false accusation, and counseled the abuse to the fair Lavinia, they scarce knew what torments sufficient to devise for him; but at last digging a hole, they set him in the ground to the middle alive, smeared him over with honey, and so, between the stinging of bees and wasps and starving, he miserably ended his wretched days. After this, to prevent the torments he expected when these things came to be known, at his daughter's request he killed her; and so, rejoicing he had revenged himself on his enemies to the full, fell on his own sword and died.

Commentaries

H. T. PRICE

from *The Authorship of "Titus Andronicus"*

The best "parallel" by which we can test authorship is construction. Phrases may be borrowed here and there, but construction refers to the planning of the work as a whole. It is the most intimate expression of the author's meaning. Lyly, indeed, taught Shakespeare certain details of balance. But the pupil soon outstripped his teacher, and the masterly use Shakespeare made of what he learned gives him a place apart among Elizabethan dramatists. The carriage of the plot and the weaving together of many motifs to form unity require a particular kind of skill without which all outside aid is futile.

The closest parallel to *Titus* is the plot of *Lear*. Here as there we have two parties, whom we may crudely call the good and the bad. In both there are different kinds of good men opposed to different kinds of bad. Some critics

From *The Journal of English and Germanic Philology*, XLII (1943). Reprinted by permission of the author and the publisher.

find that the plot of *Titus* is weakened because the leadership of the "bad" party varies. It is now in the hands of Tamora, now with Aaron. I do not think this criticism has any force, since this variation does nothing to impede the sweep and rush of the play. In any case there is the same thing in *Lear*. Sometimes it is Goneril, sometimes it is Edmund, who takes the lead against Lear. In both plays the effect is the same. The forces of evil, no matter who embodies them, work with unabated intensity until the climax is reached.

If then one is looking for parallels, the only parallel to the plot of *Titus* is to be found in the other works of Shakespeare. Greene and Peele are so loose and episodic, so naïve in construction that it is incredible that they should have achieved anything so good as *Titus*. Nor is there any plot of Marlowe's so intricate, so varied, or so well sustained. *Titus* is the expression of a conflict intenser than anything the Elizabethan stage had as yet known. Shakespeare applies in *Titus* those principles of balance and contrast which he had learned from Lyly and had already tested in comedy. He sets up against one another two parties, each led by formidable characters. It is the play of fence between the high incensed points of these mighty opposites that makes the drama. There is nothing like this in Marlowe, whose supermen dominate his plays and dwarf everybody else in them. There is nothing like it in Greene and Peele, who indeed lacked the personality to create a drama of tense conflict.

Titus then resembles Shakespeare's other work, both comedy and tragedy, in that it is built upon the principle of contrast. We have the contrasting pairs or groups: Titus-Aaron, Lavinia-Tamora, Saturninus-Bassianus, the sons of Titus—the sons of Tamora. Not only are members of the opposite party contrasted, there are also contrasts within the same party. Marcus, as we shall see, by his mildness throws into higher relief the sterner traits of Titus. Contrast dominates the play and informs every scene of it. As we have already noted, whatever is fine in the Romans appears finer still in comparison with the vices of their opposites. On the one hand we have courage, stern probity, honor, but also stubbornness, hardness, and stupidity; on the other hand, slipperiness, trickiness, intrigue, the lie, foulness of every sort. None of the dramatists who are supposed to have had a hand in the play could conceive a plan so intricate or adhere to it so closely, once it was conceived. But Shakespeare goes farther. He uses contrast to heighten incident and situation as well as character. Act II.ii and iii are admirable examples of Shakespeare's technique. The delightful freshness of dawn and the beauty of the woods are not described for their own sake, still less are they, as some critics assert, a homesick reminiscence of Stratford. They are written in cold blood with the deliberate purpose of accentuating by contrast the horrors that follow. Shakespeare is again borrowing from the technique of Seneca.

There are few things in the play so characteristic of Shakespeare as the function of Marcus. In a world of hard, fierce, revengeful men, he alone is given to gentleness and moderation. Shakespeare often employs this device of a character who embodies a principle standing in stark contrast to the motives that rule the other persons of the play. We have, for instance, Falstaff in *1Henry IV*. Marcus resembles most closely Henry VI in *2, 3 Henry VI*, the mild, kind king, averse to slaughter and, like Marcus, helpless among so many Kiplingesque heroes. Frequently scholars declare that characters thus marked off are the "mouthpiece" of Shakespeare. However that may be, the technique is just what we should expect to find in a play by Shakespeare. We do not expect to find it in Marlowe, Greene, or Peele.

There is a school of critics who apply the "law of variation" to this technique. They ignore the part that contrast plays in Shakespeare's genuine work and they fasten upon the contrasting elements in *Titus* as evidence of multiple authorship. They usually say that the "poetic" passages, especially the speeches of Marcus, cannot be by the same hand as the rest of the play. Or they declare that the rhetorical speeches of Act I are so different from the imaginative verse of Aaron that there must be two poets at work. Anybody who is inclined to follow their lead should study Titania-Bottom, The Nurse-Juliet, Hotspur-Falstaff, Iago-Othello, and then, if he dares, set limits to the unparalleled versatility of Shakespeare.

Act I is often condemned as being utterly un-Shakespearean. Anglo-Saxon critics are inclined to apply a verbal yardstick to drama and to ignore construction. The act is not finely enough phrased for such people and so they reject it. Technically it is one of the finest first acts that Shakespeare wrote. It is full of incident and yet it is never confused. It announces the subject boldly and unmistakably, it exploits to the full every device that the staging of those days offered, and it has swiftness, surprise, and a well-sustained interest. It leads up to an effective close. Nothing in the work of Shakespeare's contemporaries can be compared to it for a moment.

The plot is superior to anything that Greene, Peele, Marlowe, or Kyd could achieve, by its quick succession of closely knit incidents, enlivened by many sudden turns and surprises, by its intricacy, in that the fates of so many persons are involved in it and yet the thread is never lost, and by the skill with which all the different threads are bound up into one knot and untied at once in the fifth act. Intricacy with clearness, a firm hand on the story, a swift succession of effective situations logically leading out of what precedes and on to what follows, these are qualities lacking in the dramatists who are supposed to have shared in the composition of *Titus*.

It must be admitted that the plot hinges on several Elizabethan conventions that are now strange to us. For instance the ruse, no matter how transparent, always succeeds, first when Titus is tricked, later when Titus himself takes to deception. Aaron eavesdrops in II.i—the Elizabethans took in this trick a childish delight which we cannot recapture. Quite suddenly Saturninus falls head over heels in love with Tamora—the Elizabethan believed in these swift and overwhelming effects of passion. Shakespeare is full of them. (See Ruth L. Anderson, *Elizabethan Psychology and Shakespeare's Plays,* Iowa, 1928, p. 120.) Every dramatist must work according to the rules of the game as it is understood in his time. The play is not less likely to be by Shakespeare because it is so full of the conventions of the theater.

We come to an important aspect of the plot which scholars tend to overlook. *Titus* is a political play, and Shakespeare is the most political of all dramatists. His work excited the admiration of statesmen like Gladstone and Bismarck, who both wondered how he managed to penetrate so many secrets of their profession. Shakespeare's political interest shows itself in various ways. He likes to connect his heroes with an action involving the fortunes of the state, he is skillful in tracing the course of political intrigue, and he delights in exposing those kinks of character or intellect which unfit even men of action for public life. The real hero of his political plays is the state. In some plays it is England, in others it is Rome. Now *Titus* centers round an affair of state, and its hero is no particular person but it is Rome herself. All the characters are viewed in their relation to Rome and they are set against Rome as a background. This theme is sustained throughout the play; it dominates the fifth act as the first. No member of that writers' syndicate—large as it is—which the revisionists credit with *Titus* has Shakespeare's deep love of the state or his understanding of the crisscross currents of politics. The intense political interest of *Titus* points to the man who wrote Shakespeare's historical and Roman plays, and it points to no one else.

But even if we grant that *Titus* could not have been written by anybody but Shakespeare, its horrible cruelty still leaves us profoundly dissatisfied. It is not only that Titus is cruel; it is more, he is cruel to the end. He is not a Lear who grows in stature as the play proceeds and whose sufferings purge his character of its baser elements until he emerges a man entirely good. Titus alone of Shakespeare's tragic heroes never arrives at healing self-knowledge. At the beginning of the play we hope that Titus will succeed against his enemies; at the end we wish that he had not. But we must not forget the task that Shakespeare has set himself. He is writing a Senecan play according to the rules, that is to say, a play in which the hero is a man who inexorably pursues revenge and who

dies in the act of taking it. Such a plan leaves no room
for change of character. Shakespeare, therefore, has been
obliged to split what he had to say between Titus and
Marcus. Roughly speaking, Lear is a Titus who becomes
a Marcus, but a revenge play necessarily precluded this
type of development. Shakespeare has not been deluded
into thinking revenge is a fine thing. He sets up Marcus
to show us the better way. The great fault of the drama
from our point of view is that Titus never finds that way.
But his stern pursuit of revenge is inherent in the revenge
play and Shakespeare could only have got round it by
making his hero a kind of Hamlet.

Now if we could absolve Shakespeare of all complicity
in the revenge play of *Titus Andronicus,* that might be a
good thing. Unfortunately, the evidence makes it quite
clear that Shakespeare is at any rate an accessory to the
crime, and that he is responsible for the play as it now
stands. It is more profitable to consider what probably
took place. Everyone knows the cant phrase that Shakespeare "played the sedulous ape" to all and sundry. Even
late in life he is asserted to have copied Beaumont and
Fletcher. In his apprentice stage he founded himself on
Lyly, on Marlowe, and went to Roman comedy, to
Plautus. In the same way, in order to learn his craft, he
went to Roman tragedy, to Seneca. To understand this,
we must remember that the Renaissance entertained an
immense admiration for Seneca and that it was the fashion
to imitate him. Shakespeare, following the mood of his
time, wrote a complete Senecan tragedy, an experiment of
unity in harshness and gross cruelty. He makes almost
everything harsh, the language, the characters, the incidents. Where he appears to be relenting toward mildness,
that is only an artistic device to make the harshness appear all the harsher. It is the very unity of the play that
is a criterion of Shakespeare's skill. It is, indeed, this
severe unity, which is difficult to achieve, that makes it
impossible to entertain the theory that this play was the
work of a syndicate of writers or of some young amateur
helped out by Shakespeare.

If we turn from the action to the character shown in

action, we are just as certainly within the realm of Shakespeare. There is no convincing parallel to the character
of Titus outside the works of Shakespeare. He owes, indeed, a few hints to Kyd's *Spanish Tragedy*. Like Kyd's
Hieronimo he is an old man angry, seeking revenge for
murder, but in the essentials of characterization he is quite
different. Titus, like the typical Shakespearean hero, falls
by a mixture of good and bad qualities. He is a soldier,
and as such, put loyalty and obedience before everything.
In his campaigns he has been accustomed both to judge
men swiftly and to act swiftly on his judgment. But he has
something of the simplicity of Othello; although he can
estimate a man's capacity in the field, he is helpless in the
hands of a dishonest schemer at home. Like Lear he is a
man grown irascible with age, tolerating no insubordina-
tion from his inferiors, from whom he demands that un-
questioning obedience which he in turn gives to lawful
authority. Shakespeare knew that there is nothing so cruel
as the wrath of age. Titus is an old man who retains the
strength but has lost the elasticity of youth. His fury,
therefore, persists with an obstinacy that it is useless to
oppose. The murders that Titus commits in Act I are
horrible, just as it is horrible of Lear to banish from his
heart Cordelia and Kent, but in neither case is the characterization improbable. Critics are inclined to find both
Titus and Lear absurd, but Shakespeare knew more about
old age than his critics.

As with many soldiers, the religion of Titus is a firm
and somewhat naïve acceptance of the usages consecrated
by tradition. He kills Alarbus not so much out of cruelty,
but because the traditional rites of religion demand it. He
makes Saturninus Emperor for much the same reason.
Sacred tradition requires that the eldest son of the Emperor should succeed. He stabs his son Mutius in wrath
but also as a soldier exacting that same obedience which
is the rule of his own life. Some German scholars doubt
whether Shakespeare meant us to approve when Titus
kills his son! (Wolfgang Keller in *Shaks. Jbch.*, LXXIV
[1938], 146). Surely in all the blunders of Titus we see
the corruption of the best turned to the worst, qualities

fine in themselves producing disaster because of Titus'
devotion to a false ideal. Further, Titus' habit of loyalty
keeps him blind to the dangers that threaten him. His own
probity makes it difficult for him to suspect duplicity in
others. When the Emperor proves false, his world breaks
down and he begins to go mad. The kaleidoscope is shifted
to show now one side of his character, and now another.
He is not like Marlowe's heroes, the incarnation of a
single quality or passion. He is a mixture of virtues and
weaknesses, and by a strange irony his virtues are the
more devastating. Tamora expresses the fatal defect in his
character when she speaks of "cruel irreligious piety."
A similar ironic treatment is found in other tragedies of
Shakespeare—but nowhere in the work of dramatists who
are supposed to have shared in *Titus*. It was indeed far
beyond their reach. This irony permeates the play so thoroughly that scholars would find it difficult to prove that
any part of *Titus* is not by Shakespeare.

Aaron's character, too, is turned round from side to
side so that we can view him from many angles. He is
the obvious villain, black like the devil, lustful, cunning,
cruel, a consummate dissembler and hypocrite, admiring
himself for his superiority in evil and taking a childlike
pleasure in contemplating his villainies. Before the days
of the dictators, the picture was probably thought to be
crude and overdrawn. Shakespeare goes on to mark off
Aaron vividly by allowing him an "Oriental" imagination. He is the only man in the play to speak lines afire
with romantic poetry (see the opening speech of Act II),
as he is the only character to delight in magnificent dress
(II.i.18–20). In this he supplies the strongest possible
contrast with the sober Romans, but he is very like the
Moorish Prince of Arragon in the *Merchant of Venice*
—another parallel that connects Shakespeare with *Titus*.
Suddenly at the end of the play another twist is given to
Aaron's character. He is a devoted father, through the
fact of fatherhood exalted by pride of race and contempt
for the white men, ready to go to any lengths to save his
offspring. Shakespeare does not make the mistake of soft-
ening Aaron to sentimentality by the sight of his child.

He remains a killer. Several of these qualities are found in some Moor or other in the Elizabethan drama, but not all together in the same person. It is his many-sidedness that makes Aaron unique. And even when we add up these characteristics we do not obtain the sum of Aaron. There is a fire, a vigor, and a concentration in his personality such as no Elizabethan villain in the early nineties had displayed. The dilemma is not that either Shakespeare or a rival poet created Aaron, it is *aut Shakespeare, aut diabolus.*

Of the minor figures I will only take young Lucius, since he closely resembles Shakespeare's other boys. His character is composed of that mingled web in which Shakespeare delights. He is on the border between child and man. He weeps at the sight of his grandfather's distress. When Lavinia wants one of his books, he runs away from the girl in fear—a touch that while adding horror to horror shows delicate perception of a child's soul. He is full of big words about the great things he is going to do when he grows up. On the other hand he delivers with courage and address the dangerous message entrusted to him, showing an impish humor that we find in other boys of Shakespeare. His speeches are suited to his age by a somewhat simple vocabulary and a certain lilt in their rhythm. This again is characteristic of Shakespeare's presentation of young boys and girls. There is so much delicacy of perception, sympathy, and humor in the portrait of Lucius that he may take rank with the best of Shakespeare's boys.

Scholars, of course, might recognize Shakespeare's hand in particular characters and still assert that he did no more than just revise the play. But if we look at the characterization broadly, we must say of it what we said of the construction, that it is beyond the reach of anybody but Shakespeare. It is in the round. On the other hand Marlowe's "figures are as one dimensional as a line," and the same is true of Greene and Peele. Besides, the characterization has the peculiar exuberance, the irrepressible vitality which we find in Shakespeare's early work and nowhere else. No other playwright of that pe-

riod could carry such a crowd of persons in his brain
and make them so different from one another and so
alive. More important than this—no other dramatist writing in 1594 could conceive or depict so intense a conflict
of character. Tamora, Aaron, and Titus are as full of
fight as an egg is of meat. Marlowe may fill one man
with consuming passion, Kyd may spin a long intrigue,
but only Shakespeare could combine these things, give
intense passions to a crowd of characters, manipulate
the action and reaction of feeling back and forth from
one character to another, and at the same time keep up
a long intrigue white hot with sustained fury. The sheer,
unflagging power of *Titus* is beyond the reach of anybody but Shakespeare.

Style now remains to be considered as a criterion.
There are two ways of approaching the question—the
philological and the aesthetic. The philologist counts and
compares—his results we have already discussed. It is
only necessary to say here that if parallels prove anything, it is that Shakespeare wrote *Titus*. Aesthetic consideration is more difficult. You cannot say of Shakespeare,
as you can of Ben Jonson and Milton, that he had one
particular style. He was the dramatist speaking through
the minds of his characters, and the words are those of
his characters, not his own. The variations of Shakespeare's style from play to play or from character to character within the same play are among the commonplaces
of criticism.

The question is complicated because Shakespeare was
a slow learner, who made his way by imitating his contemporaries. His early work therefore contains many passages written in the prevailing fashion which just for that
reason offend our taste. Even the great parting scene at
dawn in *Romeo and Juliet* is spoiled for us by lines which
we find too "conceited" or too fantastic. Indeed, ideas
of decorum have changed so much that I doubt if we
can read a single play of Shakespeare's without constantly
being pulled up by passages that are hard for us to accept.

Let us see what the author of *Titus* was doing. He
was writing, as it were, an artificial play, that is one in

a particular mode, according to strict, conventional rules. He is writing the rhetorical drama of Seneca. Professor W. F. Schirmer has worked out for us the rhetorical pattern of this play (*Shaks. Jbch.,* LXXI [1935], pp. 11–31). Professor Schirmer shows that Marcus's speech (I.i.18–45) is exactly divided out into three parts. Two of 7 lines each, consisting of a single sentence, frame a middle part of 14 lines. Part 1 reproaches the Romans for their factional spirit and recommends Titus. Part 2 emphasizes his great merits, his noble character, his achievements, the death in battle of his sons. Part 3 seeks to calm down the rivals. Schirmer points out how this exact logical construction corresponds to the best rules of Quintilian or Cicero (p. 19). There is no room here to follow Schirmer further. It is enough to say that he has shown that a large part of the play is severely rhetorical and that in this respect it resembles much of Shakespeare's early work. Indeed, Shakespeare never completely succeeded in freeing himself from the influence of rhetoric. It not only colors his poetry but it also inspires some of his greatest prose speeches. We all recognize that the sheer beauty of Falstaff's style is the result of a training in rhetoric. Intricately designed speech such as we have in *Titus* is common throughout Shakespeare. If we are looking for affinities, I suggest one that is too often neglected—*Titus,* like *Julius Caesar* and *Coriolanus,* is a political play, in which the hero is Rome, and in which a crisis is time and again resolved by rhetoric. The author of all three plays was a fine historian and a fine rhetorician. I submit that it would be difficult to find an affinity more convincing.

But the style, though rhetorical, is not therefore entirely undramatic. The Romans, the Goths, Aaron, all speak a different language. At this period Shakespeare conceived the Romans as a forthright people, direct in expression, cultivating simplicity in language as in all things. On great occasions their speech can be noble, pity or indignation can move them to poetry, but they are not in the habit of indulging in highfalutin stuff which would lead to a succession of poetical speeches. It is true that in trying to be plain Shakespeare is occasionally flat. But on the whole we can say that the language of the Romans is neat in its plainness and at times it even achieves a kind of monumental dignity. In all his Roman plays Shakespeare aims at some kind of simplicity for his Romans. It is not the same in each play, but then his art ripens.

As we have already noticed, Aaron the Moor speaks with more imagination than anybody else in the play. His ordinary language, however, is full of blunt and coarse expressions that are never to be found in the Roman speeches. Chiron and Demetrius are even coarser than Aaron. They are marked off by their extensive use of rustic proverbs. The Romans do not use proverbs in this way. Tamora, as Professor Schirmer has shown, is all deceit and she can sing any tune. She speaks the language of the man she is talking to. Such differentiation is not to be found in Shakespeare's rivals of the nineties. Other playwrights had their own style, which they gave, together with a characteristic rhythm, to all their persons alike. Shakespeare, on the other hand, takes great pains to differentiate, so that when in the 1590's we find characters carefully distinguished by their style, we may with confidence look upon that as a sign of Shakespeare's authorship. This assertion is so painfully obvious that it would not be worth saying if scholars had not applied the law of variation to the style of *Titus* and attempted to make it prove multiple authorship.

H. B. CHARLTON

from *Shakespearian Tragedy*

Titus Andronicus is melodrama, the crudest of Shakespeare's tragedies, magnificent only in this, that its language is always adequate to its own dramatic and theatrical demands, crude or low, spectacular or sentimental, as on varying occasion they may be. But as drama it can never disguise its own quality. It is a rudimentary type of tragedy. It appeals only to the eye and to the other senses. Response to it is confined to the nervous system. Its thrills and throbs are not transmissible to the mind in forms more intellectual than mere sensation. They induce a nightmare of horrors. As sensations of horror, if they are felt as such at all and not laughed off by man's sense of the ludicrous, they strike so heavily and so frequently that the mind is incapacitated from attempting to translate them into its own discursive idiom. So great is the weight of horror that the response of the senses themselves is finally stunned to stupor, and the disabled sensibility is deprived of the power to prompt mind and imagination to cope with such tremendous issues as are the essence of tragedy, the ultimate mysteries of human

From *Shakespearian Tragedy* by H. B. Charlton. London and New York: Cambridge University Press, 1948. Reprinted by permission of Cambridge University Press.

destiny. "Those who employ spectacular means to create a sense not of the terrible, but only of the monstrous, are strangers to the purpose of Tragedy."[1]

As a piece of serious drama, *Titus Andronicus* has little of worth except its theatrically stirring situations. Even these occur in isolation. A momentary spectacle can be given as much conviction as is needed for the achievement of its stage effect by craftsmanship of no higher order in the art of poetry than is the stage carpenter's in the art of drama. But a sustained representation of human action in a continuous dramatic plot makes greater demands. As Aristotle put it, what happens must happen according to the law of the probable and the necessary. As human action, it must be intelligible. The men and women in the play must act as human beings do act. When their action seems to be spontaneously prompted by passion or by instinct rather than by considered choice, those passions and instincts must be shown to be of that sort which in our experience of life seems likely to break out in that way. When the doers of such deeds plead also the sanction of deliberate choice, the systems of conduct to which they appeal must appear to have impetus vital enough to make their compulsion inevitable. However, a qualification must here be made. Sanctions, like the systems of law and morality which give them their warrant, are but rarely eternal and are often flagrantly ephemeral. *Omnia mutantur, nos et mutamur in illis. Autres temps, autres mœurs.* But in drama, sanctions which are pleaded as constraints to a decisive course of action must have something more than a merely historic warrant to give them effective dramatic force. The compulsion must be felt by the audience as a power which might well compel human beings to such deeds.

It is in respects such as this that the greatest French classical drama seems to an Englishman less universal and therefore less tragic than Shakespeare's tragedies. Their preference for pitting love against honor in the tragic conflict appears, to a modern, to commit them to a contest between unequally matched opponents. The dic-

[1] Aristotle, *Poetics*, XIV, 2 (Butcher).

tates of love may vary from era to era; its nature may swing through a whole range between lust and the lyric love which is half-angel: but love is a passion, an affection deeply rooted even in the physiological genes of spiritual man. There is no limit to its potential urgency as an impulse to action. On the other hand, honor is a code of human construction, and the course of its formulation can be easily watched through a relatively short stretch of historic time. Its taboos and its injunctions are the patent outcome of particular forms of society at particular periods of history. Hence its content embraces manners as much as, and often more than, morals. Its edicts tend therefore to seem arbitrary and even factitious; and as imperatives they have but temporary and local authority. They lack the absoluteness of a universal tragic sanction. Sometimes one of the opposing stresses is formulated in a phrase which seems a limitedly localized or a dialectal idiom; but often this is only the accident of phrase or of manner, and the real significance is clear. Antigone must bury her exiled brother; but the burial itself is only the ritual action symbolizing the real compunction by which the act itself is categorically imperative, the absolute obligation of fraternal duty. Contrast Racine; though the surge of his Phèdre's love can sweep us into conviction of its fury, and, on the other hand, the obligation on her to suppress it or to die can be felt as the command of a code of honor with foundations firmly based in the depths of morality, yet the momentousness of such contending and mighty opposites suffers a sharp collapse on our discovery that the honor of Phèdre, whilst permitting her maid to make wicked charges against Hippolyte, can recover itself by laying all the blame onto this poor servant whose only motive was devotion to her mistress. Often, to drive his action forward with the sense of irresistible compulsion, the dramatist will invoke an impetus from sources outside the will, blind or deliberate, of his persons. At worst, he may allege any extraneous and intrusive determinant as a mere chance, relying on his audience superstitiously to identify chance within some pattern or other of purposive destiny. No great tragedian, however, fails to introduce amongst the operant powers which direct the stream of his plot those cosmic forces which lie beyond human personality and outside the established formularies of human cognition. In the dramatist's summoning of these great mysteries as actors in his drama, his tragic genius is revealed in its deepest qualities. His greatness as a tragedian depends on the extent to which he can invest these superhuman arbiters with the absoluteness of ultimate Necessity. In Shakespeare, this dramatic ultimacy inheres in and also exists outside his characters. For him the stern necessity of character and the resistless compulsion of circumstance are a form of what John Morley called "the modern and positive expression for the old Destiny of the Greeks."

With a mind conscious of these considerations, turn to *Titus Andronicus* and inquire how far its action is autonomously and organically propelled. Very soon, its nominal hero, Titus, is a comparative pawn in the theatrical game, and the real protagonists are the villains, Aaron and Tamora. The incidents of the play, and especially the more theatrical of them, proceed in the main as the deliberate purposes of the villains' evil designs. These purposes are those of sinners whose prevalent passion is lust, than which no passion is more deeply seated in the human animal, none more primary or more insatiable. The dramatist can therefore permit to them the extremest of enormities; the law of human probability can be pleaded for suspending for them its own normal requirements; as Aristotle says, "such an event is probable in Agathon's sense of the word: 'it is probable,' he says, 'that many things should happen contrary to probability.' "[2] Moreover, with such human devils as these for the outstanding figures, other characters and episodes in the play can be stretched to extravagant limits. Titus in his turn can execute his own son. In these ways, the dramatist is easily provided with a string of melodramatic incidents in unbroken sequence. But it is merely the sequence of succession, each item owing its occurrence not

2 *Poetics*, XVIII, 6 (Butcher).

to what has gone immediately before, but as the accidental next in the cumulative outcome of the bestial passions of the main contrivers.

There is, however, some attempt to give to this succession a specious appearance of causal sequence. Action is sometimes expressed, not as the spontaneous consequence of passion, but as the recognizable manifestation of some sort of world order.

The first scene sets up the façade of the universe in which its action is to occur. The "righteous heavens," "the gods of Rome" preside over it; priests minister at their solemn services, sometimes with "holy water," sometimes with "sacrificial rites"; its men lift up their "vows to heaven," and "sumptuously" maintain the sacred "monuments" in which their dead are solemnly interred. But it is a mere façade. The moral system which would give such a universe a credible substance manifests itself as an incoherent chaos. There is talk of "virtue" and "nobility," yet they appear to comprise nothing but a primitive valor in martial enterprise. "Piety" is named; but it gives nothing beyond a moment's historic authenticity to a Roman father's right to kill his son, and such historic authentication may even be an obstacle to dramatic plausibility: "the poet should prefer probable impossibilities to improbable possibilities."[3] In *Titus Andronicus* the standard of moral currency most in use is "honor." The word occurs a score of times in the scene in which Titus kills his son; it is made more prominent by another half-score instances of its opposite, "dishonor." But it is utterly impossible to define the content of the moral concept implied, and quite impossible therefore to assess its potency as a moral agent in motivating action. Titus is "dishonored" because his sons do not immediately obey his edict, and no less "dishonored" because Bassianus, with what appear to be highly honorable intentions, marries Titus' daughter. Saturninus is "dishonored" because someone has revealed the flagrant truth that he is a scoundrel, and even more "dishonored" because others have helped him to secure the throne in-

3 *Ibid.*, XXIV, 10.

stead of recognizing his right to it without help. The audience, with more justice than Falstaff, may well inquire "what is this honor?" The play gives no answer, for nothing consistently recognizable as "honor" animates its action. Hence its incidents sink to melodrama. There are crucial examples in this first scene.

Take one which relies on an alleged ancient practice: the noblest prisoner taken must be sacrificed to appease "the groaning shadows of the slain." Tamora's son is the victim chosen by Titus' sons, and they will "hew his limbs and on a pile *Ad manes fratrum* sacrifice his flesh." Tamora appeals, with far less ancient terms and with more intelligible instinct, for the exercise of the "sweet mercy which is nobility's true badge." But Titus is placidly unmoved: for "their brethren slain" his sons "religiously ask a sacrifice"; they have marked her son for this, and "die he must." He is haled away by Titus' sons with fervent zeal, and in a twinkling they return to tell that his "limbs are lopped,"

> And entrails feed the sacrificing fire
> Whose smoke, like incense, doth perfume the sky.

As a mere record in human archaeology, such a scene can doubtless be freely paralleled; but its persons have not here inspired the psychological resuscitation which would give them dramatic personality. Their motives, therefore, implicit and explicit, are dramatically inert; the "must" of "die he must" is merely arbitrary and void of all power to excite in the audience a willing concurrence in its compulsiveness. Or take the incident in which Titus, exercising the Roman *jus patrium,* slays his son Mutius for a single act of sudden disobedience. Mutius' action is completely intelligible in common sense and in the simplest psychology; moreover, it commands enough moral sympathy to make it instantly credible to the audience. So, in despite of assurances from historical record, it is impossible for the audience to slip into a requisite and subconscious understanding of Titus. For them he is a lay figure, humanly, and therefore dramatically, unreal.

As in its first scene, so throughout the whole play. There is no inner world to it. Hence its plot is factitious; its people are mechanized puppets wearing masks of human faces, but seldom reacting even with a faint semblance of humanity except when their deeds are crimes which are prompted by a primitive human passion, crimes such as are still occasionally committed by the more bestial members of the human race. It is sheer melodrama and not tragedy; for, as *The New British Theatre* even as long ago as 1814 distinguished them, "in tragedy and comedy, the final event is the effect of the moral operations of the different characters, but in melodrama the catastrophe is the physical result of mechanical stratagem." And melodrama, lacking an inner world, can have none of the philosophic significance which is the peculiar function of tragedy; it can throw no light on the great mysteries of human fate.

RICHARD DAVID

Drams of Eale

Their virtues else—be they as pure as grace,
As infinite as man may undergo—
Shall in the general censure take corruption
From that particular fault: the dram of evil
Doth all the noble substance of a doubt
To his own scandal.

Hamlet's analysis applies to productions of Shakespeare as well as to men. The 1955–56 season promised marvels and in performance displayed an infinity of individual virtues. And yet the total impression was one of disappointment. There was always a dram of evil that finally undermined the most notable production.

Peter Brook's *Titus Andronicus* at Stratford (which came too late for inclusion in my last report) was certainly that. Brook had not only produced the play but had designed scenery, costumes, and musical accompaniment, and he achieved a quite extraordinary unity and concentration of effect. The staging was powerfully simple: three great squared pillars, set angle-on to the audience, fluted, and bronzy-gray in color. The two visible sides could be swung back, revealing inner recesses that might be used as entrances or, in the central pillar, as

From *Shakespeare Survey 10* (1957), edited by Allardyce Nicoll. Reprinted by permission of Cambridge University Press.

a two-storied inner stage. This was the tomb of the Andronici, somber and shadowy against the vivid green of
the priests' robes and mushroom hats; festooned with
lianes it became the murder pit and the forest floor above
it; stained a yellowish natural-wood color, it provided
a background of Roman frugality to the bereaved and
brooding Titus at his family table; blood-red, it made
a macabre eyrie of the upper chamber from which the
Revenger peers out upon his victims, come in fantastic
disguise to entrap him. In the court scenes the closed
pillars, supported by heavy side gratings of the same
color and hangings of purple and green, richly suggested
the civilized barbarity of late imperial Rome.

Within this frame the whole phantasmagoria unrolled
without hitch or hesitation—from the opening, when the
citizens, in ruffed gowns of shot satin and dark fustian,
broke off their rival acclamations to perform the obsequies for Titus' sons, marching and countermarching
with obstinate purposefulness in a dirgelike quadrille;
to the closing scene, when in the glare of the torches the
victims topple forward in succession across the dinner
table like a row of ninepins skittled from behind. It was
as if the actors were engaged in a ritual at once fluent
from habitual performance and yet still practiced with
concentrated attention. There was something puppetlike
about them; but puppets manipulated by a master whose
genius for improvisation constantly enlivened his expert
routine.

The compulsive and incantatory nature of the production (which sent some spectators off into faints before
ever a throat was cut) was reinforced by the musical
effects, all of a marvelous directness. The overture was
a roll of drum and cymbal, the dirge for the slain Andronici, so strange and powerful, no more than the first
two bars of *Three Blind Mice,* in the minor and endlessly
repeated. A slow seesaw of two bass notes, a semitone
apart, wrought the tension of the final scene to an unbearable pitch, and ceased abruptly, with breath-taking
effect, as the first morsel of son-pie passed Tamora's lips.
Even more harrowing were the hurrying carillon of elec-

tronic bells that led up to the abduction of Lavinia and
the slow plucking of harp strings, like drops of blood
falling into a pool, that accompanied her return to the
stage.

In speaking of the actors as puppets of the producer's
conception, I do not mean to imply that there were not
performances of strong individuality but only that, like
the dyer's hand, they were all loyally subdued to what
they worked in. The freest, from the very nature of his
part in the play, is Aaron the Moor, and to him Antony
Quayle brought a rich gusto, as fetching in the creamy
slyness that cheats Titus of his hand as in the bounce and
glory of the defense of his black baby. But Aaron is a
nice fat part for anyone; that Laurence Olivier should
succeed in giving equal richness to the stock Revenger,
Titus, was a more unexpected feat. At his first entry
one might almost have accused him of mugging, so hard
did he work with swallowing and pursing, wrinkling and
charming to build up, on the bare bones of the part, a
Great Man, cantankerous, choleric, and at the same time
compelling. Yet by making Titus a "character," in every
sense, he was able not only to gloss over some of the
play's awkwardnesses but to rise (when, all too seldom,
the chance was there) into a freer air than that of Grand
Guignol. We could accept the conqueror's, and patriot's,
blazing rage, that with "Barr'st me my way in Rome?"
sweeps his youngest son out of existence. And the great
central scene, where Titus stands

> as one upon a rock
> Environ'd with a wilderness of sea,
> Who marks the waxing tide grow wave by wave,

so grew and proliferated in the astonishing variety of
his reactions to disaster (the enormous physical agony
of the severed hand was almost unbearable) that with
the crowning frenzy of "I am the sea" Olivier seemed to
break through the illusion and become, not old Hieronimo run mad again, but madness itself.

As with individual performances, so with individual

scenes. Who could forget the return of the ravishers with
Lavinia? They bring her through the leafy arch that was
the central pillar and leave her standing there, right arm
outstretched and head drooping away from it, left arm
crooked with the wrist at her mouth. Her hair falls in
disorder over face and shoulders, and from wrist and
wrist-and-mouth trail scarlet streamers, symbols of her
mutilation. The two assassins retreat from her, step by
step, looking back at her, on either side of the stage.
Their taunts fall softly, lingeringly, as if they themselves
were in a daze at the horror of their deed; and the air
tingles and reverberates with the slow plucking of harp
strings. Another peak was the scene in which Titus makes
his followers shoot arrows into the sky with messages for
the gods. Here Brook cheated, bringing on the yokel,
who seems to come in answer to the prayers, in a basket
from the flies, and writing in a line about "fetching down
his pigeons from the walls" to make this plausible. It
was certainly in keeping, and added a crowning touch
of fantasy to a most fantastical invention.

It was the whole, however, the one extended conjuring
trick that held the spectator spellbound—spellbound and
yet quite unmoved. What was it that in the last analysis
made the evening so unrewarding, the effect so cold beside that of the perhaps more run-of-the-mill *Macbeth?*
It was the conviction, unsought but growing irresistibly
as the play proceeded, that this piece on which so much
labor and ingenuity had been lavished, and to which
we had been invited to attend for two and a half hours,
was—twaddle. Perhaps this would have been less apparent if producer and company had not worked so hard
to persuade us that it was otherwise. The Cambridge
Marlowe Society's production in 1954, a shortened version played with frank gusto and dash, had prepared
me to find in the play itself a straightforward blood-and-
thunder entertainment. In striving to make it more than
this Brook made it less than nothing. The blood was,
we have seen, turned to favors and to prettiness. Severed
heads were not allowed to appear unless decently swathed
in black velvet and enclosed in ornate funerary caskets.

Titus' hand, so swaddled and coffered, was decorously cradled in Lavinia's arms, not carried off between her teeth as the text directs. The pig killing of Chiron and Demetrius occurred offstage and (perhaps to compensate the audience with one maiming in place of another) Titus' final cry of triumph,

Why, there they are both, baked in that pie,

was lopped of its last four words. But no amount of sandpapering and gilding can turn this old shocker into high tragedy à la Racine. Has Shakespeare's *Titus* really any life left in it? The question is not yet answered. Certainly Brook's romantic play of the same name was stillborn.

GERMAINE GREER

The Royal Shakespeare Company's "Titus Andronicus," 1972

Titus Andronicus has found its way into the Stratford Roman series under false pretenses. To be sure the play is set in Rome and the country near it, but it is not historic Rome. *Titus Andronicus* is no more a play about history or politics than *Measure for Measure* is a play about Vienna. It is a play about decadence and cruelty, but not about the historical pressures which give rise to such manifestations. The marvellous clarity of the current Stratford production of *Julius Caesar* casts the lineaments of Rome as a police state, vivid with banners and demagoguery and the rhythms of marching feet, sharply through the verse which is their substance, adding immeasurably to understanding of the play, and of history and of ourselves.

All productions of all plays are for the times in which they take place, no matter how meticulous the reproduction of vanished conventions might imagine itself to be. Trevor Nunn's production of *Julius Caesar* related Shakespeare's profound insight into Plutarch's story to our own understanding of half a century of minority rebellion and dictatorship: it was timely but not trendy. It did not reiterate this month's rhetoric about fascism, but exposed something essential and eternal about human political

Reprinted from *Plays and Players*, Dec. 1972, pp. 39–40. (Original title: *Titus Andronicus*.)

institutions; the play itself gained resonance from our own
painful struggle to fend off totalitarianism.

Behind Trevor Nunn's production of *Titus Andronicus*,
however, there lies a much more banal and quite suspect
conception of degeneracy as a historical pressure, an idea
which is chiefly useful in justifying the plagues of fascism
and national regeneration, *le nouvel ordre* and uniforms
and health camps for the young. The hysteria behind such
notions was amply illustrated by an absurd statement
which Trevor Nunn made to *Plays and Players* in the
September issue about the rape of Lavinia in *Titus Andronicus*: 'A girl is raped, her hands cut off, her tongue cut
out. It happens on the American sidewalks every day.'
Certes rapes do happen, and in America too, but rarely on
sidewalks, and hands are cut off and tongues are cut out,
but seldom are all these conditions fulfilled at once.
Indeed, I may venture to say that no such case has ever
been reported in American history. In falling for such
gutter press sensationalism Trevor Nunn loses his chance
of dealing sensibly with this play, in which not only do
extravagant concepts of violence appear, but people utter
extravagantly figured verse in response to them, something
that never happens today even in America, and never
happened anywhere at all ever except on a particular kind
of stage.

Janet Suzman's Lavinia appeared in a fashion which
has been praised as realistic, for she was soiled, bloodstained, crouching convulsed with shame, but the very
fact that she was able to walk or run at all, when blood-
loss would have killed her within minutes, was an absurdity, if we are to consider it in crassly realistic terms. The
mild rusty stains on her sleeves were an off-hand gesture
towards the gore that would have flowed down her stiff-
ened skirts. With such considerations crowding into mind,
Shakespeare's jewelled ikon of violence, modelled upon
the kind of hunting frieze which makes decoration of
suffering and death, foundered in a morass of irrelevancy,
typified as always in misconceived Stratford productions
of which there have been a great many, by an attempt to

avoid the verse utterly, and frenzied concentration on more irritating detail, such as the difficulty of sawing Titus' hand off. As Grand Guignol, *Titus Andronicus* is a relentless bore. At times like those, the harrassed critic remembers sourly that a goodly portion of the Stratford takings comes from folk who couldn't understand the verse, even if the actors took time off from biting blood capsules and grunting and falling about actually to utter any of it clearly.

Shakespeare's poetry embalms the action of *Titus Andronicus*, like a Laocoön carved in a block of crystal or an oyster's illness transfixed in pearl. Each artifice of horror is surrounded by calm, intricately patterned verse, a *da capo* aria transforming suffering into delight—an aesthetic exercise quite unlike anything Shakespeare is concerned to do in the History Plays. This is just one facet of the celebration of Lavinia's mutilation, six lines out of sixty:

> Alas! a crimson river of warm blood
> Like to a bubbling fountain stirr'd with wind,
> Doth rise and fall between thy rosed lips,
> Coming and going with thy honey breath.
> But sure, some Tereus hath deflowered thee,
> And, lest thou should detect him, cut thy tongue.

The Platonic exercise of the power of art to make beauty out of gross sin and ugliness could well have seemed uninteresting to the minds who were forging the Shakespearian view of Roman history into a whole which was more than the sum of its parts, however worthwhile each part in itself. It would have been better to have left the play out of the series altogether than to have obliterated its distinctive form by crude references to current stereotypes; equipping Chiron and Demetrius with black leather suits, studded and belted, in which to effect Lavinia's rape and mutilation, was merely tricky and banal. Thinking of the court of Saturnine as a cross between something from the cutting room floor of the Fellini

Satyricon and Alice Cooper on *Top of the Pops* is the least provocative way of regarding it. Beneath such spectacle, Shakespeare's mottling of the play's surface into the veins of light and dark, of Venus and Saturn, gold and lead faded with the eclipse of the verse, and more delicate perceptions about decadency and elegance, ripeness and rottenness, were lost.

There can be no point in enumerating performances in such a misconceived production, for in a director's theatre like the Royal Shakespeare an actor cannot rise above the general notion of the play, a fact for which one is usually grateful. Only Aaron (Calvin Lockhart), of whose part the current interpretation could make no sense at all, seemed to derive some amusement from his own charming depiction of preposterous wickedness, of the paradox of *perfect* evil. Something of the character of the play shone forth for an instant, when the smiling Moor beguiled Titus of his hand, but was instantly obliterated by the crunching of the blade against the bone-floor. The rest of the actors projected huge unhappiness into the murky auditorium, and it seems unkind to lumber them for the dreariness of a production which was not their fault at all. Colin Blakely's Titus might have made part of a good Lear, but the unsatisfactory reminiscence does havoc to the lesser play.

SYLVAN BARNET

Titus Andronicus on the Stage

In 1987 the Royal Shakespeare Company's production
of *Titus Andronicus*, at the Swan Theatre, Stratford-upon-
Avon, was extremely well received. Reviewers asserted
that the play really was quite effective, even highly impressive, and audiences agreed. Much of the public seemed
surprised, but older theatergoers remembered that Peter
Brook's production at Stratford in 1955 also was hailed
for showing that *Titus* had been unjustly neglected.

There is no question that *Titus* has undergone long
periods of neglect, but it has also had its periods of popularity—and the second half of the twentieth century may
be one of them. What is especially interesting, however, is
that we cannot claim to have rescued from obscurity a
neglected play; *Titus* was popular in its own day. The first
record of a specific performance is on January 23, 1594,
but the title page of the first edition, published sometime
in 1594, says that the play has been acted by three theatrical companies, which suggests that *Titus* had already
been on the stage for at least a couple of years. In addition to a few other references to specific public performances in London early in 1594, there is a record of a
private performance at Christmas festivities given in
Rutland in 1596, in the country house of Sir John Haring-
ton of Exton. Nor was this early popularity simply a
matter of the appeal that any new play might make. *Titus*
was reprinted in 1600 and in 1611—a sign that there

must have been a market for it—each time with the assertion that it had been acted by prominent theatrical companies. Moreover, four years after the third printing of
Titus, in the Induction to *Bartholomew Fair* Ben Jonson
cites *Titus* as an enduring favorite of a public with low
tastes.

We can't say exactly how *Titus Andronicus* was performed on the Elizabethan stage, but clues in the text
indicate that it took advantage of all three performing
levels: the platform stage, an upper acting area, and (in
II.iii) a trap. The first stage direction in the earliest
printed text runs thus:

> Enter the Tribunes and Senators aloft; and then enter
> Saturninus and his followers at one door, and Bassianus
> and his followers with drums and trumpets.

Pretty clearly if Saturninus enters "at one door," Bassianus enters at another, since they represent opposed
forces. (The De Witt drawing of the Swan [discussed on
page xiv] shows two doors at the rear of the thrust stage,
with an overhanging gallery.) Possibly one of the stage
doors—perhaps equipped with black drapery or with a
cloth painted to represent an architectural facade—
served also as the tomb, though conceivably the tomb was
represented by some sort of structure erected at the rear
of the platform. The upper stage was not used only for
the initial entrance, "aloft," of the tribunes and senators;
at line 63 Bassianus and Saturninus *"go up into the Senate
house."* An upper playing area is also used in V.ii; although no stage directions in this scene specify that the
action is "aloft," it is clear that when Tamora addresses
Titus in his "study," Titus is above, since she asks him to
"come down." And in V.iii.130–33, Marcus's words
("headlong hurl ourself / And on the ragged stones beat
forth our souls") suggest that he and Lucius are on an
upper level. Also worth mentioning is the emphasis on
spectacle, implicit in the reference to "drums and trumpets" in the first stage direction. One sometimes reads that

the Elizabethan stage was bare, but in fact a good deal
of attention was paid to highly visual effects; here the
"drums and trumpets" imply at least some dressing up of
the stage with supernumeraries, and one may assume that
such characters were attractively dressed.

We also get some sense of Elizabethan stage spectacle
from a late sixteenth-century illustration of *Titus Andronicus*, the only contemporary drawing illustrating a play
by Shakespeare. This pen drawing, in the papers of the
Marquis of Bath at Longleat, shows Tamora in the center,
crowned and robed, kneeling before Titus, to the left, who
wears what passes for a Roman costume. Behind Tamora,
at the right, kneel two of her sons, their hands tied, and
still further to the right stands a coal-black Aaron brand-
ishing a sword. At the extreme left, behind Titus, stand
two attendant soldiers in Elizabethan garb. The drawing
is important evidence that for plays set in classical times
the Elizabethans used both classical and contemporary
clothing, classical clothing for the chief characters, and
Elizabethan clothing for the lesser ones. Although the
drawing is accompanied by some forty lines of text from
several parts of the play, in fact it does not precisely
illustrate any scene in the play. Obviously it evokes the
first part of the play, when Tamora pleads for her son
Alarbus—but why is Aaron (a captive) armed, and why
are there not three sons (as the text specifies) rather than
two? And why are not Titus's sons shown, since in the
play they are present when Tamora pleads for Alarbus?
Even if a viewer interprets the picture as showing a
slightly later episode, after Alarbus has been sent off to
his death, the problem of an armed Aaron remains. In all
probability the drawing is based on a somewhat faulty
memory of a performance of the play; but it probably does
give us a good idea of Elizabethan costuming and of the
Elizabethan presentation of the Moor.

From 1642 until 1660, that is, during the Civil War
and the reign of Cromwell, until the restoration of King
Charles II in 1660, the theaters in England were closed,
but they reopened in 1660 and *Titus* may have been

performed occasionally during the 1660s; in any case it was mentioned, and it appears in a list of plays assigned to one of the theaters. In 1678 Edward Ravenscroft adapted the play, calling his work *Titus Andronicus or the Rape of Lavinia*. The adaptation, probably performed in 1678, was not published until 1687, when it included an address "To the Reader" in which Ravenscroft claims that he has extensively revised "a heap of rubbish":

> However as if some great Building had been design'd, in the removal we found many Large and Square Stones both usefull and Ornamental to the Fabrick, as now Modell'd: Compare the Old Play with this, you'l finde that none in all that Authors Works ever receiv'd greater Alterations or Additions, the Language not only refin'd but many scenes entirely New; Besides most of the Principal Characters heighten'd, and the Plot much encreas'd.

This version was revived in the mid 1680s, and continued on the stage until 1724. Curiously, despite Ravenscroft's claim, his revisions are relatively slight, at least when compared to other revisions of the period, such as John Dryden's version of *Troilus and Cressida* and Nahum Tate's revision of *King Lear*. He modernizes some of the language, reassigns or moves some speeches (he heightens Aaron's part in I.i by giving him lines that Shakespeare gave to Tamora and Demetrius), invents some new speeches, and sends Titus offstage to chop off his hand, but Ravenscroft pretty much follows the original, except that he ends with Aaron, tied to the rack, being set afire.

To this point the stage history of the play, though not exceptional, was respectable. But after the 1724 production of Ravenscroft's version, with the eminent James Quin as Aaron, *Titus Andronicus*—in the original form and in Ravenscroft's adaptation—seems to have vanished from the stage until 1839, when it was given in Philadelphia in an adaptation by the American actor Nathaniel Harrington Bannister. No text of Bannister's adaptation survives, but a commentator wrote that Bannister "excluded the horrors with infinite skill." As we will see, excluding the horrors, or at least modifying them, continues to be a preoccupation of most directors of the play.

In England (and in Scotland and Ireland) Ira Aldridge, a black American who went to England because he could not find work with white companies in the United States, played the role of Aaron between 1849 and 1860. Aldridge did not confine himself to black roles, but earlier he had been especially successful as Othello, and so it seems natural for him to have added Aaron to his repertoire. His version of the play does not survive, but fairly full references to it make it clear that it was heavily adapted. Not surprisingly, the part of Aaron—already in many ways highly attractive—was made more attractive, and, equally unsurprisingly, the violence was muted. But the changes in Tamora and her children come as a surprise. A reviewer of a production in Hoxton, in 1857, wrote:

> The deflowerment of Lavinia, cutting out her tongue, chopping off her hands, and the numerous decapitations and gross language which occur in the original are totally omitted and a play not only presentable but actually attractive is the result. Aaron is elevated into a noble and lofty character. Tamora, the Queen of Scythia, is a chaste though decidedly strong-minded female, and her connection with the Moor appears to be of a legitimate description; her sons Chiron and Demetrius are dutiful children, obeying the behests of their mother . . . . Thus altered, Mr. Aldridge's conception of the part of Aaron is excellent—gentle and impassioned by turns; now burning with jealousy as he doubts the honor of the Queen; anon, fierce with rage as he reflects upon the wrongs which have been done him—the murder of Alarbus and the abduction of his son; and then all tenderness and emotion in the gentle passages with his infant.

After Aldridge's final production of the play in 1860,

Titus (even in adapted forms) disappeared from the stage until 1923, when the Old Vic put it on, thereby completing its production of the entire canon. The director, Robert Atkins, sought to do the play in a more or less Elizabethan manner, with few properties and with an emphasis on pageantry. The reviews on the whole were favorable, although the rapid sequence of deaths in the last scene (Titus kills Lavinia and then kills Tamora; Saturninus kills Titus, and Lucius kills Saturninus, all within twenty lines) evoked some laughter. Putting aside productions chiefly of local interest (e.g. a version done at Yale University in 1924), *Titus* next appeared in 1951, in a thirty-minute version by Kenneth Tynan and Peter Myers, staged in London as one of six pieces in an evening of Grand Guignol in London. (Later, in a review of Peter Brook's production of *Titus* in 1955, Tynan said that he "always had a soft spot for *Titus Andronicus*," a play that is "tragedy naked, godless, and unredeemed, a carnival of carnage in which pity is the first man down. We have since learned how to sweeten tragedy, to make it ennobling, but we would do well to remember that *Titus* is the raw material, 'the thing itself,' the piling of agony on to a human head until it splits.") Curiously, Aaron was omitted. In 1953 the play was performed by the Marlowe Society at Cambridge, and (as part of a cycle of Shakespeare's classical plays) by the Antioch Shakespeare Festival at Yellow Springs, Ohio, but the great production of the 1950s was Peter Brook's, at Stratford-upon-Avon in 1955, with Laurence Olivier as Titus, Vivien Leigh as Lavinia, Maxine Audley as Tamora, and Anthony Quayle as Aaron. Richard David's somewhat cool report of the production is reprinted in the Signet Classic edition of the play, but a few details may be added here. Brook cut about 650 lines, dropping a hundred and fifty from the first scene. Moreover, he occasionally rearranged speeches. For instance, in I.i he put Lavinia's rejection of Saturninus before Saturninus's expression of interest in Lavinia, thus making Lavinia's rejection contribute to Saturninus's interest in Tamora. As Richard David points out, Brook

muted or stylized much of the violence, for instance by
not displaying Titus's severed hand, and by using scarlet
ribbons to represent Lavinia's bloody stumps. He also
used such visual devices to replace some of the ornate
poetry, in this case Marcus's speech (II.iv.11–57) describing the maimed Lavinia as a "conduit with three issuing
spouts." Still, it should be pointed out that although Brook
relegated the deaths of Chiron and Demetrius to offstage,
he did keep the other seven onstage murders of the play.
In short, although he did not attempt a faithful, museum-
piece production, he did demonstrate that Shakespeare's
play (with some touching up) could powerfully move an
audience. In 1957 he took the production on a tour of
six continental capitals, and then brought it to London for
thirty-six performances; these, with the 1955 performances, gave the play a total of ninety performances,
probably the longest run the play has had.

Other productions in the 1950s included two performances at the Oregon Shakespeare Festival in Ashland in
1956, done without an intermission (i.e. Elizabethan
style) on a stage that approximated an Elizabethan stage
(a neutral platform with a permanent architectural background), fifteen performances at Joseph Papp's New
York Shakespeare Festival in 1956, and a highly cut version done in 1957 by the Old Vic, on a double bill with an
abridged *Comedy of Errors*. The Old Vic production was
set in an inn courtyard; Elizabethan strolling players
entered, and then, wearing a combination of Elizabethan
and classical costume, gave a version of *Titus* that ran
about an hour and a half.

In 1963 the Birmingham Repertory performed the play,
and in 1967 a Baltimore company staged it in a modern
setting: Saturninus, with a retinue of Blackshirts, re-
sembled Mussolini, Titus was dressed like a Prussian officer, and the Goths—envisioned as a liberating army
—wore costumes reminiscent of the clothing of American
forces in World War II. Also in 1967 Joseph Papp in New
York returned to the play, offering a version directed by
Gerald Freedman and starring Moses Gunn as Aaron.

Freedman's production was somewhat like Peter Brook's
in that it ritualized the play, though Freedman went
further, using masks, a chorus, and silver and black costumes of no particular period or culture. Freedman explained that he turned to such devices because he had
found the 1967 Baltimore modern version unsuccessful;
its realism, in his view, called attention to the *un*reality of
the play. *Titus Andronicus,* Freedman said, needs to be
stylized if it is to be "meaningful and emotional to a contemporary audience," and if the multiple deaths are to be
acceptable rather than ridiculous. (Brook had already
said he presented the play in an "unrealistic" manner in
order to make the violence of the play "totally real.")
Mildred Kuner, in a brief review in *Shakespeare Quarterly*
(Autumn 1967) gives a sample of the staging:

> At the end, when the principals meet their death in the
> banquet scene, the chorus, from the shadows, wove about
> the victims a red cloth which turned into a black shroud;
> the dead, in turn, did not collapse but remained upright,
> as though transformed into stone. Symbolism rather than
> gory realism was what made this production so stunning.

One other detail of Freedman's production may be cited:
when the emperor sends Titus the severed heads of two
of his sons, the heads were simply the masks on a platter.
It is reported that the audience gasped at the sight of the
empty masks.

The 1970s saw several productions of *Titus,* including
one by the Royal Shakespeare Theatre in 1972, directed
by Trevor Nunn, where, with *Coriolanus, Julius Caesar,*
and *Antony and Cleopatra,* it was done as part of a
series of Roman plays. Nunn said that Shakespeare used
Roman settings in order to examine "political motives
and social organization," and that the Roman plays "are
speaking directly to us now." What did he think *Titus* was
saying? In the program, Nunn wrote that "Shakespeare's
Elizabethan nightmare has become ours," and that we may
already be experiencing a "convulsion which heralds a fall

greater than Rome's." The governing idea was that Titus's Rome has become decadent (Saturninus was an effete weakling) and is about to fall. Despite this unpromising reading of the play, there were some successes, notably Colin Blakely's grand, battered Titus, which received considerable praise.

The play has fared better in the 1980s, though not in John Barton's production of 1981, done in a "presentational" rather than a "representational" manner (e.g. actors when not performing sat in the shadows onstage). In practice, Barton's production seemed to mock the play, giving us a fatuous Titus and a Tamora who spoke with a ludicrous accent. A production at Brown University, however, directed by David Burr in 1984, was extremely effective, using a black-and-silver-metal set and presenting Titus and the old guard in leather, against a new world of upstart punks. Unfortunately this production attracted little attention outside of the university. An earlier punk production in New York in a lounge in the lower East Village in 1983, directed by Kestutis Nakas, was far less successful. Nakas chose to present the play in as ridiculous a fashion as possible: effeminate soldiers equipped with plastic weapons and shields made grand gestures, and meat snacks were served to the audience. The director justified the production by claiming, "If the humor is openly recognized, it'll be gruesome, black humor adding to the tragedy rather than destroying it—which is what happens when you play it straight." The experiment was, as one might have easily predicted, a failure.

The most recent production at the time of writing this essay was given in the Swan at Stratford-upon-Avon in 1987, directed by Deborah Warner and starring Brian Cox as Titus and Estelle Kohler as Tamora. The stage was relatively bare except for a large aluminum ladder, to which Tamora's defeated sons were tied when they enter Rome, and which was used again when Aaron is hanged. Ritual was *not* used to distance the horrors; although blood was kept to a minimum, the mutilations were realistic. Perhaps more than any other production of the play in the twentieth century this production showed that a relatively straight version can be deeply moving.

Bibliographic note: There are two valuable essays on the stage history of *Titus Andronicus*: G. Harold Metz's "Stage History of *Titus Andronicus*," *Shakespeare Quarterly* 28 (1977), 154–69, and Eugene M. Waith's somewhat less detailed but more up-to-date account (1984) in Waith's edition of *Titus* in the Oxford Shakespeare. The notes in these two accounts will direct a reader to fuller commentaries on some productions. Reviews of most productions in the second half of the twentieth century can be found in issues of *Shakespeare Quarterly* and *Shakespeare Survey*. J. Dover Wilson illustrates and discusses the sixteenth-century drawing of *Titus* in *Shakespeare Survey 1* (1948), 17–22; Waith also discusses it in his Oxford edition of the play.

William Shakespeare

The Life of
TIMON OF ATHENS

Edited by Maurice Charney

Contents

Introduction

There is general agreement that *Timon of Athens* is an unfinished play. In an influential article in the *Review of English Studies* (1942), Una Ellis-Fermor described *Timon* as "a play such as a great artist might leave behind him, roughed out, worked over in part and then abandoned; full of inconsistencies in form and presentation, with fragments (some of them considerable) bearing the unmistakable stamp of his workmanship scattered throughout." The roughnesses of the play are obvious to any conscientious reader of Shakespeare. The blank verse is often extremely irregular, with many lines that do not fit into the iambic pentameter pattern. There are strange eruptions of prose in verse passages, and there are many inept repetitions of words and phrases from one line to the next. Characters appear, such as the Fool and Page (II.ii), who are not properly integrated into the action; there are two conflicting epitaphs for Timon in Act V; and the Poet and Painter announced at IV.iii.355 do not arrive until almost two hundred lines later. The subplot of Alcibiades and his revenge on Athens is so loosely related to the main action which it is intended to parallel that some have suspected a lost scene. We know that the murderer for whom Alcibiades is pleading in Act III, Scene v, cannot be Timon, but he is not anyone else in the play, and it is more than an idle curiosity which seeks to know his name.

One detail in the play is the subject of a fascinating study. In "Shakespeare Learns the Value of Money,"

Terence Spencer discusses the inconsistency in the references to talents. A talent was an ancient coin frequently mentioned in Plutarch and the Bible, and generally taken to be worth half a hundredweight of silver, or well over $1000 in its modern equivalent. The sum of 1000 talents that Timon seeks from the Senators (II.ii) is an absurdly large one (more than $1,000,000), and it is possible that Shakespeare really did not know how much a talent was worth. At some point he learned its true value and corrected the references at the beginning of the play, but left others uncorrected. The request for "fifty five hundred talents" in Act III, Scene ii, seems to mean either fifty or five hundred, depending on how much a talent is worth, and the references to "so many talents" in the same scene should be replaced by actual sums.

This example of the talents is a very neat one for demonstrating that many details in *Timon* need to be revised and corrected and that the play lacks the sort of polishing and tidying up that one would expect from a final draft. The circumstances surrounding the printing of *Timon* (discussed in the Textual Note) lend further support to this idea. There can be no doubt that the play as it appears in Shakespeare's First Folio of 1623 is unfinished. But Miss Ellis-Fermor's thesis has done great harm to the appreciation of *Timon* because it suggests that the play is not only unfinished (in the sense of its lacking any final revision), but that it is a mere collection of jottings and rough sketches without any integral coherence. I would strongly disagree with this point of view. It seems to me that *Timon* is completely finished in conception: its structure makes good sense as a whole, its characters are well adapted to the overall plan, and its style, tone, imagery, and dramatic handling all contribute to a unified imaginative vision.

Because *Timon* is an unusual play, it would be more profitable to try to understand its uniqueness than to compare it unfavorably with the great tragedies that preceded it. The structure of the play is that of a dramatic fable, divided into two sharply contrasted parts. By dramatic fable I mean what other critics have called a morality play or an allegory—that is, a structure that does not proceed rationally and causatively from point to point, but rather one that progresses by a series of unmotivated leaps from one imaginative state to another. We are not meant to examine the credibility of Timon's financial extravagance, or his total unawareness of his bankruptcy, or his sudden discovery of an inexhaustible supply of gold. We accept these improbabilities as part of our willing suspension of disbelief. The testing of the three false friends in Act III moves as in a folktale to its inevitable conclusion, and the faithful servant who remains true while all others are false is a familiar fairy-tale figure. The exact cause of Timon's death is left poetically obscure, and no attempt at all is made to give his sudden change from philanthropy to misanthropy a psychological basis. The structure of the play is schematic, and the dramatic action separates itself into a series of well-defined episodes related to each other analogically rather than causally. One scene is not the source or cause or motive for another, but is, rather, a parallel to it and serves as a comment on it. I should like to look more closely at the structure of *Timon* in order to show that the play is complete and fully imagined within the meaning of a dramatic fable. For this purpose, I will survey the action scene by scene and offer an account of "what happens in *Timon*."

The first sequence of ninety-four lines before Timon appears is of crucial importance for establishing the tone and mood of the play as well as announcing its major themes. We have a Poet and Painter, a Jeweler and Merchant, who have come to peddle their wares to Timon, as patron of the arts and general connoisseur. None of these characters is named, and they represent, as in an allegory, the type functions of their names. Behind the elaborate compliment and self-deprecation of this scene lies a blatant hucksterism that well expresses the rottenness of Athens. The meretriciousness of the Poet and Painter is particularly disturbing, since we expect them

to aim higher than merely "to propagate their states."
Shakespeare seems nowhere else to have put artists in
such an unfavorable light.

The controlling element in the scene is the Poet's allegory of Fortune, which serves as a central fable for the
play. The goddess Fortune and her capricious ways much
occupied the mind of men in the Middle Ages and Renaissance, and great efforts were made to reconcile the
Roman myth with Christian morality. Wealth and all
material benefits are the fortuitous and insubstantial gifts
of Fortune, the blindfolded goddess who is forever turn-
ing the wheel on which her worshipers are placed (the
wheel in a gambling casino derives from this one).
Timon's alliance with Fortune early in the play clearly
foreshadows his ruin, "When Fortune in her shift and
change of mood/ Spurns down her late beloved."

Thus, when Timon enters at line 94 with great ceremony, *"addressing himself courteously to every suitor,"*
we are already prepared not to accept his munificence at
its face value. The pack of suppliants is itself so mixed
in degrees of worth that we cannot help agreeing with
Dr. Johnson, who said that the play is a "warning against
that ostentatious liberality which scatters bounty but confers no benefits, and buys flattery but no friendship."
Timon is at his height in this scene, reveling in his phil-
anthropic role. There is, of course, something dreamlike
about this early scene, with its mixture of charity, prodigality, and enormous public display. The entrance of
Apemantus at line 175 restores some measure of reality,
since he at least speaks the truth, however churlish and
snarling he may be in his personal manner. He warns
Timon of his waste and extravagance, but Apemantus
is so unsympathetic in his role of satiric, malcontent railer
that he is almost never believed; this is another disturbing
element in the play. The young military hero, Alcibiades,
also appears in Act I, Scene i, but aside from his elaborate military costume, he is a colorless figure and, with
the single exception of Act III, Scene v, remains so
throughout.

In Act I, Scene ii, Timon is still high and godlike as

he presides over an elaborate banquet for his friends. There is a strong visual emphasis on the fact that Timon's bounty shows itself in hedonism and high living more than in old-fashioned benevolence. His ideal of friendship is inseparable from the clubby atmosphere of good food and drink and the Gemütlichkeit of mutual compliment. As Apemantus had said earlier, "He that loves to be flattered is worthy o' th' flatterer." The Masque of Amazons in this scene is an element of spectacle common in Shakespeare's later plays and not very closely related to the action. Incidentally, the only women in the play are these Amazons and the prostitutes, Phrynia and Timandra; the world of Athens is distinctly a man's world.

It is in Act I, Scene ii, that Flavius, the always loyal steward of Timon, tells us that his master is bankrupt, everything is mortgaged, and utter ruin is imminent. Flavius resembles Apemantus in speaking the truth, but he has a fund of compassion for Timon—"I bleed inwardly for my lord"—while Apemantus cynically delights in misfortune.

The first scene of Act II takes us back to the opening of the play, and once again we are plunged into the icy reality of Athens, in which all values are on a strictly cash basis. A Senator who is not named is counting up Timon's debts and is impatiently dispatching his servant to dun him for the money. He loves and honors Timon, of course, "But must not break my back to heal his finger." The most shocking aspect of this scene is the contempt in which the Senator holds Timon for his generosity:

> If I want gold, steal but a beggar's dog
> And give it Timon—why the dog coins gold.
>   (II.i.5–6)

The Senator is only elaborating on Timon's own formula: "there's none/ Can truly say he gives, if he receives." But Timon's rejection of reciprocity in giving leaves him terribly vulnerable.

The next scene (II.ii) marks a new stage in the action, for Timon is now finally aware of his bankruptcy. In an effort to avoid the overwhelming truth, Timon will test his friends by seeking to borrow money from them. This process is accomplished in three satiric scenes in Act III, written in vivid colloquial style. They are all brief vignettes, very different from each other, and designed to show the varieties of evasive ingenuity. The scene with Lucullus (III.i) is so masterfully done that we are almost convinced that "this is no time to lend money, especially upon bare friendship without security." In the next scene (III.ii), three Strangers are introduced to serve as choral commentators on what is happening and to arouse our sympathies for Timon. These Strangers are merely non-Athenians without any further specification (although one of them is called Hostilius); they are in no way connected with the plot and appear only to vindicate Timon.

In Act III, Scene iv, the creditors' servants are again assembled at the house of Timon as they were in Act II, Scene ii. When Timon enters *"in a rage,"* we have a new development in the action, since Timon now has been stripped of his illusions. His misanthropy proper begins at this point, and he speaks in the highly emotional, freely associative style reserved for those distracted. Timon seems to be on the road to that bitter self-knowledge demanded by tragic recognition, yet he never progresses any further, and the tragedy, at least from the point of view of Aristotle's *Poetics*, remains truncated and fragmentary. In his hysterical, martyrlike sufferings, Timon does not turn inward as do so many of Shakespeare's tragic protagonists; instead, he begins to gloat over the possibility of being brilliantly and histrionically revenged in a mock-banquet.

Act III, Scene v, is the first and only full scene of the subplot. It is well written and fully written, with a carefully developed oration by Alcibiades for a friend and fellow soldier who has killed a man to defend his honor. This speech is, by the way, in the direct tradition of the "mercy" speeches of Portia in *The Merchant of Venice* and Isabella in *Measure for Measure*. Although the scene has no plot links with what precedes, it does have a strong thematic connection with it. The Athenian senators show the same ingratitude to a benefactor of their state as they did to Timon. This scene plays an important part in developing the tone and mood of Athens, so that when Timon's mock-banquet and revenge follow in the next scene, we are glad to see the tables turned on the greedy, usurious senators. Alcibiades' banishment in this scene foreshadows the self-exile of Timon at the end of the next scene.

The final scene of Act III is carefully written up to provide an effective climax for the first part of the play: "Uncover, dogs, and lap." This is a memorable line, and the dramatic skill with which the discovery and reversal are managed shows Shakespeare at his best. It is a great moment for Timon, who has once again recovered his former stature. One interesting structural element is that Timon in this scene is beginning to take over the role of Apemantus: his grace echoes Apemantus' bitter benediction in Act I, Scene ii, and in Acts IV and V the verbal echoes become more marked. Another striking feature is the reaction of the guests to Timon's revenge. Here we have an excellent example of the use of sharp contrast to establish an effect. The friends are as untouched by Timon's towering pronouncements as the dunning servants were in Act III, Scene iv. After having their souls seared by Timon's revelations of their inner corruption, they respond with utter banality: "Push, did you see my cap?", "I have lost my gown," "He gave me a jewel th' other day, and now he has beat it out of my hat. Did you see my jewel?" This anticlimax of high comedy concludes when the lost items have been recovered.

Timon's soliloquy outside the walls of Athens in the next scene (IV.i) has none of the meditative, soul-searching qualities of the soliloquies in *Hamlet* or *Macbeth;* it is purely an oration by one with no onstage audience. Timon's vision of chaos in this scene is so radical that it fails to be convincing. It is perhaps not more extreme than Lear's speeches on the heath, but it has no psychological terror and passion to support the violent rhetoric, and the intensity of the language seems to be separated from any occasion which might have caused it. This leads to some odd side effects, even to an irreverent feeling of sick humor in some of the most hysterical imprecations:

> Son of sixteen,
> Pluck the lined crutch from thy old limping sire,
> With it beat out his brains.   (IV.i.13–15)

One of the drawbacks in the writing of a dramatic fable is that one deliberately rejects the kind of psychological thickness that is needed to support statements like the above. The fourth and fifth acts of *Timon* are unsuccessful partly because the impassioned rhetoric cannot sustain itself without an impassioned action.

The brief second scene of Act IV shows us Timon's servants, "All broken implements of a ruined house," still faithful to him in adversity. They are the counterparts of the false friends, and they modify our possible contempt for Timon. Along with the three Strangers of Act III, Scene ii, they prevent the play from becoming out-and-out satire.

Act IV, Scene iii, a long and miscellaneous scene, consists chiefly of a series of encounters with Timon. It is worth noting that Timon's cave in the woods seems to be as easily accessible as a good midtown office. These encounters all meet with predictable failure, as we might expect in a dramatic fable, so that their main function seems to be to exhibit Timon's misanthropy in a number of different guises. One new movement, however, is the sense of world-weariness that comes over Timon, accompanied by a desire to die. It begins at line 380 and culminates in the moving speech:

> My long sickness
> Of health and living now begins to mend,
> And nothing brings me all things.   (V.i.187–89)

At the beginning of Act IV, Scene iii, Timon's parable of the "Twinned brothers of one womb" shows us that he now believes in the Poet's vision of Fortune in the first scene of the play. "All's obliquy," everything is crooked and perverse, and the law of nature no longer rules man. Timon's hate would not be so disturbing if it did not include a petulant self-hate by which he forfeits all neutral ground. He is not the one just man bearing witness against corruption, but as worthless and corrupt as the rest. His primitivism, then, is a mere sham, and there is ironic justification for his finding gold rather than roots. He will use it to fulfill his evil vision and make "Destruction fang mankind."

The appearance of Alcibiades with a brace of whores undercuts his heroic pretensions, and the slangy directness of the whores makes them more interesting than their noble captain. Like other realists in the play, Phrynia and Timandra humor Timon in the hope of gain: "More counsel with more money, bounteous Timon." In their plainspeaking refusal to flatter, they make explicit a theme from the earlier part of the play: "Believe't that we'll do anything for gold."

The word-slinging wit-combat with Apemantus has some of the best and some of the worst speeches in the play. The absolute low point, it seems to me, is the series of insults they hurl at each other. There is not enough inventiveness in either calumniator to go beyond Timon's "Would thou wert clean enough to spit upon"—my entry for the worst line in the play, which gains an added point from Timon's insufferable snobbishness. But the mutual judgments that Timon and Apemantus make of each other are excellently done, and they show an old-fashioned character analysis rare in this play. Apemantus' case against Timon is made so explicitly that we cannot possibly mistake Timon for Shakespeare's mouthpiece. Timon is a naturally disdainful man, who feigns misanthropy out of pique with Fortune; he is an absolutist who cannot make any compromises with the human condition. As Apemantus says, "The middle of humanity thou never knewest, but the extremity of both ends." This hits home, but Timon's account of Apemantus' meanness and envy and essentially servile nature also strikes its mark and draws blood.

The meeting with the anonymous Banditti is full of improbability, and their sententiousness and lack of ferocity are disappointing. The encounter with Flavius that closes the scene shows Timon again at his worst, since he is grudgingly forced to admit that there is one honest man. Shadwell got around this difficulty in his version of the play (1678) by introducing an honest woman, Evandra, who is able to regenerate Timon. At this point in the structure of Shakespeare's play, it is clear that Timon must soon die, if only to satisfy the exacerbation of the audience. He has reached such an extreme position that he can go no further in negation. Being a static and flat character, he has already involved himself in tedious repetition.

Act V, Scene i, continues the previous scene, with the Poet and Painter forming another exhibit of why Timon took to the woods; we are pleased to see them laboring so hard for rewards they will not receive. The mission from Athens at the end of the scene suggests that some changes have occurred in the city since Timon's departure, although the elaborate, unnecessarily complicated rhetoric of the Senators hints that these changes could not have been very profound. The "heaps and sums" and "figures of their love" inevitably imply that the Senators are ready to offer Timon a handsome bribe. After the announcement of Timon's death and the discovery of his epitaph, the play ends conventionally with a sense of the purgation of evil and the possibility of a new and better life in the once corrupted city.

At the risk of reviewing the plot, I have gone into some detail about the structure of *Timon* in order to show that it is a coherent whole with carefully developed analogies between its parts, and not a mere hodgepodge of first thoughts, jottings, roughings-out, or fragments. Although it has many flaws, it does seem to me a completed play, and one that can satisfactorily be acted in its present form (as it has been in recent years by the Old Vic—

twice, the Stratford Festival Company of Canada, and many others). There is no doubt that *Timon* could be improved, but it does make good sense dramatically as it now stands. I would not try to push the argument further than that. A dramatic fable by its very nature has many weaknesses in psychological characterization and tragic development, but it can produce some striking effects of simplicity, symmetry, and dramatic intensity. These excellences of *Timon* have perhaps been best appreciated by William Hazlitt, who in *The Characters of Shakespear's Plays* said that the play

> always appeared to us to be written with as intense a feeling of his subject as any one play of Shakespear. It is one of the few in which he seems to be in earnest throughout, never to trifle nor go out of his way. He does not relax in his efforts, nor lose sight of the unity of his design.

The imagery of *Timon* has an inner consistency that reflects the completeness of the play as a work of the imagination. Images of disease, especially venereal disease, pervade the action, evoking the sort of disgust one finds in *Hamlet* and *Troilus and Cressida*. Man's nature is infected and the soul of the world is sick. Timon's misanthropy itself rages as virulently as any disease. Animal imagery and predatory images of food and eating combine with those of disease to strengthen its negative aspect. In Timon's tirades, especially, all mankind is reduced to Hobbes's fearful state of nature, where the law of the jungle once more prevails. There is much elaborate play on the dog image, since Apemantus was himself a Cynic philosopher, a school derived from the Greek word for dog and thought to have currish properties. William Empson has discussed some of the overtones of this image in the play, and Caroline Spurgeon has pointed to the typical fawning image-cluster of dogs licking candy. The imagery of gold is too obvious to dwell on, but one should remember its double sense of evil and blessing. There are also traditional themes of winter and summer, cold and hot, constriction and flow, which follow the movement of the dramatic action.

Shakespeare seems to be completely in control of the style of *Timon,* which, if it has rough places that need to be revised, has also some extraordinary felicities. The play is not lyric in intent, so that some of the most vivid lyric effects are used negatively to support Timon's cruel imagination. The best passage of this sort is Timon's advice to Alcibiades to wage total war and spare none, for all are hypocritical dissemblers:

> Let not the virgin's cheek
> Make soft thy trenchant sword: for those milk paps,
> That through the window-bars bore at men's eyes,
> Are not within the leaf of pity writ,
> But set them down horrible traitors.   (IV.iii.115–19)

"Window-bars" has sometimes been interpreted to mean the open-work squares on the bodice of a woman's frock, but its literal reference to the bars outside a window seems more natural. We have the image of a young virgin mewed up in her chamber, whose disturbing sexuality as she stands at her window transfixes men and pierces them through. One must struggle against one's natural instincts to overcome these charms, and the lyric expression is used for derogatory purposes. Another more shocking example of twisted lyricism is Timon's advice to Flavius:

> Hate all, curse all, show charity to none,
> But let the famished flesh slide from the bone
> Ere thou relieve the beggar.   (IV.iii.536–38)

The physical force of the image is not buried in faded metaphor. Its cruelty is stark and unadorned.

One other stylistic excellence in *Timon* is its epigrammatic conciseness, the ability to pack a complex meaning into a brief phrase. There are many examples of this, some of them, as "feast-won, fast-lost," founded on prov-

erbs. Flavius' defense of Timon also suggests a proverb,
although it is not a recorded one: "Never mind/ Was
to be so unwise to be so kind." The effect of compression
probably depends upon the multiple connotations of
"kind" and "unwise"; a paraphrase would demand a good
deal of amplification. The most numerous examples of
this kind of writing are, I think, in Act III, Scene v. Here
the conciseness is part of the dramatic plan, and the
Senators' brusque questions are ominous in their brevity:
"Now, captain?", "What's that?", "How?", "What?",
and then the explicit: "Do you dare our anger?" which
precedes Alcibiades' banishment. In the carefully articu-
lated rhetoric of Alcibiades' oration, there are many of
these pregnant phrases. When the First Senator states
as his guiding principle, "He forfeits his own blood that
spills another," Alcibiades simply cannot believe what
he has heard: "Must it be so? It must not be." The repetition gives special point to the line, as it also does in
Alcibiades' final soliloquy:

> I'm worse than mad; I have kept back their foes,
> While they have told their money, and let out
> Their coin upon large interest. I myself
> Rich only in large hurts. All those, for this?
>
> (III.v.105–08)

The ironic echoing of "large" prepares us for the antithesis
of the final question. The deliberate ambiguity of "this"
suggests a wide range of meanings: this banishment, this
debasement, this travesty of justice, this perversion of
honor and merit—in sum, this evil, corrupt, tyrannical
city governed by cynically usurious Senators.

Timon has many of the qualities of satire and high
comedy. In the attempt to depict the sophisticated, morally corrupt, and completely money-oriented life of
Athens, Shakespeare uses a sharp realism of style expressed in easy colloquial speech. The scenes with the
false friends in Act III (i, ii, iii) are the best sustained
examples of this style. Lucullus' reply to Flaminius' request for money shows an unabashed ironic scorn: "La,

la, la, la! 'Nothing doubting,' says he? Alas, good lord,
a noble gentleman 'tis, if he would not keep so good a
house." Lucullus is completely at his ease, and his use
of contracted speech forms throughout this scene indicates
an assumed and contemptuous familiarity. Another example of Shakespeare's mastery of the colloquial style
is Flavius' report of how the Senators reacted to his request for a loan:

> They answer in a joint and corporate voice,
> That now they are at fall, want treasure, cannot
> Do what they would, are sorry; you are honorable,
> But yet they could have wished—they know not;
> Something hath been amiss—a noble nature
> May catch a wrench—would all were well—'tis pity—
> And so, intending other serious matters,
> After distasteful looks, and these hard fractions,
> With certain half-caps and cold-moving nods,
> They froze me into silence.   (II.ii.214–23)

"These hard fractions" show Shakespeare's skill at imitating, by syntax and phrase, the halting dishonesty of
the Senators. The fragments are those of actual speech,
and their disconnectedness is intended to soften the blow
on Timon. Even such a glorious spender as Timon "May
catch a wrench" and go broke, and, as Lucullus says,
"this is no time to lend money, especially upon bare
friendship without security."

Another approach to the integrity of *Timon* is to consider the play in the context of Shakespeare's other works.
Timon has most often been compared with *King Lear*.
Coleridge called it an "after vibration" of *Lear,* and
A. C. Bradley compared the two plays extensively in his
study of Shakespearean tragedy. Both deal with the
theme of ingratitude and its overpowering effects on Lear
and Timon, who both react with a fierce indictment of
man and society. But in *Lear* this indictment touches the
protagonist, too, and leads him to a bitter self-awareness
which is not present in *Timon*. There is no inward-turning
in the latter play, no soul-searching of any sort, which

gives it the effect of satire rather than tragedy. Both Lear and Timon are first shown in an atmosphere of false flattery and public adoration. They are soon reduced to primitive nature, but in Lear's case this stripping-down has a necessity lacking in Timon's, who chooses self-exile in the woods and perversely persists in it even after he has found gold. One may also compare Kent and Flavius, the unshakably loyal servants who minister to their masters in adversity, but Kent is individualized as a character by a keen, blunt-speaking wit, whereas Flavius only fulfills a type function. In both plays, the frequent contrast of "nothing" and "all" identifies the extreme nature of the tragic action, which eschews any happy mean between prosperity and adversity.

Timon is especially close to those dark, satirical plays that put a strong emphasis on sexual corruption: Measure for Measure, Hamlet, and Troilus and Cressida. While Timon conveys the strongest sense of sexual disease, it shares a disillusioned view of human nature and an overpowering sense of deceit and hypocrisy with these other plays. It has been suggested that all of these plays (except Hamlet) were written for the more fastidious audiences of the Inns of Court or the private theaters. That would help to explain the difficult, closely reasoned, and abstract character of many of their speeches.

There is a specific connection between Timon and Troilus and Cressida in the characters of Apemantus and Thersites. Both are scurrilous, churlish, and thoroughly unattractive truth-speakers, who, like professional fools, prick the illusions in their plays. Their own reality is never intended to be any alternative to the pretensions they attack, since they are both base and mean-spirited. Perhaps Apemantus, by his profession of Cynic philosophy, is a somewhat more attractive figure than the completely servile Thersites.

The relation of Timon to Coriolanus is so close that it deserves particular attention. Both plays are based on North's Plutarch for their essential details, and the exile of Alcibiades with his return to conquer his native city is very like the career of Coriolanus. The two are, in fact, parallel lives in Plutarch. The banishment of Alcibiades and Coriolanus is manipulated by a politically and morally corrupt group, whose mediocrity is disturbed by the presence of military heroes. The subsequent plea of the Senators to spare their city is also similar in the two plays. In structure both plays are divided into two distinct parts, one showing the wrong or evil, the other the revenge for it. The opening fable of Fortune's hill in *Timon* parallels the fable of the belly and the members in *Coriolanus;* both provide a convenient set of ideas by which to interpret the action, and both foreshadow what will eventually occur.

One could enumerate many similarities in detail between the two plays, but the larger similarities in conception are more important. *Timon* and *Coriolanus* are both tragedies that cannot be judged by the standards of Aristotle's *Poetics*: in neither play does the tragic protagonist have much awareness of what is happening to him, and there is no tragic recognition at all. Neither Timon nor Coriolanus has any sense of the middle state of man, the mean, the human condition. They are both absolutists, extremists, harsh individualists who wish to be either god or beast, but nothing in between. They are equally insensitive to human failings and weaknesses— even Timon's philanthropy is always public, never personal. Both plays put strong emphasis on public display and have many large scenes of crowded activity. There are very few personal or domestic scenes, and almost no attention at all is devoted to romantic heroines. The soliloquies in both plays are never used for purposes of self-analysis or self-exploration. Stylistically, both plays seem very objective and impersonal, and there are excellent examples in both of a condensed and telegraphic dramatic speech without lyric amplification. Both plays also have a good deal of satire, which draws on an extensive imagery of disease, animals, and food.

In the absence of any external evidence, I agree with E. K. Chambers in placing *Timon* after *Coriolanus* as the last of Shakespeare's tragedies, written sometime around 1608. However, Chambers' dating of *Timon* (in

William Shakespeare, Vol. I), is based on assumptions about Shakespeare's psychological and physical condition at the time of composition that are difficult to accept:

> Both *King Lear* and *Timon of Athens* seem to show symptoms of mental disturbance. But mental disturbance may come in waves. It may very likely only be a whimsy of my own that during the attempt at *Timon of Athens* a wave broke, then an illness followed, and that when it passed, the breach between the tragic and the romantic period was complete.

Timon has always been a favorite candidate for the "mythical sorrows of Shakespeare," and Chambers only echoes more than a century of romantic speculation on the dark corners of Shakespeare's soul. Georg Brandes in his *William Shakespeare* said much the same thing in a more rapturous and unrestrained form:

> all that, in these years, Shakespeare has endured and experienced, thought and suffered, is concentrated into the one great despairing figure of Timon of Athens, "misanthropos," whose savage rhetoric is like a dark secretion of clotted blood and gall, drawn off to assuage pain.

Recently, a number of medical critics have stated that Timon is suffering from the classic symptoms of syphilis, which reach the stage of paresis by Act IV. Perhaps we must then postulate that Shakespeare himself was suffering from the French malady in order to be able to write about it. This is the same order of fallacy as attributing Shakespeare's birdlore and flowerlore to his close observation of the Warwickshire countryside, despite the fact that they have figured in literary traditions at least as old as the ancient Greeks.

Shakespeare surely tried to protect himself from being taken for a Timonist by making Timon so unattractive and unsympathetic. "Yond despised and ruinous man" is a lost soul, self-exiled and self-damned by his own evil vision of reality. We cannot have become so uncritically enamored of the power of blackness not to see the truth of Apemantus' judgment:

> Thou hast cast away thyself, being like thyself:
> A madman so long, now a fool.   (IV.iii.221–22)

We would not want to accept this, however, as a final appraisal of Timon, whose fierce energy and passion redeem him from the pettiness and rancor of his accusers. "Friendship's full of dregs," but to escape the humdrum complications of the common fate by trying to be either god or beast can be a more agonizing experience. Both Shakespeare's and Molière's misanthrope fascinate us and repel us because their attempt is so heroic, so uncompromising, and so inhuman.

MAURICE CHARNEY
Rutgers University

The Life of Timon of Athens

The Actors' Names

Timon of Athens
Lucius, and } two flattering lords
Lucullus
Sempronius, another flattering lord
Ventidius, one of Timon's false friends
Apemantus, a churlish philosopher
Alcibiades, an Athenian captain
Poet
Painter
Jeweler
Merchant
[Flavius, steward to Timon]
Flaminius, one of Timon's servants
Servilius, another
[Lucilius, another]
Caphis
Philotus
Titus
Hortensius } several servants to usurers
[Servant to] Varro
[Servant to] Lucius
[Servant to Isidore]
[An Old Athenian]
[Three Strangers]
[A Page]
[A Fool]
[Phrynia
[Timandra } mistresses to Alcibiades]
Certain Maskers [as] Cupid [and Amazons]
Certain Senators, certain Thieves, with divers other Servants and Attendants, [Lords, Officers, Soldiers]

[*Scene:* Athens and the neighboring woods]

The Life of Timon of Athens

ACT I

Scene I. [*Athens. Timon's house.*]

*Enter Poet, Painter, Jeweler, Merchant
at several*° *doors.*

Poet. Good day, sir.

Painter. I am glad y'are well.

Poet. I have not seen you long; how goes the world?

Painter. It wears,° sir, as it grows.

Poet. Ay that's well known.
But what particular rarity? What strange,
Which manifold record° not matches? See,   5
Magic of bounty,° all these spirits thy power
Hath conjured to attend. I know the merchant.

Painter. I know them both; th' other's a jeweler.

---

1 The degree sign (°) indicates a footnote, which is keyed to the
text by line number. Text references are printed in **bold** type; the
annotation follows in roman type.
I.i.s.d. several separate (the Poet and Painter enter at one door, the
Jeweler and Merchant at another)   **3 wears** wears out   **5 manifold
record** many and varied records, history ("record" accented on
second syllable)   **6 bounty** generosity

41

Merchant. O 'tis a worthy lord.

Jeweler.　　　　　　　　　　　　Nay that's most fixed.°

Merchant. A most incomparable man, breathed,° as it
10　　　were,
To an untirable and continuate° goodness.
He passes.°

Jeweler.　　　　I have a jewel here—

Merchant. O pray let's see't. For the Lord Timon, sir?

Jeweler. If he will touch the estimate.° But for that—

Poet. [*Aside to Painter*] When we for recompense
15　　　have praised the vild,°
It stains the glory in that happy° verse
Which aptly sings the good.

Merchant. [*Looking at the jewel*] 'Tis a good form.

Jeweler. And rich. Here is a water,° look ye.

Painter. You are rapt, sir, in some work, some dedication
To the great lord.

20　*Poet.*　　　　　　　A thing slipped idly from me.
Our poesy is as a gum, which oozes
From whence 'tis nourished. The fire i' th' flint
Shows not till it be struck; our gentle flame
Provokes itself,° and like the current flies
25　　　Each bound it chases.° What have you there?

Painter. A picture, sir. When comes your book forth?

Poet. Upon the heels of my presentment,° sir.
Let's see your piece.

---

9 **fixed** certain　10 **breathed** exercised, trained　11 **continuate** uninterrupted　12 **passes** surpasses　14 **touch the estimate** offer the
expected price　15 **vild** vile　16 **happy** fortunate　18 **water** luster
(of a jewel)　23–24 **our gentle flame/Provokes itself** i.e., the inspiration of poets is spontaneous, not externally provoked like the "fire
i' th' flint"　25 **Each bound it chases** i.e., the stream flows towards
the shore but rebounds upon contact　27 **presentment** presentation
(to Timon)

Painter.　　　　　　　　'Tis a good piece.

Poet. So 'tis; this comes off well and excellent.

Painter. Indifferent.°

Poet.　　　　　　　　Admirable. How this grace　　30
Speaks his own standing!° What a mental power
This eye shoots forth! How big° imagination
Moves in this lip! To th' dumbness° of the
　gesture
One might interpret.°

Painter. It is a pretty mocking° of the life.　　35
Here is a touch—is't good?

Poet.　　　　　　　　I will say of it,
It tutors nature; artificial strife°
Lives in these touches, livelier than life.

> *Enter certain Senators,* [*who pass over the
> stage and exeunt*].

Painter. How this lord is followed!

Poet. The senators of Athens, happy men!　　40

Painter. Look, moe!°

Poet. You see this confluence, this great flood of visi-
　tors:
I have in this rough work shaped out a man
Whom this beneath world° doth embrace and hug
With amplest entertainment. My free drift　　45
Halts not particularly,° but moves itself
In a wide sea of wax;° no leveled° malice

---

30 **Indifferent** neither good nor bad　31 **standing** dignity, social
status　32 **big** (adverb)　33 **dumbness** silence (as in a dumb show)
34 **interpret** supply words　35 **mocking** imitation　37 **artificial strife**
the striving of art to outdo nature　41 **moe** more　44 **beneath
world** sublunary world (Timon as the moon)　46 **particularly** at
individuals　47 **sea of wax** (either a sea of inspiration as easily
molded as wax—not limited to a mere writing tablet of wax—or
perhaps a waxing sea swelling with inspiration)　47 **leveled** aimed
(at one person)

Infects one comma in the course I hold,
But flies an eagle flight, bold and forth on,
50 Leaving no tract° behind.

Painter. How shall I understand you?

Poet.   I will unbolt to you.
You see how all conditions,° how all minds,
As well of glib and slipp'ry creatures as
Of grave and austere quality, tender down°
55 Their services to Lord Timon. His large fortune,
Upon his good and gracious nature hanging,
Subdues and properties° to his love and tendance°
All sorts of hearts; yea, from the glass-faced°
    flatterer
To Apemantus, that few things loves better
60 Than to abhor himself—even he drops down
The knee before him, and returns in peace
Most rich in Timon's nod.

Painter.   I saw them speak together.

Poet. Sir, I have upon a high and pleasant hill
Feigned° Fortune to be throned. The base o' th'
    mount
65 Is ranked with all deserts,° all kind of natures
That labor on the bosom of this sphere
To propagate their states.° Amongst them all,
Whose eyes are on this sovereign lady fixed,
One do I personate of Lord Timon's frame,°
70 Whom Fortune with her ivory hand° wafts to her,

---

50 **tract** (either "trace" or "track")   52 **conditions** (1) social classes
(2) temperaments   54 **tender down** offer (as one offers money)
57 **properties** appropriates   57 **tendance** attendance   58 **glass-faced**
mirror-faced   64 **Feigned** imagined   65 **deserts** degrees of worth
67 **propagate their states** increase their possessions   69 **frame** (1)
disposition (2) physical stature   70 **ivory hand** hand white and
smooth as ivory (this is the right hand of Fortune, with which she
distributes her favors; with the left or dark hand she takes them
away)

Whose present° grace° to present slaves and ser-
     vants
Translates° his rivals.

Painter.   'Tis conceived to scope.°
This throne, this Fortune, and this hill, methinks,
With one man beckoned from the rest below,
Bowing his head against the steepy mount   *75*
To climb his happiness, would be well expressed
In our condition.

Poet.   Nay, sir, but hear me on.
All those which were his fellows but of late,
Some better than his value, on the moment
Follow his strides, his lobbies fill with tendance,   *80*
Rain sacrificial whisperings° in his ear,
Make sacred even his stirrup, and through him
Drink° the free air.

Painter.   Ay marry,° what of these?

Poet. When Fortune in her shift and change of mood
Spurns down her late beloved, all his dependants   *85*
Which labored after him to the mountain's top,
Even on their knees and hands, let him slip down,
Not one accompanying his declining foot.

Painter. 'Tis common.
A thousand moral paintings° I can show   *90*
That shall demonstrate° these quick° blows of
     Fortune's
More pregnantly than words. Yet you do well
To show Lord Timon that mean° eyes have seen
The foot above the head.°

71 **present** (1) existing now (2) immediate   71 **grace** graciousness,
generosity   72 **Translates** transforms   72 **to scope** to the purpose,
just right 81 **sacrificial whisperings** (lines 81–83 suggest the hieratic
atmosphere surrounding Timon, now high in Fortune's favor)   83
Drink breathe   83 **marry** indeed (originally "By Mary")   90 **moral
paintings** allegorical pictures (especially wall hangings)   91 **demonstrate** (accented on second syllable)   91 **quick** (1) swift (2) full
of life   93 **mean** lowly   94 **The foot above the head** i.e., in the
quick changes that Fortune brings, the foot of the lowliest may
suddenly appear above the head of the highest

Trumpets sound. Enter Lord Timon, addressing him-
self courteously to every suitor; [a Messenger from
Ventidius talking with him; Lucilius and other servants
following].

Timon.　　　　　　　　Imprisoned is he, say you?

95 *Messenger.* Ay, my good lord; five talents° is his debt,
　　His means most short, his creditors most strait.°
　　Your honorable letter he desires
　　To those have shut him up, which failing,
　　Periods° his comfort.

Timon.　　　　　　　Noble Ventidius—well.
100 I am not of that feather° to shake off
　　My friend when he must need me. I do know him
　　A gentleman that well deserves a help,
　　Which he shall have. I'll pay the debt and free him.

Messenger. Your lordship ever binds° him.

105 *Timon.* Commend me to him; I will send his ransom,
　　And being enfranchised bid him come to me.
　　'Tis not enough to help the feeble up,
　　But to support him after. Fare you well.

Messenger. All happiness to your honor.　　　*Exit.*

Enter an Old Athenian.

Old Athenian. Lord Timon, hear me speak.

110 *Timon.*　　　　　　　　Freely, good father.

Old Athenian. Thou hast a servant named Lucilius.

Timon. I have so. What of him?

Old Athenian. Most noble Timon, call the man before
　　thee.

Timon. Attends he here or no? Lucilius!

115 *Lucilius.* Here at your lordship's service.

95 **five talents** (see Introduction, p. xxii)　96 **strait** strict　99 **Periods**
puts an end to　100 **feather** character　104 **binds** attaches by ties of
gratitude (with play on "free" in line 103)

Old Athenian. This fellow° here, Lord Timon, this thy
  creature,°
 By night frequents my house. I am a man
 That from my first have been inclined to thrift,
 And my estate deserves an heir more raised
 Than one which holds a trencher.°

Timon.   Well; what further? *120*

Old Athenian. One only daughter have I, no kin else,
 On whom I may confer what I have got.
 The maid is fair, a° th' youngest for a bride,
 And I have bred her at my dearest cost
 In qualities of the best. This man of thine   *125*
 Attempts her love. I prithee, noble lord,
 Join with me to forbid him her resort;°
 Myself have spoke in vain.

Timon.   The man is honest.

Old Athenian. Therefore he will be,° Timon.
 His honesty rewards him in itself;   *130*
 It must not bear° my daughter.

Timon.   Does she love him?

Old Athenian. She is young and apt.
 Our own precedent° passions do instruct us
 What levity's in youth.

Timon.   Love you the maid?

Lucilius. Ay, my good lord, and she accepts of it. *135*

Old Athenian. If in her marriage my consent be missing,
 I call the gods to witness, I will choose

---

116 **fellow, creature** (terms of contempt) 120 **trencher** wooden
plate or shallow dish on which meat is served (a servant who waits on
tables would hold a trencher) 123 **a** (a worn down form for "of")
127 **her resort** resort or access to her 129 **Therefore he will be** i.e.,
since Lucilius *is* honest (or honorable), he will therefore show his
honesty by not pursuing the Old Athenian's daughter 131 **bear**
carry away 133 **precedent** former (accented on second syllable)

Mine heir from forth the beggars of the world,
And dispossess her all.°

Timon.   How shall she be endowed,
140   If she be mated with an equal° husband?

Old Athenian. Three talents on the present;° in future,
all.

Timon. This gentleman of mine hath served me long.
To build his fortune I will strain a little,
For 'tis a bond° in men. Give him thy daughter;
145   What you bestow, in him I'll counterpoise,°
And make him weigh with her.

Old Athenian.   Most noble lord,
Pawn me to this your honor, she is his.

Timon. My hand to thee, mine honor on my promise.

Lucilius. Humbly I thank your lordship; never may
150   That state or fortune fall into my keeping,
Which is not owed° to you.
                  Exit [Lucilius, with Old Athenian].

Poet. Vouchsafe° my labor, and long live your lordship.

Timon. I thank you; you shall hear from me anon.
Go not away. What have you there, my friend?

155 *Painter.* A piece of painting, which I do beseech
Your lordship to accept.

Timon.   Painting is welcome.
The painting is almost the natural man;
For since dishonor traffics° with man's nature,
He is but outside.° These penciled° figures are

---

139 **all** completely   140 **equal** (either socially or financially)   141 **on
the present** at once   144 **bond** obligation   145 **counterpoise** coun-
terbalance   151 **owed** (1) acknowledged to you as the cause of it (2)
due to you as a debt   152 **Vouchsafe** deign to accept   158 **traffics**
deals (pejorative sense)   159 **but outside** merely external, a false
semblance   159 **penciled** painted

Even such as they give out.° I like your work,   160
And you shall find I like it. Wait attendance
Till you hear further from me.

Painter.   The gods preserve ye.

Timon. Well fare you, gentleman. Give me your hand;
We must needs dine together. Sir, your jewel
Hath suffered under praise.°

Jeweler.   What, my lord, dispraise?   165

Timon. A mere° satiety of commendations.
If I should pay you for't as 'tis extolled,
It would unclew° me quite.

Jeweler.   My lord, 'tis rated
As those which sell would give.° But you well
    know,
Things of like value, differing in the owners,   170
Are prizèd by their masters.° Believe't, dear lord,
You mend° the jewel by the wearing it.

Timon. Well mocked.°

Merchant. No, my good lord; he speaks the common
    tongue°
Which all men speak with him.   175

                Enter Apemantus.

Timon. Look who comes here; will you be chid?

Jeweler. We'll bear with your lordship.

Merchant.   He'll spare none.

---

160 **Even such as they give out** i.e., painting, in contrast with human
nature, is honest; it makes no pretense to be something other than
what it appears to be   165 **under praise** in being praised, since the
jewel is beyond praise (but the Jeweler takes it in the sense of "dispraise")   166 **mere** absolute   168 **unclew** undo   169 **As those
which sell would give** i.e., at the wholesale price   171 **Are prizèd
by their masters** are valued according to the social status of their
owners   172 **mend** improve   173 **mocked** simulated (i.e., I know
your flattery is only part of your sales talk)   174 **speaks the common
tongue** says what everyone is saying

Timon. Good morrow to thee, gentle° Apemantus.

Apemantus. Till I be gentle, stay thou for thy good
    morrow—
180   When thou art Timon's dog, and these knaves
    honest.

Timon. Why dost thou call them knaves, thou know'st
    them not?

Apemantus. Are they not Athenians?

Timon. Yes.

Apemantus. Then I repent not.

185 *Jeweler.* You know me, Apemantus?

Apemantus. Thou know'st I do, I called thee by thy
    name.

Timon. Thou art proud, Apemantus.

Apemantus. Of nothing so much as that I am not like
190   Timon.

Timon. Whither art going?

Apemantus. To knock out an honest Athenian's
    brains.

Timon. That's a deed thou't die for.

195 *Apemantus.* Right, if doing nothing be death by th'
    law.

Timon. How lik'st thou this picture, Apemantus?

Apemantus. The best, for the innocence.°

Timon. Wrought he not well that painted it?

200 *Apemantus.* He wrought better that made the painter,
    and yet he's but a filthy° piece of work.

---

178 **gentle** (1) well-born (a conventional complimentary epithet) (2)
mild   198 **innocence** (1) harmlessness (2) foolishness   201 **filthy**
contemptible

Painter. Y'are a dog.°

Apemantus. Thy mother's of my generation.° What's she, if I be a dog?

Timon. Wilt dine with me, Apemantus?   205

Apemantus. No. I eat not lords.

Timon. And° thou shouldst, thou'dst anger ladies.

Apemantus. O they eat lords; so they come by great bellies.°

Timon. That's a lascivious apprehension.   210

Apemantus. So, thou apprehend'st it, take it for thy labor.

Timon. How dost thou like this jewel, Apemantus?

Apemantus. Not so well as plain-dealing, which will not cost a man a doit.°   215

Timon. What dost thou think 'tis worth?

Apemantus. Not worth my thinking. How now, poet?

Poet. How now, philosopher?

Apemantus. Thou liest.

Poet. Art not one?   220

Apemantus. Yes.

Poet. Then I lie not.

Apemantus. Art not a poet?

Poet. Yes.

---

202 **dog** (Apemantus is a Cynic philosopher; "cynic" is derived from the Greek word for dog)   203 **generation** (1) breed (2) persons born at about the same time   207 **And** if   208–09 **come by great bellies** become pregnant   215 **doit** a small Dutch coin worth less than a farthing (used as a type expression for any very small sum)

225 *Apemantus.* Then thou liest.° Look in thy last work,
where thou hast feigned him° a worthy fellow.

Poet. That's not feigned, he is so.

Apemantus. Yes, he is worthy of thee, and to pay thee
for thy labor. He that loves to be flattered is worthy
230 o' th' flatterer. Heavens, that I were a lord!

Timon. What wouldst do then, Apemantus?

Apemantus. E'en as Apemantus does now: hate a lord
with my heart.

Timon. What, thyself?

235 *Apemantus.* Ay.

Timon. Wherefore?

Apemantus. That I had no angry wit to be a lord.°
Art not thou a merchant?

Merchant. Ay, Apemantus.

240 *Apemantus.* Traffic° confound thee, if the gods will
not.

Merchant. If traffic do it, the gods do it.

Apemantus. Traffic's thy god, and thy god confound
thee.

Trumpet sounds. Enter a Messenger.

245 *Timon.* What trumpet's that?

Messenger. 'Tis Alcibiades and some twenty horse,°
All of companionship.°

Timon. Pray entertain them, give them guide to us.
[Exeunt some Attendants.]
You must needs dine with me. Go not you hence

225 **liest** (a play on the old idea that poetry is a *mimesis*, imitation,
mocking, or feigning of reality and therefore a lie)   226 **him** i.e.,
Timon   237 **no angry wit to be a lord** no more wit in my anger than
to wish to be a lord (?)   240 **Traffic** trade, business   246 **horse**
horsemen   247 **All of companionship** all of the same party

Till I have thanked you. When dinner's done   250
Show me this piece. I am joyful of your sights.°

Enter Alcibiades with the rest.

Most welcome, sir.

Apemantus.   So, so.
Their° aches° contract and starve° your supple
    joints!
That there should be small love amongst these
    sweet knaves,
And all this courtesy! The strain of man's bred out   255
Into baboon and monkey.

Alcibiades. Sir, you have saved° my longing, and I
    feed
Most hungerly on your sight.

Timon.   Right welcome, sir.
Ere we depart, we'll share a bounteous time
In different pleasures. Pray you let us in.   260
           Exeunt [all but Apemantus].

Enter two Lords.

First Lord. What time a day is't, Apemantus?

Apemantus. Time to be honest.

First Lord. That time serves still.°

Apemantus. The most accursèd thou that still omit'st°
    it.   265

Second Lord. Thou art going to Lord Timon's feast?

Apemantus. Ay, to see meat fill knaves and wine heat
    fools.

Second Lord. Fare thee well, fare thee well.

---

251 **of your sights** at the sight of you   253 **Their** i.e., of Alcibiades
and his soldiers   253 **aches** (the reference is probably to venereal
disease—"aches" is dissyllabic, pronounced "aitches")   253 **starve**
destroy   257 **saved** anticipated and so prevented   263 **still** always
264 **omit'st** neglects

270 *Apemantus.* Thou art a fool to bid me farewell twice.

Second Lord. Why, Apemantus?

Apemantus. Shouldst have kept one to thyself, for I
    mean to give thee none.

First Lord. Hang thyself!

275 *Apemantus.* No, I will do nothing at thy bidding.
    Make thy requests to thy friend.

Second Lord. Away, unpeaceable° dog, or I'll spurn
    thee hence.

Apemantus. I will fly like a dog the heels a th' ass.
                                                    [*Exit.*]

First Lord. He's opposite to° humanity. Come, shall
280   we in
    And taste Lord Timon's bounty? He outgoes
    The very heart of kindness.

Second Lord. He pours it out. Plutus, the god of gold,
    Is but his steward; no meed° but he repays
285 Sevenfold above itself. No gift to him
    But breeds the giver a return exceeding
    All use of quittance.°

First Lord.   The noblest mind he carries°
    That ever governed man.

Second Lord.   Long may he live
    In fortunes. Shall we in?

First Lord.   I'll keep you company. *Exeunt.*

---

277 **unpeaceable** quarrelsome   280 **opposite to** (1) hostile to (2) the
reverse of   284 **meed** (1) merit, desert (2) gift (?)   287 **All use of
quittance** all the customary returns made in repayment of debts (one
meaning of "use" is "interest")   287 **carries** bears

[Scene II. *Timon's house.*]

Hautboys° playing loud music. A great banquet served
in; and then enter Lord Timon, the States,° the
Athenian Lords, Ventidius (which Timon redeemed
from prison), [and Alcibiades. Steward and others attending.] Then comes dropping after all, Apemantus,
discontentedly, like himself.

Ventidius. Most honored Timon,
　It hath pleased the gods to remember my father's
　　age,
　And call him to long peace.
　He is gone happy, and has left me rich.
　Then, as in grateful virtue I am bound　　　　　　　5
　To your free° heart, I do return those talents
　Doubled with thanks and service, from whose help
　I derived liberty.

Timon.　　　　　　O by no means,
　Honest Ventidius. You mistake my love;
　I gave it freely ever, and there's none　　　　　　　10
　Can truly say he gives, if he receives.
　If our betters° play at that game, we must not dare
　To imitate them; faults that are rich are fair.°

Ventidius. A noble spirit.

Timon. Nay, my lords, ceremony° was but devised at
　　first　　　　　　　　　　　　　　　　　　　　15
　To set a gloss on faint deeds, hollow welcomes,
　Recanting goodness, sorry ere 'tis shown.

I.ii.s.d. **Hautboys** oboes　　s.d. **the States** persons of state, the Senators
6 **free** generous　12 **our betters** those of higher rank　13 **faults that
are rich are fair** i.e., the faults of rich persons are made to seem
attractive because of their wealth　15 **ceremony** ceremonious attitudes

But where there is true friendship, there needs none.
Pray sit; more welcome are ye to my fortunes
20   Than my fortunes to me.

First Lord. My lord, we always have confessed it.

Apemantus. Ho, ho, confessed it? Hanged it,° have
    you not?

Timon. O Apemantus, you are welcome.

Apemantus. No, you shall not make me welcome.
25   I come to have thee thrust me out of doors.

Timon. Fie, th'art a churl, y'have got a humor° there
    Does not become a man; 'tis much to blame.
    They say, my lords, *Ira furor brevis est,*° but yond
    man is ever angry. Go, let him have a table by
30   himself, for he does neither affect° company, nor is
    he fit for't indeed.

Apemantus. Let me stay at thine apperil,° Timon.
    I come to observe, I give thee warning on't.

Timon. I take no heed of thee. Th'art an Athenian,
35   therefore welcome. I myself would have no power;°
    prithee let my meat make thee silent.

Apemantus. I scorn thy meat; 'twould choke me, for I
    should ne'er flatter thee.° O you gods! What a num-
    ber of men eats Timon, and he sees 'em not! It grieves
40   me to see so many dip their meat in one man's
    blood, and all the madness is, he cheers them up
    too.
    I wonder men dare trust themselves with men.
    Methinks they should invite them without knives:°
45   Good for their meat, and safer for their lives.

22 **confessed it? Hanged it** (an allusion to the proverb "Confess and
be hanged")   26 **humor** temperamental quirk (in the old physiological sense of the four humors)   28 **Ira furor brevis est** anger is
a brief fury or madness (Horace, *Epistles,* I.ii.62)   30 **affect** (1) like
(2) seek out   32 **apperil** peril   35 **no power** i.e., to force you to be
silent   37–38 **'twould … thee** i.e., Apemantus would prefer to choke
on Timon's meat than to flatter him   44 **knives** (dinner guests normally brought their own knives)

There's much example for't; the fellow that sits
next him, now parts bread with him, pledges the
breath of him in a divided draught,° is the readiest
man to kill him. 'T'as been proved. If I were a
huge° man, I should fear to drink at meals,   50
Lest they should spy my windpipe's dangerous
    notes;°
Great men should drink with harness° on their
    throats.

Timon. My lord, in heart;° and let the health go
    round.

Second Lord. Let it flow this way, my good lord.

Apemantus. Flow this way? A brave° fellow. He keeps   55
his tides° well. Those healths will make thee and
thy state° look ill, Timon.
Here's that which is too weak to be a sinner,
Honest water, which ne'er left man i' th' mire.
This and my food are equals, there's no odds;   60
Feasts° are too proud to give thanks to the gods.

Apemantus' Grace.

Immortal gods, I crave no pelf;°
I pray for no man but myself.
Grant I may never prove so fond°
To trust man on his oath or bond,   65
Or a harlot for her weeping,
Or a dog that seems a-sleeping,
Or a keeper° with my freedom,
Or my friends if I should need 'em.
Amen. So fall to't: 70

---

48 **a divided draught** a drink from a cup that is passed around the
table   50 **huge** important   51 **Lest . . . notes** i.e., lest men should
cut my throat when my head is tilted backward (with additional
allusion to the windpipe as a musical instrument, like a bagpipe)
52 **harness** armor   53 **My lord, in heart** (a toast)   55 **brave** excellent
56 **tides** times (with play on the usual sense, linked to "flow")
57 **state** estate, fortune   61 **Feasts** i.e., those who give feasts   62 **pelf**
possessions   64 **fond** foolish   68 **keeper** jailer

Rich men sin, and I eat root.   [*Eats and drinks.*]
Much good dich° thy good heart, Apemantus.

Timon. Captain Alcibiades, your heart's in the field
now.

75 *Alcibiades.* My heart is ever at your service, my lord.

Timon. You had rather be at a breakfast of° enemies
than a dinner of friends.

Alcibiades. So° they were bleeding new, my lord,
there's no meat like 'em; I could wish my best
80   friend at such a feast.

Apemantus. Would all those flatterers were thine enemies then, that then thou mightst kill 'em—and
bid° me to 'em.

First Lord. Might we but have that happiness, my
85   lord, that you would once use our hearts,° whereby
we might express some part of our zeals, we should
think ourselves for ever perfect.°

Timon. O no doubt, my good friends, but the gods
themselves have provided that I shall have much
90   help from you: how had you been my friends else?
Why have you that charitable° title from° thousands, did not you chiefly belong to my heart? I
have told more of you to myself than you can
with modesty speak in your own behalf; and thus
95   far I confirm° you. O you gods, think I, what
need we have any friends, if we should ne'er have
need of 'em? They were the most needless creatures
living should we ne'er have use for 'em, and
would most resemble sweet instruments hung up
100   in cases, that keeps their sounds to themselves.
Why I have often wished myself poorer that I

72 **dich** may it do (?)   76 **of** consisting of (but later in the sentence
it means "with")   78 **So** provided that   83 **bid** invite   85 **use our
hearts** i.e., make trial of the feelings in our hearts   87 **perfect** i.e., in
our happiness in demonstrating our love for Timon   91 **charitable**
loving, kindly   91 **from** from among   95 **confirm** sanction, cor-
roborate (your claims as friends)

might come nearer° to you. We are born to do
benefits; and what better or properer can we call
our own than the riches of our friends? O what a
precious comfort 'tis to have so many like brothers   105
commanding one another's fortunes. O joy's e'en
made away ere't can be born.° Mine eyes cannot
hold out water,° methinks. To forget their faults,°
I drink to you.

Apemantus. Thou weep'st to make them drink,°
Timon.   110

Second Lord. Joy had the like conception° in our eyes,
And at that instant like a babe sprung up.°

Apemantus. Ho, ho! I laugh to think that babe a bastard.

Third Lord. I promise you, my lord, you moved me
much.

Apemantus. Much.   *Sound tucket.*°   115

Timon. What means that trump?

                    Enter Servant.

                                        How now?

Servant. Please you, my lord, there are certain ladies
most desirous of admittance.

Timon. Ladies? What are their wills?

Servant. There comes with them a forerunner, my   120
lord, which bears that office to signify their pleasures.°

102 **nearer** (1) closer to your hearts (2) closer to your financial status
106–07 **e'en . . . born** i.e., our weeping for joy seems to destroy joy
before it properly exists   108 **hold out water** keep out tears   108
faults defects   110 **to make them drink** (1) to provide drink for
them (they drink up your tears, and you and your estate, too) (2) to
furnish a pretext for their carousing   111 **the like conception** a similar birth (i.e., accompanied with tears)   112 **like a babe sprung up**
i.e., the sight of Timon's joy immediately caused the birth of a like
joy in the eyes of his friends   115 s.d. **tucket** a flourish on a trumpet
121–22 **pleasures** wishes

Timon. I pray let them be admitted.

[*Enter Cupid.*]

Cupid. Hail to thee, worthy Timon, and to all
125   That of his bounties taste. The five best senses
    Acknowledge thee their patron, and come freely
    To gratulate° thy plenteous bosom. Th' ear,
    Taste, touch, all, pleased from thy table rise;
    They only now come but to feast thine eyes.°

Timon. They're welcome all; let 'em have kind admit-
130   tance.
    Music° make their welcome.   [*Exit Cupid.*]

First Lord. You see, my lord, how ample y'are be-
    loved.

[*Music.*] *Enter Cupid with the Masque° of Ladies [as]
Amazons,° with lutes in their hands, dancing and
playing.*

Apemantus. Hoy-day!°
    What a sweep° of vanity comes this way.
135   They dance? They are madwomen.
    Like° madness is the glory° of this life,
    As this pomp shows to° a little oil and root.
    We make ourselves fools to disport° ourselves,
    And spend our flatteries to drink° those men
140   Upon whose age we void° it up again
    With poisonous spite and envy.°
    Who lives that's not depravèd or depraves?°
    Who dies that bears not one spurn° to their graves

127 **gratulate** (1) greet (2) gratify, please   129 **but to feast thine eyes**
i.e., only to appeal to the sense of sight, whereas at Timon's banquet
all the senses were gratified   131 **Music** i.e., let music   132 s.d.
Masque an elaborate allegorical show or entertainment with emphasis on spectacle, music, and dance   132 s.d. **Amazons** legendary
female warriors   133 **Hoy-day** (exclamation of surprise)   134 **sweep**
(in reference to the sweeping motion of the dancers)   136 **Like** similar   136 **glory** vainglory   137 **to** compared to   138 **disport** amuse
139 **drink** drink the health of   140 **void** vomit   141 **envy** malice
142 **depravèd or depraves** slandered or a slanderer   143 **spurn** insult

Of their friends' gift?°
I should fear those that dance before me now   145
Would one day stamp upon me. 'T'as been done.
Men shut their doors against a setting sun.

> *The Lords rise from table, with much
> adoring of° Timon, and to show their
> loves, each single out an Amazon, and
> all dance, men with women, a lofty
> strain or two to the hautboys, and cease.*

Timon. You have done our pleasures much grace, fair
    ladies,
Set a fair fashion on° our entertainment,
Which was not half so beautiful and kind.°   150
You have added worth unto't and luster,
And entertained me with mine own device.°
I am to thank you for't.

First Lady. My lord, you take us even at the best.°

Apemantus. Faith, for the worst is filthy, and would 155
    not hold taking,° I doubt me.°

Timon. Ladies, there is an idle banquet° attends you,
    Please you to dispose yourselves.°

All Ladies. Most thankfully, my lord.
                    Exeunt [Cupid and Ladies].

Timon. Flavius.   160

Flavius. My lord.

Timon.   The little casket bring me hither.

Flavius. Yes, my lord. [*Aside*] More jewels yet?

---

144 **gift** giving   147s.d. **adoring of** paying homage to   149 **Set a
fair fashion on** given a pleasant semblance to   150 **kind** gracious
152 **mine own device** (suggests that Timon designed the masque or at
least had the idea for it)   154 **take us even at the best** judge us in the
most favorable and complimentary way   155–56 **would not hold
taking** i.e., sexual "taking" is not possible because of rottenness
caused by venereal disease   156 **doubt me** fear, suspect (reflexive)
157 **idle banquet** trifling dessert or light collation   158 **Please you to
dispose yourselves** if you please to take your places

There is no crossing him in's humor,°
Else I should tell him well, i' faith I should,
When all's spent, he'd be crossed° then, and° he
165   could.
'Tis pity bounty had not eyes behind,
That man might ne'er be wretched for his mind.°
                                                        Exit.

First Lord. Where be our men?

Servant. Here, my lord, in readiness.

170 *Second Lord.* Our horses.

          Enter Flavius [with the casket].

Timon. O my friends,
          I have one word to say to you. Look you, my good
               lord,
          I must entreat you honor me so much
          As to advance° this jewel; accept it and wear it,
175   Kind my lord.

First Lord. I am so far already in your gifts—

All. So are we all.

          Enter a Servant.

Servant. My lord, there are certain nobles of the
          senate newly alighted, and come to visit you.

180 *Timon.* They are fairly° welcome.

Flavius. I beseech your honor, vouchsafe me a word;
          it does concern you near.

Timon. Near? Why then another time I'll hear thee. I
          prithee let's be provided to show them entertain-
185   ment.

Flavius. [*Aside*] I scarce know how.

---

163 **no crossing him in's humor** no thwarting him in his capricious
disposition   165 **crossed** (1) thwarted (2) have his debts canceled
("crossed" off a list) (3) be given money (have his palm "crossed")
165 **and if**   167 **for his mind** for his generous inclinations   174 **advance** enhance in value (by your wearing it)   180 **fairly** courteously

Enter another Servant.

Second Servant. May it please your honor, Lord
   Lucius,
   Out of his free love, hath presented to you
   Four milk-white horses, trapped in silver.°

Timon. I shall accept them fairly. Let the presents   190
   Be worthily entertained.°

Enter a third Servant.

                                   How now? What news?

Third Servant. Please you, my lord, that honorable
   gentleman Lord Lucullus entreats your company
   tomorrow to hunt with him, and has sent your
   honor two brace° of greyhounds.   195

Timon. I'll hunt with him, and let them be received
   Not without fair reward.

Flavius. [*Aside*]   What will this come to?
   He commands us to provide, and give great gifts,
   And all out of an empty coffer;
   Nor will he know his purse, or yield° me this,   200
   To show him what a beggar his heart is,
   Being of no power to make his wishes good.
   His promises fly so beyond his state°
   That what he speaks is all in debt; he owes for
      ev'ry word.
   He is so kind that he now pays interest for't;   205
   His land's put to their books.° Well, would I were
   Gently put out of office before I were forced out.
   Happier is he that has no friend to feed
   Than such that do e'en enemies exceed.°
   I bleed inwardly for my lord.   *Exit.*   210

---

189 **trapped in silver** with harness coverings adorned in silver
191 **worthily entertained** appropriately received   195 **two brace** two
pairs   200 **yield** grant   203 **state** estate, possessions   206 **put to
their books** mortgaged (entered on creditors' account books)
209 **Than such that do e'en enemies exceed** (1) than such a number
that surpasses the number of one's enemies (2) than such sort of
friends whose demands go beyond those of one's enemies

Timon. You do yourselves much wrong,
You bate° too much of your own merits.
Here, my lord, a trifle of our love.

Second Lord. With more than common thanks I will
receive it.

215 *Third Lord.* O he's the very soul of bounty.

Timon. And now I remember, my lord, you gave good
words the other day of a bay courser° I rode on.
'Tis yours because you liked it.

First Lord. O I beseech you pardon me, my lord, in
220 that.°

Timon. You may take my word, my lord, I know no
man can justly praise but what he does affect.° I
weigh° my friend's affection with° mine own. I'll
tell you true, I'll call to you.°

225 *All Lords.* O none so welcome.

Timon. I take all and your several° visitations
So kind to heart, 'tis not enough to give.°
Methinks I could deal° kingdoms to my friends,
And ne'er be weary. Alcibiades,
230 Thou art a soldier, therefore seldom rich;
It° comes in charity to thee, for all thy living°
Is 'mongst the dead, and all the lands thou hast
Lie in a pitched field.°

Alcibiades. Ay, defiled° land, my lord.

235 *First Lord.* We are so virtuously bound—

Timon. And so am I to you.

212 **bate** abate, undervalue   217 **bay courser** reddish-brown stallion
219–20 **in that** in accepting your gift (because I seemed to solicit it)
222 **affect** like, desire to possess   223 **weigh** consider   223 **with**
equal with   223–24 **I'll tell you true, I'll call to you** I assure you I
will call on you   226 **all and your several** the sum total (an inten-
sive form)   227 **'tis not enough to give** i.e., mere gifts, no matter
how great, cannot truly express the feeling in my heart   228 **deal**
distribute   231 **It** what you receive, a gift   231 **living** (1) existence
(2) property (3) livelihood   233 **pitched field** field prepared for a
battle   234 **defiled land** (a quibble on the proverb, "He that toucheth
pitch shall be defiled," *Ecclesiasticus* 13:1)

Second Lord. So infinitely endeared°—

Timon. All to you.° Lights, more lights!

First Lord. The best of happiness, honor, and fortunes
Keep with you, Lord Timon.   240

Timon. Ready for his friends.   *Exeunt Lords.*

Apemantus.   What a coil's° here,
Serving of becks° and jutting out of bums!°
I doubt whether their legs° be worth the sums
That are given for 'em. Friendship's full of dregs;
Methinks false hearts should never have sound
legs.°   245
Thus honest fools lay out their wealth on curtsies.°

Timon. Now Apemantus, if thou wert not sullen,
I would be good to thee.

Apemantus. No, I'll nothing; for if I should be bribed
too, there would be none left to rail upon° thee,   250
and then thou wouldst sin the faster. Thou giv'st so
long, Timon, I fear me thou wilt give away thyself in paper° shortly. What needs these feasts,
pomps, and vainglories?

Timon. Nay, and you begin to rail on society once, I   255
am sworn not to give regard to you. Farewell, and
come with better music.   *Exit.*

Apemantus. So. Thou wilt not hear me now, thou
shalt not then.°
I'll lock thy heaven° from thee.
O that men's ears should be   260
To counsel deaf, but not to flattery.   *Exit.*

---

237 **endeared** indebted   238 **All to you** i.e., I am all of these things
to you rather than vice versa   241 **coil** fuss, bustle, confusion
242 **Serving of becks** offering of nods or curtsies   242 **bums** posteri-
ors   243 **legs** (1) bows (cf. "to make a leg") (2) the limbs themselves
245 **sound legs** i.e., legs healthy enough to make obeisances   246
curtsies (1) bows (2) courtesies (a different spelling of the same word)
250 **rail upon** revile   253 **in paper** i.e., in promissory notes and other
paper records of debts   258 **thou shalt not then** you will not be able
to listen to me later, when you are bankrupt   259 **thy heaven** i.e.,
the advice by which I might have saved you from ruin

[ACT II

Scene I. *A Senator's house.*]

Enter a Senator.

Senator. And late° five thousand. To Varro and to
    Isidore
He owes nine thousand, besides my former sum,
Which makes it five and twenty. Still° in motion
Of raging waste? It cannot hold,° it will not.
5 If I want gold, steal but a beggar's dog
And give it Timon—why the dog coins gold.
If I would sell my horse and buy twenty moe
Better than he—why give my horse to Timon;
Ask nothing, give it him, it foals me straight,°
10 And able horses. No porter° at his gate,
But rather one that smiles, and still invites
All that pass by. It cannot hold; no reason
Can sound his state in safety.° Caphis, ho!
Caphis, I say!

Enter Caphis.

Caphis.　　　　　Here, sir, what is your pleasure?

Senator. Get on your cloak, and haste you to Lord
　　Timon;　　　　　　　　　　　　　　　　　　　15
　Importune him for my moneys; be not ceased
　With slight denial; nor then silenced when
　"Commend me to your master" and the cap
　Plays in the right hand, thus°—but tell him,
　My uses° cry to me; I must serve my turn　　20
　Out of mine own;° his days and times° are past,
　And my reliances on his fracted° dates
　Have smit my credit. I love and honor him,
　But must not break my back to heal his finger.
　Immediate are my needs, and my relief　　　25
　Must not be tossed and turned to me in words,
　But find supply immediate. Get you gone;
　Put on a most importunate aspect,°
　A visage of demand; for I do fear,
　When every feather sticks in his own wing,°　30
　Lord Timon will be left a naked gull,°
　Which flashes now a phoenix.° Get you gone.

Caphis. I go, sir.

Senator. Ay, go sir! Take the bonds along with you,
　And have the dates in.° Come!

Caphis.　　　　　　　　　I will, sir.

Senator.　　　　　　　　　　　　Go!　　35
　　　　　　　　　　　　　　　　Exeunt.

18–19 **"Commend me . . ."** . . . **thus** (examples of anticipated ceremonious delays by Timon) 20 **uses** financial needs 21 **mine own**
i.e., my own money 21 **days and times** due dates of his debts
22 **fracted** broken 28 **aspect** (accented on second syllable) 30
sticks in his own wing is returned to the bird to which it belongs
(i.e., when Timon's debts, and the security he has given for them, are
settled) 31 **gull** (1) unfledged bird (2) credulous dupe 32 **phoenix**
a rare legendary bird which immolated itself and was reborn from
its own ashes; a unique or matchless person 35 **have the dates in**
put in the exact dates when the bonds fall due

[Scene II. *Timon's house.*]

*Enter [Flavius, the] Steward, with many bills in
his hand.*

Flavius. No care, no stop, so senseless of expense
That he will neither know how to maintain it,
Nor cease his flow of riot.° Takes no accompt
How things go from him, nor resumes no care°
5 Of what is to continue. Never mind
Was to be so unwise to be so kind.°
What shall be done he will not hear, till feel.
I must be round° with him, now he comes from
    hunting.
Fie, fie, fie, fie!

*Enter Caphis, [with the Servants of] Isidore
and Varro.*

Caphis. Good even, Varro. What, you come for
10   money?

Varro's Servant. Is't not your business too?

Caphis. It is; and yours too, Isidore?

Isidore's Servant. It is so.

Caphis. Would we were all discharged.°

15 *Varro's Servant.* I fear it.°

Caphis. Here comes the lord.

Enter Timon and his Train, [and Alcibiades].

Timon. So soon as dinner's done, we'll forth again,

II.ii.3 **riot** extravagance, irresponsible reveling **4 resumes no care**
has no concern **6 to be so kind** (1) as to be so generous (2) in order
to be so generous **8 round** blunt **14 discharged** paid (of a debt)
15 I fear it I doubt it

My Alcibiades. [*To Caphis*] With me, what is your
will?

Caphis. My lord, here is a note of certain dues.

Timon. Dues? Whence are you?

Caphis.   Of Athens here, my lord. 20

Timon. Go to my steward.

Caphis. Please it your lordship, he hath put me off
To the succession of new days° this month.
My master is awaked by great occasion
To call upon his own, and humbly prays you 25
That with your other noble parts you'll suit°
In giving him his right.

Timon.   Mine honest friend,
I prithee but repair° to me next morning.

Caphis. Nay, good my lord—

Timon.   Contain thyself, good friend.

Varro's Servant. One Varro's servant, my good lord— 30

Isidore's Servant. From Isidore; he humbly prays
your speedy payment.

Caphis. If you did know, my lord, my master's
wants—

Varro's Servant. 'Twas due on° forfeiture, my lord, 35
six weeks and past.

Isidore's Servant. Your steward puts me off, my lord,
and I am sent expressly to your lordship.

Timon. Give me breath.
I do beseech you, good my lords, keep on;° 40
I'll wait upon you instantly.
                    [*Exeunt Alcibiades and Lords.*]

---

23 **To the succession of new days** from one day to the next 26 **That
. . . suit** i.e., that you will act in accordance with your other noble
qualities 28 **repair** return 35 **on** on penalty of 40 **keep on** go
ahead

[*To Flavius*] Come hither. Pray you,
How goes the world,° that I am thus encount'red
With clamorous demands of broken bonds,
And the detention° of long since due debts
Against my honor?

45 *Flavius.*   Please you, gentlemen,
The time is unagreeable to this business.
Your importunacy° cease till after dinner,
That I may make his lordship understand
Wherefore you are not paid.

50 *Timon.* Do so, my friends. See them well entertained.
                                            Exit.

Flavius. Pray draw near.   [*Exit.*]

            Enter Apemantus and Fool.

Caphis. Stay, stay, here comes the fool with Ape-
      mantus.
    Let's ha' some sport with 'em.

Varro's Servant. Hang him, he'll abuse us.

55 *Isidore's Servant.* A plague upon him, dog!

Varro's Servant. How dost, fool?

Apemantus. Dost dialogue with thy shadow?

Varro's Servant. I speak not to thee.

Apemantus. No, 'tis to thyself. [*To the Fool*] Come
60   away.

Isidore's Servant. [*To Varro's Servant*] There's the
      fool hangs on your back already.

Apemantus. No, thou stand'st single,° th'art not on
      him yet.

65 *Caphis.* Where's the fool now?

Apemantus. He last asked the question. Poor rogues
      and usurers' men, bawds between gold and want.

42 **How goes the world** what is going on   44 **detention** withholding
payment   47 **importunacy** urgent solicitation   63 **single** alone

All Servants. What are we, Apemantus?

Apemantus. Asses.

All Servants. Why?   70

Apemantus. That you ask me what you are, and do
  not know yourselves. Speak to 'em, fool.

Fool. How do you, gentlemen?

All Servants. Gramercies,° good fool. How does your
  mistress?   75

Fool. She's e'en setting on water to scald° such chickens as you are. Would we could see you at
  Corinth.°

Apemantus. Good, gramercy.

Enter Page.

Fool. Look you, here comes my mistress' page.   80

Page. [*To the Fool*] Why, how now, captain? What
  do you in this wise company? How dost thou,
  Apemantus?

Apemantus. Would I had a rod° in my mouth, that
  I might answer thee profitably.°   85

Page. Prithee, Apemantus, read me the superscrip-
  tion° of these letters. I know not which is which.

Apemantus. Canst not read?

Page. No.

Apemantus. There will little learning die then that   90
  day thou art hanged. This is to Lord Timon, this
  to Alcibiades. Go, thou wast born a bastard, and
  thou'lt die a bawd.

74 **Gramercies** thanks   76 **scald** a method of removing feathers from
chickens (with suggestions of loss of hair in venereal disease, and of
sweating in a heated tub, which was one of the treatments of venereal
disease)   78 **Corinth** ancient city noted for licentiousness (hence a
cant term for brothel or red-light district)   84 **rod** stick to beat you
85 **profitably** for your profit or improvement   86–87 **superscription**
address

Page. Thou wast whelped a dog, and thou shalt fam-
95   ish a dog's death.° Answer not, I am gone.   *Exit.*

Apemantus. E'en so thou outrun'st grace.° Fool, I
    will go with you to Lord Timon's.

Fool. Will you leave me there?

Apemantus. If Timon stay at home. You three serve
100   three usurers?

All Servants. Ay; would they served us.

Apemantus. So would I—as good a trick as ever
    hangman served thief.

Fool. Are you three usurers' men?

105 *All Servants.* Ay, fool.

Fool. I think no usurer but has a fool to his servant.
    My mistress is one, and I am her fool. When men
    come to borrow of your masters, they approach
    sadly,° and go away merry; but they enter my
110   mistress' house merrily, and go away sadly. The
    reason of this?

Varro's Servant. I could render one.

Apemantus. Do it then, that we may account thee a
    whoremaster and a knave, which notwithstanding,
115   thou shalt be no less esteemed.

Varro's Servant. What is a whoremaster, fool?

Fool. A fool in good clothes, and something like thee.
    'Tis a spirit; sometime't appears like a lord, some-
    time like a lawyer, sometime like a philosopher,
120   with two stones° moe than's artificial one.° He is
    very often like a knight; and generally, in all shapes

94–95 **famish a dog's death** die by famishing, a mean death appropriate for a dog   96 **E'en so thou outrun'st grace** i.e., by leaving
now and not listening to my profitable answer, you will never receive
grace   109 **sadly** gravely   120 **stones** testicles   120 **artificial one**
philosopher's stone (a highly refined substance which could turn
base metals into gold)

that man goes up and down in, from fourscore to
thirteen, this spirit walks in.

Varro's Servant. Thou are not altogether a fool.

Fool. Nor thou altogether a wise man. As much fool- 125
ery as I have, so much wit thou lack'st.

Apemantus. That answer might have become Apemantus.

    Enter Timon and [Flavius, the] Steward.

All Servants. Aside, aside, here comes Lord Timon.

Apemantus. Come with me, fool, come. 130

Fool. I do not always follow lover, elder brother, and
woman;° sometime the philosopher.

Flavius. Pray you, walk near: I'll speak with you
anon.° *Exeunt [Apemantus, Fool, and Servants].*

Timon. You make me marvel wherefore ere this time
Had you not fully laid my state° before me, 135
That I might so have rated° my expense
As I had leave of means.°

Flavius.   You would not hear me.
At many leisures° I proposed—

Timon.   Go to.°
Perchance some single vantages° you took
When my indisposition° put you back, 140
And that unaptness° made your minister°
Thus to excuse yourself.

Flavius.   O my good lord,
At many times I brought in my accompts,

131–32 **lover, elder brother, and woman** (persons who might be expected to be generous) 133 **anon** soon 135 **state** financial situation
136 **rated** regulated 137 **As I had leave of means** as my means
would allow 138 **At many leisures** i.e., when you were at leisure
138 **Go to** nonsense (an exclamation of impatience) 139 **vantages**
opportunities 140 **indisposition** disinclination 141 **unaptness** un-
readiness to listen 141 **minister** ministration, prompting

Laid them before you; you would throw them off,
145　And say you found them in mine honesty.
When for some trifling present you have bid me
Return so much, I have shook my head and wept;
Yea 'gainst th' authority of manners,° prayed you
To hold your hand more close. I did endure
150　Not seldom, nor no slight checks,° when I have
Prompted° you in the ebb of your estate
And your great flow of debts. My loved lord,
Though you hear now, too late, yet now's a time:
The greatest of your having° lacks a half
To pay your present debts.

155　*Timon.*　　　　　　　　　Let all my land be sold.

Flavius. 'Tis all engaged,° some forfeited and gone,
And what remains will hardly stop the mouth
Of present dues. The future comes apace.°
What shall defend the interim? And at length
160　How goes our reck'ning?

Timon. To Lacedaemon did my land extend.

Flavius. O my good lord, the world is but a word;
Were it all yours to give it in a breath,
How quickly were it gone!

Timon.　　　　　　　　You tell me true.

165　*Flavius.* If you suspect my husbandry or falsehood,°
Call me before th' exactest auditors,
And set me on° the proof. So the gods bless me,
When all our offices° have been oppressed°
With riotous feeders,° when our vaults° have wept
170　With drunken spilth° of wine, when every room
Hath blazed with lights and brayed with minstrelsy,

---

148 **th' authority of manners** the dictates of good manners　150
checks rebukes　151 **Prompted** (in its theatrical sense)　154 **The
greatest of your having** your worth estimated at the highest possible
figure　156 **engaged** mortgaged　158 **apace** swiftly　165 **suspect
my husbandry or falsehood** suspect me of false husbandry or dishonest management　167 **on** to　168 **offices** service rooms of a
household　168 **oppressed** crowded　169 **feeders** servants　169
vaults wine cellars　170 **spilth** spilling

I have retired me to a wasteful cock,°
And set mine eyes at flow.°

Timon.   Prithee no more.

Flavius. Heavens, have I said, the bounty of this lord!
How many prodigal bits° have slaves and peasants   *175*
This night englutted!° Who is not Timon's?
What heart, head, sword, force, means, but is
    Lord Timon's?
Great Timon, noble, worthy, royal Timon!
Ah, when the means are gone that buy this praise,
The breath is gone whereof this praise is made.   *180*
Feast-won, fast-lost;° one cloud of winter show'rs,
These flies are couched.°

Timon.   Come, sermon me no further.
No villainous bounty° yet hath passed my heart;
Unwisely, not ignobly, have I given.
Why dost thou weep? Canst thou the conscience°
    lack   *185*
To think I shall lack friends? Secure° thy heart.
If I would broach the vessels° of my love,
And try the argument° of hearts by borrowing,
Men and men's fortunes could I frankly° use
As I can bid thee speak.

Flavius.   Assurance° bless your thoughts.   *190*

Timon. And in some sort these wants of mine are
    crowned,°
That I account them blessings; for by these

---

172 **wasteful cock** spigot (of a wine cask) that has not been shut off
173 **And set mine eyes at flow** i.e., following the example of the
"wasteful cock," I have added my tears to the general riot and
superfluity   175 **prodigal bits** wasteful morsels   176 **englutted**
gulped down   181 **Feast-won, fast-lost** the friendship that is won by
giving feasts is quickly lost (with pun on "fast" as noun and adverb)
182 **couched** lying hidden   183 **villainous bounty** generosity for evil
purposes   185 **conscience** reasonableness   186 **Secure** make free
from care or apprehension   187 **broach the vessels** tap the casks
188 **try the argument** test the theme or contents   189 **frankly** freely
190 **Assurance** i.e., may assurance   191 **crowned** given a royal dignity

Shall I try friends. You shall perceive how you
Mistake my fortunes; I am wealthy in my friends.
195 Within there! Flaminius! Servilius!

Enter [Flaminius, Servilius, and Third Servant].

Servants. My lord, my lord.

Timon. I will dispatch you severally.° [*To Servilius*]
You to Lord Lucius, [*to Flaminius*] to Lord Lucullus you; I hunted with his honor today. [*To Third
200 Servant*] You to Sempronius. Commend me to their
loves; and I am proud, say, that my occasions°
have found time to use 'em toward a supply of
money. Let the request be fifty talents.

Flaminius. As you have said, my lord.
[*Exeunt Servants.*]

205 *Flavius.* [*Aside*] Lord Lucius and Lucullus? Humh!

Timon. Go you, sir, to the senators,
Of whom, even to the state's best health,° I have
Deserved this hearing. Bid 'em send o' th' instant
A thousand talents to me.

Flavius.   I have been bold,
210 For that I knew it the most general° way,
To them to use your signet° and your name;
But they do shake their heads, and I am here
No richer in return.

Timon.   Is't true? Can't be?

Flavius. They answer in a joint and corporate voice,
215 That now they are at fall,° want treasure, cannot
Do what they would, are sorry; you are honorable,
But yet they could have wished—they know not;
Something hath been amiss—a noble nature

---

197 **severally** separately   201 **occasions** needs   207 **even to the state's best health** i.e., Timon, because of his own generosity to the state in the past, now deserves a loan from them to the very outer-most limit they can pay (?)   210 **general** usual   211 **signet** signet ring (as sign of authority to act)   215 **at fall** at ebb tide

May catch a wrench°—would all were well—'tis
   pity—
And so, intending° other serious matters,   220
After distasteful looks, and these hard fractions,°
With certain half-caps° and cold-moving° nods,
They froze me into silence.

Timon.   You gods reward them!
Prithee man look cheerly. These old fellows
Have their ingratitude in them hereditary.   225
Their blood is caked, 'tis cold, it seldom flows;
'Tis lack of kindly° warmth they are not kind;
And nature, as it grows again toward earth,°
Is fashioned for the journey, dull and heavy.
Go to Ventidius. Prithee be not sad;   230
Thou art true and honest; ingeniously° I speak,
No blame belongs to thee. Ventidius lately
Buried his father, by whose death he's stepped
Into a great estate. When he was poor,
Imprisoned, and in scarcity of friends,   235
I cleared him with five talents. Greet him from me,
Bid him suppose some good necessity°
Touches his friend, which craves to be rememb'red
With those five talents. That had, give't these
   fellows
To whom 'tis instant° due. Nev'r speak or think   240
That Timon's fortunes 'mong° his friends can sink.

Flavius. I would I could not think it; that thought is
   bounty's foe.
Being free° itself, it thinks all others so.   *Exeunt.*

219 **catch a wrench** accidentally be twisted from its natural bent
220 **intending** pretending   221 **hard fractions** harsh fragments of
speech (conveyed in the broken syntax)   222 **half-caps** half-courte-
ous salutations   222 **cold-moving** producing cold, frigid   227 **kindly**
(1) natural (2) generous   228 **grows again toward earth** approaches
death and the grave   231 **ingeniously** ingenuously, candidly   237 **good
necessity** valid need   240 **instant** instantly, immediately   241 **'mong**
in the midst of   243 **free** bounteous

[ACT III

Scene I. *Lucullus' house.*]

*Flaminius waiting to speak with Lord [Lucullus]
from his Master, enters a Servant to him.*

Servant. I have told my lord of you; he is coming
down to you.

Flaminius. I thank you, sir.

Enter Lucullus.

Servant. Here's my lord.

5   **Lucullus.** [*Aside*] One of Lord Timon's men? A gift
I warrant. Why this hits right; I dreamt of a silver
basin and ewer tonight.°—Flaminius, honest Flaminius, you are very respectively° welcome, sir.
Fill me some wine. [*Exit Servant.*] And how does

10   that honorable, complete,° free-hearted gentleman
of Athens, thy very bountiful good lord and master?

Flaminius. His health is well, sir.

III.i.7 **tonight** last night   8 **respectively** respectfully   10 **complete**
fully equipped or endowed, perfect

Lucullus. I am right glad that his health is well, sir.
And what hast thou there under thy cloak, pretty°   15
Flaminius?

Flaminius. Faith, nothing but an empty box, sir,
which in my lord's behalf I come to entreat your
honor to supply;° who, having great and instant
occasion to use fifty talents, hath sent to your lord-   20
ship to furnish him, nothing doubting your present°
assistance therein.

Lucullus. La, la, la, la! "Nothing doubting," says he?
Alas, good lord, a noble gentleman 'tis, if he would
not keep so good a house.° Many a time and often   25
I ha' dined with him, and told him on't, and come
again to supper to him of purpose to have him
spend less, and yet he would embrace no counsel,
take no warning by my coming. Every man has
his fault, and honesty° is his. I ha' told him on't,   30
but I could ne'er get him from't.

Enter Servant, with wine.

Servant. Please your lordship, here is the wine.

Lucullus. Flaminius, I have noted thee always wise.
Here's to thee.

Flaminius. Your lordship speaks your pleasure.°   35

Lucullus. I have observed thee always for a towardly
prompt spirit,° give thee thy due, and one that
knows what belongs to reason; and canst use the
time well, if the time use thee well.° Good parts°
in thee. [*To Servant*] Get you gone, sirrah. [*Exit*   40
Servant.] Draw nearer, honest Flaminius. Thy
lord's a bountiful gentleman, but thou art wise,
and thou know'st well enough, although thou

---

15 **pretty** (vague epithet of praise)   19 **supply** fill   21 **present** immediate   25 **so good a house** such lavish hospitality   30 **honesty**
generosity   35 **speaks your pleasure** is pleased to say so   36–37 **towardly prompt spirit** well-disposed and well-inclined person   39 **if
the time use thee well** if you strike good fortune   39 **parts** qualities

com'st to me, that this is no time to lend money,
45   especially upon bare friendship without security.
Here's three solidares° for thee. Good boy, wink°
at me, and say thou saw'st me not. Fare thee well.

Flaminius. Is't possible the world should so much
differ,°
And we alive that lived?° Fly, damnèd baseness,
50   To him that worships thee.
                              [*Throws back the money.*]

Lucullus. Ha? Now I see thou art a fool, and fit for
thy master.   *Exit.*

Flaminius. May these° add to the number that may
scald° thee.
Let molten coin be thy damnation,°
55   Thou disease of a friend, and not himself.
Has friendship such a faint and milky heart
It turns° in less than two nights? O you gods!
I feel my master's passion.° This slave
Unto his honor° has my lord's meat° in him;
60   Why should it thrive and turn to nutriment
When he is turned to poison?
O may diseases only work upon't,
And when he's sick to death, let not that part of
nature°
Which my lord paid for be of any power
65   To expel sickness, but prolong his hour.°   *Exit.*

---

46 **solidares** (perhaps Shakespeare was referring to the Roman "sol-
idus," which was used in England for a shilling)   46 **wink** shut your
eyes   48 **differ** change   49 **And we alive that lived** i.e., the world
changes so swiftly, it is hard to believe that the same people are still
alive   53 **these** (the rejected coins)   53 **scald** i.e., in hell   54 **thy
damnation** the torment you will suffer in hell (perhaps a reference to
the pouring of molten gold down the throat of Marcus Crassus by
the Parthians, thought of as a punishment in hell for avarice)
57 **turns** curdles   58 **passion** anger, suffering (trisyllabic)   58–59
slave/Unto his honor (ironical: "this man who claims to be so devoted to honor")   59 **meat** food (in general, in contradistinction to
"drink")   63 **that part of nature** i.e., that part of his body nourished
by Timon's food   65 **but prolong his hour** i.e., may he have a lin-
gering death

[Scene II. *A public place.*]

Enter Lucius, with three Strangers.°

Lucius. Who, the Lord Timon? He is my very good
friend and an honorable gentleman.

First Stranger. We know him for no less, though we
are but strangers to him. But I can tell you one
thing, my lord, and which I hear from common   5
rumors: now Lord Timon's happy hours are done
and past, and his estate shrinks from him.

Lucius. Fie, no, do not believe it; he cannot want for
money.

Second Stranger. But believe you this, my lord, that   10
not long ago, one of his men was with the Lord
Lucullus to borrow so many talents,° nay urged
extremely for't, and showed what necessity be-
longed to't, and yet was denied.

Lucius. How?   15

Second Stranger. I tell you, denied, my lord.

Lucius. What a strange case was that! Now before
the gods I am ashamed on't. Denied that honorable
man? There was very little honor showed in't. For
my own part, I must needs confess, I have received   20
some small kindnesses from him, as money, plate,°
jewels, and suchlike trifles, nothing comparing to
his;° yet had he mistook him° and sent to me, I
should ne'er have denied his occasion° so many
talents.   25

III.ii.s.d. **Strangers** foreigners, non-Athenians   12 **so many talents**
(an indefinite number probably intended to be replaced, in revision,
by a definite number)   21 **plate** utensils for domestic use, especially
of gold or silver   23 **his** i.e., Lucullus'   23 **mistook him** made a
mistake   24 **occasion** need

Enter Servilius.

Servilius. See, by good hap, yonder's my lord; I have
sweat to see his honor. My honored lord.

Lucius. Servilius? You are kindly met, sir. Fare thee
well; commend me to thy honorable virtuous lord,
30   my very exquisite friend.

Servilius. May it please your honor, my lord hath
sent—

Lucius. Ha? What has he sent? I am so much en-
deared° to that lord; he's ever sending. How shall
35   I thank him, think'st thou? And what has he sent
now?

Servilius. Has only sent his present occasion now, my
lord, requesting your lordship to supply his instant
use with so many talents.

40   *Lucius.* I know his lordship is but merry with me,
He cannot want° fifty five hundred talents.°

Servilius. But in the meantime he wants less, my lord.
If his occasion were not virtuous,
I should not urge it half so faithfully.

45   *Lucius.* Dost thou speak seriously, Servilius?

Servilius. Upon my soul 'tis true, sir.

Lucius. What a wicked beast was I to disfurnish myself against° such a good time, when I might ha'
shown   myself   honorable!   How   unluckily   it
50   happ'ned that I should purchase the day before for
a little part,° and undo a great deal of honor!°
Servilius, now before the gods I am not able to
do—the more beast, I say! I was sending to use

33–34 **endeared** indebted   41 **want** (1) be without, lack (2) need,
desire   41 **fifty five hundred talents** a huge sum (see Introduction,
p. xxii)   47–48 **disfurnish myself against** to allow myself to be un-
provided for   50–51 **for a little part** for a little business transaction
(deliberately vague)   51 **undo a great deal of honor** i.e., lose the
anticipated honor of lending to Timon

Lord Timon myself, these gentlemen can witness;
but I would not for the wealth of Athens I had　55
done't now. Commend me bountifully to his good
lordship, and I hope his honor will conceive the
fairest° of me, because I have no power to be kind.
And tell him this from me, I count it one of my
greatest afflictions, say, that I cannot pleasure such　60
an honorable gentleman. Good Servilius, will you
befriend me so far as to use mine own words to
him?

Servilius. Yes, sir, I shall.

Lucius. I'll look you out a good turn, Servilius.　65
　　　　　　　　　　　　　　　Exit Servilius.
True, as you said, Timon is shrunk indeed,
And he that's once denied will hardly speed.°　*Exit.*

First Stranger. Do you observe this, Hostilius?

Second Stranger.　　　　　　　　　　Ay, too well.

First Stranger. Why this is the world's soul, and just
　of the same piece°
Is every flatterer's sport.° Who can call him his
　friend　　　　　　　　　　　　　　　　　　　70
That dips in the same dish? For in my knowing
Timon has been this lord's father,
And kept his° credit with his° purse;
Supported his estate; nay, Timon's money
Has paid his men their wages. He ne'er drinks　75
But Timon's silver treads° upon his lip,
And yet—O see the monstrousness of man
When he looks out in an ungrateful shape°—
He does deny him, in respect of his,°
What charitable men afford to beggars.　　　80

Third Stranger. Religion groans at it.

57–58 **conceive the fairest** think the best　67 **speed** be successful,
prosper　69 **piece** sort, kind　70 **sport** mockery, diversion (as Lucius
has just made sport of Timon)　73 **kept his** sustained Lucius'
73 **his** i.e., Timon's　76 **treads** presses　78 **shape** form　79 **in respect of his** in relation to what Lucius is worth

First Stranger.   For mine own part,
   I never tasted° Timon in my life,
   Nor came any of his bounties over me
   To mark me for his friend. Yet I protest,
85   For his right° noble mind, illustrious virtue,
   And honorable carriage,°
   Had his necessity made use of me,
   I would have put my wealth into donation,°
   And the best half should have returned° to him,
90   So much I love his heart. But I perceive
   Men must learn now with pity to dispense,
   For policy° sits above conscience.   *Exeunt.*

[Scene III. *Sempronius' house.*]

*Enter a Third Servant [of Timon] with
Sempronius, another of Timon's friends.*

Sempronius. Must he needs trouble me in't—humh!—
   'bove all others?
   He might have tried Lord Lucius or Lucullus,
   And now Ventidius is wealthy too,
   Whom he redeemed from prison. All these
   Owes their estates unto him.

5 *Third Servant.*   My lord,
   They have all been touched° and found base metal,
   For they have all denied him.

Sempronius.   How? Have they denied him?
   Has Ventidius and Lucullus denied him,
   And does he send to me? Three? Humh!
10   It shows but little love or judgment in him.

82 **tasted** experienced the qualities of 85 **right** very 86 **carriage**
moral conduct 88 **put my wealth into donation** i.e., treated my
fortune as a gift from Timon 89 **returned** been given back 92 **policy** cunning III.iii.6 **touched** tested (by being rubbed on a touchstone; unlike base metals, gold and silver produced the proper
colored streak)

Must I be his last refuge? His friends, like physi-
cians,
Thrive, give him over.° Must I take th' cure upon
me?
Has much disgraced me in't; I'm angry at him
That might have known my place.° I see no sense
for't,
But his occasions° might have wooed me first;   15
For, in my conscience, I was the first man
That e'er received gift from him.
And does he think so backwardly° of me now
That I'll requite it last? No.
So it may prove an argument° of laughter   20
To th' rest, and I 'mongst lords be thought a fool.
I'd rather than the worth of thrice the sum,
Had° sent to me first, but for my mind's sake;°
I'd such a courage° to do him good. But now re-
turn,
And with their faint reply this answer join: 25
Who bates° mine honor shall not know my coin.
                                             Exit.

Third Servant. Excellent. Your lordship's a goodly
villain. The devil knew not what he did when he
made man politic;° he crossed himself by't:° and
I cannot think but in the end the villainies of   30
man will set him clear.° How fairly° this lord
strives to appear foul!° Takes virtuous copies to be
wicked.° Like those° that under hot ardent zeal

---

12 **Thrive, give him over** i.e., prosper on his money while they are
giving him up for dead (?)   14 **my place** i.e., before Lucullus, Lucius,
and Ventidius   15 **occasions** needs   18 **backwardly** (1) poorly (2)
near the end, late   20 **argument** occasion, subject   23 **Had** i.e., he
had (perhaps "H'ad"?)   23 **but for my mind's sake** if only to express
my good will towards him   24 **courage** desire   26 **bates** abates,
undervalues   29 **politic** cunning   29 **he crossed himself by't** i.e.,
the devil thwarted his own purposes by making man his rival in
shrewdness and guile   31 **will set him clear** will make the devil appear innocent (when compared with the "villainies of man")   31
How fairly with what a beautiful appearance   32 **foul** ugly   32–33
Takes virtuous copies to be wicked i.e., models himself on exemplars
of virtue to serve as disguise for his wickedness   33 **those** i.e., religious fanatics (perhaps "zeal" suggests an allusion to Puritans)

would set whole realms on fire, of such a nature is
35 his politic love.
This was my lord's best hope; now all are fled
Save only the gods. Now his friends are dead,
Doors that were ne'er acquainted with their wards°
Many a bounteous year, must be employed
40 Now to guard sure° their master.
And this is all a liberal° course allows;
Who cannot keep his wealth must keep his house.°
Exit.

[Scene IV. *Timon's house.*]

*Enter Varro's [two Servants], meeting others. All
[the Servants of] Timon's creditors to wait for
his coming out. Then enter [the Servant of]
Lucius; [then Titus] and Hortensius.*

Varro's First Servant. Well met; good morrow, Titus
and Hortensius.

Titus. The like to you, kind Varro.

Hortensius.   Lucius!
What, do we meet together?

Lucius' Servant.   Ay, and I think
One business does command us all;
For mine is money.

5 *Titus.*   So is theirs and ours.

Enter Philotus.

Lucius' Servant. And, sir, Philotus' too!

Philotus.   Good day at once.°

38 **wards** locks   40 **sure** securely   41 **liberal** generous   42 **keep his
house** remain at home (for fear of being arrested for debt)   III.iv.6
at once to you all

Lucius' Servant. Welcome, good brother. What do
   you think the hour?

Philotus. Laboring for nine.

Lucius' Servant. So much?

Philotus.   Is not my lord seen yet?

Lucius' Servant.   Not yet.

Philotus. I wonder on't; he was wont to shine at seven.   10

Lucius' Servant. Ay, but the days are waxed° shorter
   with him.
  You must consider that a prodigal course
  Is like the sun's,
  But not like his recoverable,° I fear.
  'Tis deepest winter in Lord Timon's purse;   15
  That is, one may reach deep enough and yet
  Find little.

Philotus.   I am of your fear for that.

Titus. I'll show you how t' observe° a strange event.
  Your lord sends now for money?

Hortensius.   Most true, he does.

Titus. And he wears jewels now of Timon's gift,   20
  For which I wait for money.

Hortensius. It is against my heart.°

Lucius' Servant.   Mark how strange it shows,
  Timon in this should pay more than he owes;°
  And e'en as if your lord should wear rich jewels
  And send for money for 'em.   25

Hortensius. I'm weary of this charge,° the gods can
  witness.

---

11 **waxed** grown   12–14 **prodigal course . . . recoverable** i.e., the
prodigal, like the sun, declines, but cannot renew himself every
day   18 **observe** observe and interpret   22 **against my heart** contrary to my natural feeling   23 **should pay more than he owes** i.e.,
he has given the gifts, and now he is also asked for the money for
them   26 **charge** task

I know my lord hath spent of Timon's wealth,
And now ingratitude makes it worse than stealth.°

Varro's First Servant. Yes, mine's three thousand
crowns. What's yours?

30 *Lucius' Servant.* Five thousand mine.

Varro's First Servant. 'Tis much deep, and it should
seem by th' sum
Your master's confidence° was above mine,°
Else surely his had equaled.

Enter Flaminius.

Titus. One of Lord Timon's men.

35 *Lucius' Servant.* Flaminius? Sir, a word. Pray is my
lord ready to come forth?

Flaminius. No, indeed he is not.

Titus. We attend his lordship; pray signify so much.

Flaminius. I need not tell him that; he knows you are
40   too diligent.   [*Exit.*]

*Enter [Flavius, the] Steward, in a cloak,
muffled.°*

Lucius' Servant. Ha! Is not that his steward muffled
so?
He goes away in a cloud.° Call him, call him.

Titus. Do you hear, sir?

Varro's Second Servant. By your leave, sir.

45 *Flavius.* What do ye ask of me, my friend?

Titus. We wait for certain money here, sir.

Flavius.   Ay,
If money were as certain as your waiting,

---

28 **stealth** stealing   32 **confidence** trust   32 **mine** i.e., my master's
40 s.d. **muffled** wrapped up, especially about the face   42 **in a cloud**
(1) in a state of gloominess and concern (2) covered with a cloud
because he is muffled

'Twere sure enough.
Why then preferred° you not your sums and bills
When your false masters ate of my lord's meat?   50
Then they could smile, and fawn upon° his debts,
And take down th' int'rest° into their glutt'nous
    maws.
You do yourselves but wrong to stir me up;
Let me pass quietly.
Believe't, my lord and I have made an end;   55
I have no more to reckon,° he to spend.

Lucius' Servant. Ay, but this answer will not serve.

Flavius. If 'twill not serve, 'tis not so base as you,
For you serve knaves.   [*Exit.*]

Varro's First Servant. How? What does his cashiered°
    worship mutter?   60

Varro's Second Servant. No matter what; he's poor,
and that's revenge enough. Who can speak
broader° than he that has no house to put his head
in? Such may rail against great buildings.

Enter Servilius.

Titus. O here's Servilius. Now we shall know some   65
answer.

Servilius. If I might beseech you, gentlemen, to re-
pair° some other hour, I should derive much
from't. For take't of my soul,° my lord leans won-
drously to discontent. His comfortable° temper has   70
forsook him, he's much out of health, and keeps
his chamber.

Lucius' Servant. Many do keep their chambers are
not sick;

49 **preferred** proffered, presented   51 **fawn upon** seek favor by
servility (used especially of dogs)   52 **th' int'rest** i.e., what they
ate was equivalent to the interest due on the money owed them
by Timon   56 **reckon** keep account of   60 **cashiered** dismissed
from employment   63 **broader** more critically   67–68 **repair**
come   69 **tak't of my soul** take it from my heart (i.e., sincere-
ly)   70 **comfortable** cheerful

And if it be so far beyond his health,
75 Methinks he should the sooner pay his debts,
And make a clear° way to the gods.

Servilius.   Good gods!

Titus. We cannot take this for answer, sir.

Flaminius. (*Within*) Servilius, help! My lord, my lord!

     Enter Timon in a rage.

Timon. What, are my doors opposed against my
  passage?
80 Have I been ever free,° and must my house
Be my retentive° enemy? My jail?
The place which I have feasted,° does it now,
Like all mankind, show me an iron heart?

Lucius' Servant. Put in° now, Titus.

85 *Titus.* My lord, here is my bill.

Lucius' Servant. Here's mine.

Hortensius. And mine, my lord.

Both Varro's Servants. And ours, my lord.

Philotus. All our bills.

Timon. Knock me down with 'em, cleave me to the
90 girdle.°

Lucius' Servant. Alas, my lord—

Timon. Cut my heart in sums.°

Titus. Mine, fifty talents.

---

76 **clear** (1) free from debt (2) innocent, unstained (because he has paid his debts) (3) untrammeled, without the obstacle of debts 80 **free** (1) generous (2) unrestrained 81 **retentive** confining 82 **The place which I have feasted** i.e., the house itself in which I have given feasts 84 **Put in** i.e., put in your claim for money 90 **Knock ... girdle** (Timon chooses to understand "bills" not as "accounts of money due," but as "weapons"—a bill had a long wooden handle with a blade or ax-shaped head at one end, and it was capable of cutting a man through to the belt) 92 **in sums** into sums of money

Timon. Tell out° my blood.

Lucius' Servant. Five thousand crowns, my lord.   *95*

Timon. Five thousand drops pays that. What yours?
    And yours?

Varro's First Servant. My lord—

Varro's Second Servant. My lord—

Timon. Tear me, take me, and the gods fall upon you.
                              Exit Timon.

Hortensius. Faith, I perceive our masters may throw   *100*
    their caps at their money;° these debts may well be
    called desperate° ones, for a madman owes 'em.
                              Exeunt.

              Enter Timon [and Flavius].

Timon. They have e'en put my breath from me,° the
    slaves.
    Creditors? Devils!

Flavius. My dear lord—   *105*

Timon. What if it should be so?

Flavius. My lord—

Timon. I'll have it so. My steward!

Flavius. Here, my lord.

Timon. So fitly?° Go, bid° all my friends again,   *110*
    Lucius, Lucullus, and Sempronius—all.
    I'll once more feast the rascals.

Flavius.   O my lord,
    You only speak from your distracted soul;
    There's not so much left to furnish out
    A moderate table.

94 **Tell out** count out   100–01 **may throw . . . money** may give up
their money for lost   102 **desperate** beyond hope of recovery (cf.
"sperate," recoverable)   103 **put my breath from me** put me out of
breath   110 **fitly** conveniently   110 **bid** invite

115 Timon.   Be it not in thy care.°
        Go, I charge thee, invite them all, let in the tide
        Of knaves once more; my cook and I'll provide.
                                        Exeunt.

[Scene V. *The Senate House.*]

*Enter three Senators at one door, Alcibiades meeting
                them with Attendants.*

First Senator. My lord, you have my voice° to't. The
        fault's
    Bloody; 'tis necessary he should die.
    Nothing emboldens sin so much as mercy.

Second Senator. Most true; the law shall bruise 'em.°

Alcibiades. Honor, health, and compassion to the
5   senate.

First Senator. Now, captain?

Alcibiades. I am an humble suitor to your virtues;
    For pity is the virtue° of the law,
    And none but tyrants use it cruelly.
10   It pleases time and fortune to lie heavy
    Upon a friend of mine, who in hot blood
    Hath stepped into the law;° which is past depth°
    To those that, without heed, do plunge into't.
    He is a man, setting his fate° aside,
15   Of comely virtues;
    Nor did he soil the fact° with cowardice
    (An honor in him which buys out° his fault),

115 **Be it not in thy care** i.e., let the feast be my concern   III.v.1
voice vote   4 **bruise 'em** crush them (possibly sinners or wrongdoers
in general?)   8 **virtue** characteristic excellence   12 **stepped into the
law** done something to bring him within the jurisdiction of the law
12 **past depth** beyond any measurable depth   14 **his fate** i.e., this one
fateful action of his   16 **soil the fact** sully the deed   17 **buys out**
redeems

But with a noble fury and fair° spirit,
Seeing his reputation touched to death,
He did oppose his foe;   20
And with such sober and unnoted° passion
He did behove° his anger, ere 'twas spent,
As if he had but proved an argument.°

First Senator. You undergo too strict a paradox,°
Striving to make an ugly deed look fair.   25
Your words have took such pains as if they labored
To bring manslaughter into form,° and set
Quarreling upon the head of valor, which indeed
Is valor misbegot, and came into the world
When sects and factions° were newly born.   30
He's truly valiant that can wisely suffer
The worst that man can breathe,°
And make his wrongs his outsides,°
To wear them like his raiment, carelessly,
And ne'er prefer° his injuries to his heart,   35
To bring it into danger.
If wrongs be evils and enforce us kill,
What folly 'tis to hazard life for ill.

Alcibiades. My lord—

First Senator. You cannot make gross sins look clear.°
To revenge is no valor, but to bear.°   40

Alcibiades. My lords, then, under favor,° pardon me,
If I speak like a captain.
Why do fond° men expose themselves to battle,
And not endure all threats? Sleep upon't,

18 **fair** excellent   21 **unnoted** not notable, i.e., calm   22 **behove** control   23 **argument** i.e., a *point d'honneur* rather than a personal passion   24 **undergo too strict a paradox** i.e., attempt to argue a position that is excessively paradoxical   27 **form** i.e., a legal and acceptable form   30 **factions** (trisyllabic)   32 **breathe** utter   33 **outsides** mere externals   35 **prefer** present   39 **clear** innocent   40 **bear** tolerate (our wrongs)   41 **under favor** by your leave (a formula of politeness)   43 **fond** foolish

45   And let the foes quietly cut their throats
     Without repugnancy?° If there be
     Such valor in the bearing, what make we
     Abroad?° Why then, women are more valiant
     That stay at home, if bearing° carry it,°
50   And the ass more captain than the lion, the fellow
     Loaden with irons wiser than the judge,
     If wisdom be in suffering. O my lords,
     As you are great, be pitifully good.°
     Who cannot condemn rashness in cold blood?
55   To kill, I grant, is sin's extremest gust,°
     But in defense, by mercy,° 'tis most just.
     To be in anger is impiety;
     But who is man that is not angry?
     Weigh but the crime with this.

Second Senator. You breathe in vain.

60   *Alcibiades.*   In vain? His service done
     At Lacedaemon and Byzantium
     Were a sufficient briber for his life.

First Senator. What's that?

     Alcibiades.   Why say,° my lords, h'as
     done fair service,
     And slain in fight many of your enemies.
65   How full of valor did he bear himself
     In the last conflict, and made plenteous wounds!

Second Senator. He has made too much plenty with
     'em.
     He's a sworn rioter;° he has a sin° that often
     Drowns him and takes his valor prisoner.
70   If there were no foes, that were enough
     To overcome him. In that beastly fury
     He has been known to commit outrages,

46 **repugnancy** resistance, fighting back   48 **Abroad** i.e., away from
home, at battle   49 **bearing** (1) enduring of wrongs (2) childbearing
(3) bearing of men in sexual intercourse   49 **carry it** win the day
53 **be pitifully good** i.e., be good in showing pity   55 **gust** (1) taste,
relish (2) strong wind or storm   56 **by mercy** in a merciful interpretation   63 **say** let us say, let us admit   68 **rioter** debauchee   68 **sin**
i.e., drunkenness

And cherish factions.° 'Tis inferred° to us
His days are foul and his drink dangerous.

First Senator. He dies.

Alcibiades.   Hard fate. He might have died
    in war.   75
My lords, if not for any parts° in him—
Though his right arm might purchase his own time,°
And be in debt to none—yet, more to move you,
Take my deserts to his, and join 'em both.
And for I know your reverend ages love   80
Security,° I'll pawn my victories, all
My honor to you, upon his good returns.°
If by this crime he owes the law his life,
Why, let the war receive't in valiant gore,
For law is strict, and war is nothing more.   85

First Senator. We are for law. He dies. Urge it no
    more,
On height of our displeasure. Friend or brother,
He forfeits his own blood that spills another.

Alcibiades. Must it be so? It must not be.
My lords, I do beseech you know me.

Second Senator.   How?   90

Alcibiades. Call me to your remembrances.

Third Senator.   What?

Alcibiades. I cannot think but your age° has forgot
    me;
It could not else be I should prove so base
To sue° and be denied such common grace.
My wounds ache at you.

First Senator.   Do you dare our anger?   95
'Tis in few words, but spacious in effect:
We banish thee for ever.

73 **cherish factions** foster dissension   73 **inferred** reported   76
parts good qualities   77 **his own time** i.e., his proper time to
die   81 **Security** (1) safety, freedom from care or apprehension
(2) collateral for a debt   82 **good returns** profit on an invest-
ment   92 **your age** i.e., you, because of your age   94 **To sue**
to beg

Alcibiades.   Banish me?
    Banish your dotage, banish usury,
    That makes the senate ugly.

First Senator. If after two days' shine Athens contain
100   thee,
    Attend our weightier judgment.° And, not to swell
      our spirit,°
    He shall be executed presently.°
                    Exeunt [Senators].

Alcibiades. Now the gods keep you old enough, that
      you may live
    Only in bone,° that none may look on you.
105 I'm worse than mad. I have kept back their foes,
    While they have told° their money, and let out
    Their coin upon large interest, I myself
    Rich only in large hurts. All those, for this?
    Is this the balsam° that the usuring Senate
110 Pours into captains' wounds? Banishment!
    It comes not ill. I hate not to be banished;
    It is a cause worthy my spleen° and fury,
    That I may strike at Athens. I'll cheer up
    My discontented troops and lay for hearts.°
115 'Tis honor with most lands to be at odds;
    Soldiers should brook° as little wrongs as gods.
                              Exit.

---

101 Attend our weightier judgment expect a more severe sentence
from us   **101 not to swell our spirit** not to allow our anger any further scope   **102 presently** at once   **104 Only in bone** i.e., be mere
hideous skeletons   **106 told** counted   **109 balsam** balm   **112 spleen**
malice, passionate hatred   **114 lay for hearts** i.e., try to win their
hearts to my cause (or, possibly, try to win the hearts of new followers)   **116 brook** endure

[Scene VI. *A banqueting hall in Timon's house.*

Music. Tables set out, Servants attending.] *Enter divers Friends* [*of Timon*] *at several doors.*

First Lord. The good time of day to you, sir.

Second Lord. I also wish it to you. I think this honorable lord did but try us this other day.

First Lord. Upon that were my thoughts tiring° when we encount'red. I hope it is not so low with him as   *5*
he made it seem in the trial of his several friends.

Second Lord. It should not be, by the persuasion of°
his new feasting.

First Lord. I should think so. He hath sent me an earnest inviting, which many my near occasions°   *10*
did urge me to put off; but he hath conjured me beyond them, and I must needs appear.

Second Lord. In like manner was I in debt to my importunate business, but he would not hear my excuse. I am sorry, when he sent to borrow of me,   *15*
that my provision° was out.

First Lord. I am sick of that grief too, as I understand how all things go.°

Second Lord. Every man here's so. What would he have borrowed of you?   *20*

III.vi.4 **tiring** feeding (especially, to tear flesh in feeding as does a bird of prey)   7 **by the persuasion of** on the evidence of   10 **many my near occasions** my many pressing social obligations   16 **provision** supply (of money)   17–18 **as I . . . go** i.e., on the evidence of his "new feasting," things seem to be picking up again with Timon

First Lord. A thousand pieces.°

Second Lord. A thousand pieces?

First Lord. What of you?

Second Lord. He sent to me, sir—

Enter Timon and Attendants.

Here he comes.

25 *Timon.* With all my heart, gentlemen both; and how
fare you?

First Lord. Ever at the best, hearing well of your lordship.

Second Lord. The swallow° follows not summer more
30   willing than we your lordship.

Timon. [*Aside*] Nor more willingly leaves winter, such
summer birds are men.— Gentlemen, our dinner
will not recompense this long stay. Feast your ears
with the music awhile, if they will fare so harshly°
35   o' th' trumpet's sound; we shall to't presently.°

First Lord. I hope it remains not unkindly with your
lordship that I returned you an empty messenger.

Timon. O sir, let it not trouble you.

Second Lord. My noble lord—

40 *Timon.* Ah my good friend, what cheer?

Second Lord. My most honorable lord, I am e'en sick
of shame that when your lordship this other day
sent to me, I was so unfortunate a beggar.

Timon. Think not on't, sir.

45 *Second Lord.* If you had sent but two hours before—

21 **pieces** gold coins worth about a pound (but probably used vaguely)
29 **swallow** (cf. the proverb: "Swallows, like false friends, fly away
upon the approach of winter") 34 **fare so harshly** feed on such
rough food   35 **we shall to't presently** we shall sit down to eat immediately

Timon. Let it not cumber your better remembrance.°
                    The banquet brought in.
Come, bring in all together.

Second Lord. All covered dishes.°

First Lord. Royal cheer,° I warrant you.

Third Lord. Doubt not that, if money and the season   50
can yield it.

First Lord. How do you? What's the news?

Third Lord. Alcibiades is banished. Hear you of it?

First and Second Lords. Alcibiades banished?

Third Lord. 'Tis so, be sure of it.   55

First Lord. How? How?

Second Lord. I pray you upon what?°

Timon. My worthy friends, will you draw near?

Third Lord. I'll tell you more anon.° Here's a noble
feast toward.°   60

Second Lord. This is the old man still.°

Third Lord. Will't hold?° Will't hold?

Second Lord. It does; but time will°—and so—

Third Lord. I do conceive.°

Timon. Each man to his stool, with that spur° as he   65
would to the lip of his mistress. Your diet° shall be
in all places alike.° Make not a city feast° of it, to

---

46 **cumber your better remembrance** burden your good memory
48 **covered dishes** (signifies food of high quality)   49 **Royal cheer**
i.e., food fit for a king   57 **upon what** for what cause   59 **anon**
soon   60 **toward** forthcoming   61 **still** ever, without change   62
Will't hold will it last   63 **time will** (presumably a platitude such
as "time will alter all things")   64 **conceive** understand   65 **spur**
spurring, speed   66 **diet** food   67 **in all places alike** the same at all
places of the table (i.e., no need for seating according to rank)   67
city feast a formal London banquet (London is the "City")

let the meat cool ere we can agree upon the first
place. Sit, sit. The gods require our thanks.

70   You great benefactors, sprinkle our society with
thankfulness. For your own gifts, make yourselves
praised. But reserve° still to give, lest your deities
be despised. Lend to each man enough that one
need not lend to another; for were your godheads to
75   borrow of men, men would forsake the gods. Make
the meat be beloved more than the man that gives
it. Let no assembly of twenty be without a score of
villains. If there sit twelve women at the table, let
a dozen of them be as they are. The rest of your
80   fees,° O gods—the senators of Athens, together
with the common leg° of people—what is amiss in
them, you gods, make suitable for destruction. For
these my present friends, as they are to me nothing,
so in nothing bless them, and to nothing are they
85   welcome.
Uncover, dogs, and lap.

> [*The dishes are uncovered
> and seen to be full of water.*]

Some speak. What does his lordship mean?

Some other. I know not.

Timon. May you a better feast never behold,
90   You knot of mouth-friends.° Smoke° and lukewarm
water
Is your perfection.° This is Timon's last,
Who, stuck and spangled° with your flatteries,
Washes it off and sprinkles in your faces
Your reeking° villainy.   [*Throws the water
                                 in their faces.*]
Live loathed and long,

72 **reserve** i.e., keep something in reserve   80 **fees** property, possessions   81 **leg** limb (as a literal part of the body politic)   90 **knot of
mouth-friends** pack of (1) friends merely in speech (2) friends won
through feeding, "trencher-friends"   90 **Smoke** (1) insubstantiality
(2) mere talk   91 **perfection** highest excellence (?) perfect likeness of
you (?)   92 **stuck and spangled** bespattered and tricked out (as if
with spangles)   94 **reeking** giving off smoke or fumes, stinking

Most smiling, smooth,° detested parasites,   95
Courteous destroyers, affable wolves, meek bears,
You fools of fortune, trencher-friends, time's flies,
Cap-and-knee slaves, vapors, and minute-jacks.°
Of man and beast the infinite° malady
Crust you quite o'er. What, dost thou go?   100
Soft, take thy physic° first; thou too, and thou.
Stay, I will lend thee money, borrow° none.
                              [*Drives them out.*]
What? All in motion? Henceforth be no feast,
Whereat a villain's not a welcome guest.
Burn house, sink Athens, henceforth hated be   105
Of° Timon man and all humanity.   *Exit.*

Enter the Senators, with other Lords.

First Lord. How now, my lords?

Second Lord. Know you the quality of Lord Timon's
    fury?

Third Lord. Push,° did you see my cap?   110

Fourth Lord. I have lost my gown.

First Lord. He's but a mad lord, and naught but
    humors° sways him. He gave me a jewel th' other
    day, and now he has beat it out of my hat. Did
    you see my jewel?   115

Third Lord. Did you see my cap?

Second Lord. Here 'tis.

Fourth Lord. Here lies my gown.

First Lord. Let's make no stay.

95 **smooth** flattering   97-98 **You fools . . . minute-jacks** you dupes
of fortune, friends won by feeding, insects that appear only in fair
weather, servile slaves always kneeling or removing caps in deference,
insubstantial creatures, and figures who strike the bell of a clock
(i.e., opportunistic persons)   99 **infinite** unlimited   101 **physic**
medicine   102 **borrow** i.e., borrow none from others (?) I will borrow none (?)   106 **Of** by   110 **Push** (an effeminate expression of
impatience)   113 **humors** whims, caprices

Second Lord. Lord Timon's mad.

120 *Third Lord.*   I feel't upon my bones.

Fourth Lord. One day he gives us diamonds, next day stones.

Exeunt the Senators [and others].

[ACT IV

Scene I. *Outside the walls of Athens.*]

Enter Timon.

Timon. Let me look back upon thee. O thou wall
 That girdles in those wolves, dive in the earth,
 And fence not Athens. Matrons, turn incontinent;
 Obedience fail in children. Slaves and fools,
 Pluck the grave wrinkled senate from the bench,   5
 And minister° in their steads. To general filths°
 Convert o' th' instant green° virginity;
 Do't in your parents' eyes. Bankrupts, hold fast
 Rather than render back;° out with your knives,
 And cut your trusters' throats. Bound° servants,
    steal;   10
 Large-handed° robbers your grave masters are,
 And pill° by law. Maid, to thy master's bed,
 Thy mistress is o' th' brothel. Son of sixteen,
 Pluck the lined° crutch from thy old limping sire,
 With it beat out his brains. Piety, and fear,   15

IV.i.6 **minister** govern 6 **filths** harlots (or, more generally, immoral
acts or corruption) 7 **green** young, inexperienced 9 **render back**
repay debts 10 **Bound** under obligation to serve for a stated period
11 **Large-handed** rapacious (usually means "generous") 12 **pill**
steal 14 **lined** padded

Religion to° the gods, peace, justice, truth,
Domestic awe,° night-rest, and neighborhood,°
Instruction, manners, mysteries,° and trades,
Degrees,° observances, customs, and laws,
20   Decline to your confounding contraries,°
And let confusion° live. Plagues incident to° men,
Your potent and infectious fevers heap
On Athens ripe for stroke. Thou cold sciatica,
Cripple our senators, that their limbs may halt°
25   As lamely as their manners. Lust and liberty°
Creep in the minds and marrows of our youth,
That 'gainst the stream of virtue they may strive,
And drown themselves in riot. Itches, blains,°
Sow all th' Athenian bosoms, and their crop
30   Be general leprosy. Breath infect breath,
That their society, as their friendship, may
Be merely° poison. Nothing I'll bear from thee
But nakedness, thou detestable° town;
Take thou that too, with multiplying bans.°
35   Timon will to the woods, where he shall find
Th' unkindest beast more kinder° than mankind.
The gods confound—hear me, you good gods all—
Th' Athenians both within and out that wall.
And grant, as Timon grows, his hate may grow
40   To the whole race of mankind, high and low.
Amen.   *Exit.*

---

16 **Religion to** religious concern for   17 **Domestic awe** the respect
appropriate to domestic relations (to parents, home, etc.)   17 **neighborhood** neighborliness   18 **mysteries** crafts, callings   19 **Degrees**
social classes   20 **confounding contraries** opposites which destroy
each other and so bring on general chaos   21 **confusion** ruin   21 **incident to** natural to   24 **halt** limp   25 **liberty** licentiousness   28
blains blisters   32 **merely** utterly   33 **detestable** (primary accent on
first syllable)   34 **multiplying bans** ever-increasing curses (?) multiple curses (?)   36 **more kinder** (1) more generous, gracious (2) more
natural, closer to the moral law of nature

[Scene II. *Athens. Timon's house.*]

Enter [Flavius, the] Steward, with two or three
Servants.

First Servant. Hear you, master steward, where's our
      master?
   Are we undone, cast off, nothing remaining?

Flavius. Alack, my fellows, what should I say to you?
   Let me be recorded° by the righteous gods,
   I am as poor as you.

First Servant.   Such a house broke?   5
   So noble a master fall'n, all gone, and not
   One friend to take his fortune° by the arm,
   And go along with him?

Second Servant.   As we do turn our backs
   From our companion thrown into his grave,
   So his familiars to his buried fortunes°   10
   Slink all away, leave their false vows with him,
   Like empty purses picked; and his poor self,
   A dedicated beggar to the air,°
   With his disease of all-shunned poverty,
   Walks like contempt alone.

                Enter other Servants.

                         More of our fellows.   15

Flavius. All broken implements of a ruined house.

Third Servant. Yet do our hearts wear Timon's livery,

IV.ii.4 **Let me be recorded** let it be recorded of me   7 **his fortune**
i.e., Timon in his ill fortune   10 **his familiars to his buried fortunes**
those who were the familiar friends of his now buried fortunes (also
suggests "familiar spirit," a personal servant from the spirit world)
13 **A dedicated beggar to the air** a beggar vowed or doomed to wander about in the open air.

That see I by our faces; we are fellows° still,
Serving alike in sorrow. Leaked is our bark,
20 And we poor mates stand on the dying deck,
Hearing the surges threat. We must all part
Into this sea of air.°

Flavius.   Good fellows all,
The latest° of my wealth I'll share amongst you.
Wherever we shall meet, for Timon's sake,
25 Let's yet be fellows. Let's shake our heads and say,
As 'twere a knell unto our master's fortunes,
"We have seen better days." Let each take some.
                            [*Gives money.*]
Nay, put out all your hands. Not one word more;
Thus part we rich in sorrow, parting poor.
                    Embrace, and part several ways.
30 O the fierce wretchedness that glory brings us!
Who would not wish to be from wealth exempt,
Since riches point to° misery and contempt?
Who would be so mocked with glory, or to live°
But in a dream of friendship,
35 To have his pomp and all what state compounds°
But only painted,° like his varnished° friends?
Poor honest lord, brought low by his own heart,
Undone by goodness. Strange, unusual blood,°
When man's worst sin is, he does too much good.
40 Who then dares to be half so kind° again?
For bounty, that makes gods, do still mar men.
My dearest lord, blessed to be° most accursed,
Rich only to be wretched, thy great fortunes
Are made thy chief afflictions. Alas, kind lord,
45 He's flung in rage from this ingrateful seat°
Of monstrous friends;

18 **fellows** fellow servants   22 **this sea of air** i.e., the open air, which
is as comfortless to us as is the sea to sailors on a sinking ship   23
latest last   32 **point to** lead to   33 **to live** i.e., who would wish to
live   35 **all what state compounds** all that worldly splendor is composed of   36 **painted** illusory   36 **varnished** fair-seeming   38
blood disposition   40 **half so kind** i.e., as Timon was, who came to
grief because of it   42 **blessed to be** i.e., blessed with wealth only to
be   45 **seat** residence

Nor has he with him to supply his life,°
Or that° which can command it.
I'll follow and inquire him out.
I'll ever serve his mind with my best will;   50
Whilst I have gold, I'll be his steward still.   *Exit.*

[Scene III. *Before Timon's cave.*]

Enter Timon in the woods.

Timon. O blessèd breeding sun, draw from the earth
    Rotten humidity;° below thy sister's orb°
    Infect the air. Twinned brothers of one womb,
    Whose procreation, residence, and birth,
    Scarce is dividant°—touch° them with several°
        fortunes,   5
    The greater scorns the lesser. Not nature,
    To whom all sores lay siege, can bear great fortune
    But by contempt of nature.°
    Raise me this beggar, and deny't° that lord,
    The senators shall bear contempt hereditary,°   10
    The beggar native° honor.
    It is the pasture lards the brother's sides,
    The want that makes him lean.° Who dares? Who
        dares

---

47 **to supply his life** i.e., he has no food and drink 48 **that** i.e.,
money IV.iii.2 **Rotten humidity** humidity that causes things to rot
2 **below thy sister's orb** beneath the moon (i.e., in the middle air
between earth and moon) 5 **dividant** divisible, separable 5 **touch**
test 5 **several** different 6–8 **Not nature . . . nature** i.e., human
nature, which is subjected to all sorts of miseries, when it encounters
good fortune rejects its own natural affection and despises mankind
9 **deny't** i.e., deny to raise 10 **hereditary** i.e., as if they were born
that way and not simply victims of fortune's caprices 11 **native** i.e.,
as if he were born with it 12–13 **It is . . . lean** i.e., the "twinned
brothers" (line 3) are distinguished by their gifts of fortune; the
rich pasture, and not any intrinsic worth, makes one brother fat and
the other lean

In purity of manhood stand upright
15 And say, this man's a flatterer? If one be,
So are they all, for every grise° of fortune
Is smoothed° by that below. The learned pate°
Ducks to the golden fool.° All's obliquy;°
There's nothing level in our cursèd natures
20 But direct villainy. Therefore be abhorred
All feasts, societies, and throngs of men.
His semblable,° yea himself, Timon disdains;
Destruction fang° mankind. Earth, yield me roots.
                         [*Digs.*]
Who seeks for better of thee, sauce° his palate
25 With thy most operant° poison. What is here?
Gold? Yellow, glittering, precious gold?
No, gods, I am no idle votarist.°
Roots, you clear° heavens! Thus much of this will make
Black, white; foul, fair; wrong, right;
30 Base, noble; old, young; coward, valiant.
Ha, you gods! Why this? What this, you gods? Why this
Will lug your priests and servants from your sides;
Pluck stout men's pillows from below their heads.°
This yellow slave
35 Will knit and break religions, bless th' accursed,
Make the hoar° leprosy adored, place° thieves,
And give them title, knee, and approbation
With senators on the bench. This is it
That makes the wappened° widow wed again;
40 She, whom the spital-house° and ulcerous sores°

---

16 grise step   **17 smoothed** flattered, facilitated by flattery   **17 pate** head   **18 Ducks to the golden fool** inclines in deference to the rich fool   **18 obliquy** obliquity, moral crookedness   **22 semblable** anything like himself   **23 fang** (1) seize, as with fangs (2) provide with fangs   **24 sauce** season   **25 operant** potent   **27 no idle votarist** i.e., I have not sworn my vow in an idle or trifling way   **28 clear** pure   **33 Pluck . . . heads** i.e., kill even strong men by sudden suffocation   **36 hoar** white   **36 place** elevate to a place or office of dignity   **39 wappened** sexually exhausted   **40 spital-house** hospital (especially for the lower classes and sufferers from loathsome diseases)   **40 ulcerous sores** i.e., those afflicted with ulcerous sores

Would cast the gorge° at, this embalms and spices
To th' April day° again. Come, damned earth,
Thou common whore of mankind, that puts odds
Among the rout of nations,° I will make thee
Do thy right nature.°

March afar off.

   Ha? A drum? Th'art quick,°   *45*
But yet I'll bury thee. Thou't go,° strong thief,
When gouty keepers of thee cannot stand.
Nay, stay thou out for earnest.° [*Keeps some gold.*]

  Enter Alcibiades, with drum and fife, in
  warlike manner; and Phrynia and Timandra.

Alcibiades. What art thou there? Speak.

Timon. A beast as thou art. The canker° gnaw thy
 heart   *50*
For showing me again the eyes of man.

Alcibiades. What is thy name? Is man so hateful to
 thee
That art thyself a man?

Timon. I am Misanthropos° and hate mankind.
For thy part, I do wish thou wert a dog,   *55*
That I might love thee something.°

Alcibiades.   I know thee well,
But in thy fortunes am unlearned and strange.°

Timon. I know thee too, and more than that I know
 thee
I not desire to know. Follow thy drum,
With man's blood paint the ground gules,° gules. *60*

---

41 **cast the gorge** vomit 41–42 **embalms and spices/To th' April day** i.e., preserves, perfumes, and generally revivifies to a springlike and youthful amorousness 43–44 **puts odds/Among the rout of nations** sets the disorderly mob of nations at strife with each other 45 **Do thy right nature** i.e., cause strife and dissension 45 **quick** (1) alive (2) speedily had and lost 46 **go** walk, move 48 **for earnest** as an installment 50 **canker** (1) ulcerous sore (2) canker-worm 54 **Misanthropos** the man-hater 56 **something** somewhat 57 **strange** ignorant 60 **gules** red (the heraldic term)

Religious canons, civil laws are cruel;
Then what should war be? This fell° whore of thine
Hath in her more destruction than thy sword,
For all her cherubin look.

Phrynia.   Thy lips rot off.

65 *Timon.* I will not kiss thee; then the rot returns°
To thine own lips again.

Alcibiades. How came the noble Timon to this
change?

Timon. As the moon does, by wanting° light to give.
But then renew° I could not like the moon;
70 There were no suns to borrow of.

Alcibiades. Noble Timon, what friendship may I do
thee?

Timon. None, but to maintain my opinion.°

Alcibiades. What is it, Timon?

Timon. Promise me friendship, but perform none.
75 If thou wilt not promise, the gods plague thee,
For thou art a man. If thou dost perform,
Confound thee, for thou art a man.

Alcibiades. I have heard in some sort of thy miseries.

Timon. Thou saw'st them when I had prosperity.

80 *Alcibiades.* I see them now; then was a blessed time.

Timon. As thine is now, held with a brace° of harlots.

Timandra. Is this th' Athenian minion,° whom the
world
Voiced so regardfully?°

---

62 **fell** destructive   65 **the rot returns** (based on a prevalent belief
that by transmitting a venereal infection to another, one loses it
himself)   68 **wanting** lacking   69 **renew** (1) to become new (2) to
extend a loan (as in the next line)   72 **maintain my opinion** i.e.,
be a misanthropist, too   81 **brace** (usually used for a pair of dogs on
a leash)   82 **minion** favorite, darling   83 **Voiced so regardfully**
spoke of with so much regard

Timon.   Art thou Timandra?

Timandra.   Yes.

Timon. Be a whore still; they love thee not that use
  thee.
  Give them diseases, leaving° with thee their lust.   *85*
  Make use of thy salt° hours. Season° the slaves
  For tubs and baths;° bring down rose-cheeked
    youth
  To the tub-fast and the diet.°

Timandra.   Hang thee, monster!

Alcibiades. Pardon him, sweet Timandra, for his wits
  Are drowned and lost in his calamities.   *90*
  I have but little gold of late, brave° Timon,
  The want whereof doth daily make revolt
  In my penurious° band. I have heard, and grieved,
  How cursèd Athens, mindless of thy worth,
  Forgetting thy great deeds, when neighbor states,   *95*
  But for thy sword and fortune, trod° upon them—

Timon. I prithee beat thy drum° and get thee gone.

Alcibiades. I am thy friend and pity thee, dear Timon.

Timon. How dost thou pity him whom thou dost
    trouble?
  I had rather be alone.

Alcibiades.   Why fare thee well.   *100*
  Here is some gold for thee.

Timon.   Keep it, I cannot eat it.

Alcibiades. When I have laid proud Athens on a
    heap—

_____

85 **leaving** i.e., while they leave   86 **salt** lustful, salacious   86 **Season**
spice   87 **tubs and baths** sweating-tubs and hot baths (used to treat
venereal disease)   88 **tub-fast and the diet** (fasting and special diet
were treatments for venereal disease)   91 **brave** excellent   93 **penuri-
ous** needy   96 **trod** i.e., would have trodden   97 **beat thy drum** i.e.,
let thy drummer give the signal for departure

Timon. War'st thou 'gainst Athens?

Alcibiades.   Ay, Timon, and have cause.

Timon. The gods confound them all in thy conquest,°
105   And thee after when thou hast conquerèd.

Alcibiades. Why me, Timon?

Timon.   That by killing of villains
Thou wast born to conquer my country.
Put up° thy gold. Go on, here's gold, go on.
Be as a planetary plague,° when Jove
110 Will o'er some high-viced city hang his poison
In the sick air. Let not thy sword skip one.
Pity not honored age for his white beard:
He is an usurer. Strike me the counterfeit matron:
It is her habit° only that is honest,°
115 Herself's a bawd. Let not the virgin's cheek
Make soft thy trenchant° sword: for those milk
      paps,
That through the window-bars° bore at men's eyes,
Are not within the leaf of pity writ,°
But set them down horrible traitors. Spare not the
      babe
Whose dimpled smiles from fools exhaust° their
120   mercy:
Think it a bastard, whom the oracle
Hath doubtfully° pronounced thy throat shall cut,
And mince it sans remorse.° Swear against objects.°
Put armor on thine ears and on thine eyes,
Whose proof° nor yells of mothers, maids, nor
125   babes,

104 **in thy conquest** i.e., in your victory over them   108 **Put up** put away   109 **planetary plague** plague caused by the planets   114 **habit** dress   114 **honest** chaste   116 **trenchant** cutting   117 **window-bars** lattice work of a window (?) open-work squares of the bodice of a woman's frock (?)   118 **within the leaf of pity writ** i.e., written down on the page with the names of those who are to be pitied and spared   120 **exhaust** draw out, elicit   122 **doubtfully** ambiguously   123 **mince it sans remorse** cut it up without pity   123 **objects** objections, accusations of cruelty   125 **proof** high quality (of armor), impenetrability

Nor sight of priests in holy vestments bleeding,
Shall pierce a jot. There's gold to pay thy soldiers.
Make large confusion;° and, thy fury spent,
Confounded be thyself. Speak not, begone.

Alcibiades. Hast° thou gold yet, I'll take the gold thou
    givest me,   *130*
Not all thy counsel.

Timon. Dost thou or dost thou not, heaven's curse
    upon thee.

Phrynia and Timandra. Give us some gold, good
    Timon; hast thou more?

Timon. Enough to make a whore forswear her trade,
And to make whores, a bawd.° Hold up, you sluts, *135*
Your aprons mountant.° You are not oathable,°
Although I know you'll swear, terribly swear
Into strong shudders and to heavenly agues
Th' immortal gods that hear you. Spare your oaths;
I'll trust to your conditions.° Be whores still,° *140*
And he whose pious breath seeks to convert you,
Be strong in whore, allure him, burn him up;
Let your close fire predominate his smoke,°
And be no turncoats. Yet may your pains six months
Be quite contrary.° And thatch   *145*
Your poor thin roofs with burdens of the dead—°
Some that were hanged, no matter.
Wear them, betray with them; whore still;

---

128 **confusion** destruction   130 **Hast** i.e., if you have   135 **And to
make whores, a bawd** i.e., and enough to make a bawd give up her
trade of making whores (or, perhaps, enough to make a whore set
herself up as a bawd, making whores instead of being one)   136
aprons mountant rising aprons (a mock heraldic phrase with sexual
overtones)   136 **oathable** capable of being placed under oath   140
conditions dispositions   140 **still** always   143 **Let . . . smoke** i.e.,
let the hidden fire of your sexuality or disease dominate over the
smoke of idle words of he who "seeks to convert you"   144–45 **Yet
. . . contrary** i.e., may you spend six months of the year in being
whores and the other six in repairing the physical damage occasioned
by your debaucheries (?)   145–46 **And thatch . . . dead** i.e., wear
wigs (or possibly false pubes) made from loads of hair taken from
the dead (venereal disease was thought to cause loss of hair)

Paint till a horse may mire° upon your face.
A pox of wrinkles!°

150 *Phrynia and Timandra.* Well, more gold. What then?
Believe't that we'll do anything for gold.

Timon. Consumptions° sow
In hollow° bones of man; strike their sharp° shins,
And mar men's spurring. Crack the lawyer's voice,
155 That he may never more false title plead,
Nor sound his quillets° shrilly. Hoar the flamen,°
That scolds against the quality of flesh°
And not believes himself. Down with the nose,°
Down with it flat, take the bridge quite away
160 Of him, that his particular to foresee,
Smells from the general weal.° Make curled-pate
ruffians bald,
And let the unscarred braggarts of the war
Derive some pain from you. Plague all,
That your activity may defeat and quell
165 The source of all erection.° There's more gold.
Do you damn others, and let this damn you,
And ditches grave° you all.

Phrynia and Timandra. More counsel with more
money, bounteous Timon.

Timon. More whore, more mischief first; I have given
you earnest.°

149 **mire** sink into the mire or mud (because of the thickness of
cosmetics)   150 **A pox of wrinkles** i.e., a pox on wrinkles, away with
wrinkles (since they can be covered with cosmetics)   152 **Consump-
tions** wasting diseases (here venereal disease)   153 **hollow ... sharp**
i.e., the disease will make the bones hollow and the shins painful   156
quillets subtle verbal distinctions   156 **Hoar the flamen** whiten the
priest with disease, or cause his hair to turn white (possible pun on
"whore")   157 **quality of flesh** the nature of the flesh, sexual pleasure   158 **Down with the nose** (an effect of syphilis)   160–61 **his
particular ... weal** i.e., to provide for his private advantage or profit,
he abandons the proper scent that contributes to the public good or
welfare   165 **The source of all erection** i.e., sexuality itself   167
grave be a grave for, bury   169 **earnest** a part payment to seal a
bargain

Alcibiades. Strike up the drum towards Athens. Fare-
    well, Timon.   *170*
  If I thrive well, I'll visit thee again.

Timon. If I hope well,° I'll never see thee more.

Alcibiades. I never did thee harm.

Timon. Yes, thou spok'st well of me.

Alcibiades.   Call'st thou that harm?

Timon. Men daily find it. Get thee away, and take   *175*
  Thy beagles with thee.

Alcibiades.   We but offend him. Strike!
[*Drum beats.*] *Exeunt* [*Alcibiades, Phrynia, and*
                                Timandra].

Timon. That nature, being sick of° man's unkindness,
  Should yet be hungry! Common mother, thou,
                          [*Digging*]
  Whose womb unmeasurable and infinite breast
  Teems° and feeds all; whose selfsame mettle,°   *180*
  Whereof thy proud child, arrogant man, is puffed,°
  Engenders the black toad and adder blue,
  The gilded newt and eyeless venomed worm,
  With all th' abhorrèd births below crisp° heaven
  Whereon Hyperion's quick'ning fire° doth shine;   *185*
  Yield him, who all the human sons do hate,
  From forth thy plenteous bosom, one poor root.
  Ensear° thy fertile and conceptious° womb;
  Let it no more bring out ingrateful man.
  Go great° with tigers, dragons, wolves, and bears,   *190*
  Teem with new monsters, whom thy upward face
  Hath to the marbled mansion all above°

172 **If I hope well** if my hopes are realized   177 **of** as a result of
180 **Teems** brings forth   180 **mettle** (1) substance (2) vigorous spirit
181 **puffed** puffed up with pride   184 **crisp** with curled clouds (?)
shining, clear (?)   185 **Hyperion's quick'ning fire** (the sun was
thought to have the power of generating some of the lower forms of
insect life)   188 **Ensear** dry up   188 **conceptious** conceiving, pro-
lific   190 **great** pregnant   192 **above** in heaven

Never presented. O, a root, dear thanks!
Dry up thy marrows,° vines and plough-torn leas,
195 Whereof ingrateful man, with liquorish draughts
And morsels unctious,° greases his pure mind,
That from it all consideration° slips—

Enter Apemantus.

More man? Plague, plague!

Apemantus. I was directed hither. Men report
200 Thou dost affect° my manners, and dost use them.

Timon. 'Tis then because thou dost not keep a dog
Whom I would imitate. Consumption° catch thee.

Apemantus. This is in thee a nature but infected,°
A poor unmanly melancholy sprung
From change of future.° Why this spade? This
205 place?
This slave-like habit° and these looks of care?
Thy flatterers yet wear silk, drink wine, lie soft,
Hug their diseased perfumes,° and have forgot
That ever Timon was. Shame not these woods
210 By putting on the cunning of a carper.°
Be thou a flatterer now, and seek to thrive
By that which has undone thee. Hinge thy knee,
And let his very breath whom thou'lt observe
Blow off thy cap;° praise his most vicious strain°
215 And call it excellent. Thou wast told thus.°

194 **marrows** (the type of a rich food, not a necessity of life, produced by the "vines" and "leas") 196 **unctious** (an obsolete variant
form of "unctuous") 197 **consideration** ability to consider 200
affect imitate 202 **Consumption** any wasting disease 203 **infected**
(1) affected, factitious (2) caught like an infection from your changed
circumstances 205 **change of future** i.e., change in your material
prospects 206 **habit** dress, garb 208 **diseased perfumes** diseased
and perfumed mistresses 210 **By . . . carper** i.e., by pretending to
the profession of a cynic or railer (which any fool can do) 213–14
let his . . . cap kneel so obsequiously close to the person you are paying court to that his breath may blow off your cap 214 **strain** quality
215 **Thou wast told thus** i.e., in your prosperity others spoke to you
in this manner

Thou gav'st thine ears, like tapsters° that bade
  welcome,
To knaves and all approachers. 'Tis most just
That thou turn rascal; hadst thou wealth again,
Rascals should have't. Do not assume my likeness.

Timon. Were I like thee, I'd throw away myself.   220

Apemantus. Thou hast cast away thyself, being like
  thyself:
A madman so long, now a fool. What, think'st
That the bleak air, thy boisterous chamberlain,°
Will put thy shirt on warm? Will these moist° trees,
That have outlived the eagle, page thy heels   225
And skip when thou point'st out?° Will the cold
  brook,
Candied° with ice, caudle° thy morning taste
To cure thy o'er-night's surfeit?° Call the creatures
Whose naked natures live in all the spite
Of wreakful° heaven, whose bare unhousèd trunks,   230
To the conflicting elements exposed,
Answer mere nature.° Bid them flatter thee.
O thou shalt find—

Timon.   A fool of thee. Depart.

Apemantus. I love thee better now than e'er I did.

Timon. I hate thee worse.

Apemantus.   Why?

Timon.   Thou flatter'st misery.   235

Apemantus. I flatter not, but say thou art a caitiff.°

---

216 **tapsters** (tavern-keepers or bartenders are proverbial for their
indiscriminate hospitality)   223 **chamberlain** one who waits on a
king or lord in his bedchamber   224 **moist** damp   226 **point'st out**
indicate your desires   227 **Candied** congealed, encrusted   227 **caudle** offer a caudle (a warm, spiced, mildly alcoholic drink given to
the sick)   228 **o'er-night's surfeit** previous night's indulgence in drink
230 **wreakful** vengeful   232 **Answer mere nature** correspond to or
reflect nature in its barest and most rigorous form   236 **caitiff**
wretch

Timon. Why dost thou seek me out?

Apemantus.   To vex thee.

Timon. Always a villain's office° or a fool's.
  Dost please thyself in't?

Apemantus.   Ay.

Timon.   What, a knave too?

240 *Apemantus.* If thou didst put this sour cold habit° on
        To castigate thy pride, 'twere well; but thou
        Dost it enforcedly.° Thou'dst courtier be again
        Wert thou not beggar. Willing misery°
        Outlives incertain pomp, is crowned before.°
245   The one is filling still,° never complete;
        The other, at high wish.° Best state, contentless,
        Hath a distracted and most wretched being,
        Worse than the worst, content.°
        Thou shouldst desire to die, being miserable.

250 *Timon.* Not by his breath° that is more miserable.
        Thou art a slave, whom Fortune's tender arm
        With favor never clasped, but bred a dog.
        Hadst thou, like us, from our first swath° proceeded
        The sweet degrees° that this brief world affords
255   To such as may the passive drudges° of it
        Freely command, thou wouldst have plunged thyself
        In general riot,° melted down thy youth
        In different beds of lust, and never learned

238 **office** duty   240 **habit** (1) garment (2) outward manner, bearing
242 **enforcedly** i.e., as if you were being forced to do it   243 **Willing
misery** voluntary poverty   244 **is crowned before** comes earlier to
the fulfillment of its desires and wishes   245 **The one is filling still**
i.e., pomp, like a leaky vessel, can never be filled (or fulfilled)   246
The other, at high wish i.e., "willing misery," because it wishes little,
can easily arrive at the height of its wishes   246–48 **Best state . . .
content** i.e., a man in even the best material condition, if he is without content or happiness, is confused and wretched, worse than a
man in the poorest condition who is contented   250 **breath** voice
253 **swath** swaddling clothes   253–54 **proceeded/The sweet degrees**
advanced from one stage to the next above it (in sense of academic
"degrees")   255 **passive drudges** submissive menial servants   257
riot debauchery

The icy precepts of respect,° but followed
The sug'red game° before thee. But myself—   *260*
Who had the world as my confectionary,°
The mouths, the tongues, the eyes, and hearts of
    men
At duty, more than I could frame employment;°
That numberless upon me stuck, as leaves
Do on the oak, have with one winter's brush°   *265*
Fell° from their boughs, and left me open, bare
For every storm that blows—I to bear this,
That never knew but better, is some burden.
Thy nature did commence in sufferance,° time
Hath made thee hard in't. Why shouldst thou hate
    men?   *270*
They never flattered thee. What hast thou given?
If thou wilt curse, thy father, that poor rogue,
Must be thy subject; who in spite put stuff
To° some she-beggar and compounded thee
Poor rogue hereditary. Hence, begone.   *275*
If thou hadst not been born the worst° of men,
Thou hadst been a knave and flatterer.

Apemantus.   Art thou proud yet?

Timon. Ay, that I am not thee.

Apemantus.   I, that I was
No prodigal.

Timon.   I, that I am one now.
Were all the wealth I have shut up in thee,   *280*
I'd give thee leave to hang it. Get thee gone.
That° the whole life of Athens were in this!
Thus would I eat it.   [*Eats a root.*]

---

259 **icy precepts of respect** i.e., the chilling rules of reason which
constitute proper social conduct   260 **sug'red game** outwardly sweet
quarry (probably whores)   261 **confectionary** a place where sweet-
meats or candy are made   263 **frame employment** invent work for
265 **winter's brush** i.e., brush of a wintry wind   266 **Fell** fallen   269
sufferance suffering   273–74 **put stuff/To** i.e., made pregnant (contemptuous)   276 **worst** i.e., in social and financial position   282
That i.e., would that

Apemantus.   Here, I will mend° thy feast.
                                    [*Offers him food.*]

Timon. First mend my company, take away thyself.

Apemantus. So I shall mend mine own, by th' lack of
283   thine.

Timon. 'Tis not well mended so, it is but botched;°
If not, I would it were.

Apemantus. What wouldst thou have to° Athens?

Timon. Thee thither in a whirlwind. If thou wilt,
290   Tell them there I have gold; look, so I have.

Apemantus. Here is no use for gold.

Timon.   The best and truest;
For here it sleeps and does no hirèd harm.

Apemantus. Where liest a nights, Timon?

Timon.   Under that's above me.°
Where feed'st thou a days, Apemantus?

295 *Apemantus.* Where my stomach finds meat, or rather
where I eat it.

Timon. Would poison were obedient and knew my
mind!

Apemantus. Where wouldst thou send it?

300 *Timon.* To sauce thy dishes.

Apemantus. The middle of humanity thou never
knewest, but the extremity of both ends. When thou
wast in thy gilt and thy perfume, they mocked thee
for too much curiosity;° in thy rags thou know'st
305   none, but art despised for the contrary. There's a
medlar° for thee; eat it.

---

283 **mend** improve   286 **botched** clumsily repaired (because Apemantus is still present—with himself)   288 **to** in   293 **that's above
me** i.e., that which is above me, the sky   304 **curiosity** carefulness,
fastidiousness   306 **medlar** a fruit like a small brown-skinned apple,
not ready to be eaten until in the early stages of decay

Timon. On what I hate I feed not.

Apemantus. Dost hate° a medlar?

Timon. Ay, though it look like thee.

Apemantus. And° th'hadst hated meddlers° sooner,   *310*
thou shouldst have loved thyself better now. What
man didst thou ever know unthrift° that was beloved after° his means?

Timon. Who, without those means thou talk'st of,
didst thou ever know beloved?   *315*

Apemantus. Myself.

Timon. I understand thee; thou hadst some means to
keep a dog.°

Apemantus. What things in the world canst thou nearest compare to thy flatterers?   *320*

Timon. Women nearest, but men—men are the
things themselves. What wouldst thou do with the
world, Apemantus, if it lay in thy power?

Apemantus. Give it the beasts, to be rid of the men.

Timon. Wouldst thou have thyself fall in the confu-   *325*
sion of men,° and remain a beast with the beasts?

Apemantus. Ay, Timon.

Timon. A beastly ambition, which the gods grant
thee t' attain to. If thou wert the lion, the fox
would beguile° thee. If thou wert the lamb, the   *330*
fox would eat thee. If thou wert the fox, the lion
would suspect thee, when peradventure° thou wert
accused by the ass. If thou wert the ass, thy dull-

---

308 hate ("eat" and "hate" were pronounced alike in Elizabethan
English)   310 And if   310 meddlers (1) the fruit (2) busybodies,
intriguers (3) those who overindulge in sexual intercourse   312 unthrift prodigal, spendthrift   313 after in accordance with (i.e., the
true love for an "unthrift" is not in proportion with his bounty)   318
a dog i.e., you had just enough to keep a dog so that something might
love you   325–26 the confusion of men i.e., the original Fall in the
Garden of Eden   330 beguile trick   332 peradventure perchance

ness would torment thee, and still thou liv'dst but
335   as a breakfast to the wolf. If thou wert the wolf,
thy greediness would afflict thee, and oft thou
shouldst hazard thy life for thy dinner. Wert thou
the unicorn,° pride and wrath would confound°
thee, and make thine own self the conquest of thy
340   fury. Wert thou a bear, thou wouldst be killed by
the horse. Wert thou a horse, thou wouldst be
seized by the leopard. Wert thou a leopard, thou
wert german° to the lion, and the spots° of thy
kindred were jurors° on thy life. All thy safety
345   were remotion,° and thy defense absence. What
beast couldst thou be that were not subject to a
beast? And what a beast art thou already, that
seest not thy loss in transformation!°

Apemantus. If thou couldst please me with speaking
350   to me, thou mightst have hit upon it here. The
commonwealth of Athens is become a forest of
beasts.

Timon. How has the ass broke the wall, that thou art
out of the city?

355 *Apemantus.* Yonder comes a poet and a painter.°
The plague of company light upon thee! I will fear
to catch it, and give way.° When I know not what
else to do, I'll see thee again.

Timon. When there is nothing living but thee, thou
360   shalt be welcome. I had rather be a beggar's dog
than Apemantus.

Apemantus. Thou art the cap° of all the fools alive.

338 **unicorn** (an untamable beast, who, in his fury to attack the treed
lion, runs his horn into the tree and puts himself at the mercy of the
lion) 338 **confound** destroy 343 **german** akin 343 **spots** (1)
markings (2) moral stains, vices 344 **jurors** witnesses (especially
false ones) 345 **remotion** removal of yourself (to a distance), re-
moteness 348 **in transformation** i.e., in seeking to be transformed
into a beast 355 **a poet and a painter** (they do not actually enter
until the beginning of Act V) 357 **give way** retire 362 **cap** chief,
summit

Timon. Would thou wert clean enough to spit upon.

Apemantus. A plague on thee, thou art too bad to
curse.

Timon. All villains that do stand by thee° are pure.   365

Apemantus. There is no leprosy but what thou
speak'st.

Timon. If I name thee.
I'll beat thee, but I should infect my hands.

Apemantus. I would my tongue could rot them off.

Timon. Away, thou issue of a mangy dog.   370
Choler° does kill me that thou art alive;
I swound° to see thee.

Apemantus. Would thou wouldst burst.

Timon. Away, thou tedious rogue, I am sorry I shall
lose a stone by thee.   [*Throws a stone at him.*]   373

Apemantus. Beast!

Timon. Slave!

Apemantus. Toad!

Timon. Rogue, rogue, rogue!
I am sick of this false world, and will love naught   380
But even the mere necessities upon't.°
Then, Timon, presently° prepare thy grave.
Lie where the light foam of the sea may beat
Thy gravestone daily. Make thine epitaph,
That death in me° at others' lives may laugh.   385
[*To the gold*] O thou sweet king-killer, and dear
divorce
'Twixt natural° son and sire, thou bright defiler
Of Hymen's° purest bed, thou valiant Mars,

365 **that do stand by thee** compared to you   371 **Choler** anger   372
swound swoon   381 **But even . . . upon't** i.e., except the bare necessities of life   382 **presently** immediately   385 **in me** by my example
387 **natural** son by birth (does not mean "illegitimate")   382 **Hymen**
Greek god of marriage

Thou ever young, fresh, loved, and delicate wooer,
390   Whose blush° doth thaw the consecrated snow
That lies on Dian's° lap. Thou visible god,
That sold'rest close impossibilities°
And mak'st them kiss; that speak'st with every
    tongue
To every purpose. O thou touch° of hearts,
395   Think thy slave man rebels, and by thy virtue
Set them into confounding odds,° that beasts
May have the world in empire.

Apemantus.   Would 'twere so,
But not till I am dead. I'll say th'hast gold.
Thou wilt be thronged to shortly.

Timon.   Thronged to?

Apemantus.   Ay.

Timon. Thy back, I prithee.

400 *Apemantus.*   Live, and love thy misery.

Timon. Long live so, and so die. I am quit.°

Enter the Banditti.

Apemantus. Moe things like men! Eat, Timon, and
    abhor them.   *Exit Apemantus.*

First Bandit. Where should he have this gold? It is
    some poor fragment, some slender ort° of his re-
405   mainder. The mere° want of gold, and the falling-
    from° of his friends, drove him into this melan-
    choly.

Second Bandit. It is noised° he hath a mass of treas-
    ure.

410 *Third Bandit.* Let us make the assay° upon him. If

---

390 **blush** glow 391 **Dian** Diana, the virgin huntress, Greek goddess
of chastity 392 **sold'rest close impossibilities** joins closely together
things thought to be irreconcilable 394 **touch** touchstone 396 **into
confounding odds** at ruinous strife 401 **quit** rid (of Apemantus)
404 **ort** leftover bit 405 **mere** sheer 405–06 **falling-from** falling-off
408 **noised** rumored 410 **make the assay** put it to the test

he care not for't, he will supply us easily; if he
covetously reserve it, how shall's get it?

Second Bandit. True, for he bears it not about him;
'tis hid.

First Bandit. Is not this he?   415

All. Where?

Second Bandit. 'Tis his description.

Third Bandit. He? I know him.

All. Save thee,° Timon.

Timon. Now, thieves?   420

All. Soldiers, not thieves.

Timon.   Both too, and women's sons.

All. We are not thieves, but men that much do want.°

Timon. Your greatest want is, you want much of
    meat.°
  Why should you want? Behold, the earth hath
    roots;
  Within this mile break forth a hundred springs;   425
  The oaks bear mast,° the briers scarlet hips;°
  The bounteous huswife° nature on each bush
  Lays her full mess° before you. Want? Why want?

First Bandit. We cannot live on grass, on berries,
    water,
  As beasts and birds and fishes.   430

Timon. Nor on the beasts themselves, the birds and
    fishes;
  You must eat men. Yet thanks I must you con°
  That you are thieves professed, that you work not
  In holier shapes; for there is boundless theft

419 **Save thee** God save thee (a conventional salutation)   422 **want**
need, lack   423 **you want much of meat** you desire (or lack) a good
deal of food (i.e., if you didn't eat so much your wants would be
smaller)   426 **mast** acorns (generally fed to swine)   426 **hips** fruit
of the rose   427 **huswife** housewife   428 **mess** meal   432 **con** offer

435 In limited° professions. Rascal thieves,
Here's gold. Go, suck the subtle° blood o' th' grape,
Till the high fever° seethe your blood to froth,
And so 'scape hanging. Trust not the physician;
His antidotes are poison, and he slays
440 Moe° than you rob. Take wealth and lives together,
Do, villain, do, since you protest° to do't.
Like workmen, I'll example you with thievery:°
The sun's a thief, and with his great attraction°
Robs the vast sea. The moon's an arrant thief,
445 And her pale fire she snatches from the sun.
The sea's a thief, whose liquid surge resolves
The moon into salt tears.° The earth's a thief,
That feeds and breeds by a composture° stol'n
From gen'ral excrement. Each thing's a thief.
450 The laws, your curb and whip, in their rough power
Has unchecked theft. Love not yourselves; away,
Rob one another. There's more gold; cut throats,
All that you meet are thieves. To Athens go,
Break open shops; nothing can you steal
455 But thieves do lose it. Steal less for this I give you,°
And gold confound you howsoe'er.° Amen.

Third Bandit. Has almost charmed me from my profession by persuading me to it.

First Bandit. 'Tis in the malice of mankind° that he
460 thus advises us, not to have us thrive in our
mystery.°

---

435 **limited** limited in numbers, restricted (as a guild)   436 **subtle** treacherous   437 **high fever** i.e., of drunkenness   440 **Moe** more   441 **protest** profess   442 **Like ... thievery** i.e., as one instructs workmen by practical example, so I will give you some precedents for your line of work, thievery   443 **attraction** drawing power   446–47 **whose ... tears** (the idea is that the sea's tides are stolen from the moon's precipitation)   448 **composture** compost, manure   455 **Steal less for this I give you** i.e., even if you steal less because of the gold I am giving you   456 **howsoe'er** nevertheless   459 **in the malice of mankind** i.e., because of the malice Timon bears to all mankind   461 **mystery** trade, profession

Second Bandit. I'll believe him as an enemy,° and
  give over° my trade.

First Bandit. Let us first see peace in Athens; there
  is no time so miserable but a man may be true.°   465
                                    Exit Thieves.

Enter [Flavius,] the Steward to Timon.

Flavius. O you gods!
  Is yond despised and ruinous° man my lord?
  Full of decay and failing? O monument
  And wonder° of good deeds evilly bestowed!
  What an alteration of honor° has desp'rate want
    made!   470
  What vilder° thing upon the earth than friends,
  Who can bring noblest minds to basest ends!
  How rarely does it meet with this time's guise,°
  When man was wished° to love his enemies!
  Grant I may ever love, and rather woo   475
  Those that would mischief me than those that do.°
  Has caught me in his eye; I will present
  My honest grief unto him, and as my lord
  Still serve him with my life. My dearest master.

Timon. Away! What art thou?

Flavius.   Have you forgot me, sir?   480

Timon. Why dost ask that? I have forgot all men.
  Then, if thou grunt'st° th'art a man,
  I have forgot thee.

462 **I'll believe him as an enemy** i.e., since he is an enemy, I'll do the
opposite of what he advises   463 **give over** give up   464–65 **there
is . . . true** i.e., you can become an honest man any time you choose
(therefore, why do it now?)   467 **ruinous** ruined   468–69 **monu-
ment/And wonder** i.e., wonderful monument (memorial or tombstone)   470 **alteration of honor** change (for the worse) in honor
471 **vilder** viler   473 **How . . . guise** i.e., how excellently does
Timon's example fit in with the moral tone of these times (spoken
ironically)   474 **wished** desired (by God)   476 **Those . . . do** i.e.,
I will love those enemies who are direct and open in their desire to
harm me better than those who harm me under the guise of friendship   482 **grunt'st** i.e., even your claim to be a man is delivered in
an animal grunt (since all men are bestial)

Flavius. An honest poor servant of yours.

485 *Timon.* Then I know thee not.
 I never had honest man about me, I; all
 I kept were knaves,° to serve in meat to villains.

Flavius. The gods are witness,
 Nev'r did poor steward wear a truer grief
490 For his undone lord than mine eyes for you.

Timon. What, dost thou weep? Come nearer. Then
  I love thee
 Because thou art a woman, and disclaim'st
 Flinty° mankind, whose eyes do never give°
 But thorough° lust and laughter. Pity's sleeping.
 Strange times, that weep with laughing, not with
495   weeping!

Flavius. I beg of you to know me, good my lord,
 T' accept my grief, and whilst this poor wealth lasts,
 To entertain° me as your steward still.

Timon. Had I a steward
500 So true, so just, and now so comfortable?°
 It almost turns my dangerous nature mild.
 Let me behold thy face. Surely, this man
 Was born of woman.
 Forgive my general and exceptless° rashness,
505 You perpetual-sober gods. I do proclaim
 One honest man. Mistake me not, but one.
 No more I pray—and he's a steward.
 How fain would I have hated all mankind,
 And thou redeem'st thyself. But all save thee
510 I fell° with curses.
 Methinks thou art more honest now than wise;
 For, by oppressing° and betraying me,

487 **knaves** (1) servants (2) villains   493 **Flinty** hardhearted   493
give weep   494 **But thorough** except through   498 **entertain** receive into service   500 **comfortable** comforting   504 **exceptless**
making no exceptions   510 **fell** cause to fall, strike down   512 **op-
pressing** distressing

Thou might'st have sooner got another service.°
For many so arrive at second masters
Upon their first lord's neck.° But tell me true—   515
For I must ever doubt,° though ne'er so sure—
Is not thy kindness subtle, covetous,
A usuring kindness, as rich men deal° gifts,
Expecting in return twenty for one?

Flavius. No, my most worthy master, in whose breast   520
Doubt and suspect,° alas, are placed too late.
You should have feared false times when you did
     feast.
Suspect still° comes where an estate is least.
That which I show, heaven knows, is merely° love,
Duty and zeal to your unmatchèd mind,   525
Care of your food and living; and believe it,
My most honored lord,
For any benefit that points° to me,
Either in hope or present, I'd exchange
For this one wish, that you had power and wealth   530
To requite me by making rich yourself.

Timon. Look thee, 'tis so. Thou singly° honest man,
Here, take. The gods out of my misery
Has sent thee treasure. Go, live rich and happy,
But thus conditioned:° thou shalt build from° men;   535
Hate all, curse all, show charity to none,
But let the famished flesh slide from the bone
Ere thou relieve the beggar. Give to dogs
What thou deniest to men. Let prisons swallow 'em,
Debts wither 'em to nothing; be men like blasted°
     woods,   540
And may diseases lick up their false bloods.
And so farewell, and thrive.

---

513 **service** position as a servant   515 **Upon their first lord's neck**
i.e., by treading down their first master and mounting on his neck
(or shoulders)   516 **doubt** suspect, fear   518 **deal** distribute   521
suspect suspicion   523 **still** always   524 **merely** entirely   528 **points**
might accrue   532 **singly** (1) uniquely (2) truly   535 **But thus conditioned** with this condition   535 **from** away from   540 **blasted**
blighted

Flavius. O let me stay and comfort you, my master.

Timon. If thou hat'st curses
545   Stay not; fly, whilst thou art blessed and free.
Ne'er see thou man, and let me ne'er see thee.
        Exit [Flavius; and exit Timon into his cave].

[ACT V

Scene I. *Before Timon's cave.*]

Enter Poet and Painter; [Timon listens from his cave, unseen].

Painter. As I took note of the place, it cannot be far where he abides.

Poet. What's to be thought of him? Does the rumor hold for true that he's so full of gold?

Painter. Certain. Alcibiades reports it. Phrynia and   5
Timandra had gold of him. He likewise enriched poor straggling soldiers° with great quantity. 'Tis said he gave unto his steward a mighty sum.

Poet. Then this breaking° of his has been but a try° for his friends?   10

Painter. Nothing else. You shall see him a palm° in Athens again, and flourish with the highest. Therefore 'tis not amiss we tender° our loves to him in this supposed distress of his. It will show honestly° in us, and is very likely to load our purposes with   15 what they travail° for, if it be a just and true report that goes of his having.°

V.i.7 soldiers i.e., the banditti, who claimed to be soldiers   9 breaking going bankrupt   9 try test   11 palm (cf. Psalm 92:11 "The righteous shall flourish like the palm-tree")   13 tender offer   14 honestly honorably   16 travail (1) labor (2) travel   17 having wealth

131

Poet. What have you now to present unto him?

Painter. Nothing at this time but my visitation; only
20　I will promise him an excellent piece.

Poet. I must serve him so too, tell him of an intent
that's coming toward him.

Painter. Good as the best. Promising is the very air
o' th' time; it opens the eyes of expectation. Per-
25　formance is ever the duller for his act,° and but
in the plainer and simpler kind of people, the deed
of saying° is quite out of use. To promise is most
courtly and fashionable; performance is a kind of
will or testament, which argues a great sickness in
30　his judgment that makes it.

Enter Timon from his cave.

Timon. [*Aside*] Excellent workman, thou canst not
paint a man so bad as is thyself.

Poet. I am thinking what I shall say I have provided
for him. It must be a personating of himself;° a
35　satire against the softness° of prosperity, with a
discovery° of the infinite flatteries that follow youth
and opulency.

Timon. [*Aside*] Must thou needs stand for° a villain
in thine own work? Wilt thou whip thine own faults
40　in other men? Do so, I have gold for thee.

Poet. Nay, let's seek him.
Then do we sin against our own estate,°
When we may profit meet, and come too late.

Painter. True.
45　When the day serves, before black-cornered night,°

25 **his act** its act, its having been put into action　26–27 **the deed of
saying** i.e., the doing of what a person says he will do　34 **personating of himself** representation of Timon and his situation　35 **soft-
ness** weakness, flabbiness　36 **discovery** revelation (a theatrical term)
38 **stand for** serve as a model for　42 **estate** fortune, material possessions　45 **black-cornered night** i.e., night which creates dark corners
and is obscure like them

Find what thou want'st by free and offered light.
Come.

Timon. [*Aside*] I'll meet you at the turn.°
    What a god's gold, that he is worshiped
    In a baser temple° than where swine feed!   50
    'Tis thou that rig'st the bark and plough'st the
        foam,
    Settlest admirèd reverence° in a slave.
    To thee be worshiped and thy saints for aye;°
    Be° crowned with plagues that thee alone obey.
    Fit I meet them.   [*Comes forward.*]   55

Poet. Hail, worthy Timon.

Painter.   Our late noble master.

Timon. Have I once° lived to see two honest men?

Poet. Sir,
    Having often of your open bounty tasted,
    Hearing you were retired,° your friends fall'n off,   60
    Whose thankless natures, O abhorrèd spirits,
    Not all the whips of heaven are large enough—
    What, to you,
    Whose star-like nobleness gave life and influence°
    To their whole being! I am rapt,° and cannot cover   65
    The monstrous bulk of this ingratitude
    With any size° of words.

Timon.   Let it go;
    Naked, men may see't the better.
    You that are honest, by being what you are,
    Make them° best seen and known.

Painter.   He and myself   70

48 **I'll meet you at the turn** i.e., I will match your tricks with better
ones of my own   50 **baser temple** i.e., the human body   52 **Settlest
admirèd reverence** establishes a wondering awe (of his master)
53 **for aye** forever   54 **Be** i.e., may they be   57 **once** indeed (an in-
tensive)   60 **retired** withdrawn   64 **influence** i.e., astrological influence   65 **rapt** carried away with emotion   67 **size** (1) magnitude
(2) starch-like glue used on cloth, especially before painting on it
70 **them** i.e., the thankless natures of his fair-weather friends

Have traveled in the great show'r of your gifts,
And sweetly felt it.

Timon.   Ay, you are honest men.

Painter. We are hither come to offer you our service.

Timon. Most honest men. Why, how shall I requite you?
75 Can you eat roots and drink cold water? No?

Both. What we can do, we'll do to do you service.

Timon. Y'are honest men. Y'have heard that I have gold,
I am sure you have. Speak truth, y'are honest men.

Painter. So it is said, my noble lord, but therefore
80 Came not my friend nor I.

Timon. Good honest men. Thou draw'st a counterfeit°
Best in all Athens. Th'art indeed the best;
Thou counterfeit'st most lively.°

Painter.   So-so, my lord.

Timon. E'en so, sir, as I say. And for thy fiction,°
85 Why thy verse swells with stuff so fine and smooth°
That thou art even natural in thine art.°
But for all this, my honest-natured friends,
I must needs say you have a little fault;
Marry,° 'tis not monstrous in you, neither wish I
You take much pains to mend.

90 *Both.*   Beseech your honor
To make it known to us.

Timon.   You'll take it ill.

Both. Most thankfully, my lord.

---

81 **counterfeit** (1) representation, picture (2) false representation
83 **most lively** in a most lifelike manner   84 **fiction** imaginative
feigning   85 **smooth** polished (with implication of flattery)   86 **thou
. . . art** (1) your writings represent a triumph of nature over art;
your art conceals itself (2) you show your evil natural self in your
artful dissimulation   89 **Marry** indeed

Timon.   Will you indeed?

Both. Doubt it not, worthy lord.

Timon. There's never a one of you but trusts a knave
  That mightily deceives you.

Both.   Do we, my lord?   *95*

Timon. Ay, and you hear him cog,° see him dis-
    semble,
  Know his gross patchery,° love him, feed him,
  Keep° in your bosom, yet remain assured
  That he's a made-up° villain.

Painter. I know none such, my lord.

Poet.   Nor I.   *100*

Timon. Look you, I love you well; I'll give you gold:
  Rid me these villains from your companies.
  Hang them, or stab them, drown them in a
    draught,°
  Confound° them by some course, and come to me,
  I'll give you gold enough.   *105*

Both. Name them, my lord, let's know them.

Timon. You that way, and you this; but two in com-
    pany.°
  Each man apart, all single and alone,
  Yet an arch-villain keeps him company.
  [*To one*] If where thou art, two villains shall not be, *110*
  Come not near him. [*To the other*] If thou wouldst
    not reside
  But° where one villain is, then him abandon.
  Hence, pack,° there's gold; you came for gold, ye
    slaves.
  [*To one*] You have work for me, there's payment.
    Hence!

---

96 **cog** cheat   97 **patchery** roguery   98 **Keep** i.e., let him dwell
99 **made-up** complete   103 **draught** privy, sink   104 **Confound** destroy   107 **but two in company** i.e., wherever either of them is, there
is both a poet (or painter) and a villain   112 **But** except   113 **pack**
be off

[*To the other*] You are an alchemist, make gold
115　　of that.
Out, rascal dogs!
　　　　　[*Beats them out, then retires into his cave.*]

Enter [Flavius, the] Steward, and two Senators.

Flavius. It is vain that you would speak with Timon,
For he is set so only to himself°
That nothing but himself, which looks like man,
Is friendly with him.

120　*First Senator.*　　　　Bring us to his cave.
It is our part and promise° to th' Athenians
To speak with Timon.

Second Senator.　　　　At all times alike
Men are not still the same; 'twas time and griefs
That framed him thus. Time with his fairer hand
125　Offering the fortunes of his former days,
The former man may make him. Bring us to him,
And chance it° as it may.

Flavius.　　　　　　Here is his cave.
Peace and content be here. Lord Timon! Timon!
Look out, and speak to friends. Th' Athenians
130　By two of their most reverend senate greet thee.
Speak to them, noble Timon.

Enter Timon out of his cave.

Timon. Thou sun that comforts, burn! Speak and be
　　hanged.
For each true word a blister,° and each false
Be as a cauterizing to the root o' th' tongue,
Consuming it with speaking.

135　*First Senator.*　　　　Worthy Timon—

Timon. Of none but such as you, and you of Timon.

118 **is set so only to himself** is so completely preoccupied with himself　121 **our part and promise** the role we promised to play
127 **chance it** may it turn out　133 **For each true word a blister** (an
ironic reversal of the proverbial belief that a lie causes a blister on
the tongue)

First Senator. The senators of Athens greet thee,
   Timon.

Timon. I thank them, and would send them back the
   plague,
   Could I but catch it for them.

First Senator.   O forget
   What we are sorry for ourselves in thee.°   140
   The senators, with one consent of love,°
   Entreat thee back to Athens, who have thought
   On special dignities, which vacant lie
   For thy best use and wearing.°

Second Senator.   They confess
   Toward thee forgetfulness too general° gross;   145
   Which now the public body,° which doth seldom
   Play the recanter, feeling in itself
   A lack of Timon's aid, hath sense withal°
   Of it own fall,° restraining° aid to Timon;
   And send forth us to make their sorrowed render,° 150
   Together with a recompense more fruitful°
   Than their offense can weigh down by the dram°—
   Ay, even such heaps and sums of love and wealth
   As shall to thee blot out what wrongs were theirs,
   And write in thee the figures° of their love,   155
   Ever to read them° thine.

Timon.   You witch° me in it;
   Surprise me to the very brink of tears.

---

140 **in thee** i.e., in the wrongs we have caused you   141 **consent of love** harmonious voice of affection   144 **For thy best use and wearing** i.e., only you are suited to fill these dignities with the proper distinction   145 **general** universally   146 **the public body** the senate as representative of the body politic   148 **withal** at the same time   149 **it own fall** its own fall from grace   149 **restraining** keeping back   150 **sorrowed render** sorrowful rendering of an account   151 **fruitful** abundant   152 **weigh down by the dram** i.e., balance in weight even if measured to the last tiny unit   155 **figures** (1) written characters (2) numerals (as in counting money) (3) images, representations   156 **them** i.e., the Athenians as represented in the "figures of their love"   156 **witch** bewitch

Lend me a fool's heart and a woman's eyes,
And I'll beweep these comforts,° worthy senators.

First Senator. Therefore so please thee to return with
160   us,
And of our Athens, thine and ours, to take
The captainship, thou shalt be met with thanks,
Allowed° with absolute power, and thy good name
Live with authority. So soon we shall drive back
165 Of Alcibiades th' approaches wild,
Who like a boar too savage doth root up
His country's peace.

Second Senator.   And shakes his threat'ning sword
Against the walls of Athens.

First Senator.   Therefore, Timon—

Timon. Well, sir, I will; therefore I will, sir, thus:
170 If Alcibiades kill my countrymen,
Let Alcibiades know this of Timon,
That Timon cares not. But if he sack fair Athens,
And take our goodly agèd men by th' beards,
Giving our holy virgins to the stain
175 Of contumelious,° beastly, mad-brained war,
Then let him know, and tell him Timon speaks it,
In pity of our agèd and our youth,
I cannot choose but tell him that I care not,
And let him take't at worst.° For their knives care
    not
180 While you have throats to answer.° For myself,
There's not a whittle° in th' unruly camp°
But I do prize it at my love° before
The reverend'st throat in Athens. So I leave you

---

159 **comforts** pleasures   163 **Allowed** endowed   175 **contumelious**
insolent   179 **take't at worst** put the worst interpretation he wishes
on it   180 **throats to answer** i.e., throats to be cut by the knives of
Alcibiades' soldiers (and voices to protest for yourselves)   181 **whit-
tle** small knife   181 **th' unruly camp** (1) the party of those revolting
against Athens (2) the disorderly, turbulent army (of Alcibiades)
182 **prize it at my love** value it in my esteem

To the protection of the prosperous° gods,
As thieves to keepers.°

Flavius.   Stay not, all's in vain.   185

Timon. Why I was writing of my epitaph;
It will be seen tomorrow. My long sickness
Of health and living now begins to mend,
And nothing° brings me all things. Go, live still;
Be Alcibiades your plague, you his,   190
And last° so long enough.

First Senator.   We speak in vain.

Timon. But yet I love my country, and am not
One that rejoices in the common wrack,°
As common bruit° doth put it.

First Senator.   That's well spoke.

Timon. Commend me to my loving countrymen.   195

First Senator. These words become° your lips as they
   pass thorough them.

Second Senator. And enter in our ears like great tri-
   umphers°
In their applauding gates.°

Timon.   Commend me to them,
And tell them that to ease them of their griefs,
Their fears of hostile strokes, their aches,° losses,   200
Their pangs of love, with other incident throes°
That nature's fragile vessel doth sustain
In life's uncertain voyage, I will some kindness do
   them;
I'll teach them to prevent° wild Alcibiades' wrath.

---

184 **prosperous** propitious   185 **As thieves to keepers** i.e., as I would
leave thieves to the protection of their jailers   189 **nothing** nothing-
ness, oblivion   191 **last** endure   193 **wrack** destruction   194 **bruit**
rumor   196 **become** befit   197 **triumphers** triumphant marchers
198 **applauding gates** i.e., city gates thronged with those applauding
the triumph   200 **aches** (two syllables, pronounced "aitches")
201 **incident throes** agonies likely to occur   204 **prevent** anticipate
(but First Senator interprets "to keep from occurring")

205 *First Senator.* I like this well; he will return again.

Timon. I have a tree which grows here in my close,°
That mine own use invites me to cut down,
And shortly must I fell it. Tell my friends,
Tell Athens, in the sequence of degree,°
210 From high to low throughout, that whoso please
To stop affliction, let him take his haste;
Come hither ere my tree hath felt the ax,
And hang himself. I pray you do my greeting.

Flavius. Trouble him no further; thus you still° shall
find him.

215 *Timon.* Come not to me again, but say to Athens,
Timon hath made his everlasting mansion
Upon the beachèd verge of the salt flood,°
Who° once a day with his embossèd° froth
The turbulent surge shall cover. Thither come,
220 And let my gravestone be your oracle.°
Lips, let four words go by and language end.°
What is amiss, plague and infection mend.
Graves only be men's works and death their gain.
Sun, hide thy beams; Timon hath done his reign.
Exit Timon.

225 *First Senator.* His discontents are unremovably
Coupled to nature.°

Second Senator. Our hope in him is dead. Let us
return,

206 **close** enclosure   209 **sequence of degree** proper order of the
social hierarchy   214 **still** always   217 **beachèd verge of the salt
flood** edge of the sea that forms a beach   218 **Who** i.e., "the beachèd
verge"   218 **embossèd** covered with foam (usually from the mouth
of a hunted animal)   220 **be your oracle** i.e., be consulted by you as
if it were an oracle (a place where divine pronouncements are made,
or the god making such pronouncements)   221 **let four words go
by and language end** i.e., speak only a few more words ("four" is
used indefinitely) and then not speak any further   226 **Coupled to
nature** a part of his nature

And strain° what other means is left unto us
In our dear° peril.

First Senator.   It requires swift foot.   *Exeunt.*

[Scene II. *Before the walls of Athens.*]

Enter two other Senators with a Messenger.

Third Senator. Thou hast painfully discovered.° Are
   his files°
As full as thy report?

Messenger.   I have spoke the least.°
Besides, his expedition° promises
Present° approach.

Fourth Senator. We stand much hazard if they bring
   not Timon.   5

Messenger. I met a courier, one mine ancient° friend,
Whom though in general part° we were opposed,
Yet our old love made a particular° force,
And made us speak like friends. This man was
   riding
From Alcibiades to Timon's cave   10
With letters of entreaty, which imported°
His fellowship i' th' cause against your city,
In part for his sake moved.°

228 **strain** exert to the utmost   229 **dear** grievous, dire **V.ii.1 Thou
hast painfully discovered** (1) your revelation was painful to us (2) you
have made your revelation in painstaking detail   1 **files** ranks
2 **spoke the least** reported the minimum   3 **expedition** speed
4 **Present** immediate   6 **ancient** former   7 **in general part** i.e., in
matters of general or public interest   8 **particular** personal   11 **im-
ported** bore as their message (with additional suggestion of "im-
portuned" or urged)   13 **moved** instigated

Enter the other Senators [from Timon].

Third Senator.   Here come our brothers.

First Senator. No talk° of Timon, nothing of him
     expect.
15   The enemy's drum is heard, and fearful scouring°
     Doth choke the air with dust. In, and prepare.
     Ours is the fall, I fear, our foes the snare.°   *Exeunt.*

[Scene III. *Before Timon's cave.*]

Enter a Soldier in the woods, seeking Timon.

Soldier. By all description this should be the place.
     Who's here? Speak, ho! No answer? What is this?°
     "Timon is dead, who hath outstretched his span.°
     Some beast read this; there does not live a man."°
5   Dead, sure, and this his grave. What's on this tomb
     I cannot read. The character I'll take with wax;°
     Our captain hath in every figure° skill,
     An aged° interpreter, though young in days.
     Before proud Athens he's set down° by this,
10   Whose fall the mark° of his ambition is.   *Exit.*

14 No talk i.e., let us not talk   15 scouring scurrying about (in
preparation for battle)   17 our foes the snare i.e., our foes are the
snare or trap which will cause the downfall of Athens   V.iii.2 What
is this (presumably the Soldier finds an inscription or trial epitaph
composed by Timon in English, which the Soldier can read, whereas
the epitaph on Timon's tomb is in Latin, which the Soldier cannot
read)   3 outstretched his span lived beyond his allotted or desired
life span   4 there does not live a man i.e., all men left alive are
merely beasts   6 The character I'll take with wax I will take a wax
impression of the letters   7 figure written character   8 aged experienced   9 set down i.e., in a siege   10 mark goal

[Scene IV. *Before the walls of Athens.*]

*Trumpets sound. Enter Alcibiades with his
powers before Athens.*

Alcibiades. Sound to this coward and lascivious town
Our terrible° approach.   *Sounds a parley.*°

The Senators appear upon the walls.°

Till now you have gone on, and filled the time
With all licentious measure,° making your wills
The scope° of justice. Till now, myself and such   5
As slept° within the shadow of your power,
Have wandered with our traversed° arms and
    breathed
Our sufferance vainly.° Now the time is flush,°
When crouching marrow in the bearer strong°
Cries, of itself, "No more." Now breathless wrong°   10
Shall sit and pant in your great chairs of ease,°
And pursy° insolence shall break his wind
With fear and horrid° flight.

First Senator.   Noble and young,
When thy first griefs° were but a mere conceit,°

V.iv.2 **terrible** terrifying 2 s.d. **Sounds a parley** i.e., by a special signal on drum or trumpet, Alcibiades calls for a conference with the
enemy to try to make peace 2 s.d. **upon the walls** i.e., upon the
upper stage 4 **With all licentious measure** with all kinds of unbridled conduct 5 **scope** extent 6 **slept** (1) were asleep, inactive
(2) lived 7 **traversed** folded across (in resignation) 7–8 **breathed/
Our sufferance vainly** spoke in vain about our sufferings 8 **flush**
ripe 9 **When . . . strong** i.e., when the resolute man's courage is
aroused 10 **breathless wrong** wrongdoers breathless through fear
11 **great chairs of ease** comfortably upholstered chairs of state
12 **pursy** short-winded 13 **horrid** horrible 14 **griefs** grievances
14 **conceit** idea

15 Ere thou hadst power or we had cause of fear,
    We sent to thee to give thy rages balm,
    To wipe out our ingratitude with loves
    Above their° quantity.

Second Senator.   So did we woo
    Transformèd Timon to our city's love
20 By humble message and by promised means.°
    We were not all unkind, nor all deserve
    The common stroke of war.

First Senator.   These walls of ours
    Were not erected by their hands from whom
    You have received your grief; nor are they such
    That these great tow'rs, trophies, and schools°
25   should fall
    For private faults in them.

Second Senator.   Nor are they living
    Who were the motives that you first went out°
    Shame that they wanted, cunning in excess
    Hath broke their hearts.° March, noble lord,
30 Into our city with thy banners spread.
    By decimation and a tithèd death,°
    If thy revenges hunger for that food
    Which nature loathes, take thou the destined tenth,
    And by the hazard of the spotted die,°
    Let die the spotted.°

35 *First Senator.*   All have not offended.
    For those that were, it is not square° to take

18 **their** (the antecedent is either "griefs" or "rages" or both)
20 **means** conditions of peace (or possibly "riches")   25 **trophies, and schools** monuments, and public buildings   27 **motives that you first went out** instigators or movers of your
original banishment   28–29 **Shame . . . hearts** i.e., their hearts
were broken with remorse for two common moral failings: lack
of a sense of disgrace for their wrongdoing and excess of crafty
deceit   31 **decimation and a tithèd death** the killing of one
person in ten   34 **by the hazard of the spotted die** by chance,
as in dice ("die" is the singular of "dice")   35 **spotted** (1) guilty
(2) those selected by the "spots" on the dice   36 **square** honest

On those that are, revenge. Crimes, like lands,
Are not inherited. Then, dear countryman,
Bring in thy ranks, but leave without° thy rage.
Spare thy Athenian cradle and those kin   40
Which in the bluster° of thy wrath must fall
With those that have offended. Like a shepherd,
Approach the fold° and cull th' infected forth,
But kill not all together.

Second Senator.   What thou wilt,
Thou rather shalt enforce it with thy smile   45
Than hew to't° with thy sword.

First Senator.   Set but thy foot
Against our rampired° gates, and they shall ope,
So° thou wilt send thy gentle heart before
To say thou't enter friendly.

Second Senator.   Throw thy glove,
Or any token of thine honor else,   50
That thou wilt use the wars as thy redress
And not as our confusion.° All thy powers°
Shall make their harbor° in our town till we
Have sealed° thy full desire.

Alcibiades.   Then there's my glove.
Descend and open your uncharg'd ports.°   55
Those enemies of Timon's and mine own
Whom you yourselves shall set out for reproof,°
Fall, and no more. And to atone° your fears
With my more noble meaning,° not a man
Shall pass his quarter,° or offend the stream   60
Of regular justice in your city's bounds,

---

39 **without** outside   41 **bluster** tempest   43 **fold** enclosure for sheep
or the flock itself   46 **hew to't** cut thy way to it   47 **rampired** forti-
fied   48 **So** provided that   52 **confusion** destruction   52 **powers**
armed forces   53 **make their harbor** be billeted   54 **sealed** solemnly
ratified (by fulfilling)   55 **uncharg'd ports** unassailed gates   57 **reproof** shame   58 **atone** appease   59 **meaning** intention   60 **quarter**
billet (?) area of duty (?)

But shall be remedied° to your public laws
At heaviest answer.°

Both Senators.   'Tis most nobly spoken.

Alcibiades. Descend, and keep your words.
          [*The Senators descend, and open the gates.*]

                    Enter a Soldier.

65 *Soldier.* My noble general, Timon is dead,
    Entombed upon the very hem° o' th' sea,
    And on his gravestone this insculpture° which
    With wax I brought away, whose soft impression
    Interprets° for my poor ignorance.

                Alcibiades reads the epitaph.°

Alcibiades. "Here lies a wretched corse,° of wretched
70   soul bereft.
    Seek not my name. A plague consume you, wicked
        caitiffs° left.
    Here lie I, Timon, who alive all living men did
        hate.
    Pass by and curse thy fill, but pass, and stay not
        here thy gait."
    These well express in thee thy latter° spirits.
75 Though thou abhorr'dst in us our human griefs,
    Scorn'dst our brains' flow,° and those our droplets
        which
    From niggard° nature fall; yet rich conceit°
    Taught thee to make vast Neptune weep for aye°
    On thy low grave, on faults forgiven. Dead
80 Is noble Timon, of whose memory
    Hereafter more. Bring me into your city,

_____

62 **remedied** turned over for remedy   63 **At heaviest answer** for the
maximum punishment   66 **hem** edge (the "beachèd verge" of
V.i.217)   67 **insculpture** inscription   69 **Interprets** acts as an in-
terpreter   69 **s.d. epitaph** (there are two epitaphs here, both from
North's *Plutarch*, and it seems very likely that one of them—probably the first—was intended to be omitted)   70 **corse** corpse   71
caitiffs wretches   74 **latter** later, more recent   76 **brains' flow** tears
77 **niggard** stingy   77 **rich conceit** fanciful imagination   78 **for aye**
forever

And I will use the olive with my sword,°
Make war breed peace, make peace stint° war, make each
Prescribe to other, as each other's leech.°
Let our drums strike.　　　　　　　　*Exeunt.*　85

FINIS

82 **use the olive with my sword** i.e., combine the olive branch of peace with the sword of war, show mercy even though I enter your city as a conqueror　83 **stint** cause to stop　84 **leech** physician

Textual Note

Our sole authority for the text of *Timon of Athens* is the First Folio of Shakespeare, published in 1623. It may only be the result of a lucky accident that the play was printed at all, since *Troilus and Cressida* was intended to follow *Romeo and Juliet* in the section of Tragedies, and three pages of *Troilus* were actually set up and printed. But difficulties over the copyright of *Troilus* probably forced Jaggard to stop work on it. He allowed a sufficient number of blank pages for it, and then went on to set up and print *Julius Caesar*. Contrary to Jaggard's expectations, the difficulties with *Troilus* were not quickly resolved. Something had to fill the space left for *Troilus,* and *Timon* was decided on. It is a relatively short play, so that it only partially fills the allotted pages. Signature ii is omitted and there is an awkward gap between pages 98 and 109 (beginning of *Julius Caesar*), despite the blown-up and elaborately decorated list of actors' names that has a page to itself at the end of *Timon*.

Whether *Timon* would have been printed at all if the difficulties with *Troilus* had not occurred is a teasing question, but the condition of its text strongly confirms its role as an afterthought or stopgap. *Timon* is full of the kind of inconsistencies and roughnesses that suggest a play that has not received any final revision (see Introduction). There is no record of a performance of the play during Shakespeare's lifetime, and the possibility seems unlikely. It is obviously not the sort of play that a business-minded publisher would be eager to include in an expensive and speculative venture like the Shakespeare Folio. The text of *Timon* was set up either directly from Shakespeare's "foul papers" (rough draft), or from a transcript of them made by a scribe.

The state of the text has an important bearing on the editing of the play. If *Timon* is indeed a play that has not received that final revision and polishing necessary to put it into actable (or printable) form, it is not the job of a modern editor to undertake this task for Shakespeare. It is not up to a modern editor, for example, to make the lines scan by piecing them out differently (a formidable task here), or to distribute specific roles to the First, Second, Third, and Fourth Lords, or to make other changes of an essentially "improving" nature. I assume that the present-day reader would like to have the play in a modernized form, but as close as possible to the way Shakespeare left it. I have therefore made very few changes in the Folio text, even at the expense of leaving loose ends or inconsistencies. (It would be wonderfully satisfying to know whom Alcibiades is pleading for in Act III, Scene v.)

Two matters of special interest are related to the nature of the text: lineation and stage directions. In the text of *Timon* there is either serious mislineation (the printing of blank verse lines in some other form, either broken in two or run together as prose), or a failure in a number of places to write regular, five-beat, iambic lines. That is, either the compositor took wide liberties with the metrics, or the author himself made errors or allowed himself a great deal of freedom. Considering the unrevised state of the text, one is forced to conclude that the printed version is probably an accurate rendering of the copy. "Mislineation" is, therefore, a misleading term. I have generally followed the lineation of the Folio, except where lines are obviously broken into two to fill up the "cast off" space (that is, the amount of space estimated to be needed for a certain quantity of copy), or run together as prose where not enough space was allowed. The Folio lineation usually makes for good speech rhythm, with important pauses at the ends of lines. To run these lines through the blank verse meat grinder would distort their quality as dramatic speech.

How one treats the Folio stage directions of *Timon* also depends upon one's attitude to the text. The indications of action in this play are of the permissive and literary sort characteristic of an author's manuscript. For example, the final part of the stage direction that opens Act I, Scene ii, reads: *"Then comes dropping after all, Apemantus, discontentedly, like himself."* This is a descriptive stage direction, which would have been put into a more practical form in a promptbook prepared by the stage manager. To change this direction to *"Then enter Apemantus, alone and at a distance"* (as Sisson does in his fine text) is to throw away a significant Shakespearean line for the sake of some imagined modern production. In an unrevised play such as *Timon* there is a special sanction for retaining the obviously authorial stage directions of the Folio, which bring us closer to the original manuscript of the play than do the colorless, clarified directions of a modern editor. I have also avoided one other type of correction in the stage directions. When it is not clear who is being addressed, I have not seen fit to supply a name. In Act V, Scene i, for example, Timon is upbraiding Poet and Painter in turn, but the text never specifies which one. I have simply indicated *To one* and *To the other,* although in a production it would obviously have to be either to Poet or Painter. Perhaps these two characters are meant to have a Rosencrantz and Guildenstern interchangeability.

In the present text spelling has been modernized, except that certain older forms have been retained when they are essentially different from their modern counterparts, for example, "vild" (for "vile"), "huswife" (for "housewife"), "a th' " (for "o' th' "). The punctuation has been modernized within limits, but I have generally been wary of introducing changes where the Folio pointing makes good sense. Even editors scrupulous about the language of the Folio seem not to feel bound by the punctuation. Capitalization has been modernized, and contractions not affecting pronunciation have been eliminated (especially in the verb forms). For stylistic reasons, I have omitted many traditional exclamation marks. The speech prefixes have been expanded and somewhat clarified. The list of actors' names is taken from the Folio, where it is printed (with one name given twice, and with the names in a slightly different order) at the end of the play.

Typographical errors have been corrected, and some stage directions have been slightly moved. Many traditional stage directions, not in the Folio, have been supplied in square brackets. The traditional act and scene divisions and scene locations have been indicated for convenience, but the reader should recall that the action of the play was continuous and the scenes often unlocalized. The Folio indicates only "Actus Primus, Scœna Prima."

Other departures from the Folio are listed below. The reading of the present text is given first, in italics, and then the reading of the Folio (F) in roman.

I.i.s.d. *Enter Poet, Painter, Jeweler, Merchant* [F adds "and Mercer"]   21 *gum, which oozes* Gowne, which vses   87 *hands* hand   87 *slip* sit   166 *satiety* saciety   215 *cost* cast   280 *Come* Comes   289 *I'll keep you company* [in F part of speech of Second Lord]

I.ii.29 *ever* verie   115 s.d. *Sound tucket* [F follows this with another s.d., "Enter the Maskers of Amazons, with Lutes in their hands, dauncing and playing," incorrectly anticipating the entry at line 132; the necessary part of this s.d. is therefore added to that of line 132]   127 *Th'ear* There   132 *First Lord* First Lord Luc.   154 *First Lady* I Lord

II.ii.4 *resumes* resume   43 *of broken* of debt, broken   80 *mistress'* Masters   110 *mistress'* Masters   138 *proposed* propose   195 *Flaminius* Flauius   195 s.d. *Enter Flaminius, Servilius, and Third Servant* Enter three Seruants

III.i.s.d. *with* with a

III.iii.21 *and I* and

III.iv.s.d. *two Servants* man   50 *ate* eate   87 *Hortensius* 1. Var.   111 *Sempronius—all* Sempronius Vllorxa

III.v.17 *An* And   67 *'em* him

III.vi.92 *with your* you with   116–17 [speech prefixes reversed]

IV.i.13 *Son* Some   21 *let* yet

IV.iii.12 *pasture* Pastour   13 *lean* leaue   88 *tub-fast* fubfast   117 *window-bars* window Barne   122 *thy* the   157 *scolds* scold'st   255 *drudges* drugges   256 *command* command'st   272 *rogue* ragge   284 *my* thy   402 *them* then   501 *mild* wilde   518 *A usuring kindness, as* If not a Vsuring kindnesse, and as

V.i.5–6 *Phrynia and Timandra* Phrinica and Timandylo   72 *men* man   116 s.d. *Beats . . . cave* Exeunt   127 *chance* chanc'd   134 *cauterizing* Cantherizing   148 *sense* since   183 *reverend'st* reuerends

V.iv.55 *Descend* Defend   64 s.d. *Soldier* Messenger

The Sources of *Timon of Athens*

The chief source for Shakespeare's play is probably
Lucian's satiric dialogue, *Timon*, written in Greek in the
second century A.D. It is unlikely that Shakespeare read
Lucian in Greek, but the earliest English translation, by
Thomas Heywood, was not published until 1637. There
may, of course, have been an earlier English translation
that has not survived, but a more likely possibility is that
Shakespeare used the French translation by Filbert Bretin
in 1582 (as Honigmann argues). A number of Italian versions were also available, as well as a Latin translation by
Erasmus. The verbal parallels between Shakespeare and
Lucian are few, but there is a striking similarity in style
and tone. Common sense insists that Lucian must be
Shakespeare's ultimate source, even though the exact
stages of transmission are not clear to us. We reprint
below the lively modern translation of Lucian by Lionel
Casson.

The most direct and commonly agreed-on source for
Timon is Sir Thomas North's translation of Plutarch, *The
Lives of the Noble Grecians and Romans,* first published
in 1579 (although Shakespeare probably used the 1595
edition). There is a brief digression in the "Life of Marcus
Antonius" which recounts how Antony, despondent after
his defeat at the battle of Actium, lived apart from men
in a house by the sea called Timoneon. Plutarch follows
Strabo's version of the story, which represents Antony as
deliberately imitating the example of Timon. In the section

reprinted below, Timon's career is briefly described to explain the erratic conduct of Antony. Timon was apparently
an actual person who lived in Athens in the fifth century
B.C., and about whose misanthropy many legends arose.
He was a favorite butt of the Greek comic dramatists.
There are a few further references to Timon in Plutarch's
"Life of Alcibiades," which was the Greek life paired
with that of the Roman Coriolanus. If *Timon* was written
around the time of *Antony and Cleopatra* and *Coriolanus,*
it is not surprising that all three plays should draw on
North's Plutarch. It is likely that Shakespeare used Plutarch more extensively than the few selections printed
below would indicate. Six names in *Timon,* for example,
come from the "Life of Marcus Antonius," and the "Life
of Lucullus" provides us with an excellent background for
the character in Shakespeare's play.

The account of Timon in William Painter's *The Palace
of Pleasure,* first published in 1566 (but Shakespeare
probably used the 1575 edition), draws on Plutarch for
its facts, but orders them with an eye to making a good
story. There is perhaps one bit of evidence of Shakespeare's literal use of Painter. Timon's epitaphs in the
play are taken over verbatim from North's Plutarch except
for one change: Shakespeare uses Painter's phrase,
"wicked caitiffs," in place of North's "wicked wretches."
Since Shakespeare probably drew on Painter for *All's Well
That Ends Well,* and possibly for *Romeo and Juliet,* it is
reasonable to suppose that he also read the brief account
of Timon. The version of the Timon story given in Sir
Richard Barckley, *A Discourse of the Felicity of Man*
(1598), is derived almost entirely from Painter.

The most controversial and puzzling source that has
been claimed for Shakespeare's play is the anonymous
Timon, which the Reverend Alexander Dyce in 1842 first
published from a manuscript for the Shakespeare Society
(now Dyce MS 52 in the Victoria and Albert Museum,
London). This is an academic play, full of self-consciously
learned allusions and quotations. It is based on Lucian,
although on at least three occasions it introduces material
not in Lucian and also used, in somewhat different form,

by Shakespeare: 1) a mock-banquet scene in which Timon serves stones painted to look like artichokes; 2) the faithful Steward Laches, who follows his master in adversity; 3) the burial by Timon of his newly discovered gold. None of these is so distinctive that it can only be accounted for by direct borrowing, but the combination suggests that Shakespeare may have seen a performance of the play, read the manuscript, or heard about the play from someone who had seen or read it. Just how this could have occurred is entirely a matter of speculation.

The date of the "old" Timon play (as it is usually called) is very uncertain. It has generally been assigned to the last quarter of the sixteenth century, but recently some scholars have argued that it may just as easily follow Shakespeare's Timon as precede it. This late date offers a simple way to account for the similarities not in Lucian, but it seems unlikely to me. It is difficult to reconstruct how the academic author could have known a Shakespearean play that was presumably never acted, never completely finished, and not published until 1623. The records may, of course, be incomplete, but then the argument has to be founded on a series of negative probabilities. Proponents of a late date for the "old" Timon play have heard echoes in it of King Lear and The Merchant of Venice, but these are questionable. One other explanation for the similarity of Timon of Athens to the "old" Timon play is that they both drew on a common source now lost. This is a convenient postulate, but not very helpful in the present case, since nothing further is known about this common source.

Two other sources for which claims have been offered have generally been rejected by scholars: Boiardo's Timone (1494) and Lyly's Campaspe (1584). In the latter play, Diogenes is rather close to Shakespeare's Apemantus, but the malcontent railer was a familiar type, and Shakespeare had already created Jaques in As You Like It and Thersites in Troilus and Cressida.

There are many allusions to Timon in Renaissance English literature. He was a stock figure for the misanthrope, whose life was often described in animal analogies. Shakespeare refers to Timon in Love's Labor's Lost, when

Berowne hypocritically berates his companions for being in love:

> O me, with what strict patience have I sat
> To see a king transformèd to a gnat!
> To see great Hercules whipping a gig,
> And profound Solomon to tune a jig,
> And Nestor play at push-pin with the boys,
> And critic Timon laugh at idle toys! (IV.iii.165–70)

LUCIAN

Timon

Timon, Zeus, Hermes, Wealth, Poverty,
Gnathonides, Philiades, Demeas, Thrasycles

*The scene is a remote spot on the border of Attica, the
district about Athens. The time is the second half of the
fifth century* B.C.

Timon. O Zeus, god of friends, strangers, comrades, the
hearth, lightning, and oaths; gatherer of the clouds,
thunderer—and whatever else the wild-eyed poets call
you (particularly when they're stumped by their meter
—with all your names strung out you're a big help to a
verse that's short; you plug the gaps in the rhythm).
Well, Zeus, where's your crashing lightning and rolling
thunder and blazing, flashing, terrifying thunderbolt
now? It's become painfully clear that this is all nonsense, just poetic hot air—the only crash and roar is the
sound of the words. That far-famed, far-flying, ever-
ready missile of yours has somehow or other fizzled
out; it's stone cold; it hasn't a spark of wrath left in it
to descend on the heads of wrongdoers. As a matter
of fact, anyone out to try his hand at perjury would get
more of a scare from an old candle stump than the flame
of that all-consuming thunderbolt of yours. You look so

From *Selected Satires of Lucian,* translated and edited by Lionel Casson. New York: Doubleday & Company, Inc. (Anchor Books). Copyright
© 1962 by Lionel Casson. Reprinted by permission of Doubleday & Company, Inc. The notes have been abridged.

much like a mere person just wagging a torch that sinners aren't the least bit afraid of the fire and smoke; the worst hurt they think they can get is a messy smudge of soot. That's why Salmoneus[1] had the nerve to set himself up as a rival thunderer—a perfectly logical thing to do, considering what a cocksure hothead he was and how slow-burning your anger is. Why shouldn't he have? You're as fast asleep as if you'd taken a narcotic; you don't hear the perjurers or notice the wrongdoers; your eyes are bleary and can't focus on what's going on; your ears are as deaf as any dotard's. When you were young and hot-tempered and in the bloom of your anger, you carried on against the wicked and the violent. You never gave them a moment's peace in those days: the thunderbolt was always in action and the aegis[2] in motion; the thunder rolled, and the lightning flashed so thick and fast it seemed to come in volleys. Quakes tossed the earth like a salad, to use the vernacular; snow came down in bucketfuls, and the hailstones were like rocks. The rain pelted fast and furious, each drop a river. Why, back when Deucalion[3] was alive, in the twinkling of an eye such a flood took place that everything was swamped and only one vessel, some sort of ark, barely came through; it grounded on a peak of Parnassus carrying human seed with its spark of life so that greater wickedness could be propagated on earth. Well, you're reaping the reward of your laziness: men don't sacrifice to you any longer or wear garlands in your honor—someone may do it as an afterthought during the Olympic games, but he hardly thinks of it as an obligation; he's just helping to keep an old tradition alive.

Little by little, my King of the Gods, they're making a second Cronus of you and shoving you off your throne. I won't bother mentioning how many times they've

---

1 Salmoneus, son of the god of the winds, imitated thunder (he rolled chariots over a bridge of brass) and insisted that men sacrifice to him as to Zeus.
2 Zeus's shield, the sight of which inspired terror.
3 The Greek Noah.

robbed your temple by now. But some have even laid hands on your very image at Olympia—and you, Almighty Thunderer, didn't have the energy to unleash the bloodhounds or call out your neighbors so they could help you catch the criminals while still packing up for the getaway. The noble Destroyer of the Giants and Master of the Titans sat still, his fifteen-foot thunderbolt motionless in his hand, while his golden locks were clipped from his head. Well, Your Highness, when are you going to stop being so careless and indifferent to all this? When are you going to punish such wrongdoing? How much fire and flood do you think you'll need to deal with this rampaging human insolence?

Let me stop talking in generalities and bring up my own case. I raised dozens of Athenians to the heights; I found them in poverty and made them rich. I lent a hand to everyone in need. Even more—I actually poured out my money in a flood to help my friends. But now that all this has left me a pauper, they don't know me any longer, they don't look in my direction—the same people who used to bow and scrape before me and hang on my every word. When I meet any of them on the street they go by me the way people go by some old tombstone overturned by time and lying on its back, without bothering to look at the epitaph. When they catch sight of me from far off they turn up another street—they feel it's a bad omen, it'll bring bad luck, to look at the man who, not so long ago, had been their savior and benefactor. Because of all these troubles I've exiled myself in this remote outpost, put on overalls, hired out as a farm hand for a dollar fifty a day, and deliver my philosophical pronouncements to the solitude and my mattock. I feel I've gained this much: I no longer have to lay eyes upon so much undeserved prosperity; of the two evils, that's by far the worse.

But when, O Lord of the World, will you shake off this deep, sound sleep—you've been at it longer than Epimenides[4]—, stoke the fire in the thunderbolt (or re-

---

4 The Greek Rip Van Winkle.

light it from Etna), get a mighty blaze going, and show
the anger that Zeus used to, in his younger days when
he was a real man. Or maybe the stories the Cretans
tell about you and your grave there are true.

Zeus. Hermes, who's that shouting? Down there in the
foothills of Mt. Hymettus in Attica. That man there in
overalls, covered with grime and dirt. He's bent over; I
think he's digging. Talkative fellow with plenty of nerve.
Must be a philosopher—otherwise he wouldn't utter
such blasphemy about us.

Hermes. Father, don't you recognize Echecratides' son
Timon? He's the one who fed us so often with top-grade
sacrificial offerings, that *nouveau riche* who served us
whole hecatombs and threw such magnificent parties
for us on your festival day.

Zeus. My, oh my, what a change! You mean the wealthy,
fine-looking fellow who always had so many friends
around? Why is he like this? Poor devil! It looks as if
he's a workman, a farm hand. That's a mighty heavy
mattock he's swinging!

Hermes. You *could* say it was his goodness and philanthropy and the way he took pity on everyone in need
that ruined him. But the truth of the matter is, it was
his senselessness, stupidity, and lack of judgment in
choosing friends. The man never realized he was indulging a pack of crows and wolves. The poor devil
imagined that all those vultures, who were tearing out
his liver, were his bosom friends, who enjoyed eating
his food because they liked him so much. When they
had stripped his bones, gnawed them clean as a whistle,
and carefully sucked out all the marrow inside, away
they went, leaving him like a withered tree trunk lopped
off at the roots. They don't know him any longer; they
won't look at him—perish the thought!—and they're
certainly not going to play savior or benefactor in their
turn. That's why you see him now in overalls, swinging
a mattock. He was ashamed to stay in the city, so he
hired out as a farm hand. He's going mad brooding over

his troubles, over the way people he made rich pass him by with their noses in the air and don't even remember whether or not his name is Timon.

Zeus. We simply cannot pass over this man or neglect him any longer. Naturally he's angry at his bad luck. Why, we'd be behaving just like those damned parasites of his if we forgot about a man who's sacrificed so many fat haunches of beef and goat on our altars. I can actually still sniff the aroma in my nostrils. You see, I've been so busy and there's been such a fuss kicked up by perjurers and ruffians and bandits, and then there's the scare the temple robbers have been giving me—there are so many of them and they're so hard to keep track of, they don't let me close my eyes for a second—that it's been ages since I last looked in on Attica. Particularly ever since philosophers and their debates became the rage there. They wrangle with each other and shout so loud I can't even listen to prayers; I either have to sit around with my ears plugged up or let them be the death of me with their endless hollering about "virtue," "incorporeal substances," and all that drivel. That's how I came to neglect this fellow, who's really not a bad sort. Hermes, go get Wealth and rush right down to the man. Tell Wealth to bring Treasure along, and tell them both to stick with Timon and not be in such a hurry to leave him this time even if, with that big-heartedness of his, he tries to chase them out of the house again. As for those scroungers and the ingratitude they showed him—I'll look into the matter again and they'll pay for what they did as soon as my thunderbolt is fixed. I broke the two biggest flashes and ruined their edge yesterday: Professor Anaxagoras[5] was trying to convince his students that we gods are just nobodies, and I threw it too hard at him. I missed—Pericles had his hand over him—and it bounced off the temple of Castor and Pollux and started a fire; it almost broke into

[5] A celebrated philosopher who argued that not gods but an intelligent force governed the world. He was brought up on charges of impiety and would have been executed had not Pericles, the all-powerful political leader of Athens at the time, intervened in his behalf.

bits on the stone. In the meantime it will be punishment enough for those parasites when they see Timon rolling in money.

Hermes (*musing as he goes to fetch Wealth*). That's what it means to have the nerve to shout and make a nuisance of yourself. Very useful. Not only in court but at prayers too. See? Because he raised a holler, said what was on his mind, and got Zeus's attention, overnight Timon will go from rags to riches. If he had stayed bent over his mattock and kept on digging without opening his mouth, he'd still be digging and nobody would be paying him the slightest attention. (*Gets Wealth and brings him before Zeus.*)

Wealth. Zeus, I won't go to him.

Zeus. My dear Wealth, why not? It's my orders, you know.

Wealth. So help me Zeus, that man insulted me. He squandered me. He cut me up into little pieces—me, an old friend of his father's. He practically booted me out of the house; he got rid of me quicker than you'd drop a hot potato. Go back there and be handed over again to a bunch of parasites, bootlickers, and whores? No, Zeus. Send me to people who'll appreciate the gift, people who'll treat me with respect, who value me and are anxious to have me. Let gulls like him stick with Poverty since they prefer her to me. Let the poor devils take the overalls and mattock she'll give them and be content to pocket their dollar and a half a day—since they so cavalierly toss away gifts worth a hundred thousand.

Zeus. Timon won't behave that way with you any longer. Unless that back of his is impervious to aches, the mattock's been a good schoolmaster and taught him that you're preferable to Poverty. But what's the matter with you, anyway? You sound to me like a born faultfinder. Now you're blaming Timon because he opened the doors wide to let you circulate freely and didn't guard you jealously under lock and key. Up to now you used to get angry at the rich for doing the reverse—you complained they locked you up so tightly with bolts, bars, and seals you couldn't see a ray of light. You were always wailing about it to me, how they were asphyxiating you in pitch-darkness. It made you look pale and worried, your fingers were cramped from counting money, and you were always threatening to run away if you ever got the chance. All in all, you felt it was a downright outrage to live a virgin's existence in a bronze or iron chamber, like Danaë, under the tutelage of those exacting and rascally schoolmasters, Interest and Bookkeeping. You kept telling me that what the rich do makes no sense; they love you madly yet, though they have every right to enjoy you, they never dare to; you're the object of their passion yet, though they have you in their power, they never lay a finger on you. They stay awake guarding you, staring at the seals and bolts without closing their eyes, thinking it enjoyment enough, not that they have the right to enjoy you, but that they have the right to exclude all others from any share, like the dog in the manger who wouldn't eat the hay himself but wouldn't let the hungry horse have any. What's more, you even used to laugh at the way they scrimp and save, at the incredible fact that they're jealous of themselves, at how it never enters their heads that some damned servant or slave driver of a steward is going to sneak in and have himself a gay party, without a thought for his miserable, despised master who's lying awake the livelong night figuring interest by the light of a dim and skimpy lamp with an oil-starved wick. These are the accusations you used to make. Now you're blaming Timon for just the opposite. I don't think that's fair.

Wealth. If you look into the truth of the matter, I think you'll find I make sense in both cases. On the one hand, Timon's squandering is, to all intents and purposes, thoughtless and not very considerate toward me. On the other hand, those who put me under lock and key and keep me in the dark, watching over me so I put on weight and become fat as a pig, never touching me or bringing me out to the light for fear someone might see me, those I've always considered not only boobs but criminals: although I've done them no harm, they let me rot in all those chains; they don't realize that, before very long, they'll pass on and leave me to some of the luckier ones in life.

No, I'm for neither type, neither these nor the ones who are so careless with me. I'm for the people who can set a limit in the situation, who neither hold on to everything nor throw everything away. That's the best system. In the name of Zeus, Zeus, tell me this. Suppose a man marries a young, beautiful woman and then doesn't keep an eye on her or act the least bit jealous. Day and night he lets her go wherever she wants and be with whomever she chooses—or, rather, actually leads her into adultery by throwing the doors open and inviting everyone in, like a pimp. Would you say that man loves her? No, you wouldn't, Zeus, and you've had plenty of experience with love. Now suppose, on the other hand, a man takes a respectable woman as his lawfully wedded wife to be the mother of his children and then, though she's a beautiful girl in the bloom of youth, he never lays a finger on her or lets another man see her but locks her up to drag out a virgin's existence, barren and childless. Let's say he even keeps telling the world he's in love with her—and he looks it, too, with his pale face, loss of weight, and sunken eyes. Wouldn't you say that such a man is mad? He ought to have children and enjoy matrimony, yet he lets a beautiful, alluring girl wither away by treating her, her whole life long, like a Vestal Virgin. Well, it's behavior like this that makes me angry—at some people because they have no respect for me and push me around or gorge on me or pour me out like water, and at others because they clap me in irons as if I were a runaway slave.

Zeus. Why be angry? Both types pay you a handsome penalty: the one, like Tantalus, goes without food or drink and, drooling at the mouth, just eyes his gold; the other, like Phineus, has the food snatched right out of his throat by Harpies. On your way now. You'll find Timon a much wiser man.

Wealth. Timon? He'll never stop acting as if he's in a leaky canoe: he'll bail me out as fast as he can, even before I finish running in; he'll try to beat the inflow so I don't flood in and swamp him. If you ask me, it'll be like filling the cask Danaë's daughters used. I'll be pouring in and getting nowhere since the thing won't hold water; what flows in will practically be out before it gets in. The outlet is so much bigger: it's a gaping hole; it's unpluggable.

Zeus. Well, if he doesn't plug that gaping hole and it stays open once and for all, it won't take you long to spill out, and he'll have no trouble finding his overalls and mattock at the bottom of the cask. But get going now, and make him rich. And, Hermes, remember on your way back to pick up the Cyclops[6] at Etna and bring them here so they can put my thunderbolt on the grindstone and fix it up. I'm going to need it good and sharp.

Hermes. Let's go, Wealth. What's this? Are you limping? My dear fellow, I had no idea you were lame as well as blind.

Wealth. Not always, Hermes. Only when I get orders from Zeus to go to someone. Then, somehow or other, I'm lame in both legs and walk so slowly I barely make it to my destination. Sometimes the person expecting me waits around till he's old and gray. But when I have to leave someone, then you see me on wings; I'm swifter than a dream. The starting signal sounds—and at that very moment you hear the announcement that I've won the race. I take the whole course in one jump. Sometimes the spectators don't even see me.

Hermes. That isn't true. I can give you lots of examples of people who yesterday didn't have a penny to buy a rope to hang themselves with and suddenly today

---

6 The one-eyed giants who, with Hephaestus as foreman, ran the celestial smithy in the fiery crater of Mt. Etna.

they're rich, they're millionaires. Before they didn't even
have a pack mule, and now they drive a team of thor-
oughbreds; they go around in silks and satins and their
fingers are full of rings. If you ask me, they themselves
find it hard to believe that all this wealth isn't a dream.

Wealth. That's different, Hermes. In those cases I don't
travel on my own legs, and the orders come, not from
Zeus, but Pluto. He's another one who likes to give
away money and make handsome gifts. You can tell it
from his name.[7] Whenever I have to move out of one
house into another, people wrap me in a will, sign and
seal me carefully, pick me up like a bundle, and transfer
me. While the corpse lies in some dark corner of the
house with an old sheet tossed over its knees and the
cats scrapping over it, the people who hope to get their
hands on me hang around in the main square with
mouth agape, like twittering swallow chicks waiting for
their mother to fly home. The seal is removed, the rib-
bon cut, the will opened, and my new master announced
—a relative, or a parasite, or some pervert of a slave boy
who, through his abilities in bed, became the master's
favorite and who still shaves to keep that boyish look;
in return for the various and multitudinous favors which,
even after he became too old for that sort of thing, he
furnished the master, our hero now reaps a munificent
reward. This unknown grabs me, will and all, quickly
changes his name from Pyrrhias or Dromo or Tibius to
Megacles, Megabyzus, or Protarchus,[8] and off he runs,
leaving behind the disappointed hopefuls looking at
each other and mourning—this time for real—because
such a fine fish, after gulping down so much of their
bait,[9] had slipped out of the bottom of the net. Well,
my new owner—a thick-skinned vulgarian who still

7 *Plouton,* the name of the god of the underworld, is very much like
the Greek word for wealth (*ploutos*).

8 Pyrrhias, Dromo, and Tibius were common names of slaves and
Megacles, Megabyzus, and Protarchus common names in the best aristo-
cratic families.

9 I.e., the presents they had given the deceased in the hope of being
remembered in the will.

shudders when he hears the clank of chains, pricks up his ears if some passer-by happens to crack a whip, and genuflects before the treadmill as if it were a shrine—once he's landed on me with both feet, becomes insufferable to everyone he meets. Respectable people he insults, and the slaves he once worked with he has whipped just to prove to himself he can do that sort of thing. He ends up either falling into the clutches of some cheap whore, or going in for breeding race horses, or handing himself over to a bunch of bootlickers who swear he's handsomer than Nireus, comes from a better family than Cecrops or Codrus, has more brains than Odysseus, and is richer than a dozen Croesuses rolled into one. Once that happens, in no time at all the poor devil squanders what took years of lying, cheating, and robbery to scrape together.

Hermes. You're right. That's about the size of it. But tell me, when you walk on your own two feet, how does a blind man like you find your way? When Zeus decides certain people should be rich and sends you to them, how do you recognize them?

Wealth. Do you think I actually track them down? God, no! In that case I never would have passed up Aristides and gone to Hipponicus and Callias and a lot of other Athenians who didn't deserve a cent.

Hermes. Well, when Zeus sends you down, what do you do?

Wealth. I walk up and down and wander around until I bunk into someone. The first person who happens to meet me takes me away with him—and offers up heartfelt thanks to you, Hermes, for the unexpected windfall.

Hermes. But Zeus is under the impression you follow his decisions and give money to the ones he thinks merit it. You mean to say you're deceiving him?

Wealth. Of course—and he's getting what he deserves. He knew I was blind and yet he kept sending me to look for something that became extinct ages ago, something so hard to track down, so small and dim that Lynceus himself would have trouble finding it. So, since there's just a handful of good people while the cities are filled with thousands of good-for-nothings, as I stumble around it's much easier for me to run across that breed and land in their clutches.

Hermes. But when you leave them, how is it you can get away so easily if you can't see where you're going?

Wealth. Somehow, when it comes to making a getaway —but only then—I become quick as a flash and my vision is perfect.

Hermes. Now explain this one last thing to me. You're blind—it's the truth, let's face it—lame in both legs, and you have a bad complexion. Yet how do you have so many lovers? Everyone has eyes only for you; if they win you they think they're in heaven, and if they lose out they can't bear to stay alive. In fact, I know of quite a few who were so desperately in love with you they went off and threw themselves into the "deep bosom of the sea" or off the "sky-towering cliffs" simply because they got the notion you were deliberately snubbing them when actually you had never even seen them. If you have any idea of what you look like, you'll admit, I'm sure, that they're out of their minds to go wild over an inamorata like you.

Wealth. Are you under the impression they see me as I really am? Lame, blind, and whatever else is wrong with me?

Hermes. They must—unless they're all blind themselves.

Wealth. My dear fellow, they're not blind. It's simply that Ignorance and Self-Deceit, two factors having the upper hand everywhere these days, dim their sight. What's more, I take steps on my own not to appear so completely ugly: when I meet them I'm dressed in embroideries and wear a lovely mask gilded and studded with jewels. They think they see my real face, fall in love with my beauty, and destroy themselves if they don't win me. Let someone strip me bare and expose me before them, and they'd kick themselves, no question about it, for being blear-eyed enough to fall in love with something so hideous.

Hermes. But, once they get rich, why do they put on a mask, too, and go on deceiving themselves? Why, if anyone were to try to take it off, they'd sooner lose their heads than that mask! Once they've seen everything underneath, you wouldn't expect them to shut their eyes to the fact that your beauty is just paint and powder.

Wealth. There are quite a few things helping me out on that score.

Hermes. Such as?

Wealth. Whenever someone meets me for the first time and throws open the door to receive me, as I enter, in sneak Delusion, Stupidity, Arrogance, Sloth, Insolence, Deceit, and a thousand others of the same ilk. And once all these take possession of his soul, he marvels at things that aren't the least bit marvelous, longs for what he should shrink from, and goggles adoringly at me—me who begat all these ills that have come over him, me the very captain of the whole band. He'll suffer anything sooner than put up with losing me.

Hermes. It's amazing how slippery-smooth you are. You're hard to hold and quick to get away. There's no way to get a good grip on you; somehow you slither through a man's fingers just like an eel or a snake. Poverty, on the other hand, is sticky and clings. She has thousands of hooks all over her body so that the minute people come near they get caught, and it's not easy to break loose. Oh, damn! During all this chatter we forgot something very important.

Wealth. What?

Hermes. We didn't bring Treasure, and we particularly need him.

Wealth. Don't worry about that. I always leave him below

on earth when I go up to you people. I give him
orders to stay inside with the door shut and, unless he
hears my voice, not to open to a soul.

Hermes. In that case let's land now on Attica. Hold on to
my coat and follow me; we're going to the frontier.

Wealth. Good idea, this leading me by the hand, Hermes.
If you got separated from me, I might wander around
and bunk into Hyperbolus or Cleon.[10] But what's that
noise? Sounds like iron on rock.

Hermes. That's Timon digging up a little piece of rocky
hillside nearby. Damn! There's Poverty with him. And
Toil and Strength and Wisdom and Manliness—the
whole gang that's under the command of Hunger. Much
better than the ones in your band.

Wealth. Hermes, why don't we get out of here as fast as
we can? We're not going to cover ourselves with glory
against a man backed up by an army like that.

Hermes. Zeus has other ideas. So let's not be cowards.

Poverty. My dear Hermes, where are you taking that fellow you're leading by the hand?

Hermes. To Timon here. Zeus's orders.

Poverty. So now Wealth comes to Timon, eh? After I
picked him up suffering from a bad case of soft living,
handed him over to Wisdom and Toil, and made him
into a fine, worth-while man? Do I seem so contemptible, so easy to wrong, that, after giving him a complete
course of training in virtue, I'm to be robbed of the only
possession I have? Robbed so that Wealth can get him
in his clutches again, turn him over to Insolence and
Delusion, and hand him back to me just as he was at
first, soft, spineless, stupid, a worn-out rag of a man?

Hermes. That's the way Zeus wants it.

Poverty. I'm leaving. Toil, Wisdom, and all the rest of

---

10 Notorious Athenian demagogues.

you, follow me. Timon here will find out soon enough
what his desertion means—that he loses a fine fellow
worker and a teacher of the best things in life. So long
as he was with me he was sound in body and sane in
mind; he lived the way a man should; he looked to no
one else for help, and his basic principle—a perfectly
valid one—was that extravagance and plenty were not
for him.

Hermes. They're leaving. Let's go up to him.

Timon. Who the hell are you? What do you mean by coming here and disturbing a workingman who has to earn
a living? You're damned nuisances, both of you. You'll
be sorry you came: in one minute I'll start heaving
clods and stones and smash the both of you.

Hermes. No, Timon, please! Put those stones down. We're
not men. I'm Hermes, and this fellow here is Wealth.
Zeus heard your prayers and sent us. So, no more of
this hard work, take your riches, and good luck to you.

Timon. Gods, are you? Well, even if you are, you're going
to be sorry for this. I hate everybody, you hear, gods
and men both. I don't know who that blind fellow is,
but I've a good mind to bash his head in with this
mattock.

Wealth. Hermes, in the name of Zeus, let's go now or I
won't get away from here under my own power. If you
ask me, the man's stark raving mad!

Hermes. Mind your manners, Timon, and stop acting like
some country bumpkin. Stretch out your hands and take
your good luck. Be rich again; be the top man in Athens.
Thumb your nose at those ingrates, and keep your fortune to yourself.

Timon. I want nothing from either of you. Don't annoy
me. This mattock is all the wealth I need. Besides, I'm
the happiest man in the world so long as no one comes
near me.

Hermes. My dear Timon, how inhuman!

This I'm to bring back to Zeus? A rejoinder so brutal
and savage?[11]

To be a man-hater is natural after all you've suffered
at their hands, but to be a god-hater is certainly not—
not after all they've done for you.

Timon. Many thanks, Hermes, to you and to Zeus for all
you've done for me—but I cannot accept your friend
Wealth here.

Hermes. Why not?

Timon. Because he's to blame for endless trouble I
went through earlier. He handed me over to parasites,
brought adventurers to my door, stirred up hatred
against me, ruined me with soft living, made people
envy me bitterly—and wound up by suddenly walking
out on me like a traitor and a hypocrite. But this wonderful woman Poverty put me in condition with the kind
of labor a man should do, spoke to me truthfully and
frankly, and provided me with the necessities of life—
so long as I worked for them; she taught me to scorn
the plethora of luxuries I once had and to depend on
my own self for all I hoped for out of life. She showed
me what my true wealth was—something no sycophant's
flattery or blackmailer's threats or mob's violence or
voter's ballots or dictator's intrigues can ever take away
from me. And so, toughened by my hardships, I now
work this field—and like it. I see nothing of the wickedness of the city, and I get the bread I need, enough to
keep me going, from this mattock. So, Hermes, turn
right around, go back to Zeus, and take Wealth with
you. If I had my way, I'd be satisfied to make everyone
on earth, young and old, howl with pain.

Hermes. My dear man, not that! They're not all suited for
it. Now stop being so cantankerous and acting like a
child and take Wealth here. Gifts from the gods aren't
to be tossed away.

Wealth. Timon, may I submit the case for my defense to

11 *Iliad* 15.202, Iris' words to the angry Poseidon.

you? Or can't you bear hearing me talk?

Timon. Go ahead. But make it short. No long-winded introductions, like those damned public speakers. For Hermes' sake I'll put up with listening to a few remarks from you.

Wealth. Considering all the accusations you've made against me, I'd be better off being long-winded. No matter. Just consider whether I've really done you wrong as you claim. In the first place, it was I who was responsible for all the very pleasant things that happened to you: honor, public recognition, medals, and everything else that goes with high society; you were famous, a celebrity, a man sought after, and all because of me. In the second place, I'm not to blame for any harm those scroungers did you—in fact, you've wronged *me* by treating me so disrespectfully and putting me at the mercy of a filthy bunch of fawning double-crossers who plotted against me in every conceivable way. And now your last point, your claim that I treacherously deserted. On the contrary, I could bring that charge against you— you did everything you could to drive me away, you tossed me out of the house on my ear. Result: that lady you think so much of, Poverty, has stripped you of your fashionable clothes and wrapped you in these overalls. Hermes here can bear witness how I pleaded with Zeus not to make me go to you, not after the unfriendly way you behaved toward me. (*Timon shrugs helplessly.*)

Hermes. See how he's changed, Wealth? Don't you worry; start living with him. Timon, keep digging just the way you are. Wealth, make Treasure go under the mattock; he'll listen to you if you call him.

Timon. I suppose I have to obey and be rich again. What can a man do when the gods put pressure on him? Look what you're getting me involved in! Of all the rotten luck! Up to now I was leading the happiest possible existence, and all of a sudden, though I haven't harmed a soul, I'm to get all this gold and have all the worries that go with it.

Hermes. Put up with it, Timon, for my sake, even if it's
hard and you can barely stand it, just to make those
bootlickers die of envy. Well, I'm off; I'm flying back
to heaven via Etna.

Wealth. I think he's gone; it feels that way from the
beating of his wings. You stay here; I'll go and send
Treasure to you. Wait—I've got a better idea. Keep digging. Treasure! Gold! I'm calling you! Listen to Timon
here and let him catch you. Dig, Timon. Sink that mattock in. Well, I'll be off now.

Timon. Come on, mattock. Put some muscle into it now
for my sake and don't weaken. Invite Treasure out of
the depths into the light of day. O god of miracles!
O god of hysterics! O Hermes, you god of windfalls!
Where did so much gold come from? Is this a dream?
I'm only afraid I'll wake up and find it's just a sack
of coal—but no, it's genuine, solid, ruddy gold, the love-
liest sight the eye can see:

> O gold! The fairest gift a man can get![12]

A blaze of light both night and day, like gleaming
fire.[13] Come to me, my sweetest beloved. Now I really
believe Zeus once turned into a shower of gold—what
girl wouldn't open her arms wide to receive such a
handsome lover trickling through the roof? Midas,
Croesus, treasures of Delphi—you're nothing compared to Timon and his wealth. Even the King of Persia
can't match it. Mattock and overalls, my old friends, if
you ask me, the best thing would be to dedicate you
to Pan here.[14] For myself I think I'll buy up this whole
frontier region right away and put up a tower over my
treasure just big enough to be my house while I live
and my tomb when I die.

Resolved that the law of my land until my demise be
as hereinafter set forth:

that Timon is to cut himself off from society, know

[12] A line from a lost play of Euripides.
[13] A paraphrase of the beginning of Pindar's first Olympic ode.
[14] As a farmer, Timon maintained a rude shrine to Pan, the farmers'
god.

nobody, and scorn everybody; that friendship, hospitality, comradeship, and the sacred obligations of pity are all a lot of nonsense;

that compassion for those in mourning and assistance to those in need are felonies as well as breaches of ethics;

that Timon is to live the life of a lone wolf and have one friend—Timon. All other people are enemies and traitors; to address a word to any shall be a crime and, if I even merely happen to see one of them, the whole day is to be officially declared a day of mourning. In a word, I am to consider them exactly as so many stone or bronze statues: I will accept no messages from them; I will make no truce with them; the desert is to be the boundary between us; "clansman," "kinsman," "fellow citizen," and "fatherland" are cold, useless terms, the prized possessions of the ignorant;

that Timon is to look down on everyone else, keep his money for himself, and live a life of luxury by and for himself, free from parasitism and vulgar flattery;

that, as his own neighbor and boundary sharer, living as far from all others as he can, Timon will conduct sacrifices and celebrate religious holidays all by himself.

Be it further resolved that, when the day comes for Timon to die, he will say good-by to himself and put the winding sheet on with his own hands. "Misanthrope" is to be the name that sounds sweetest in his ears, and his characteristic traits are to be grouchiness, roughness, meanness, temper, and unsociability. If I see someone burning to death and he begs me to put out the fire, I am to put it out—with pitch and oil. If a winter torrent sweeps someone off and he stretches out his hands and beseeches me to take hold, I am to push the victim under water head first to prevent his ever coming up again. That's the way to give them what they deserve.

The foregoing was moved by Timon, son of Eche-cratides, and seconded by the aforesaid Timon. The ayes have it. So ordered—and may I abide by the provisions like a man. And yet I'd give a good deal to have people know I'm a millionaire; they'd be fit to be tied at the news. Wait—what's this? Lord, how quick! They're pouring in from all sides, out of breath and covered with dust. Somehow or other they caught the scent of my money. Now how about climbing this hill so I can drive them away by laying down a barrage of stones? Or should I break my own law code just to the extent of speaking to them once, so I can show my contempt and make them even madder? That's a better idea, I think. All right, Timon, stand your ground and receive them. Let's see, who's coming first? That scrounger Gna-thonides,[15] the one who told me to go hang myself when I asked for a loan the other day. And he used to puke up whole barrels of my wine at my house! I'm glad he's come—he'll be the first to howl.

Gnathonides. Didn't I always say that heaven wouldn't neglect a good man like Timon? Hail, Timon, the best-looking, best-tempered, best all-around good fellow alive.

Timon. Hail, Gnathonides, the most greedy, most damna-ble bloodsucker alive.

Gnathonides. Always had to have your little joke, didn't you? Well, where's the party? I've got a new song to sing for you. One of the latest hits.

Timon. Song? You'll be singing funeral dirges. And with real pathos—this mattock will see to it.

Gnathonides. What's this? An attack! I'm calling wit-nesses. . . . Ow! I'll sue you for assault and battery.

Timon. Stick around a little longer—you'll be able to make the charge murder.

---

[15] The sycophants are given common Greek names which Lucian has carefully chosen for their etymological associations: Gnathonides, "cheeky"; Philiades, "friendly"; Demeas, "public servant"; Thrasycles, "nervy"; Blepsias, "shark"; Laches, "share-seeker"; Gnipho, "skinflint."

Gnathonides. I should say not! But at least heal my injuries, will you? Just sprinkle a little gold on them. That medicine has a marvelous way of stopping bleeding.

Timon. Still here, are you?

Gnathonides. No, no, I'm on my way. You're going to be sorry you turned into such a brute. You used to be a wonderful fellow.

Timon. Who's the bald pate coming up? Philiades—the most repulsive bootlicker of all. Once I sang a song and nobody applauded except him; he raved about it and swore my voice was sweeter than an angel's. I paid for this flattery with one whole farm plus sixty thousand dollars to provide a dowry for his daughter. Yet the other day, when I came to him for help and he saw I was sick, the noble soul gave me the back of his hand.

Philiades. Disgraceful! So you all recognize Timon now, do you? So Gnathonides is his bosom friend now, is he? The ingrate! He got just what was coming to him. Even though Timon and I are old, old friends—we went to school together and later were neighbors—I'm taking it easy—I don't want to look as if I'm being pushy. Hello, sir! I warn you to watch out for all these damned bootlickers. They're only mealtime friends; the rest of the time they behave like a flock of crows. You can't trust anybody nowadays; men are ungrateful good-for-nothings, every last one of them. Now *I* was about to bring you ten thousand dollars so you'd have a little something to cover pressing expenses. I was on my way and had almost gotten here when I heard the news that you were rich, a millionaire. I came anyway so I could give you my word of caution. But a smart man like you doesn't need any advice from me—you could tell even Nestor[16] what to do in a tight spot.

Timon. I'll take your advice, Philiades. But come over here; I want to greet you—with this mattock.

Philiades. Help! I give the man some good advice—and the ingrate bashes my head in!

16 An aged chieftain in the *Iliad*, the giver of counsel par excellence.

Timon. Look, here comes a third one, Demeas the politician. He's carrying a copy of some resolution and telling everybody he's my cousin. In one day that man paid the government a fine of a hundred and fifty thousand dollars—with my money. He'd been tried and convicted and, since he couldn't pay, was thrown in jail. I took pity on him and bought him his release. Yet the other day, when it was his turn to issue free theater tickets to all the people in my neighborhood and I came up and asked for mine, he claimed he didn't know I was a citizen.

Demeas. Hail, Timon, benefactor of our people, guardian of Athens, bulwark of Greece! The House, Senate, and Cabinet are in session and they've been waiting for you for hours. But first listen to the resolution I'm going to present in your honor:

> Whereas Timon, son of Echecratides, is not only a gentleman and scholar but the wisest man in all Greece,
>
> and whereas he has devoted a lifetime bestowing benefactions on his country,
>
> and whereas in one day at the Olympic games he took first prize in boxing, wrestling, running, two chariot events—

Timon. But I've never even seen the Olympics.

Demeas. What's the difference? You will sometime. It sounds better when we tack on a lot of things like that.

> and whereas last year he distinguished himself for gallantry in action at Acharnae and cut down two regiments of Spartans—

Timon. How? I couldn't afford a suit of armor, so I wasn't even in the army.

Demeas. You're too modest. We'd be ingrates if we were to forget what you did.

> and whereas he rendered great service on behalf of his country as legislator, administrator, and military commander,
>
> be it therefore resolved by House, Senate, Supreme

Court, counties, and wards, both individually and collectively, that, in return for such services, there be set alongside the statue of Athena on the Acropolis a statue of Timon in gold bearing a thunderbolt in the right hand and a halo around the head, and be it further resolved that he receive as award seven gold crowns of honor and that public announcement to this effect be made at the customary time, to wit, prior to the presentation of new plays at the Festival of Dionysus—and in his honor we're to shift the date of the festival to today.

Respectfully submitted by Demeas the public speaker, Timon's next of kin and his pupil as well, inasmuch as Timon is an expert in public speaking—and whatever else he cares to take up.

Well, that's my resolution in your behalf. I wanted to bring my son to see you. I've named him Timon in your honor.

Timon. Son? You're not even married as far as I know.

Demeas. But, god willing, I'll get married next year, have a child, and, since it's to be a boy, I hereby name my prospective son Timon.

Timon. Listen, you, I'm not so sure you'll be interested in getting married—not after this lands on you.

Demeas. Ow! What's going on here? Trying to be a dictator, are you? The son of a slave beating up free citizens, eh? You'll pay for this, and soon. For burning down the Acropolis too.

Timon. Damn you, the Acropolis hasn't burned down. So it's clear—you're blackmailing me.

Demeas. Well, then, you got all this money by breaking into the treasury.

Timon. No one's broken into the treasury—so you won't get away with that either.

Demeas. Then you'll do it later. But you've already got everything that was inside there.

Timon. For that you get another wallop.

Demeas. Oh, my back!

Timon. Stop your yelling or you'll get a third one. The man who, unarmed, cut down two regiments of Spartans not able to break the bones of one godforsaken runt? Ridiculous idea! Those Olympic championships in boxing and wrestling wouldn't mean a thing.

Now what's this? Isn't this Thrasycles the philosopher? Exactly who it is. Here he comes with that flowing beard, those eyebrows up in the air, and that pile of hair on his head, swaggering along, wrapped in his thoughts, and glaring like a Titan—the image of Boreas or Triton in one of Zeuxis' paintings. He dresses in perfect taste, wears a plain dark-colored coat, has a dignified walk, and, from the crack of dawn on, never stops extolling virtue—he's all for the simple life and against anyone who enjoys a bit of pleasure. But, as soon as he's had his bath and sat down to dinner and the waiter's handed him his drink—a double-sized one, the stiffer the better—you'd think he'd had a swig of Lethe's waters. He proceeds to demonstrate exactly the opposite of the morning's sermons. He swoops down on the dishes like a vulture, elbows his tablemate aside, spills gravy all over his beard, bolts his food like a dog, hunches over his plate as if he expected to find there that virtue he talks about, and wipes the bowls clean as a whistle with his finger so he won't lose a drop of sauce. He can get the whole of a cake or roast all to himself and still not be satisfied—the price a person pays for insatiable gluttony. He's a drunk, too, the kind that doesn't stop with singing and dancing but gets wild and calls people names. What's more, even in his cups he babbles on about temperance and good behavior—that's when he does most of his talking on the topic. He'll hold forth when he's already three sheets to the wind and has such trouble getting the words out it's ridiculous. After all this he'll throw up; they'll finally lift him off the floor and cart him away—and he'll make a grab with both hands for the girl playing the flute as he goes. But, drunk or sober, he yields the palm to no one in lying, nerve, or avarice. He's the king of sycophants, the man most ready to perjure himself; deceit walks before him and shamelessness by his side—in a word, the cleverest thing on two legs, not a flaw anywhere, letter-perfect in all sorts of roles. Well, we'll have some howls from this pattern of virtue in a few moments.

Thrasycles, what's the matter? Why so late in coming to see me?

Thrasycles. I haven't come for the same reasons as this mob here. They're entranced by your money; they've scurried here en masse, hoping for silver and gold and for fancy parties, prepared to put on a full show of flattery before a simple soul like yourself who's so ready to share everything he owns. But you know very well that a crust of bread is a whole dinner for me, that my favorite dish is a bit of thyme or cress or, when I feel like indulging myself, a pinch of salt. And for drink just cold water. This threadbare coat I prefer to any purple robes. In my opinion gold has no more value than the pebbles on a beach. I've come purely for your sake— to keep your wealth from destroying you. It's the world's worst possession, the one people scheme for most; it's been responsible for irremediable harm to thousands, thousands of times. Now, if you'll listen to me, you'll throw it all into the sea—a good man who can discern philosophy's treasures doesn't need it. But, my dear Timon, not where it's deep. Go into the water just up to your hips and toss it a little beyond the line of breakers—with only me watching. If you don't like this way, I have another, even better, way: hurry and bring the money out of your house—all of it; don't keep a penny for yourself—and distribute it among the needy, a few dollars to this one, a few hundred to that, a couple of thousand to a third. If there are any philosophers it's only fair they get a double or triple share. As for me, I ask nothing for myself but just some to hand out to my needy friends. If you'll fill this sack—it holds less than four bushels—that'll be quite enough. Philosophers should live simply and frugally—and give no thought to anything beyond what's in their sack.

Timon. I fully agree, Thrasycles. But, if you don't mind, before I fill your sack let me fill your head with fists— after I test its capacity with this mattock.

Thrasycles. What's happened to our laws? Where's our democracy? This is a free country and this damned rascal is beating me up!

Timon. My dear Thrasycles, why so angry? I didn't cheat you, did I? All right, here's half a bushel more for good measure.

What's going on here? They're coming in droves! There's Blepsias and Laches and Gnipho—an army of potential howlers. Why don't I climb on this rock, give my mattock a rest—it's put in a hard day—lay in a supply of stones, and pelt them at long range?

Blepsias. Timon! Stop! We'll leave!

Timon. Not before I draw blood you won't!

from *The Lives of the Noble Grecians and Romans*

Antonius followeth the life and example of Timon Misanthropus, the Athenian.

Antonius, he forsook the city and company of his friends and built him a house in the sea, by the Isle of Pharos, upon certain forced mounts which he caused to be cast into the sea, and dwelt there, as a man that banished himself from all men's company: saying that he would lead Timon's life, because he had the like wrong offered him that was before offered unto Timon, and that for the unthankfulness of those he had done good unto and whom he took to be his friends, he was angry with all men and would trust no man. This Timon was a citizen of Athens that lived about the war of Peloponnesus, as appeareth by Plato and Aristophanes' comedies, in the which they mocked him, calling him a viper and malicious man unto mankind to shun all other men's companies but the company of young Alcibiades, a bold and insolent youth, whom he would greatly feast and make much of, and kissed him very gladly. Apemantus, won-

From *The Lives of the Noble Grecians and Romans,* translated by Sir Thomas North (1579).

dering at it, asked him the cause what he meant to make so much of that young man alone and to hate all others. Timon answered him, "I do it," said he, "because I know that one day he shall do great mischief unto the Athenians." This Timon sometimes would have Apemantus in his company, because he was much like of his nature and conditions, and also followed him in manner of life. On a time when they solemnly celebrated the feasts called Choae at Athens (to wit, the feasts of the dead, where they make sprinklings and sacrifices for the dead), and that they two then feasted together by themselves, Apemantus said unto the other: "O, here is a trim banquet, Timon." Timon answered again, "Yea," said he, "so thou wert not here."

It is reported of him also that this Timon on a time (the people being assembled in the marketplace about dispatch of some affairs) got up into the pulpit for orations, where the orators commonly use to speak unto the people: and silence being made, every man listening to hear what he would say, because it was a wonder to see him in that place, at length he began to speak in this manner: "My Lords of Athens, I have a little yard in my house where there groweth a fig tree, on the which many citizens have hanged themselves: and, because I mean to make some building on the place, I thought good to let you all understand it, that, before the fig tree be cut down, if any of you be desperate, you may there in time go hang yourselves."

He died in the city of Hales and was buried upon the seaside. Now it chanced so, that the sea getting in, it compassed his tomb round about that no man could come to it, and upon the same was written this epitaph:

> Here lies a wretched corse, of wretched soul bereft.
> Seek not my name; a plague consume you wicked wretches left.

It is reported that Timon himself when he lived made this epitaph, for that which is commonly rehearsed was not his, but made by the poet Callimachus:

Here lie I, Timon, who alive all living men did hate.
Pass by and curse thy fill, but pass, and stay not here thy
  gait.

Many other things could we tell you of this Timon, but
this little shall suffice at this present. [from *The Life of
Marcus Antonius*]

And on a day as he [Alcibiades] came from the council
and assembly of the city, where he had made an excellent
oration to the great good liking and acceptation of all
the hearers, and by means thereof had obtained the thing
he desired, and was accompanied with a great train that
followed him to his honor: Timon, surnamed Misanthropus (as who would say, Loup-garou, or the manhater),
meeting Alcibiades thus accompanied, did not pass by
him nor gave him way (as he was wont to do to all
other men), but went straight to him, and took him by
the hand and said: "O, thou dost well, my son, I can
thee thank that thou goest on and climbest up still, for
if ever thou be in authority, woe be unto those that follow thee, for they are utterly undone." When they had
heard these words, those that stood by fell a-laughing.
Other reviled Timon; other again marked well his words
and thought of them many a time after, such sundry
opinions they had of him for the unconstancy of his life
and waywardness of his nature and conditions. [from *The
Life of Alcibiades*]

WILLIAM PAINTER

from *The Palace of Pleasure*

*Of the strange and beastly nature of Timon of Athens,
enemy to mankind, with his death, burial, and epitaph.
The xxviii Novel.*

All the beasts of the world do apply themselves to
other beasts of their kind, Timon of Athens only excepted, of whose strange nature Plutarch is astonied in
the life of Marcus Antonius. Plato and Aristophanes do
report his marvelous nature, because he was a man but
by shape only; in qualities he was the capital enemy of
mankind, which he confessed frankly, utterly to abhor
and hate. He dwelt alone in a little cabin in the fields not
far from Athens. Separated from all neighbors and company, he never went to the city or to any other habitable
place except he were constrained. He could not abide
any man's company and conversation. He was never seen
to go to any man's house, ne yet would suffer them to
come to him. At the same time there was in Athens
another of like quality, called Apemantus, of the very
same nature, different from the natural kind of man, and
lodged likewise in the midst of the fields. On a day they
two being alone together at dinner, Apemantus said unto
him: "O Timon, what a pleasant feast is this, and what

From *The Palace of Pleasure* (1566).

a merry company are we, being no more but thou and I." "Nay," quoth Timon, "it would be a merry banquet indeed if there were none here but myself."

Wherein he showed how like a beast indeed he was. For he could not abide any other man, being not able to suffer the company of him which was of like nature. And if by chance he happened to go to Athens, it was only to speak with Alcibiades, who then was an excellent captain there, whereat many did marvel. And therefore Apemantus demanded of him why he spake to no man but to Alcibiades. "I speak to him sometimes," said Timon, "because I know that by his occasion the Athenians shall receive great hurt and trouble." Which words many times he told to Alcibiades himself.

He had a garden, adjoining to his house in the fields, wherein was a fig tree, whereupon many desperate men ordinarily did hang themselves. In place whereof he purposed to set up a house, and therefore was forced to cut it down, for which cause he went to Athens, and in the marketplace he called the people about him, saying that he had news to tell them. When the people understood that he was about to make a discourse unto them, which was wont to speak to no man, they marveled, and the citizens on every part of the city ran to hear him. To whom he said that he purposed to cut down his fig tree to build a house upon the place where it stood. "Wherefore," quoth he, "if there be any man amongst you all in this company that is disposed to hang himself, let him come betimes before it be cut down."

Having thus bestowed his charity amongst the people, he returned to his lodging, where he lived a certain time after without alteration of nature. And because that nature changed not in his lifetime, he would not suffer that death should alter or vary the same. For like as he lived a beastly and churlish life, even so he required to have his funeral done after that manner. By his last will, he ordained himself to be interred upon the seashore, that the waves and surges might beat and vex his dead carcass. Yea, and that if it were possible, his desire was to be buried in the depth of the sea; causing an epitaph to be made wherein was described the qualities of his brutish life. Plutarch also reporteth another to be made by Callimachus, much like to that which Timon made himself, whose own soundeth to this effect in English verse:

> My wretched caitiff days,
>   expired now and past.
> My carren corpse interred here
>   is fast in ground.
> In waltring waves of swel-
>   ling sea, by surges cast,
> My name if thou desire,
>   the gods thee do confound.

Commentaries

WILLIAM RICHARDSON

On the Dramatic Character of Timon of Athens

Shakespeare, in his *Timon of Athens,* illustrates the consequences of that inconsiderate profusion which has the appearance of liberality and is supposed even by the inconsiderate person himself to proceed from a generous principle, but which, in reality, has its chief origin in the love of distinction. Though this is not the view usually entertained of this singular dramatic character, I persuade myself, if we attend to the design of the poet in all its parts, we shall find that the opinion now advanced is not without foundation.

The love of distinction is asserted to be the ruling principle in the conduct of Timon; yet it is not affirmed, nor is it necessary to affirm that Timon has no goodness of heart. He has much goodness, gentleness, and love of society.— These are not inconsistent with the love of distinction; they often reside together, and in particular, that love of distinction which reigned in the conduct of Timon, may easily be shown to have received its particular bias and direction from original goodness. For, with-

From *Essays on Shakespeare's Dramatic Characters.* 2nd ed., 1785.

out this, what could have determined him to choose one method of making himself conspicuous rather than another? Why did he not seek the distinction conferred by the display of a military or of a political character? Or why did he not aspire after pageantry and parade, the pomp of public buildings, and the ostentation of wealth, unconnected with any kind of beneficence?

In general, our love of fame or distinction is directed and influenced by some previous cast of temper or early tendency of disposition. Moved by powers and dispositions leading us to one kind of exertion rather than another, we attribute superior excellence to such exertion. We transfer the same sentiment to the rest of mankind. We fancy that no preeminence can be attained but by such talents as we possess, and it requires an effort of cool reflection before we can allow that there may be excellence in those things which we cannot relish, or merit in that conduct to which we are not inclined. Guided by early or inherent predilection, men actuated by the love of distinction seek the idol of their desires in various situations— in the bustle of active life or in the shade of retirement. Take the following examples. The son of Olorus was present, while yet a boy, at the Olympic games. All Greece was assembled; many feats of dexterity, no doubt, were exhibited, and every honor that assembled Greece could bestow was conferred on the victors. Moved by a spectacle so interesting and so inspiriting, the Spartan, Theban, or Athenian youth, who were not yet of vigor sufficient to strive for the wreath, longed, we may readily suppose, for maturer years and became, in their ardent imaginations, skilful wrestlers and charioteers. The son of Olorus, if we may judge by the consequence, felt little emotion; no sympathetic longings; and no impatience to drive a chariot. —But hearing Herodotus, on that occasion, reciting his history, he felt other sensations: his heart throbbed, and the tears descended. The venerable historian observed him weeping, and comprehending his character, "I give thee joy," said he to his father, "for the happy genius of thy son." Now, the son of Olorus became a historian no less renowned than Herodotus—for Herodotus and Thucydides are usually named together. The celebrated Turenne, in his early days, was an admirer, no less passionate, of Quintus Curtius, than the son of Olorus was of Herodotus; and we are told by Ramsay, from D'Ablancourt, that when not yet twelve years of age, he challenged an officer who called his favorite history a romance. But this admiration was not so much for the graces of flowery composition which abound in the Roman historian as for the valiant actions of Alexander. These drew his attention and soon after, his imitation. Though his breast heaved and his eyes sparkled in the perusal of favorite passages, he was not led to write fine descriptions like Curtius, but to break horses like the son of Philip.

Now, since those that are actuated by the love of distinction are led, by early or inherent predilection, to one kind of action rather than another, we have no difficulty in allowing principles of goodness and humanity to have reigned early, or originally, in the breast of Timon. Nay, after losing their authority, they continued for some time to attend him and resided in that breast where they formerly reigned. They became like those eastern princes, or those early sovereigns of a neighboring country, who grew so indolent and passive that they lay immured in their apartments and left the management of the state to some active minister, an ambitious vizier, or mayor of the palace. Some of these ministers acted for a while under the banner of the sovereign's authority, but afterwards, having left him but the shadow of power, they promoted themselves, became supreme and despotic.

Here, however, we are led to inquire, how happens it that a principle inherent in the soul, and once an active principle, becomes passive, suffers others to operate in its stead; not only so, but to perform similar functions, assume corresponding appearances, and, in general, to be guided apparently to the same tenor of conduct? Did the energy of the inherent affection suffer abatement by frequent exercise? Or were there no kindred principles in the soul to support and confirm its authority? Could not reason, or the sense of duty, support, and the power of active habit confirm? How came the sultan to submit to the vizier?

In general, original principles and feelings become passive if they are not, in their first operation, confirmed by reason and convictions of duty, and if the passion which springs up in their place assumes their appearance and acts apparently as they would have done. Nothing is more imposing than this species of usurpation. It is not the open assault of a foe, but the guile of pretended friendship. Nothing contributes more to dangerous self-deception. Applying this remark to our present subject and following the lights of observation, we shall briefly illustrate how early or inherent goodness may be subverted by the love of distinction. A person of good dispositions, inclined by his temper and constitution to perform acts of beneficence, receives pleasure in the performance. He also receives applauses. He has done good and is told of it. Thus he receives pleasure, not only from having gratified a native impulse, but from the praise of mankind and the gratitude of those whom he may have served. The applauses he receives are more liberally bestowed by designing and undeserving persons than by the deserving and undesigning. The deserving depend too much on the permanency of the original principle, independent of encouragement and may therefore be too sparing in their approbation. Gustavus Adolphus used to say that valor needed encouragement and was therefore unreserved in his praises. The same may be said of every virtue. But designing or undeserving persons, transferring their own dispositions to other men, and of course apprehensive lest the wheels and springs of benevolence should contract rust, are oiling them forever with profuse adulation. Meantime, our man of liberality begins to be moved by other principles than fine feelings and constitutional impulse. The pleasure arising from such actions as these produce is too fine and too delicate compared with the joys conferred by loud and continued applauses. Thus his taste becomes vitiated; he not only acquires an undue relish for adulation, but is uneasy without it; he contracts a false appetite and solicits distinction, not so much for the pleasure it yields him, as to remove a disagreeable craving. Thus, such benevolent actions as formerly proceeded from constitutional goodness have now their origin in the love of praise and distinction. Goodness may remain in his breast a passive guest and having no other power than to give countenance to the prevailing principle. It may thus reign in his language and reveries, but the love of distinction directs his conduct. The superseded monarch enjoys the parade of state and annexes his signature and sanction to the deeds of his active minister.

Perhaps it may now seem probable that a man of constitutional goodness may perform beneficent actions not from principles of humanity, though these may actually reside in his breast, but from the desire of being distinguished as a generous person, and that in the meanwhile, not discerning his real motives, he shall imagine himself actuated by pure generosity. That such characters may exist is all that is hitherto asserted. That Shakespeare has exhibited an illustration, accurately defined and exquisitely featured, in his *Timon of Athens,* we will now endeavor to show. We will endeavor to ascertain and trace in the conduct of Timon the marks of that beneficence which proceeds from the love of distinction. We will, at the same time, endeavor to trace the causes of the strange alteration that took place in his temper, and delineate the operations of those circumstances that changed him from being apparently social, and full of affection, into an absolute misanthrope.

I. Real goodness is not ostentatious. Not so is the goodness of Timon. Observe him in the first scene of the tragedy: trumpets sound; Timon enters; he is surrounded with senators, poets, painters, and attendants, chooses that moment to display his beneficence, and accompanies his benefits with a comment on his own noble nature.

> I am not of that feather to shake off
> My friend when he most needs me.

II. He is impatient of admonition. Knowing that he was formerly influenced by sentiments of humanity, he supposes that their power is abiding and that as he continues to do good, his principles of action are still the same. He is exposed to this self-imposition not only by the tendency which all men have to deceive themselves, but by the flatteries and praises he is fond of receiving.— Of consequence, he would suffer pain by being undeceived: he would lose the pleasure of that distinction which he so earnestly pursues; the prevailing passion would be counteracted; thus, there is a disposition in his soul which leads him to be displeased with the truth, and who that is offended with the truth can endure admonition?

> Ap. Thou giv'st so long, Timon, I fear me, thou
> Wilt give away thyself in paper shortly:
> What need these feasts, pomps, and vain glories?
> Tim. Nay,
> If you begin to rail once on society,
> I am sworn not to give regard to you.
> Farewell, and come with better music.
> Ap. So——
> Thou wilt not hear me now.
> ————Oh, that men's ears should be
> To counsel deaf, but not to flattery.

III. The same self-deceit which renders him deaf to counsel renders him solicitous and patient of excessive applause. He endures even the grossest adulation. Notwithstanding the covering which hides him from himself, he cannot be quite confident that his principles are just what he wishes and imagines them to be. The applauses he receives tend to obviate his uncertainty, and reconcile him to himself. Yet, it is not affirmed that the man of conscious merit is either insensible of fame or careless of reputation. He feels and enjoys them both, but having less need of external evidence to strengthen him in the belief of his own integrity, he is less voracious of praise and more acute in the discernment of flattery.

IV. The favors bestowed by Timon are not often of such a kind as to do real service to the persons who receive them. Wishing to be celebrated for his bounty, he is liberal in such a manner as shall be most likely to draw attention and particularly to provoke the ostentation of those, on account of his munificence, whom he is inclined to benefit. He is therefore more liberal in gratifying their passions, and particularly their vanity, than in relieving their wants, and of contributing more to flatter their imaginations than to promote their improvement. Though he performs some actions of real humanity, and even these he performs in a public manner, yet his munificence appears chiefly in his banquets and showy presents.

V. He acts in the same manner in the choice he makes of those whom he serves and on whom he confers his favors. He is not so solicitous of alleviating the distress of obscure affliction as of gratifying those who enjoy some degree of distinction or have it in their power to proclaim his praises. He is not represented as visiting the cottage of the fatherless and widow, but is wonderfully generous to men of high rank and character. He is desirous of encouraging merit, but the merit must be already known and acknowledged. Instead of drawing bashful worth from obscurity, he bestows costly baubles on those eminent or reputable persons who shall be attended to if they publish his praises. These are such displays of beneficence as a man of genuine goodness would be apt to avoid. Yet, the persons whom Timon honors and obliges are loquacious poets, flattering painters, great generals, and mighty elders.

> Tim. I take all, and your several visitations,
> So kind to heart, 'tis not enough to give;
> Methinks I could deal kingdoms to my friends,
> And ne'er be weary. Alcibiades,
> Thou art a soldier, therefore seldom rich;
> It comes in charity to thee; for all thy living
> Is 'mongst the dead; and all the lands thou hast
> Lie in a pitched field.——

Yet, this seeming want of discernment in Timon is not to be considered as a proof of weak understanding. Our poet, who has omitted nothing to render the features of this character, though perhaps not obvious, yet so distinct, consistent, and perfectly united that there is scarcely a lineament too little or too much, has guarded him from this objection and represents him as a man of ability. When the state, and rulers of Athens, in the hour of extreme urgency and distress, are threatened with an assault by Alcibiades, whom they had treated with disrespect, they have recourse for advice and assistance to no other than Timon. They tell him in terms of humble entreaty:

> Therefore, so please thee to return with us,
> And of our Athens (thine and ours) to take
> The Captainship, thou shalt be met with thanks,
> Allow'd with absolute power, and thy good name
> Live with authority; so soon shall we drive back
> Of Alcibiades the approaches wild,
> Who, like a boar, too savage, doth root up
> His country's peace.——

VI. Timon is not more ostentatious, impatient of admonition, desirous of applause, injudicious in his gifts, and undistinguishing in the choice of his friends than he is profuse. Desirous of superlative praises, he endeavors, by lavish beneficence, to have unbounded returns.

> ———He outgoes
> The very heart of kindness——
> ———Plutus, the god of wealth,
> Is but his steward.

The poet, with judicious invention, deduces the chief incident in the play, namely the reverse of Timon's fortune, from this circumstance in his conduct. The vanity of Timon renders him profuse, and profusion renders him indigent.

VII. The character we are describing sets a greater value on the favors he confers than they really deserve. Of a mind undisciplined by reason and moved by a strong desire, he conceives the state of things to be exactly such as his present mood and desire represent them. Wishing to excite a high sense of favor, he believes he has done so and that the gratifications he bestows are much greater than what they are. He is the more liable to this self-imposition, that many of those he is inclined to gratify are no less lavish of their adulation than he is of his fortune. He does not perceive that the raptures they express are not for the benefit they have received, but for what they expect, and imagines that while his chambers

> Blaze with lights, and bray with minstrelsy;

while his cellars weep "with drunken spilth of wine;" while he is giving away horses, and precious stones; entertaining the rulers and chief men of Athens, he fondly fancies that he is kindling in their breasts a sense of friendship and obligation. He fondly fancies that in his utmost need, he will receive from them every sort of assistance, and without reserve or reluctance, lays immediate claim to their bounty.

> ————You to Lord Lucius;
> To Lord Lucullus, you—You to Sempronius:
> Commend me to their loves—and I am proud, say,
> That my occasions have found time to use them
> Toward a supply of money: let the request
> Be fifty talents.————
> Go you, Sir, to the senators,
> (Of whom, even to the state's best health, I have
> Deserved this hearing), bid them send on th' instant,
> A thousand talents to me.

VIII. Need we be surprised that Timon, and men of his character, should meet with disappointment? Howsoever they may impose upon themselves, and believe they are moved by real friendship, and believe that they are conferring real benefits, the rest of mankind discern, and disapprove of their conduct. Even those very persons who, by adulation and a mean acceptance of favors, have contributed to their delusion, feel, or conceive themselves, under no obligation. The benefits they received were unsolicited, or unimportant, and the friendship of their benefactor was not so genuine as he believed. Thus, then, Timon demands a requital of his good deeds—he meets with refusal; when he solicits the affections of his professing friends, he is answered with coldness.

> STR. Why, this is the world's sport;
> And just of the same piece is every flatt'rer's soul.
> —Timon has been this Lord's father—
> He ne'er drinks,
> But Timon's silver treads upon his lip;
> And yet, (O see the monstrousness of man,
> When he looks out in an ungrateful shape),
> He does deny him, in respect of his,
> What charitable men afford to beggars.

There is no one passage in the whole tragedy more happily conceived and expressed than the conduct of Timon's flatterers. Their various contrivances to avoid giving him assistance show diversity of character, and their behavior is well contrasted by the sincere sorrow and indignation of Timon's servants. They are held out to deserved scorn by their easy belief that the decay of their benefactor's fortunes was only pretended and by their consequent renewal of mean assiduities.

IX. It remains to be mentioned that such disappointment, in tempers like that of Timon, begets not only resentment at individuals, but aversion at all mankind.

Timon imposes on himself, and while he is really actuated by a selfish passion, fancies himself entirely disinterested. Yet he has no select friends and no particular attachments. He receives equally the deserving and undeserving, the stranger and the familiar acquaintance. Of consequence, those persons with whom he seems intimate have no concern in his welfare; yet, vainly believing that he merits their affections, he solicits their assistance, and sustains disappointment. His resentment is roused, and he suffers as much pain, though perhaps of a different kind, as, in a similar situation, a person of true affection would suffer. But its object is materially different. For against whom is his anger excited? Not against one individual, for he had no individual attachment, but against all those who occasioned his disappointment—that is, against all those who were, or whom he desired should be, the objects of his beneficence; in other words, against all mankind. In such circumstances, the violence of resentment will be proportioned to original sensibility; and Shakespeare, accordingly, has represented the wrath of Timon as indulging itself in furious invective, till it grows into lasting aversion.

> TIM. Who dares, who dares,
> In purity of manhood stand upright,
> And say, this man's a flatterer? If one be,
> So are they all; for every greeze of fortune
> Is smother'd by that below: the learned pate
> Ducks to the golden fool: all is oblique—
> ————Then be abhorr'd,
> All feasts, societies, and throngs of men!
> His semblable, yea himself, Timon disdains;
> Destruction phang mankind! Earth give me roots!
> Who seeks for better of thee, sauce his palate
> With thy most operant poison.

The symptoms already mentioned are numerous and indicate to the attentive observer that the state of Timon's mind is more distempered with a selfish passion than he believes; yet the poet, by a device suited to his own masterly invention, contrives an additional method of conveying a distinct and explicit view of the real design. Apemantus, a character well invented and well supported, has no other business in the play than to explain the principles of Timon's conduct. His cynic surliness, indeed, forms a striking contrast to the smoothness of Timon's flatterers, but he is chiefly considered as unveiling the principal character. His manners are fierce, but his intentions are friendly; his invectives are bitter, but his remarks are true. He tells the flattering poet, who had written a panegyric on Timon, that he was worthy of him and adds, even in Timon's presence, "He that loves to be flattered,

is worthy of the flatterer." He tells Timon, inviting him
to his banquet—"I scorn thy meat; 'twould choke me, for
I should ne'er flatter thee." Elsewhere he gives him ad-
monitions to the very same purpose, and finding his advice
undervalued, he subjoins—"I will lock thy heaven from
thee"—meaning, as a commentator has well explained it,
the pleasure of being flattered. He afterwards tells him,
having followed him, nevertheless, into his solitude, with
intentions of rendering him some assistance:

> ——————What, thinkest
> That the bleak air, thy boist'rous chamberlain,
> Will put thy shirt on warm? Will those moss'd trees,
> That have outliv'd the eagle, page thy heels,
> And skip when thou point'st out? Will the cold brook,
> Candied with ice, caudle thy morning taste,
> To cure thy o'er-night's surfeit? Call the creatures
> Whose naked natures live in all the spite
> Of wreckful heaven, whose bare unhoused trunks
> To the conflicting elements exposed,
> Answer mere nature—bid them flatter thee—
> O! thou shalt find——

There are few instances of a dramatic character executed
with such strict regard to unity of design as that of Timon.
This is not all. It is not enough to say that all the parts of
his conduct are consistent, or connected with one general
principle. They have a union of a more intimate nature.
All the qualities in his character and all the circumstances
in his conduct lead to one final event. They all co-operate,
directly or indirectly, in the accomplishment of one general
purpose. It is as if the poet had proposed to demonstrate
how persons of good temper and social dispositions may
become misanthropical. He assumes the social dispositions
to be constitutional and not confirmed by reason or by
reflection. He then employs the love of distinction to bring
about the conclusion. He shows its effects in superseding
the influence of better principles, in assuming their appearance, and so, in establishing self-deceit. He shows its effects in producing ostentation, injudicious profusion, and

disappointment. And lastly, he shows how its effects contributed to excite and exasperate those bitter feelings which estranged Timon from all mankind. Timon, at the beginning of the drama, seems altogether humane and affectionate; at the end he is an absolute misanthrope. Such opposition indicates inconsistency of character, unless the change can be traced through its causes and progress. If it can be traced, and if the appearance shall seem natural, this aspect of the human mind affords a curious and very interesting spectacle. Observe, in an instance or two, the fine lineaments and delicate shadings of this singular character. The poet refuses admission even to those circumstances which may be suitable and consistent enough with the general principle, but which would rather *coincide* with the main design than *contribute* to its consummation. Timon is lavish, but he is neither dissolute nor intemperate. He is convivial, but he enjoys the banquet not in his own, but in the pleasure of his guests. Though he displays the pomp of a masquerade, Phrynia and Timandra are in the train not of Timon, but of Alcibiades. He tells us, alluding to the correctness of his deportment,

> No villainous bounty yet hath pass'd my heart;
> Unwisely, not ignobly, have I given.

We may observe, too, that he is not so desirous of being distinguished for mere external magnificence as of being distinguished for courteous and beneficent actions. He does some good, but it is to procure distinction; he solicits distinction, but it is by doing good.

Upon the whole, "Shakespeare, in his *Timon of Athens,* illustrates the consequences of that inconsiderate profusion which has the appearance of liberality, and is supposed by the inconsiderate person himself to proceed from a generous principle, but which, in reality, has its chief origin in the love of distinction."

ROY WALKER

from *Unto Caesar: A Review of Recent Productions*

Major Shakespearian productions run from knight to knight. The Old Vic 1956–7 season opened with a production by the theatre's director, Michael Benthall, which brought back Sir Ralph Richardson to Shakespeare's stage in *Timon of Athens*. The final production of the Stratford-upon-Avon 1957 season restored Sir John Gielgud's Prospero (much changed since he was seen at the Old Vic in 1940) in a production of *The Tempest* by Peter Brook which had Drury Lane stamped all over it and was to transfer to that capacious cavern for what was once the pantomime season.

Sir Ralph's Timon and Sir John's Prospero were cousins once removed. Richardson's misanthrope in the wilderness was no vituperative, half-naked poor Tom. In his sheepskin coat he was protected against rough weather if not from man's ingratitude. His revulsion from human greed for gold was a molten melancholy that seethed inside him, not a volcano spitting scalding satire on all comers. Gielgud's Prospero came halfway back to meet him. Until the end this was no rich-robed and short-tempered magician but an ascetic hermit in brief tunic, burning with resentment of past wrongs which threatened to overthrow his reason altogether. These two performances, in fact,

From *Shakespeare Survey 11* (1958), pp. 128–32. Reprinted by permission of the author and of the Cambridge University Press.

invited some reconsideration of the transition from one play to the other in Shakespeare's mind, the dive from the beached verge of the salt flood and the not altogether sea-changed surfacing on the shores of the enchanted isle. . . .

By cutting some 500 of its 2300 lines, Michael Benthall ran through *Timon of Athens* in two hours, including a single interval of fifteen minutes. The deletions included what may be regarded as the definitive announcement of the theme of the play and a whole scene of some importance. Some minor characters were amalgamated and the ending of the play was boldly remodeled.

The first heavy stroke of the producer's pencil made Timon's entry cut short the opening dialogue of the Painter and Poet. There was no talk of artistic images of the fall of the truly great man when the mood of Fortune changes. It might be argued that modern audiences do not want the moral of a dramatic fable at the outset. But can any actor of Timon spare the tribute, spoken before he comes on (and not, therefore, in flattery), to "his good and gracious Nature"? And can any satisfactory production of the play dispense with the preliminary raising of the particular instance which we are to see into a general rule: " 'Tis common." The effect, if not also the intention, of omitting this choric opening dialogue is to slant the drama away from its theme of man's ingratitude towards the tragedy of a particular fault in the protagonist which invites a general censure. The producer's trimming of Timon's exchanges with Apemantus and excision of the dialogue of abuse between the two Lords and that churlish philosopher, which should close the first scene, does no such damage, except to deprive the scene of its deliberate final emphasis on Timon (who has left the stage and, again, is not being flattered): "The noblest mind he carries, That ever govern'd man."

In the banquet scene which follows, Apemantus' carbolic commentary was reduced, and Act II lost little by cutting out the dialogue in which Apemantus and the Fool are involved with the creditors. In fact the scene gained by leaving the crucial interview between Timon and his Steward uninterrupted. There is no dramatic difficulty in

taking the Steward's proper presentation of his accounts
for granted, and the sole function of the indifferent dialogue with the Fool seems to be to mark time while that
statement of accounts is supposed to take place.

The action so far had been acceptably staged in the hall
of Timon's house, on one side of which was placed a tall
and somewhat awe-inspiring statue of a goddess, presumably a stand-in for Fortune. Now a drop curtain depicting
the outer walls of the city was lowered and lighted, but
no scene was played before it. After a few moments it rose
to reveal a street scene of which the main feature was the
central portal and steps of Timon's house. The range of
three steps was the same as for the interior scene, and was
not enough to allow any symbolic effect of moving down
the steps as reverses of Fortune followed thick and fast.
This open-air scene worked very well to give a free flow
to the first five scenes of Act III. Instead of three servants,
this production entrusted all the begging to Timon's
Steward, who was of course addressed as Flavius where
the text names the others. A climax to the three dialogues
in the street was provided by bringing on Sempronius in a
palanquin where he was lounging with a paramour. No
pause or scene change was necessary for the fourth scene,
in which the creditors pounded upon Timon's door, with
Flavius taking the lines of Servilius and Timon appearing
in a plain gray robe which made an effective contrast with
the rich crimson he wore in the earlier scenes. The dialogue between the Senators (accompanied by a bald,
stripped, dark-skinned executioner who seemed to have
wandered in from *Hassan*) and Alcibiades was also played
in the street. The drop curtain was used as before, with
no action in front of it, while the scene was shifted back
to Timon's hall for the mock-banquet.

Timon, in red robes again, served not water but only
clouds of steam; he overturned tables, pulled down curtains and set the house afire. As he finally advanced to the
forestage the drop curtain was lowered once more, semi-
transparent where it was lighted from behind, to produce
a most effective stage picture. Through the walls of
Athens, outside which Timon now stood, could be seen to

one side the ruins of the banquet in the lurid light of
flames flickering offstage. On the other side the enigmatic
white goddess gazed inscrutably on the scene of destruction. Timon went straight on from his speech near the end
of Act III to the denunciation that opens Act IV. Throwing aside his cloak only, he made his departure from this
City of Destruction by descending into the pit at the front
of the stage, and the curtain fell for the single long interval.

The producer's decision to give a clear visual contrast
between the city scenes of the first half and the wilderness
scenes of the second half dictated the omission of IV, ii,
the scene in which the steward shares his own remaining
coins among Timon's other former servants. Instead the
curtain rose upon the wilderness, or as the stage direction
has it "in the woods." As soon as this scene was revealed
it became evident that the production had not only cut the
lines but missed the poetic point about the hero who is
spurned down the slope of Fortune's Hill and ignored by
those who had previously been his beneficiaries. Timon in
Athens was on the same level as his fellows throughout,
but for the insignificant range of three or four steps. Timon
in exile had the vantage of a central rocky mound, to the
top of which he frequently resorted. If the intention had
been to show that Timon's last state was, despite appearances, better than his first, the placing might have been justified. But if this was in the producer's mind it was hardly
the impression Sir Ralph Richardson left on his audience.
The general effect of the scene, which included a long
brown fringe of what looked rather like seaweed hung up
to dry, and of the actor's armless sheepskin coat and bare
cross-gartered legs, was more reminiscent of Robinson
Crusoe than of the naked outcast Timon.

Sir Ralph's delivery of Timon's long speeches and his
judgments on those who came to visit him were spoken
with a quiet irony more effective than the negligent extravagance of the first half. After the name-calling contest
with Apemantus, which culminated in a vigorous exchange
of stones, the churlish philosopher did not stay to bandy
further insults. Instead, there was a brief blackout in which
the festoon was raised and the rocky buttress was now

seen against a cyclorama sky. This might or might not have been at the verge of the salt sea; there was neither sight nor sound of the ocean.

Timon had set up on his rocky stronghold a huge slab, like a tombstone, on which he was carving his epitaph as he spoke the lines up to "make thine Epitaph, That death in me, at others' lives may laugh." A cut of some twenty lines allowed the three Bandits to interrupt the speech at this point. Richardson's uncanny stillness as he sat looking down unseen upon them, listening to their avaricious interchanges, gave him a memorable moment of moral superiority, which the thieves sensed when they looked up and met his quietly accusing gaze.

In the next interview, the last long speech of the Steward was omitted, and there was a cut of some thirty lines early in the scene with the Poet and the Painter. The Steward and the Senators departed sadly on "Trouble him no further . . . " and Timon resumed his chiseling for his final speech, "Come not to me again . . . let my gravestone be your Oracle . . . Timon hath done his reign," in a last ray of the setting sun.

There was a blackout while the actor left the stage, and to preserve unity of place the short scene of the Senators' report back to Athens (V, ii) was omitted. Only the first two lines of V, iii were spoken by the Soldier, who was interrupted by the entry of Alcibiades and his forces, not before Athens but at the base of Timon's rocky retreat, where they were confronted by the frightened Senators and people who enter from the opposite side of the stage. Alcibiades rejected the Athenian pleas for mercy and ordered the assault; but at this moment the Soldier, who had climbed up to examine the inscription, called urgently to him and Alcibiades halted the attack to read the epitaph himself. It was this reminder of human mortality that melted the banished general to pity, a bold rehandling of the end of the play which at least tied the main and subplots together in a theatrically effective way.

In the text of the play as we have it, Alcibiades relents for no dramatically adequate reason, and Michael Benthall's solution therefore deserves serious consideration.

But whether the change which makes Timon's death the cause of that change of heart is an acceptable image of the death of misanthropy bringing forth new mercy, or whether it is only a last irony that the man who willed the destruction of Athens should be the inadvertent means of saving the city, remains a dangerous dramatic ambiguity.

Whatever its intention, the impression made by this production on audiences who had small knowledge of the play was that Timon was entirely to blame. The early scenes suggested to them not the noble magnanimity of a largess universal like the sun, only a reckless extravagance. Yet it was presumably the poet's intention to show how selfish society drives out true generosity (and makes of it a judgment on itself); much as, in the preceding play, the mob drives out military heroism and discipline in Coriolanus, whose story is echoed (with a happier ending) in the Alcibiades subplot of *Timon of Athens*. Modern middle-class audiences have been indoctrinated with ideals of prudence and economy and are, moreover, suffering the effects of inflation and a credit squeeze! But something more might be done for Timon's credit by making the friendship of his beneficiaries seem plausible while they can still feed on Timon's means, so that we share some of his disillusionment at their unmasking.

Michael Benthall certainly avoided the gross mistake of Tyrone Guthrie's production at the Old Vic four years earlier, when the cultural *élite* of Athens was a pack of comic scarecrows. Nor was Richardson, as André Morell had been, like some devout peasant who had won a chariot-pool and set up as a one-man Athenian Arts Council, a fool and his money soon parted. But if the role of Timon calls for a display of active magnanimity, like Antony's, in the first part, and an active agony, like Philoctetes', in the second, Richardson remained too near the middle of the road throughout. His negligent prodigality at first and his half-amused irony later failed to scale the heights or reach the depths of the poetry, and his occasionally careless delivery, as well as that of a company far from strong even by recent Old Vic standards, came in for deserved censure from some critics. . . .

DAVID COOK

"Timon of Athens"

As is well known, there are certain major themes which
Shakespeare handles again and again throughout his plays,
ideas which form the framework of his thinking as it con-
tinually develops. One such concept is, of course, that of
order: the elaborate consideration of social order in the
history plays leads to an investigation of emotional and
moral order, in *Measure for Measure* for instance, in *Lear*,
and finally, with a different emphasis, in the last romances.
I find another recurrent theme in the consideration of
human pride, and the difficulty of distinguishing proper
pride, which is essential to human dignity and which keeps
a firm hold on certain fundamental values, from presumptuous, fiercely egotistical pride, which is a denial of
human contact. This duality is particularly apparent in
Shylock; Iago strikes a different balance. Othello is destroyed by positive pride, and so in his death positive
values are more important than the wastage of life; Macbeth, in his negative pride, destroys himself and rejects
humanity. Cordelia properly asserts human dignity, and
so can serve as the instrument to winnow what is destructive from what is constructive in Lear's pride. *Timon of
Athens, Coriolanus, Measure for Measure* and *All's Well
That Ends Well* investigate more specifically the distinc-

From *Shakespeare Survey 16* (1963), pp. 83–94. Reprinted by permission of the author and of the Cambridge University Press.

tion, often a fine one, between negative and positive pride: in doing so they move towards the resolution of the human dilemma which Shakespeare offers as an alternative to tragedy in the final romances. Of these plays, *Timon of Athens* analyzes pride most objectively, and offers least resolution of the issues raised.

It is the magnificent scale of Timon's presumption which determines his dramatic stature. But his extreme self-assertion is made possible only by an equal self-blindness which, unlike that of Coriolanus, is irremediable even in the last resort; thus it is impossible for Timon to pass beyond the limitations set by his pride and by his ignorance of himself; he can arrive at no fundamental self-knowledge nor meet any new dispensation in death, as do the greater tragic figures.

It will already be clear that I do not share the view of *Timon of Athens* which sees its "theme" as the depiction of "the ruin of a frank and generous soul by ingratitude, public and private."[1] The manner of the play is certainly homiletic and many of the minor characters are shown in a fiercely sardonic light. But homily is the coil rather than the core; if such simple moralizing were the main subject, then this would indeed be a naïve and uninteresting work. Incidentally, Shakespeare handles ingratitude far more powerfully in the persons of Regan and Goneril. But the whole concept of Timon as a saintly man who, being wronged, understandably comes to hate mankind, runs quite counter, I am sure, to the actual dramatic impact. In fact, Timon is pictured as flagrantly wrongheaded in both halves of the play. Our untrammeled reaction is surely to feel that at first he is a well-meaning fool, and that later his misanthropy, however provoked, is perverse. Even in the play's still unfinished form, we possess enough to see clearly that such are the effects which Shakespeare intends, and consequently there can be no solemn moralization running counter to this strong dramatic current. I am inclined to agree with J. C. Maxwell that seeing Timon as an embodiment of overtaxed virtue results from a "subservience to classification and theory—to the traditional classification of *Timon* as a tragedy, and to quasi-philosophical theories . . . of what tragedy should be."[2] The critics who were more concerned in attributing parts of the play to various playwrights of their own choice than in assessing it as a whole found a spur to their activities in the obvious absurdities and contradictions inherent in this conventional view.

As I see it, *Timon of Athens* is an investigation of aberrations from natural order in the individual promoted by subtle forms of pride, just as *Troilus and Cressida* concerns itself with similar aberrations in the state. The backbone of Shakespeare's public thinking is the medieval, neoclassical conception of a universal hierarchy, embodied in Ulysses' best-known speech (and perhaps most coherently propounded for later generations in Pope's *Essay on Man*). E. M. W. Tillyard, describing this interpretation of the cosmos in *Shakespeare's History Plays*,[3] quotes a characteristic passage from I.K.'s 1598 translation of Hannibal Romei's *Courtier's Academy*,[4] which conveniently expounds that part of the theory which seems to me relevant to *Timon of Athens*:

Creatures live after the laws of nature: man liveth by reason, prudence and art. Living creatures may live a solitary life: man alone, being himself insufficient and by nature an evil creature, without domestical and civil conversation cannot lead other than a miserable and discontented life. And therefore, as the philosopher saith very well, that man which cannot live in civil company either he is a god or a beast, seeing only God is sufficient of himself, and a solitary life best agreeth with a beast.

2. "Timon of Athens," *Scrutiny*, xv, 3 (1948), 196. In reading (and sometimes re-reading) *Timon* criticism, I find that I have agreed fairly closely with J. C. Maxwell on a number of specific points; and elsewhere with O. J. Campbell and A. C. Collins.

3. P. 14. I have adopted Tillyard's modernized spelling and punctuation, except for two commas.

4. P. 247.

"This passage . . . ," comments Tillyard, "would have been accepted without question by every educated Elizabethan." This familiar concept is, I suggest, the framework for *Timon of Athens*. In the first half of the drama Timon plays the god, far above all other men, aloof and indiscriminately munificent; in the second half he becomes the animal, alone and rejecting all fellow contact. In neither case will Timon consider or accept man's real condition. As Alcibiades declares in his funeral speech for Timon:

> Thou abhorr'dst in us our human griefs.[5]

The burden of the play, positively expressed in Alcibiades, is the need to accept and love man as he is, and to acknowledge our human condition. Thus *Timon* is closely linked in theme with *Measure for Measure*, in the demand that fallible man shall, without being pandered to, nevertheless be loved and forgiven, a train of thought which eventually leads to *The Tempest*. In *Timon*, however, it is a secondary character who embodies this positive idea, while the protagonist acts out its obverse: Timon is negative. Macbeth too is negative, but *Macbeth* is perhaps Shakespeare's only tragedy of waste (a much abused term) and so the hero remains the controlling figure in presenting the dramatic idea; whereas Timon, when measured against the very different idea which is central to his play, is found wanting. Did this subject, apparently so apt, prove in fact to be too negative to match Shakespeare's dramatic thinking at this time? Was this the reason why his impulse flagged so that he did not finish revising the play? This can be no more than a conjecture.

In the closer analysis of the play which follows I shall not normally distinguish between the polished and unpolished parts of the text. I believe the play can be interpreted as a whole. Those passages which are clearly only in draft form may carry somewhat less weight critically, but they take their place in the general pattern of the play.

5. Quotations are from *Timon of Athens*, ed. H. J. Oliver (Arden Shakespeare, 1959).

As a result of naïve blandness rather than of deliberate presumption, Timon has assumed a godlike status, a role which is clearly reflected in the phrasing and imagery. The poet announces

> I have in this rough work shap'd out a man,
> Whom this beneath world doth embrace and hug.

Timon is irresistible to all men:

> You see how all conditions, how all minds,
> As well of glib and slipp'ry creatures as
> Of grave and austere quality, tender down
> Their services to Lord Timon.

And it is by an act of grace that Timon is seen winning his opponents to join the throng of followers:

> Whose present grace to present slaves and servants
> Translates his rivals.

This line of imagery intensifies, till the sycophants whispering in Timon's ear breathe only by his allowance:

> Rain sacrificial whisperings in his ear,
> Make sacred even his stirrup, and through him
> Drink the free air.

True the painting carries a moral, the warning that pride goes before a fall, but significantly Timon does not consider this when he later receives the work. At the end of the scene the second lord declares that Pluto is merely Timon's steward. The masque symbolically sets Timon again above mere mankind who have to war with the human condition:

> The five best senses acknowledge thee their patron,
> and come freely to gratulate thy plenteous bosom.

The original stage direction tells us that the Lords "rise

from the table, with much adoring of Timon." And the Steward's bitter regrets carry a double meaning:

> His promises fly so beyond his state.

And even in his long speech at the mock-banquet Timon still, by implication but unmistakably, draws a parallel between himself and the gods.

Timon is not discriminatingly or positively generous. The opening of the play presents a repulsive picture of the competing toadies who bask in Timon's favor. They are willing to travesty art to please him, and to fawn on others whom he approves. He is too beneficent to be in real contact with lesser mortals, whom he advances regardless of their worth or worthlessness. And we see him buying a jewel with the same casualness as that with which he relieves a friend. In short, he emulates the indiscriminate generosity of an abstract deity like Fortune. The real difference is that Timon proves to have feet of clay. As Lucius' servant dryly comments:

> You must consider that a prodigal course
> Is like the sun's,
> But not, like his, recoverable.

The only two figures at Timon's court who retain their self-respect are Apemantus, who refuses his gifts, and the Steward, who well earns his comparatively slight rewards.

Timon does not stop to consider the shallowness of the friendship which he virtually buys. Apemantus is unheeded:

> That there should be small love amongst these sweet knaves,
> And all this courtesy!

But Timon is pleasant enough in all his dealings for us to be both disappointed that he should allow himself to be so duped, and chagrined by his blindness. For, however sour his manner, we must surely second Apemantus in

He that loves to be flattered is worthy o' th' flatterer.

If Timon is easily deceived, the audience is not, and is not meant to be. We mark the warnings that Timon wilfully ignores: "I take no heed of thee." He sweeps aside the reasonable consideration of his own affairs with an imperious and dramatic selflessness similar to Julius Caesar's:

Steward. . . . it does concern you near.
Timon. Near? Why, then, another time I'll hear thee.

Act I, the act that sets out the situation ends with an authoritative, impersonal rhymed couplet:

O that men's ears should be
To counsel deaf, but not to flattery.

Timon allows riches to isolate him in a privileged position, so he remains ignorant of the truth about men, and about himself. "Why," he vapidly laments, "I have often wish'd myself poorer that I might come nearer to you." This is an idle and complacent comment, proper only to hypocrisy or extreme ingenuousness, the more so as the sentence is rounded out with, "we are born to do benefits": Timon takes it for granted that the traffic between himself and others is in effect one-way. He pays lip service to community: "O what a precious comfort 'tis to have so many like brothers commanding one another's fortunes"; but we do not have to await the event to realize what simple self-delusion this is. We can hardly admire a man who cultivates such "brothers," or who understands so little about men; nor feel unqualified pity when his own conduct overtakes him and he stands aghast in wide-eyed innocence.

The refusal of Ventidius' repayment finally drives home a number of these points. This is an unconsidered demonstration of bounty, part of the culpable display of recklessness that shocks his Steward:

> Takes no accompt
> How things go from him, nor resumes no care
> Of what is to continue.

He is not here doing Ventidius any particular kindness,
since we are to understand that Ventidius' father has left
him an ample fortune. On the contrary, he is withstanding
the one proffered *exchange* of friendship and mutual hon-
orableness which he talks so much of. This can be nothing
but a gesture; a view which is confirmed by Timon's readiness to talk of things which should be unspoken:

> Nay, my lords, ceremony was but devis'd at first
> To set a gloss on faint deeds, hollow welcomes,
> Recanting goodness, sorry ere 'tis shown;
> But where there is true friendship, there needs none.

Timon clearly means well: but that is not enough. His
well meaning favors knaves, smothers real friendship, and
ruins his own estate, thus preventing the judicious and
constructive generosity he could be offering.
      What is the faithful Steward's view of this so-called
munificence?

> When all our offices have been oppress'd
> With riotous feeders, when our vaults have wept
> With drunken spilth of wine, when every room
> Hath blaz'd with lights and bray'd with minstrelsy,
> I have retir'd me to a wasteful cock
> And set mine eyes at flow.

The constant impression is that the result of Timon's
ready dispensing of cash is drunkenness, debauchery, orgy
and waste:

> No care, no stop; so senseless of expense,
> That he will neither know how to maintain it,
> Nor cease his flow of riot.

Timon squanders money to maintain his own conception
of himself:

You may take my word, my lord, I know no man
Can justly praise but what he does affect.
I weigh my friend's affection with mine own,
I'll tell you true. I'll call to you.

This is the vanity of giving:

I take all and your several visitations
So kind to heart, 'tis not enough to give:
Methinks I could deal kingdoms to my friends,
And ne'er be weary.

Timon's bounty is seen as a "humor," a wilful obsession:
"There's no crossing him in's humor" declares the
Steward. And while Timon thinks himself loved for his
generosity, he is despised and made fun of:

If I want gold, steal but a beggar's dog
And give it Timon—why, the dog coins gold.

It is impossible to exaggerate the importance of such a line
as,

Never mind
Was to be so unwise, to be so kind.

The play thus embodies truisms familiar to the neoclas-
sicist. J. C. Maxwell declares that of all Shakespeare's
works *Timon* "falls most easily within the framework of an
Aristotelian scheme, and Timon, both before and after his
fall, is clearly an example of excess."[6]

The liberal man [says Aristotle] will give to the right
people, the right amounts, and at the right time. . . .
Nor will he neglect his own property, since he wishes
by means of this to help others. And he will refrain
from giving to anybody and everybody, that he may
have something to give to the right people, at the right
time, and where it is noble to do so. . . . For as has

6. "Timon of Athens," *Scrutiny*, xv, 3 (1948), 197.

been said, he is liberal who spends according to his
substance and on the right objects; and he who exceeds
is prodigal.[7]

Certainly there are important qualifications to be made
in Timon's favor: within his own limited vision, he is
sincere and constantly imagines himself to be acting ideal-
istically. Shakespeare does not suggest that Timon is
always wrong in giving. His brief replies to the Old Man
whose daughter he marries to his servant show immediate
right feeling. He does indeed in some sort display generous
friendship, especially to Ventidius in need, and at an early
stage one almost imagines he might be a benevolent des-
pot. There is, again, a certain splendor in his high-minded
view of man, even if it rests on a failure to consider the
evidence, and on childlike vanity. As Peter Alexander
says, he has "a god-like image of a man in his heart." His
behavior may be culpable, but it is not despicable. He is an
"honest fool."

And so Timon is, on the one hand, wholly admirable
to men who know no intimate facts about him, the
strangers; while, on the other, to his Steward, who knows
the individual behind the godlike façade, he is truly
lovable. If the Steward weeps over Timon's folly, he is
weeping for one for whom he feels real affection. Yet the
emphasis remains on Timon's lack of self-control. He is
indiscriminate. He does good at random; and naïvely
squanders more than he wisely distributes. The scene at
the end of Act II between steward and master is revealing. With the coming of disaster, Timon abandons all ful-
someness; his tone is now direct and honest; but he is
altogether at a loss. He is here like a hurt child beside the
sorrowing maturity of his own overseer.

But whatever Timon's limitations, his society has, of
course, no justification for treating him as it does: society
is, in fact, ruthlessly and painstakingly indicted in the first
half of the play. However, in considering Timon himself

7. *Ethica Nicomachea*, IV, i, 1020^a, 24–1020^b, 25, translated by W. D.
Ross, *The Works of Aristotle* (Oxford, 1915), IX.

we are bound to remember that these are the very men he has chosen and fostered with his superficial beneficence, uncontrolled by reason or prudence, blindly presuming beyond man's proper scope to play the role of all-dispensing Fortune. Thus, Timon has no cause to blame Fate or mankind in general for what he wilfully brings on himself: his reaction to adversity is unwarrantably negative, just as his reaction to prosperity has been dangerously irresponsible and presumptuous.

The most difficult role to assess in this first part of the play is Apemantus. He is crabbed and uncouth, but his sour comments come close to the mark. His jibing is sometimes faintly reminiscent of the searching, cross talk from the Fool in *Lear,* who in his asperity also dismisses cliché and conventional attitudinizing:

Timon.   Good morrow to thee, gentle Apemantus.
Apemantus. Till I be gentle, stay thou for thy good morrow,
          When thou art Timon's dog, and these knaves
          honest.

Fools in Shakespeare are constantly in league with truth; so that, though the scene is little more than a rough draft, it is not insignificant that Apemantus is on more friendly terms with the Fool when they are together than with any other character. At one point he praises a riposte from the Fool by claiming, "That answer might have become Apemantus"; and the Fool says immediately afterwards, "I do not always follow lover, elder brother and woman; sometime the philosopher."

Critics who have seen Timon himself as a monument of wronged virtue have had to play down the caustic accuracy of Apemantus' social observation; and since he is not a warm or directly likable character, they have been able to do so by emphasizing his harshness at the expense of his insight. Nevertheless, Apemantus seems to be cast in the philosophical tradition of a Diogenes; he serves as the relentless mentor in the play. He is neither taken in by the glitter of society, nor does he withdraw from it, but stays to warn and moralize. His view of his fellows, if sometimes almost as black as Timon's is at the last, remains philo-

sophic rather than petulant or personal; and he is engaged
throughout in moral and prophetic admonition, never in
self-glorification or self-pity. Shakespeare, as so often, had
set himself a nice problem: how to introduce the voice of
reason into the play without hopelessly weakening the
protagonist's dramatic status. I do not think he has solved
the problem altogether, simply by giving sanity such a
rugged exterior. The result is to confuse the issue (as it
would have been confused in *Lear* if the king had ultimately resisted the rebukes of the Fool and Kent), since
Timon is still necessarily left in a negative position; but by
this device Shakespeare at least makes his play viable,
however tenuously.

The dividing line between the positions of Timon and
Apemantus in the second half of the play is a fine one, a
distinction which is not always dramatically clear in detail,
though in the main the two voices remain in subtle contrast, except in the apparently unrevised passage wherein
Apemantus makes Timon confound himself: here Apemantus' role becomes blurred; but I shall return to this
point. In the whole design one can perceive that Apemantus is cast as the homilist: often his words become so impersonal that he seems to speak for the play rather than
for himself.

One of Shakespeare's many structural experiments in his
later plays was to adopt a simple form divided into two
clearly marked halves boldly and significantly contrasted
against each other. This is perhaps most subtly effected in
Coriolanus, and most daringly in *The Winter's Tale*, where
the duality is pinpointed in the words

thou met'st with things dying, I with things new-born.

A similar division is also explicitly summarized in *Timon:*

One day he gives us diamonds, next day stones.

In his days of prosperity, instead of trying to understand
men and work on them positively with his wealth, Timon
has lived immoderately: now he flies to the opposite ex-

treme. The malcontent was, of course, a fashionable stage figure at this time; as ever Shakespeare takes the popular fabric and cuts it to his own design.

That Timon's "love" is so soon converted into hate bespeaks the empty and pretentious nature of his "generosity." A truly benevolent man could never be brought deliberately to cry down such vengeance upon his race; anyone might come to say such things in a state of hysteria, but Timon maintains them steadily from now till his death:

> Slaves and fools,
> Pluck the grave wrinkled senate from the bench,
> And minister in their steads! To general filths
> Convert, o'th'instant, green virginity!
> Do't in your parents' eyes! Bankrupts, hold fast;
> Rather than render back, out with your knives,
> And cut your trusters' throats! Bound servants, steal!
> Large-handed robbers your grave masters are,
> And pill by law. Maid, to thy master's bed;
> Thy mistress is o'th'brothel! Son of sixteen,
> Pluck the lin'd crutch from thy old limping sire;
> With it beat out his brains!

The malcontent is also indicting himself—the very excess makes this apparent. There is no poetic conviction in this opening speech of Act IV: compare it with the more savage passages of *The Revenger's Tragedy*. Shakespeare does not seem really to have entered into this wild loathing of mankind. Whatever Timon's state, he has certainly no more grounds for such indiscriminate denunciation than he had for his equally indiscriminate generosity. To underline this fact we are introduced at once to the innocent and openhearted victims of Timon's excesses—the Steward and his fellows. Timon's unbridled damning of man must include these patient followers. Their direct feeling and real, simple generosity discredit Timon's megalomaniac ravings. Those Timon has cause to hate, he himself has bred up to it; while he forgets those who patently deserve his consideration. The Steward can see Timon's career in clear perspective:

Who would be so mock'd with glory, or to live
But in a dream of friendship. . . ?

But he has no bitter word, only sympathy and affection:

Poor honest lord, brought low by his own heart,
Undone by goodness.

And he concludes, "I'll ever serve his mind, with my best
will": here is an unassuming nobility to which Timon cannot aspire.

So when Timon cries:

Who dares, who dares,
In purity of manhood stand upright,
And say this man's a flatterer? If one be,
So are they all,

we are reminded that his cynicism is culled from narrow
and self-induced experience; and when he complains that
"the learned pate Ducks to the golden fool," we remember
that such is the conduct Timon has courted. When he concludes,

all's obliquy;
There's nothing level in our cursed natures
But direct villainy,

we ask, "What of the Steward, of Alcibiades, the Servants,
the Strangers, and their like?" At last we see Timon's fury
as a private jaundice resulting from his failure to buy love
by means of lavish distribution of favors.

When Timon finds his new supply of gold, his condemnation of the malpractices it could foster is eloquent,
but he conveniently overlooks the fact that his own abuse
of wealth is to be included in the indictment. To hide the
coin is moral escapism, not a solution. Can he conceive it
doing no good, simply because it breeds nothing but selfish
greed in flatterers? And so Apemantus appears, to shake
Timon from his complacent world of private hatred.

The frequency of animal imagery in the play has often been noticed. It should be added that in the early acts it is used almost exclusively by or of Apemantus, his role being contrasted with Timon's superhuman elevation. It is immediately after this dialogue in I, i,

Second Lord. Away, unpeaceable dog, or I'll spurn thee hence!
Apemantus. I will fly, like a dog, the heels o'th'ass.
First Lord. He's opposite to humanity,

that Timon is again raised to godhead, the opposite extreme:

He pours it out. Plutus the god of gold
Is but his steward.

We are kept aware of the two states outside the human condition. But Timon, when forced to abandon the one, eagerly adopts the other:

Alcibiades. What art thou there? Speak.
Timon. A beast as thou art.

Timon turns away friend and enemy alike; and he himself is utterly ungrateful in his petulance, while in the very act of brooding upon the ingratitude of others:

Alcibiades. Here is some gold for thee.
Timon. Keep it, I cannot eat it.

The tables are turned: Timon is thankless and incapable of responding to the generosity of others. He has forgotten his own words earlier: "Oh what a precious comfort 'tis, to have so many like brothers commanding one another's fortunes."

Apemantus immediately attacks Timon as a fake cynic who has turned misanthrope in an enormous huff because his irrational dreams about human nature have proved false:

Men report thou dost affect my manners . . . putting on

the cunning of a carper. . . . Thou wast told thus. . . .
Do not *assume* my likeness.

The argument which Apemantus here presents is often
misrepresented. He is not saying that Timon would re-
nounce poverty if he had the chance: we know that he
has already found a fresh supply of gold. Shakespeare is
not merely concerned to show that Apemantus does not
know what he is talking about; far from it. What he says
is that Timon, being an escapist from reality, always seeks
an extreme, where issues are simplified into being either
rosy or without hope:

> Thou'dst courtier be again
> Wert thou not beggar. Willing misery
> Outlives incertain pomp—

in short, in hoping for nothing and dismissing mankind,
Timon has found a much more secure retreat than in his
previous dream of perfect living. When his glittering world
crashed about his ears, he was bound to be involved; when
his lonely indulgence in loathing is shown to be ill-
founded, he can, and does, shut his eyes, as we have seen.
Thus, like Richard II and Coriolanus, though for different
reasons, Timon cannot bear mediocrity: he must be all-
significant or a cipher; life must appear a utopia or a hell.
Timon will not accept the human condition with its confusions and compromises. He must be more, or less, than
man. If he cannot be a god, he will become a beast.

It is in Act IV that the distinction between Apemantus
and Timon, the caustic, satirical philosopher and the
spoilt child sulking in the face of a fate he has brought
on himself, is most important, and also most difficult to
make dramatically. Timon has been "a madman so long,
and now a fool." In his own defense he enters on a long
speech of self-pity, to which Apemantus trenchantly replies, "Art thou proud yet?" Apemantus exposes the
falsity of Timon's values which have led him to confuse
gratitude with love, and comes to the heart of the whole
play in the sentence, "The middle of humanity thou never

knewest, but the extremity of both ends." Eventually
Apemantus adopts some of Timon's own arguments and
attitudes ("Give it to the beasts, to be rid of men," and
so on): presumably he is drawing Timon on. Already
in the first act Timon has been made to condemn his
own future conduct in terms exactly appropriate to the
play, when he berates Apemantus' churlishness:

> Fie, th'art a churl, y'have got a humor there
> Does not become a man.

Now, as Apemantus plays devil's advocate, Timon is
again made to condemn his own imitation of bestial life
in even rounder terms:

> What beast couldst thou be that were not subject to a
> beast? And what a beast art thou already, that seest not
> thy loss in transformation!

It may seem like special pleading to argue that Apemantus here changes sides to draw Timon out and make
him condemn himself. But one should consider that it is
in fact Timon who truly adopts the "solitary life" which
"best agreeth with the beast": it is Apemantus who sought
the interview, and it is Apemantus who returns to mankind, to live in society as its moral mentor. His final "Live
and love thy misery" shows him as having accurately
sized up Timon's whole situation.

For now Timon proceeds to the final rejection of man.
He hates life: "I am sick of this false world." And he
dedicates the globe to the beasts: "that beasts May have
the world in empire." He reaches a new pitch of cynicism
when he advises the Banditti not only to hate others but
even to "love not yourselves." The climax of this sequence
falls in the scene with the Steward. Against all the evidence Timon at first tries to cling to his total rejection of
man:

> Steward. An honest poor servant of yours.
> Timon. Then I know thee not.
> I never had honest man about me, I; all
> I kept were knaves, to serve in meat to villains.

But the play pursues him and pins him down till he is
forced to acknowledge "One honest man." Is this, we
wonder, to be the beginning of a new vision for him? By
no means, for it proves the nadir of his wilful introver-
sion. Timon is no longer dealing with men whom he can
convince himself are contemptible: but how does he
reward this honest man? He offers him gold, the gold
which Timon, however wrongheadedly, believes to be
evil, and which, as employed in the play, has become
the symbol of destructive materialism: he exhorts him
to hatred:

> Hate all, curse all, show charity to none;

and ends the act with the ominous words:

> Ne'er see thou man, and let me ne'er see thee.

Shakespeare shows great technical daring in planning
the construction of the second half of *Timon* as a series
of duologues or interviews. These are not simply repeti-
tive but pile one on top of another to build, as it were,
a negative climax. The aim is to achieve a powerful
austerity in contrast with the shifting effects of the first
half of the play, but also parallel to the successive appeals to Timon's "friends" in Act III. The manner is
severe and classical; but its success is only partial.

There is an attempt to dramatize Timon's last denial
of mankind differently and more fully in Act V. This
depends on the appeal to Timon by the city of Athens in
time of crisis to come and save them, and Timon's refusal.
Unfortunately, there is no previous evidence in terms of
the play that Timon has ever been a crucial figure in the
state. So that, unlike the decision which is forced on
Coriolanus, with the whole dramatic weight of the play
behind it, the situation in *Timon* appears contrived, and
largely fails of its effect. But the dramatic intention is
clear enough: Timon's position is now represented by
the words "I care not." His abandonment of life is negative, the confirmation and consummation of all that has
gone before. Timon the absolutist could find no place on

earth. This absolutism was at first innocent, and remains sufficiently naïve for him to retain a certain nobility, though a barren and inhuman nobility. In order to strengthen the presentation of Timon's death, his epitaph is introduced twice, not altogether successfully in dramatic terms; but the pattern is now complete.

The action centered on Alcibiades is no mere irrelevant incident. I agree with Peter Alexander that Act III, sc. v is central to the whole play, though I would interpret it rather differently. The Senate admit that Alcibiades' friend has been subjected to wrongs, but they smugly declare, "He's truly valiant that can wisely suffer," and they advocate the wearing of one's injuries "carelessly." Alcibiades then reasonably asks why, if they believe this, they should possess an army instead of being pacifists. The First Senator's reply, "Nothing emboldens sin so much as mercy," recalls the debate between Isabella and Angelo. This passage is highly relevant to the whole play. The issue is concentrated in Alcibiades' lines,

> To be in anger is impiety;
> But who is man that is not angry?
> Weigh but the crime with this.

In short, he insists that man's fallibility must be taken into account in balancing justice against mercy. Surely there is no doubt that Alcibiades has, and is meant to have, our sympathy in this scene. He is felt to be right because he accepts man as man, with all his limitations and weaknesses. Thus Timon is paralleled with the Senate: each demands or assumes an unattainable absolute standard of conduct. The self-protective canker in the state is legislation by fear; Timon's canker, that of the individual, is fear of living in actuality and facing the complexity of man's condition.

To say this is not to argue that the two plots have been neatly integrated. But it now becomes quite clear why Alcibiades' action is allowed to conclude the play. Alcibiades, like Timon, has been betrayed and has reacted violently, but, unlike Timon, he comes to terms with life.

When forced in turn to make his moral choice, his decision is positive; he accepts man and his limitations; and in the light of this acceptance can exercise mercy. The line of argument on which Alcibiades yields is:

> We were not all unkind, nor all deserve
> The common stroke of war,

which forcefully reminds us how oversimplified was Timon's judgment in condemning all men alike by a rule of thumb. "All have not offended"; and, by corollary, if the state does not consist exclusively either of good or bad members, so the individual is neither perfect nor utterly vile. In burying his anger, Alcibiades acts like a wise, merciful, and humanly inconsistent being, not like a god or a beast. This emphasis on the need to accept, minister to, correct and forgive fallible human nature links *Timon* to a far greater work, *Measure for Measure,* and points the way once again towards the final romances.

So the idea is rounded out. It has been powerfully conceived, but not realized in fully developed dramatic terms. The suggestion, often made both on textual and critical grounds, that we have no more than an advanced draft of *Timon,* seems convincing. It is easy to see why Shakespeare might seize on the subject of Timon in a period of troubled thinking and warring moods, and might modify his material along the lines I have suggested. And it is, further, quite feasible that the reason he failed to finish the work was that, in the event, the hero proved too negative a vehicle for his thinking, and the whole fabric of the play too destructive at a time when his thoughts were slowly gestating the new positive ideas of the final group of plays. It is interesting that Shakespeare's only other fundamentally negative play, *Troilus and Cressida* (though in a much more advanced state of revision than *Timon* and altogether more effective and disturbing), also lacks finish. Perhaps not only the treatment but also the rejection of the Timon motif may contribute to our understanding of the whole body of Shakespeare's thought.

SUSAN HANDELMAN

Timon of Athens:
The Rage of Disillusion

Shakespeare's characters frequently express an obsession with the problems of creation, illusion, boundaries, dreams. The anxiety that the symbolic world will break down, vanish and leave not a rack behind, is present in all the plays, and perhaps accounts for their obsessive self-reflexiveness—their constant reflection on their own origins, their own natures as plays. The anxiety of the artist's ego is another variant of the primal shock to our universal narcissism. But with those characters who insist on retaining and trying obstinately to recapture that original state, Shakespeare is often not kind.

The inability to accept loss may express itself in the creation of higher narcissistic illusions or heightened rage. In Lear, both reactions exist simultaneously—holding dead Cordelia in his arms, he cries, "Never, never, never," etc. etc., and yet looks for signs of breath on her lips—"The feather stirs; she lives! If it be so,/It is a chance which does redeem all sorrows/that ever I have felt (V.iii.264–68). Timon of Athens follows Lear and is a play so close and yet so far from Lear because it asks the question: How do we go on living after Cordelia is dead? In Timon of Athens disillusion is absolute, no

From American Imago, 36 (1979), 45–68. Reprinted by permission of the author and of American Imago. About half of the original essay is herewith reprinted.

substitute is acceptable, there are no rituals of atonement, no provisions for mourning. The play is less about the experience of loss itself than a demonstration of the rage which refuses to accept loss. Perhaps this is why it is generally considered to be a bad play—it does not do what we expect of art in general: help us to accept loss.

All the questions about its authorship, which stem from the many confusions and disjunctions in the text, indicate an unfinished play which somewhere broke down, would not allow itself to be composed. But that indeed, I think, is itself what the play is about—a breakdown of all those ways in which rage, pain, and loss can somehow be accepted, made sense of, transformed into life-affirming energies. That transformation indeed requires a magic power, and the magic of art which is always engaged in denying loss by making something from nothing, making dead matter live, conjuring presences, thieving immortality from time, does not work in this play—both structurally and symbolically.

In *Timon*, Shakespeare does not believe in his own art, and that is why the play is unfinished. *Timon* tells us something that the artist himself cannot dwell on too long: that mourning is never finished, that we can't and don't really know how to accept or redeem loss, that we are always pained and enraged. Says Alcibiades, "To be in anger is impiety;/But who is man that is not angry?" (III.v.57–58). . . .

In the world of *Timon* nothing can redeem sorrow. Nothing can come of nothing. There are no acceptable substitutes; loss is irrevocable. Therefore, Timon does not mourn, he rages. In a world without Cordelia, without an embodied ideal of love, art, nature, man himself is not man, but a beast. What Apemantus says also applies to the modern city: "The commonwealth of Athens is become a forest of beasts." What Timon asks him is also the question of contemporary history: "What beast couldst thou be, that were not subject to a beast? And what a beast art thou already, that sees not thy loss in transformation!" (IV.iii.345–53).

That the embodied principle of good is often an idealized woman in Shakespeare is significant. In *Timon*, there is neither good art nor good women. The play itself is in part about the cultural and individual disaster of execution of the female. A world without women is a world not only without art, but without order. In *Lear*, the good woman, the ideal of pure love, was exiled, but not murdered until the end of the play. In *Timon*, she never existed; there is no feminine representative of goodness and constancy. When woman as nourisher is perceived as devourer, and relation with her as feared dependency; when the wish for a gratifying union with her is seen as threatening destruction only; when she is not only banished, but hated and murdered, then there can be neither manhood nor brotherhood, neither human being nor society. That is the condition of the world in *Timon of Athens*.

Accepting woman, however, means accepting loss, accepting not only the gap between self and other, but also the gap between self and self—recognizing the illusion of narcissistic omnipotence, knowing that one is limited, imperfect, dependent and not projecting that part of one's nature onto a conveniently hated and abhorred weak, false female. The world cannot be split, as Timon originally splits it, into a male brotherly good and a female fatal bad. Woman herself cannot be split, as the cultural myth splits her, into the Sacred Virginal Good and Profane Prostitute Bad. Accepting woman means accepting art itself. The world which excludes woman splits itself apart; the man who denies the female divides his own self and like Timon becomes his opposite, Misanthropos, monster, and beast. In *Timon of Athens*, there is no way back to humanity.

Thus, the world of *Timon* is a world of negations, mutually destructive oppositions—male-female, good-bad, love-hate, man-beast, friend-enemy, forgiveness-revenge. Contraries do not mutually exist, differences and separations are not tolerated; the gap between self and other, presence and absence, ideal and real, loss and recovery, is unbridgeable. The adjoining "bonds" are broken. The structure of the play itself operates on the principle of splitting, of incorporation and expulsion, orally ambivalent perception. The first half of the play centers around Timon's communal feasts, the second half around his solitary exile; the imagery turns from the intake of nourishing food to the vomiting of poison and disease. In place of an internal principle of integration which Timon lacks and cannot find, he had depended on a false, external, reified, material means of mutuality: money. . . .

In *Timon*, money has replaced the mediating power of the idealized woman (Blake's Emanation which joins man to man, but for him ultimately hermaphroditic), but instead of providing a way for contraries to mutually exist, marry, mingle, and create, money destructively converts opposites into negations of each other and Timon becomes Misanthropos. Marx, like Shakespeare, perceives that money is a psychological structure of alienated exchanges. When economics is conceived in terms of man's relation to man, and society as a system of exchanges, Marx asks what motivates the buying and selling of private property and answers:

> Need and want. The other person is also a property owner, but of another object which I lack and which I neither can nor want to be without, an object which seems to be something *needed* for the reintegration of my existence and the realization of my nature. . . .For the need of an object is the most evident and irrefutable proof that the object belongs to my nature and that the existence of the object for me and its *property* are the property appropriate to my essence.[1]

The problem of loss is the problem of need and want, the problem of wholeness, an integrated and not split identity. Art, money, law, love, all bonds and means of exchange between men, civilization itself, are means to

[1] Karl Marx, "Comments on James Mill, *Élémens d'économie politique*," *Karl Marx/Frederick Engels Collected Works* (New York: International Publishers, 1975), III, 218.

recover loss. Timon's primitive communism is a dream of restored communion, an attempt to defend against primal loss, to become both Self and Other, to be fed by his friends' flattery and feed them from the overflow of his bounty—to be simultaneously the passive nursing one, and the beneficent nourishing Mother. Yet he can only replace the flow of female milk with the rigid exchange of male money. Timon's attempted identification with the role of the Mother is a way to deny the loss of that primal one who gratified the infant's every wish, and to thereby be autonomous, not dependent on any female, not in need or vulnerable to any woman. But his primitive communism is, in fact, a feudal lordship, a narcissistic dream of adoration from his retainers under the guise of a Holy Brotherhood, one which admits no women. . . .

Loss can be denied by identification with the lost object and by attempted appropriation of female magic. For Shakespeare, Timon's magic, however, is impotent because it is narcissistic, substitutive, cannibalistic, and not transformative. Coins, jewels, food, are nonhuman, inert matter that cannot gratify the wish to be at one. The failure of all narcissistic substitutions leads to expulsion, spitting, and vomiting out all with which Timon had identified—women, friends, food, money, art:

> Therefore, be abhorred
> All feasts, societies, and throngs of men!
> His semblable, yea, himself, Timon disdains.
> Destruction fang mankind! (IV.iii.20–24)

> *Alcibiades*: Why, fare thee well:
> Here is some gold for thee.
> *Timon*:   Keep it, I cannot eat it. (IV.iii.100–101)

Timon, who had the world as his "confectionary" (IV.iii. 261), would change his feast of love to devouring hate: "Get thee gone./That the whole life of Athens were in this!/Thus would I eat it."/(IV.iii.281–82), eating a root. (Root possibly as phallic power and genital organization

as opposed to oral ambivalence.) That which is orally
incorporated is both loved and hated, united with and
destroyed. As Timon's servant tells him: "Feast won, fast-
lost" (II.ii.181).

The first scene of the play contains in miniature the
critique of the impossible feast of civilization in its art,
love, money and law. The poet in lines 5–7 exclaims,
"See,/Magic of bounty/All these spirits thy power/Hath
conjured to attend." The poet, too, though, is in attendance not because of free love, nor is his art a free gift,
but rather a counter to be exchanged for monetary recompense. The painter's art is described as a "pretty mocking
of the life" (l. 35). The mentality of art as imitation is the
same mentality as literal, externalized substitution—as
the mentality of money and the merchant. Art mocks
nature by holding up the mirror, by copying and aping.
In Renaissance thought, over against this kind of art, is
the idealized power of Nature—the divinely created order
of things, the procreative power which art might tutor or
tame, but which art does not possess itself. To transfer the
belief in that kind of natural transformative and freely
creative power to Art, as we have done since the Roman-
tics, and as Shakespeare plays with doing especially in the
later works, signifies the loss of the divinely ordered
scheme (and not incidentally the rise of bourgeois capi-
talism). . . .

The inability to accept change as the inability to accept
difference is also the Shakespearian theme of loss as ingratitude—of betrayal as lack of faith and constancy.
Woman is the first betrayer of constancy, not only because
she is different, but because she forces separation from
her body, through birth and weaning, and because she
cannot be possessed by the child as the father possesses
her. Thus it is that the changes and petulance of "Fortune" are personified, especially in the Renaissance, as
female. Fortune is a fickle and false lady; the poet in the
first scene of *Timon* likewise portrays Timon's ascent and
fall from Fortune as a climbing of a female body: Fortune
sits on a "mount," her followers "labour on her bosom"

"to propagate" their states. Timon, "bowing his head against the steepy mount/To climb his happiness" (I.i. 64–76) is pursued by followers who "rain sacrificial whisperings in his ear. . .Drink the free air." The images are oral and phallic, having the sense of a small boy mounting and climbing a large woman to drink and copulate, and being spurned.

Timon's own first word as he enters the play is "Imprison'd" and, one might say, he is indeed imprisoned in his own narcissism, his desire to have the love of the whole world, to devour and incorporate all into his own body. His first act in the play is to "free" a friend from "debt." "Your lordship ever binds him," says the messenger (I.i.104). Timon's acts of beneficence *bind* other men to him, defend against separation, dissolve boundaries, as Marx showed it was the particular property of money to do. Timon's next act is to put up money for his servant to equally "weigh" with a woman of higher status, "For 'tis a bond in men" (I.i.144). Bounty, Boundary, and Bond are all significantly related both in sound and sense. Timon wants the binding power of his money to be magically omnipotent. . . .

I think it makes more sense in terms of the play itself to see Timon's raging waste, communal feasts, oral ambivalence, in terms of the superfluous sacred rather than in terms of Freud's conception that the totem feast is a response to a primal murder of the father, a mutual sharing of guilt. And the superfluous sacred means at-one-ment, diffuse union with an original lost mother instead of guilt over the jealous murder of the father. . . .

Timon's love gifts (and Shakespeare's as well perhaps) are an attempt at orgiastic giving and a denial of the need to receive, a fear of passive dependence and a desire for it, a wish to dissolve the differences between self and other: "You mistake my love; I gave it freely ever; and there's none/Can truly say he gives if he receives (I.ii.9–11). . . O, what a precious comfort 'tis to have so many, like brothers, commanding one another's fortunes" (I.ii. 104–106).

When Timon discovers that his idealized brotherly communion is a cannibalistic mutual devouring, his response is not guilt or shame as it would be in the case of Freud's totemistic brotherhood, but rage and primitive hatred (what in Freud would precede the murder of the father). This rage is directed against and placed in terms of women, not men; the breeding and feeding generosity or the mother must be accepted as beneficent bounty or it becomes detested as parasitic dependence. Before he can give his gift, Timon needs to learn how to accept and receive the gift of nature, love, grace; he must accept the power of women. Instead, he tries to omnipotently become the woman and nourisher himself. He refuses to accept generation from the female, and thus *all* generation, all creation of something from nothing, is detestable debt and abhorred birth. . . .including the breeding of capital:

> He pours it out: Plutus, the god of Gold,
> Is but his steward. No need but he repays
> Sevenfold above itself; no gift to him
> But *breeds* the giver a return exceeding
> All use of quittance. (I.i.287–91)

> If I want gold, steal but a beggar's dog
> And give it Timon; why the dog coins gold   (II.i.5–6)

The birth of man is an excrescence: "If thou wilt curse, thy father, that poor rogue,/Must be thy subject, who in spite put stuff/To some she-beggar and compounded thee/Poor rogue hereditary" (IV.iii.272–75). Timon curses Mother Nature: "Ensear thy fertile and conceptious womb; Let it no more bring out ingrateful man!" (IV.iii.188–89). . . .

Outside of the two whores who appear briefly with Alcibiades in Act IV, the only women in the play are, significantly, Amazons in a masque—threatening, warlike women placed under formalized and ritual control through art (the same defensive strategy used in *The Tempest*). "They dance? They are mad women," says Apemantus, "I should fear those that dance before me now/would one day stomp upon me." (I.ii.135–46). Women, he says, "eat lords; so they come by great bellies" (I.i.209). After he loses his money, devoured by his debts, woman becomes also for Timon a ravenous destroyer:

> This fell whore of thine
> Hath in her more destruction than thy sword,
> For all her cherubin look. (IV.iii.62–64)

> Strike me the counterfeit matron;
> It is her habit only that is honest, herself's a bawd.
> Let not the virgin's cheek
> Make soft thy trenchant sword; for those milk paps
> That through the window [bars] bore at men's eyes,
> Are not within the leaf of pity writ.
> But set them down horrible traitors. (IV.iii.113–119)

The taking in of nourishing milk reverses to the vomiting of poison; communion with the mother and the other is now a source of corruption and syphillitic disintegration. But Timon's hatred, while it is a schizophrenic reversal is itself still a refusal to accept loss, a refusal to reconstruct, and recover new objects, to transform or metamorphose. He cannot find a substitute ideal. His rage remains primitively narcissistic. His hatred is as orgasmic, diffuse, and undifferentiated as his love. It contains both the desire to control and enclose the whole world, and the desire passively to see oneself as a victim of universal corruption. On the one hand, it represents an all-or-nothing split between ideas of good and evil, pure and impure, and the outward projection of the primitive hatred at the recognition of the discrepancy between self and other into the outside world. The original unity of love and hate in oral ambivalence becomes undone and in place of incorporation is expulsion. Yet Timon's curses all center around the confusion of opposites and boundaries, the collapse of splitting divisions:

> To general filths
> Convert o' th 'instant green virginity. . . .

> Instruction, manners, mysteries, and trades,
> Degrees, observances, customs, and laws,
> Decline to your confounding contraires,
> And let confusion live! (IV.i.6–21)

To convert everything into its opposite means to negate
and destroy one term of the existing contraries; such was
the original aim of Timon's love and his use of money.
His hate has the same purpose of destroying difference,
of denying mourning and recovery. His split ego, even in
its construction of a nightmare world, is seeking still a way
back to primal undifferentiated unity. . . .

Yet how is Timon to react to betrayal, ingratitude, in-
constancy? In the Alcibiades sub-plot, the alternative to
hatred and vengeance, which is mourning, is identified
with unacceptable womanishness. The idealized chaste
virtue of a good woman, one who like Cordelia suffers,
yet forgives full of pity and love, does not exist in this
play, and is excluded from the code the men live by, and
by which they control the world. Alcibiades argues for
the pity of the law to absolve a man who revenged himself according to the noble male political and civil code of
honor; that is, who made good his loss by a compensatory
act. Says the Senator,

> To revenge is no valor, but to bear. (III.v.40)
> He's truly valiant that can wisely suffer
> The worst that man can breathe. (III.v.31–32)

Alcibiades points out the contradiction of these words in
one who dispenses retaliation under the words "Justice"
and "War."

>   If there be
> Such valor in the bearing, what make we
> Abroad? Why then, women are more valiant
> That stay at home, if bearing carry it;
> And the ass more captain than the lion, the fellow
> Loaden with irons wiser than the judge,
> If wisdom be in suffering. (III.v.46–52)

The Senator who calls for forbearance also stands for the law of capital retaliatory punishment: "Friend or brother/ He forfeits his own blood that spills another" (III.v.87–88). Justice in its abstract disguise as a noble civil order is at bottom bloody revenge—the *lex talionis*, the economics of exchange based on a false reduction of human value to market value, of human life to dead coin and literalism. This same law exalts murder in war as valorous; the boundaries which demarcate the acceptable place of hatred, vengeance, and murder are false and confused. The cultural sanction of retaliation leads finally only to self-devouring.

In the world of Timon, as in the world at large, the nobility which defines itself in terms of the frozen exchanges of retaliatory violence, of life for life, destroys itself in the end; the society which sanctions mercantile exchange as a model for law ends by confusing the boundaries between the pure and impure, the permissible and inviolate. Alcibiades' giving of himself in the noble, altruistic pursuit of war to destroy his society's enemies is at bottom the same kind of narcissistic love feast in which Timon devours his friends. As Timon says to him in I.ii.76, "You had rather be at a breakfast of enemies than a dinner of friends." Alcibiades: "So they were bleeding-new, my lord, there's no meat like'm/I could wish my best friend at such a feast" (ll.78–80).

Love and war are not opposites; politics is erotic. Destruction seeks to unite with its object by devouring incorporation, to have and to be the other. One can escape only through positing the superfluous sacred value, the idealized object, above recompense, revenge, law. In Shakespeare, this idealized vision of the feminine virtues of pity and forgiveness means also a kind of sacrifice of male selfhood. When there is no acceptance of woman or what woman represents, there is also no mediation between men. The idealized value of woman as mercy and selfless love becomes the bond between men, the surplus which allows man to unite to man. In *Timon*, this surplus love is found in the faithful servant, who seeks Timon out despite his poverty and exile to serve him without price. Weeping in front of Timon, Timon can exempt him from the general hatred and curse because of the servant's tears: "What, dost thou weep? Come nearer. Then I love thee,/Because thou art a woman and disclaim'st/Flinty mankind (IV.iii. 491–93). Yet this singular act of the one poor servant is not enough in this play. Isolated acts of forgiveness exist, but do not redeem the world from the general curse. . . .

MAURICE CHARNEY

"Timon of Athens" on Stage and Screen

There is no indication that *Timon* was acted during Shakespeare's lifetime; and if Shakespeare did not regard the play as finished, it is not surprising that it was not staged. The first recorded performance is of Thomas Shadwell's version, *The History of Timon of Athens, the Man-Hater*, at Dorset Garden in 1678. Thomas Betterton played Timon; new female characters, Evandra and Melissa, were played by Mrs. Betterton (Mary Sanderson) and Mrs. Shadwell (Anne Gibbs). This adaptation was extremely successful, continuing on into the late eighteenth century with minor modifications. Shadwell claimed that his play was a "Scion grafted upon Shakespeare's stock," which is flattering to Shakespeare, but *The Man-Hater* is essentially Shadwell's play modeled on *Timon of Athens* with occasional direct quotes from Shakespeare. In his dedication to the Duke of Buckingham, Shadwell says with some admiration that *The Man-Hater* "has the inimitable hand of Shakespeare in it, which never made more Masterly strokes than in this. Yet I can truly say, I have made it into a Play."

Aside from changing the names and social function of all of the Senators, Shadwell's major alteration was to introduce two women, Melissa and Evandra, who pursue Timon. Melissa is a Restoration flirt who connives with her maid Chloe for Timon's wealth and power: "I am always true/To interest and to myself." She deserts Timon in adversity, but Evandra, a faithful and true friend (like the steward Flavius in Shakespeare), offers Timon all her money. When he dies in the final scene, Evandra stabs herself and dies with him. Everything is smoothed out and refined from Shakespeare, and even Apemantus is more of a gentleman than Shakespeare's snarling character. The original production of *The Man-Hater* in 1678 had music by Henry Purcell, which figured importantly in the performance, as well as dancing.

Shakespeare's text, heavily cut, returns with George Lamb's version presented at Drury Lane in 1816 with Edmund Kean as Timon. The cuts are chiefly those dictated by "refinement of manners." Alcibiades' whores, Phrynia and Timandra, who are not essential to the action, disappear, and so does Timon's withering sexual diatribe that shapes the last two acts. It is hard to see how Shakespeare's *Timon*, without severe distortion, could be made into a refined play. Audiences were fascinated by Edmund Kean's passionate acting, and we have Leigh Hunt's eyewitness account, but Hunt did not think that the role of Timon offered "sufficient variety and flexibility" for Kean's talents. It was an electrifying performance, but not as satisfying overall as Kean's Shylock, Hamlet, or Richard III. Hunt says that Kean as Timon often mistakes vehemence for intensity. Kean's biographer, F. W. Hawkins, affirms that his acting "throughout was deep in feeling, intense, varied, and powerful." This enabled him to make the second part of the play more fascinating than the first, a difficult feat for an actor. Hunt thought that the earlier part was presented with a stately languor rather than with the "ardent animal spirits" that Kean undoubtedly possessed.

Samuel Phelps's production in 1851 (thirty-one performances), revived in 1856 (ten performances), restored most of Shakespeare's text, with about 20 percent of the play (463 lines) cut. This is not a great deal of cutting even by modern standards. Victorian expurgation was still at work on Phrynia and Timandra, although they did appear onstage, and Timon's curses were severely modified. In the ending, Phelps tended to idealize Timon and to present Alcibiades as a redemptive, conquering hero, a tendency that is still at work in modern productions (as in that of Ron Daniels at The Other Place in Stratford in 1980). Phelps himself was a dignified actor, slow in speech and without the intensity of Kean. He played Timon as a misunderstood aristocrat, deeply hurt in adversity, and never really a hater of mankind and a committed misanthrope. The reviewer for the *Athenaeum* observed that in Phelps's performance the misanthropy seemed affected, "something alien to his disposition, the expression of which severely tasks his capacity and is but ill accomplished after all." It is difficult to conceive the play without an effective despair and hatred of mankind, but in this respect Phelps's performance seems to resemble that of Ralph Richardson's, discussed below.

I will skip the details of the many productions of *Timon* in the later nineteenth and earlier twentieth centuries and concentrate on six productions after the Second World War: Tyrone Guthrie (1952), Michael Benthall (1956), Peter Coe and Michael Langham (1963), John Schlesinger (1965), Peter Brook (1974), and Jonathan Miller (1981). There seems to be a remarkable revival of interest in *Timon* as a play for our time.

Tyrone Guthrie's *Timon* in 1952 at the Old Vic in London was a satire rather than a tragedy. With characteristic gusto, Guthrie offered us a diatribe against the absurdity of riches and materialism. There is no pity and fear in all of this, and the last two acts of the play lag, but the play was brilliantly staged by Tanya Moiseiwitsch. Guthrie "vitalised the play with his usual turbulence and comic invention," and the symbol of gold flooded our consciousness. André Morell as Timon was not an unmixed success, since critics thought he was not powerful enough to sustain the part. Roy Walker, in a review reprinted (in part) in the Signet Classic edition, describes him "like some devout peasant who had won a chariot-pool and set up as a one-man Athenian Arts Council, a fool and his money soon parted" (p. 212). Apemantus was memorably played by Leo McKern, who was vitriolic, proud, and spiky.

This production raises vividly the sense of *Timon* as a two-part play that needs a different sort of staging in each part. How can a director unify these two segments? Guthrie's satiric brilliance in the first part worked against him in the second, when tragic values are invoked. How can we sustain interest in the play as a whole without feeling an inevitable falling-off as Timon wallows and indulges himself in his adversity? The play does nothing to mitigate our sense of a radical split between prosperity and adversity, as if it were a moral fable. How are we, then, to deal with this difficulty onstage?

Michael Benthall's *Timon* at the Old Vic in 1956 was radically cut (about 500 lines) and rearranged. The strongly satirical elements were reduced in the part of Apemantus and the Poet and Painter, and much in the play was moralized and idealized, especially the ending. Alcibiades and his army are made to enter before Timon's very visible tomb with its prominent epitaph. At this moment, they meet the frightened, pleading senators and citizens of Athens who enter from the other side of the stage. Alcibiades orders the assault on Athens, but he is cut short when he reads Timon's epitaph, which impels him to take mercy on his native city. This sentimental, nineteenth-century ending moralizes the play and makes a mockery of Timon's monumental despair.

Ralph Richardson's playing of Timon was similarly mitigated, without the fierceness inherent in the role. Kenneth Tynan spoke mockingly of the performance as "the story of a scoutmaster betrayed by his troop," and Muriel St. Clare Byrne thought that Richardson did not believe in the last two acts, which are a meditation rather than a curse. "On his own view of life, generosity, tolerance, a sweet reasonableness, and a natural philanthropy will keep breaking in. . . ." As the London *Times* critic remarked, Richardson's Timon was "as gently intoxicated as Richard II." Critics seem to be in general agreement against Richardson's sweetening the part of Timon. As

Roy Walker says about Richardson's representation of Timon in exile, the actor, in his "armless sheepskin coat and bare cross-gartered legs, was more reminiscent of Robinson Crusoe than of the naked outcast Timon." Unlike Timon, who never knew the middle of humanity, Richardson avoided the extremes of active magnanimity and active agony and chose to remain throughout the play in the middle range of emotional expression. In the second part, he replaced fury and despair with a quiet irony.

Peter Coe and Michael Langham's modern-dress *Timon* at the Stratford Shakespeare Festival in Canada in 1963 was an explosive satire on the contemporary implications of the play. *Timon* lends itself to modern-dress productions because of its emphasis on an affluent and decadent society, but there is a danger that the parallels will be pursued for their own sake. Howard Taubman, the theater critic of *The New York Times*, complained that this production called attention to its own cleverness rather than to Shakespeare. A lavish dinner party showed Timon dressed in a dinner jacket of red brocade, and Apemantus was represented as a newspaperman with a cigarette dangling from his lips and with a photographer constantly in tow. The music was composed by Duke Ellington, and a trumpeter serenaded the guests at Timon's dinner party. John Colicos played Timon and the veteran William Hutt played Alcibiades. At one point, Alcibiades fired a shot at Apemantus for annoying him. Modern dress, of course, facilitated the satirical attack on the corruption of society, but there is a problem in representing Timon's despair and misanthropy. This is hardly a matter of dress, modern or period, and this is precisely where this production broke down. If it is a morality play for our times, the wit and cleverness and the use of contemporary stereotypes of character and costume hardly contribute to the morality effect.

John Schlesinger's production of *Timon* for the Royal Shakespeare Company in 1965 starred Paul Scofield as Timon. This was a memorable performance, extending the range of Scofield's Lear for Peter Brook in 1962 and endowing the two parts of *Timon* with equal fervor. No one spoke of Scofield excelling in prosperity or adversity, and this is a measure of his power as an actor. The *Times* critic said: "His way of handling verse often suggests a man struggling to lift a heavy weight, or being carried along by its momentum; and this part gives stupendous exercise to his technique." Even more eloquently, Robert Speaight observes that in Scofield's playing of the later scenes, "the excess of his misanthropy was the measure of his growth." The tragic effects were achieved without any exaggerated satire or contemporaneity in a style reminiscent of Samuel Beckett. For the scenes in the wilderness, Timon's cave was located in a barren waste like the heath in *King Lear*, with a single gnarled tree that reminded audiences of *Waiting for Godot*. Ralph Koltai designed a striking set of tragic significance.

The most important production of *Timon* in our time is that of Peter Brook, a veteran director of the Royal Shakespeare Company, in the Bouffes du Nord Theater in Paris in 1974. This was a plush and gilt Victorian theater built in 1876, but out of use as a theater since 1950. It was abandoned in June 1952 because of a disastrous fire, but Brook in 1974 put it to use pretty much as it stood, with the stage burned out and with gaping holes and gashes in the plaster of the walls. It was located in the unfashionable 10th district near the Gare du Nord—all in all, as David Williams calls it, "a lost theater for a lost play." Brook's experience with the Bouffes du Nord was used in the Majestic Theater in Brooklyn, which he reopened for *The Mahabharata* and *The Cherry Orchard*. Pierre Schneider said of the Bouffes du Nord: "Every spectator at once knows that he is sitting inside a symbol of the decline of the West."

Timon was translated into French by Jean-Claude Carrièee, in consultation with Brook and the cast. The translation simplifies and modernizes the play, making it immediately comprehensible to the audience. In producing *Timon*, Brook draws upon the collective experience of his international company, which he had assembled in

1970 at the Centre International de Recherche Théâtrale. The staging is very Brechtian: the play is given a storytelling aspect with special emphasis on the circle, as in Brecht's *The Caucasian Chalk Circle*. The costumes, designed by Michel Launay, are simple and naive, but strikingly symbolic and vivid. Underneath and still visible, the actors wear their own clothes. The staging is intense and concentrated on a few simple points.

The young actor François Marthouret played Timon with radiance and excitement, his beautiful white suit in rags in the second part of the play. Most striking was the role of Apemantus, played by Malick Bagayogo, an African, as a choric fool of bitter cynicism. Dressed as a North African street beggar in an Army surplus overcoat and boots, he represented a Third World anti-type to Timon. Alcibiades, played by Bruce Myers, was in military fancy dress like a Mediterranean general and adventurer in the style of Colonel Quadaffi of Libya. At the end of the play, Alcibiades cynically takes over the decayed society of Athens.

Jonathan Miller's version of *Timon* for the BBC-TV series in 1981 is not an impressive production, but it is widely available to students. Miller's introductory remarks are so apologetic and dismissive of the play that we are not surprised to find a fairly tepid and not clearly thought out production. I most objected to the toning down of Apemantus, played by Norman Rodway. He is now an acerbic courtier, who amuses his fellow aristocrats and rich hangers on with his witty remarks, but he is hardly a counterweight to Timon and a gruff and biting truth speaker. Timon is well played by Jonathan Pryce. At first he is naïve and idealistic, believing in some outmoded and ill-starred concept of friendship. In his adversity, he is excessively hysterical, but also very static, hardly moving from his sitting-up position in the right corner of the television screen. We feel that Timon's despair has been reduced to empty rhetoric.

The Poet, Painter, and Jeweler are rendered in a simplified, affected style, and their remarks (especially those of the Poet) fail to make a strong impression in our sense of the play. The costuming very artfully uses italianate ruffs and black doublets in the style of Veronese. It is interesting that Jonathan Miller in his introduction said that the play could be done effectively in modern dress. It's a pity that he didn't take up his own suggestion, which might have made this production more lively. One notable minor performance in this *Timon* was John Welsh's Flavius, an old man whose gravity and whose loyalty to Timon were impressive. There is a moving reunion with his master toward the end.

Shakespeare's *Timon of Athens* is a difficult play to stage, and it is not surprising that there should be so few successful productions of it. Of all those we have considered, only the presentations of John Schlesinger and Peter Brook seem to have aroused the full enthusiasm of critics. Margaret Webster, the American director, never mounted *Timon* herself, but her comments on the play in *Shakespeare Without Tears* are typical:

> Timon is a great operatic part; but the mind of the plain man recoils before the pitiless, raging bitterness of the play. It is surmised that Shakespeare, with all these "plays unpleasant," was going through some experience of extreme personal disillusionment and that with *Timon* he reached the breaking point. There can be very little doubt that he was in some way spiritually and intellectually rudderless when he wrote it; and this lack of mental stability deprived him of his sure dramatic sense. *Timon* is bad philosophy and bad theater, however brilliant the writing.

This was written in 1942, but since that time we have a different sense of *Timon*. The play, with its intense bitterness, disillusion, and despair, now seems more appropriate for our world, and we may look forward to more sympathetic and challenging productions in the future.

Bibliographic note: There is an excellent study of the stage history of this play by Gary Jay Williams in Rolf Soellner, *Timon of Athens: Shakespeare's Pessimistic Tragedy* (1979). A list of theater studies and reviews may be found in the bibliography by John J. Ruszkiewicz (1986), but the reader is warned that this bibliography has many errors. More specifically, the following material has been used in the preparation of this essay. On Shadwell: Hazelton Spencer, *Shakespeare Improved* (1927). On Kean: F. W. Hawkins, *The Life of Edmund Kean* (1869) and *Leigh Hunt's Dramatic Criticism 1808–1831*, ed. Lawrence H. and Carolyn W. Houtchens (1949). On Phelps: Shirley S. Allen, *Samuel Phelps and Sadler's Wells Theatre* (1971). On Guthrie: Kenneth Tynan, *Curtains* (1971) and Audrey Williamson, *Old Vic Drama 2, 1947–1957* (1957). On Benthall: Tynan, *Curtains*; Williamson, *Old Vic Drama 2*; Muriel St. Clare Byrne, "The Shakespeare Season at the Old Vic, 1956–1957 and Stratford-Upon-Avon, 1957," *Shakespeare Quarterly*, 8 (1957), 461–92; and review in the London *Times*, September 6, 1956. On Langham: David E. Jones, "Shakespeare Festivals, 1963: Stratford, Ontario," *Drama Survey*, 3 (1963), 301–4; Arnold Edinborough, "The Stratford Shakespearean Festival," *Shakespeare Quarterly*, 14 (1963), 433–36; and review by Howard Taubman in *The New York Times*, July 31, 1963. On Schlesinger: Robert Speaight, *Shakespeare on the Stage* (1973); Robert Speaight, "Shakespeare in Britain," *Shakespeare Quarterly*, 16 (1965), 313–24; and E. Martin Browne, "Theatre Abroad . . . ," *Drama Survey*, 4 (1965), 272–76. On Brook: Articles by Marienstras and Banu (with many photographs) in *Les Voies de la Création Théâtrale* (1977); David Williams, " 'A Place Marked by Life': Brook at the Bouffes du Nord," *New Theatre Quarterly*, 1 (1985), 39–74; Eric Shorter, " 'Timon of Paris,' " *Drama*, 115 (1974), 21–27; and review by Mel Gussow in *The New York Times*, August 10, 1975.

Suggested References

The number of possible references is vast and grows alarmingly. (The *Shakespeare Quarterly* devotes one issue each year to a list of the previous year's work, and *Shakespeare Survey*—an annual publication—includes a substantial review of recent scholarship, as well as an occasional essay surveying a few decades of scholarship on a chosen topic.) Though no works are indispensable, those listed below have been found especially helpful.

1. Shakespeare's Times

Byrne, M. St. Clare. *Elizabethan Life in Town and Country*. Rev. ed. New York: Barnes & Noble, 1961. Chapters on manners, beliefs, education, etc., with illustrations.

Joseph, B. L. *Shakespeare's Eden: The Commonwealth of England, 1558–1629*. New York: Barnes & Noble, 1971. An account of the social, political, economic, and cultural life of England.

Schoenbaum, S. *Shakespeare: The Globe and the World*. New York: Oxford University Press, 1979. A readable, handsomely illustrated book on the world of the Elizabethans.

Shakespeare's England. 2 vols. Oxford: Oxford University Press, 1916. A large collection of scholarly essays on a wide variety of topics (e.g. astrology, costume, gardening, horsemanship), with special attention to Shakespeare's references to these topics.

Stone, Lawrence. *The Crisis of the Aristocracy, 1558–1641*, abridged edition. London: Oxford University Press, 1967.

2. Shakespeare

Barnet, Sylvan. *A Short Guide to Shakespeare*. New York:

Harcourt Brace Jovanovich, 1974. An introduction to all of the works and to the dramatic traditions behind them.

Bentley, Gerald E. *Shakespeare: A Biographical Handbook.* New Haven, Conn.: Yale University Press, 1961. The facts about Shakespeare, with virtually no conjecture intermingled.

Bush, Geoffrey. *Shakespeare and the Natural Condition.* Cambridge, Mass.: Harvard University Press, 1956. A short, sensitive account of Shakespeare's view of "Nature," touching most of the works.

Chambers, E. K. *William Shakespeare: A Study of Facts and Problems.* 2 vols. London: Oxford University Press, 1930. An invaluable, detailed reference work; not for the casual reader.

Chute, Marchette. *Shakespeare of London.* New York: Dutton, 1949. A readable biography fused with portraits of Stratford and London life.

Clemen, Wolfgang H. *The Development of Shakespeare's Imagery.* Cambridge, Mass.: Harvard University Press, 1951. (Originally published in German, 1936.) A temperate account of a subject often abused.

Granville-Barker, Harley. *Prefaces to Shakespeare.* 2 vols. Princeton, N. J.: Princeton University Press, 1946–47. Essays on ten plays by a scholarly man of the theater.

Harbage, Alfred. *As They Liked It.* New York: Macmillan, 1947. A long, sensitive essay on Shakespeare, morality, and the audience's expectations.

Kernan, Alvin B., ed. *Modern Shakespearean Criticism: Essays on Style, Dramaturgy, and the Major Plays.* New York: Harcourt Brace Jovanovich, 1970. A collection of major formalist criticism.

————. "The Plays and the Playwrights." In *The Revels History of Drama in English,* general editors Clifford Leech and T. W. Craik. Vol. III. London: Methuen, 1975. A book-length essay surveying Elizabethan drama with substantial discussions of Shakespeare's plays.

Schoenbaum, S. *Shakespeare's Lives.* Oxford: Clarendon Press, 1970. A review of the evidence, and an examination of many biographies, including those by Baconians and other heretics.

————. *William Shakespeare: A Compact Documentary Life.* New York: Oxford University Press, 1977. A readable presentation of all that the documents tell us about Shakespeare.

Traversi, D. A. *An Approach to Shakespeare.* 3rd rev. ed. 2 vols. New York: Doubleday, 1968–69. An analysis of the plays beginning with words, images, and themes, rather than with characters.

Van Doren, Mark. *Shakespeare.* New York: Holt, 1939. Brief, perceptive readings of all of the plays.

3. Shakespeare's Theater

Beckerman, Bernard. *Shakespeare at the Globe, 1599–1609.* New York: Macmillan, 1962. On the playhouse and on Elizabethan dramaturgy, acting, and staging.

Chambers, E. K. *The Elizabethan Stage.* 4 vols. New York: Oxford University Press, 1945. A major reference work on theaters, theatrical companies, and staging at court.

Cook, Ann Jennalie. *The Privileged Playgoers of Shakespeare's London, 1576–1642.* Princeton, N. J.: Princeton University Press, 1981. Sees Shakespeare's audience as more middle-class and more intellectual than Harbage (below) does.

Gurr, Andrew. *The Shakespearean Stage: 1574–1642.* 2d edition. Cambridge: Cambridge Univresity Press, 1981. On the acting companies, the actors, the playhouses, the stages, and the audiences.

Harbage, Alfred. *Shakespeare's Audience.* New York: Columbia University Press, 1941. A study of the size and nature of the theatrical public, emphasizing its representativeness.

Hodges, C. Walter. *The Globe Restored.* London: Ernest Benn, 1953. A well-illustrated and readable attempt to reconstruct the Globe Theatre.

Hosley, Richard. "The Playhouses." In *The Revels History of Drama in English,* general editors Clifford Leech and T. W. Craik. Vol. III. London: Methuen, 1975. An essay of one hundred pages on the physical aspects of the playhouses.

Kernodle, George R. *From Art to Theatre: Form and Convention in the Renaissance.* Chicago: University of Chicago

Press, 1944. Pioneering and stimulating work on the symbolic and cultural meanings of theater construction.

Nagler, A. M. *Shakespeare's Stage.* Trans. Ralph Manheim. New Haven, Conn.: Yale University Press, 1958. A very brief introduction to the physical aspects of the playhouse.

Slater, Ann Pasternak. *Shakespeare the Director.* Totowa, N. J.: Barnes & Noble, 1982. An analysis of theatrical effects (e.g., kissing, kneeling) in stage directions and dialogue.

Thomson, Peter. *Shakespeare's Theatre.* London: Routledge & Kegan Paul, 1983. A discussion of how plays were staged in Shakespeare's time.

4. Miscellaneous Reference Works

Abbott, E. A. *A Shakespearean Grammar.* New Edition. New York: Macmillan, 1877. An examination of differences between Elizabethan and modern grammar.

Bevington, David. *Shakespeare.* Arlington Heights, Ill.: A. H. M. Publishing, 1978. A short guide to hundreds of important writings on the works.

Bullough, Geoffrey. *Narrative and Dramatic Sources of Shakespeare.* 8 vols. New York: Columbia University Press, 1957–75. A collection of many of the books Shakespeare drew upon, with judicious comments.

Campbell, Oscar James, and Edward G. Quinn. *The Reader's Encyclopedia of Shakespeare.* New York: Crowell, 1966. More than 2,600 entries, from a few sentences to a few pages, on everything related to Shakespeare.

Greg, W. W. *The Shakespeare First Folio.* New York: Oxford University Press, 1955. A detailed yet readable history of the first collection (1623) of Shakespeare's plays.

Kökeritz, Helge. *Shakespeare's Names.* New Haven, Conn.: Yale University Press, 1959. A guide to the pronunciation of some 1,800 names appearing in Shakespeare.

————. *Shakespeare's Pronunciation.* New Haven, Conn.: Yale University Press, 1953. Contains much information about puns and rhymes.

Muir, Kenneth. *The Sources of Shakespeare's Plays.* New Haven, Conn.: Yale University Press, 1978. An account of Shakespeare's use of his reading.

The Norton Facsimile: The First Folio of Shakespeare. Prepared by Charles Hinman. New York: Norton, 1968. A handsome and accurate facsimile of the first collection (1623) of Shakespeare's plays.

Onions, C. T. *A Shakespeare Glossary.* 2d ed., rev., with enlarged addenda. London: Oxford University Press, 1953. Definitions of words (or senses of words) now obsolete.

Partridge, Eric. *Shakespeare's Bawdy.* Rev. ed. New York: Dutton, 1955. A glossary of bawdy words and phrases.

Shakespeare Quarterly. See headnote to Suggested References.

Shakespeare Survey. See headnote to Suggested References.

Shakespeare's Plays in Quarto. A Facsimile Edition. Ed. Michael J. B. Allen and Kenneth Muir. Berkeley, Calif.: University of California Press, 1981. A book of nine hundred pages, containing facsimiles of twenty-two of the quarto editions of Shakespeare's plays. An invaluable complement to *The Norton Facsimile: The First Folio of Shakespeare* (see above).

Smith, Gordon Ross. *A Classified Shakespeare Bibliography 1936–1958.* University Park, Pa.: Pennsylvania State University Press, 1963. A list of some twenty thousand items on Shakespeare.

Spevack, Marvin. *The Harvard Concordance to Shakespeare.* Cambridge, Mass.: Harvard University Press, 1973. An index to Shakespeare's words.

Wells, Stanley, ed. *Shakespeare: Select Bibliographies.* London: Oxford University Press, 1973. Seventeen essays surveying scholarship and criticism of Shakespeare's life, work, and theater.

5. *Titus Andronicus*

Baker, Howard. *Induction to Tragedy.* Baton Rouge: Louisiana State University Press, 1939.

Hamilton, A. C. *"Titus Andronicus*: The Form of Shakespearian Tragedy," *Shakespeare Quarterly* 14 (1963), 201–13.

Hill, R. F. "The Composition of *Titus Andronicus,*" *Shakespeare Survey 10,* ed. Allardyce Nicoll. New York and London: Cambridge University Press, 1957, pp. 60–70.

Hunter, G. K. "Sources and Meanings in *Titus Andronicus,*"

in *The Mirror up to Nature*, ed. J. C. Gray. Toronto: University of Toronto Press, 1983, pp. 171–88.

Metz, G. Harold. "Stage History of *Titus Andronicus*," *Shakespeare Quarterly* 28 (1977), 154–69.

Miola, Robert S. *Shakespeare's Rome*. Ithaca: Cornell University Press, 1983.

Sommers, Alan. " 'Wilderness of Tigers': Structure and Symbolism in *Titus Andronicus*," *Essays in Criticism* 10 (1960), 275–89.

Spivack, Bernard. *Shakespeare and the Allegory of Evil*. New York: Columbia University Press, 1958.

Tricomi, Albert H. "The Mutilated Garden in *Titus Andronicus*, *Shakespeare Studies 9*, ed. J. Leeds Barroll III. New York: Burt Franklin, 1976.

Waith, Eugene M. "The Metamorphosis of Violence in *Titus Andronicus*," *Shakespeare Survey 10*, ed. Allardyce Nicoll. New York and London: Cambridge University Press, 1957. pp. 39–49.

6. *Timon of Athens*

Bradbrook, M. C. *Shakespeare the Craftsman*. London: Chatto & Windus, 1969.

Brill, Lesley W. "Truth and *Timon of Athens*," *Modern Language Quarterly*, 40 (1979), 17–36.

Butler, Francelia. *The Strange Critical Fortunes of Shakespeare's "Timon of Athens."* Ames, Iowa: Iowa State University Press, 1966.

Campbell, Oscar James. *Shakespeare's Satire*. Hamden, Conn.: The Shoe String Press, Inc. (Archon Books), 1963. First published by Oxford University Press, 1943.

Collins, A. S. *"Timon of Athens:* A Reconsideration," *Review of English Studies*, 22 (1946), 96–108.

Dowden, Edward. *Shakspere, A Critical Study of His Mind and Art*. New York: Harper & Brothers, 1881; London: H. S. King, 1875.

Ellis-Fermor, Una. *"Timon of Athens:* An Unfinished Play," *Review of English Studies*, 18 (1942), 270–83. Reprinted in her: *Shakespeare the Dramatist*, ed. Kenneth Muir. New York: Barnes & Noble; London: Methuen & Co., 1961. .

Empson, William. *The Structure of Complex Words*. Norfolk, Conn.: New Directions; London: Chatto & Windus, 1951.

Farnham, Willard. *Shakespeare's Tragic Frontier*. Berkeley, Calif.: University of California Press; London: Cambridge University Press, 1950.

Hazlitt, William. *Liber Amoris and Dramatic Criticisms*. London: Peter Nevill, 1948. *The Characters of Shakespear's Plays*, first published 1817.

Honigmann, E. A. J. "Timon of Athens," *Shakespeare Quarterly*, 12 (1961), 3–20.

Knight, G. Wilson. *The Wheel of Fire*. New York and London: Oxford University Press, 1930.

Maxwell, J. C. (ed.). *Timon of Athens*. London: Cambridge University Press, 1957.

Oliver, H. J. (ed.). *Timon of Athens*. (Arden Shakespeare). Cambridge, Mass.: Harvard University Press; London: Methuen, 1959.

Ruszkiewicz, John J. *"Timon of Athens": An Annotated Bibliography*. New York: Garland, 1986.

Slights, William W. E. "*Genera mixta* and *Timon of Athens*," *Studies in Philology*, 74 (1977), 39–62.

Soellner, Rolf. *"Timon of Athens": Shakespeare's Pessimistic Tragedy*. Columbus, Ohio: Ohio State University Press, 1979. With a stage history by Gary Jay Williams.

Spencer, Terence. "Shakespeare Learns the Value of Money: The Dramatist at Work on *Timon of Athens*," *Shakespeare Survey 6* (1953), 75–78.

Williams, Stanley T. "Some Versions of *Timon of Athens* on the Stage," *Modern Philology*, 18 (1920), 269–85.